W9-BRW-100

PRAISE FOR *Enter Helen*

"Engaging. . . . Nimble-footed. . . . Amusing. . . . Throughout, Hauser weaves in passages connecting Brown to her contemporaries and the cultural landscape of the 1960s . . . [to] situate her life in the context of its times."   —*New York Times Book Review*

"Brown deserves the biography that Brooke Hauser has written, *Enter Helen*. It is entertaining, thoughtfully researched and—the ultimate encomium where HGB was concerned—fun."

—*Washington Post*

"Legendary, inimitable *Cosmopolitan* editor and *Sex and the Single Girl* author Helen Gurley Brown comes alive in Hauser's hands."

—*Entertainment Weekly*, "Must List"

"Encapsulates the colorful life of a woman who rocked minis well into her eighties."   —*Los Angeles Times*

"A must-read piece of proto-feminist history."

—Lena Dunham's *Lenny Letter*

"Hauser deftly pulls out fascinating details. . . . Some truly juicy moments. . . . Hauser dives into her youth and her early career in advertising far more than these years have been explored previously, setting the stage much more firmly for understanding how Brown accomplished all that she did."   —*Jezebel*

"*Enter Helen* is a *Wizard of Oz* story about a feisty girl from the Ozarks, the original *Sex and the City* gal Helen Gurley Brown. Brooke Hauser enters her life like slipping into a pair of Helen's infamous fishnets, weaving a compelling drama about a determined woman and *Cosmopolitan* editor, and revealing how powerful (and threatening) a female in command of her pocketbook, sexuality, and career can really be."

—Lily Koppel, *New York Times* bestselling author of *The Astronaut Wives Club* and *The Red Leather Diary*

"Hauser dives deep into the life of our former HBIC and uncovers what drove her to revolutionize the way we live and date today. HGB, we TY." —*Cosmopolitan*

"Excellent." —*The Week*

"As Brooke Hauser's lively biography . . . reveals, [Helen Gurley Brown] was as comfortable championing single 'career girls' as she was giving them tips on how to catch a man—and her own contradictory, have-it-all life proved to be as compelling as the era she helped define." —*OK Magazine*

"Reading *Enter Helen* was like being at a party, and I'm sorry it had to end. With this sexy, riveting book, Brooke Hauser takes us on a joy ride through the 1960s and '70s of Helen Gurley Brown's life. It feels light and breezy, but—like Brown herself—Hauser's story is engaging and important."

—Linda Wells, founding editor in chief of *Allure*

"A riveting . . . complex biography. . . . Such a great read. *Enter Helen* is neither hagiographic nor damning."

—*Washington Independent Review of Books*

"Journalist Brooke Hauser's breezy and entertaining new biography . . . chronicles Brown's remarkable story, which is also a social history of two decades—the sixties and the seventies—whose cultural impact remains significant." —Acculturated.com

"It is to be hoped that Brooke Hauser's excellent biography and a film in the works will give *Sex and the Single Girl* another lease on life." —*New York Journal of Books*

ENTER HELEN

ALSO BY BROOKE HAUSER

The New Kids:
Big Dreams and Brave Journeys
at a High School for Immigrant Teens

ENTER HELEN

The Invention of Helen Gurley Brown
and the Rise of the Modern Single Woman

BROOKE HAUSER

HARPER

NEW YORK ● LONDON ● TORONTO ● SYDNEY

A hardcover edition of this book was published in 2016 by HarperCollins Publishers.

ENTER HELEN. Copyright © 2016 by Brooke Hauser. All rights reserved. Printed in the United States of America. No part of this book may be used or reproduced in any manner whatsoever without written permission except in the case of brief quotations embodied in critical articles and reviews. For information, address HarperCollins Publishers, 195 Broadway, New York, NY 10007.

HarperCollins books may be purchased for educational, business, or sales promotional use. For information, please e-mail the Special Markets Department at SPsales@harpercollins.com.

P.S.™ is a trademark of HarperCollins Publishers.

FIRST HARPER PAPERBACKS EDITION PUBLISHED 2017.

Designed by Fritz Metsch

Library of Congress Cataloging-in-Publication Data

Names: Hauser, Brooke, author.
Title: Enter Helen : the invention of Helen Gurley Brown and the rise of the modern single woman / Brooke Hauser.
Description: New York : Harper, 2016.
Identifiers: LCCN 2015038742| ISBN 9780062342669 (hardback) | ISBN 9780062342690 (ebook)
Subjects: LCSH: Brown, Helen Gurley. | Women—New York (State)—New York—Biography. | Single women—New York (State)—New York—Biography. | BISAC: BIOGRAPHY & AUTOBIOGRAPHY / Women. | BIOGRAPHY & AUTOBIOGRAPHY / Rich & Famous.
Classification: LCC HQ1439.N6 H38 2016 | DDC 306.81/53092—dc23 LC record available at http://lccn.loc.gov/2015038742

ISBN 978-0-06-234267-6 (pbk.)

17 18 19 20 21   OV/LSC   10 9 8 7 6 5 4 3 2 1

To my parents, Terry and Michelle Hauser, the best of partners;
and to my husband, Addison MacDonald,
whom I lean on and look forward to seeing every day.

Funny business, a woman's career—the things you drop on your way up the ladder so you can move faster. You forget you'll need them again when you get back to being a woman. That's one career all females have in common, whether we like it or not: being a woman. . . . And in the last analysis, nothing's any good unless you can look up just before dinner or turn around in bed, and there he is. Without that, you're not a woman. You're something with a French provincial office or a book full of clippings, but you're not a woman.

—*Margo Channing (Bette Davis), in* All About Eve, *1950*

She is such a feeling person that her work is almost surely colored by her own sensitivities. But her work is her kingdom, alas, only eight hours per day. As mentioned above, she is a feeling being. She is completely aware of her own longings—to be needed, to be reassured that she is attractive and desirable, to belong intimately somewhere to someone. She is all Woman.

—*from a 1957 job evaluation of Miss Helen Marie Gurley, a copywriter at Foote, Cone & Belding*

CONTENTS

ENTER
HELEN

PROLOGUE

"Oh well he's got that je ne sais quoi
While I, my dear, am from Arkansas"

—from an early poem by Helen Gurley

In the early Seventies, Helen Gurley Brown began working on a musical about her life, tracing her rise from a mousy girl from Little Rock, Arkansas, to the legendary editor of *Cosmopolitan* magazine. It was a story she had told countless times before, but this time her writing partner, a *Cosmo* contributor named Lyn Tornabene, was helping her to turn it into a spectacle worthy of Broadway.

They envisioned a play about "a lady who knew—all out of the context of her time—the power of sex." Set in Depression-era Arkansas, Los Angeles, and New York, it would unfold in several acts, with razzle-dazzle musical numbers like "Going All the Way" (one of the worst sins a girl could commit); "Sex Is Power" (followed by a series of "passion" ballets, featuring beds onstage and male dancers as Helen's favorite ex-lovers); and "Helen," an ode to the patron saint of single girls, the editor of *Metropolitan* magazine (subbing for *Cosmopolitan*), and the ultimate authority on such subjects as how to boff in a wig or bag a rich man. Over the course of the play, many different characters would walk on and off the stage, though the most important stage direction of all was the simplest: "Enter, Helen."

But which one? There was the young Helen: scrawny, flat-chested, and acne-ridden with crooked teeth and limp, brown hair, a timid and pitiful creature. And then there was the grown Helen: a sophisticated, stylish, and sexy woman who had transformed herself from a "mouseberger" into the most famous editor in the world, a woman who, in one scene, tells her fawning secretary, "Anybody can be me. You just have to work at it."

In a flash of inspiration, the playwrights decided to create a duet for both Helens. Picture the scene: The grown Helen begins singing to herself as she primps in the mirror, putting on false eyelashes and a hair fall. Meanwhile, a soft light illuminates another spot on the stage. Pale and frail-looking in her cap and gown on graduation day, young Helen appears, lamenting her "blah" looks and wondering aloud, in her small, shaky voice, what will become of her future self. They called this song "Look at Me," aka "The Mouseberger Blues."

Over the years, Lyn spent countless hours interviewing Helen, digging out the backstory that would become the basis of the play. Once, at Helen's Park Avenue apartment, "she made supper," Lyn says, "a salad with lemon juice and *mineral oil*—it's also a laxative! She had a little jar of Bacos, and then she made one scrambled egg that we shared. And Diet Jell-O."

Other times, Lyn went into the city to pick Helen up and take her back to her house in Greenwich, Connecticut. After Helen did her morning floor exercises in Lyn's guest room upstairs—thump, thump, thump—they got to work. They talked about single girls and sex and men and affairs and consequences. Helen remembered girls she'd known who had come to her after getting pregnant; girls she had listened to and counseled through abortions and rejections, after the men went back to their wives. But mostly, she remembered the girl she had been.

During those sessions, they talked about Helen's childhood in Arkansas. Helen told Lyn about the tragic death of her father, Ira, and the fog of depression her mother, Cleo, never quite escaped, even after remarrying. (She later took the last name Bryan.) Other characters they chose not to develop, like Helen's older sister, Mary, who lived in Oklahoma. A victim of polio who spent most of her life in a wheelchair, Mary was quietly determined in her own way, but Helen and Lyn decided she would be better as a foil—a muted, gentle soul to bring out the sparkle of Helen's personality.

They titled the musical *Helen* and eventually shared the beginnings of a script with an agent, who shopped it around. But it never sold. "It was too soon. The producing world is a man's world on Broadway. They weren't ready to worship Helen," Lyn says. "It's so sad. She wanted it very badly."

Helen filed the idea away, but she never forgot about it. Nearly two decades after they started writing *Helen*, she brought it up with Lyn once again. "Nothing's doing with the musical," she said, "but I'm still trying."

Enter Helen.

(1)

REAL ESTATE
1958

"All my life, ever since I was a little girl,
I've always had the same dream. To marry a zillionaire."

—Loco Dempsey (Betty Grable)
in *How to Marry a Millionaire*, 1953

Helen Gurley loved the idea of David Brown long before she loved him. What wasn't to love? As head of the story department at 20th Century Fox, he was one of the most eligible bachelors in Hollywood, and according to a mutual friend, Ruth Schandorf, charming, intellectual, and "gentle as a baby lamb." He had been something of a whiz kid after graduating from Stanford and the Columbia School of Journalism—editor-in-chief of *Liberty* magazine and then managing editor at *Cosmopolitan*. Twice divorced, he had a son with his first wife, a teenage boy who was almost old enough to go to college. Perhaps most intriguingly of all, David lived in an elegant house in the Pacific Palisades section of Los Angeles, and he made an annual income of $75,000. *Not* including expense accounts.

When Helen first heard that David was single again, she felt her hopes flit around in her rib cage. At forty-two, he was what she had begun to think of as "collector's-item age," more worldly than her bachelor friends in their meager twenties, with less mileage than widowers in their thick-in-the-middle sixties.

David Brown was clearly marriage material, but the first time Helen asked Ruth to fix them up, she advised against it. "It's too soon," Ruth said. "You should wait until he's ready for a sensible girl like you." David's second wife, Wayne Clark, had left him for another man, and in the aftermath he had been finding some comfort in the arms of starlets.

No one who knew Helen Gurley well would have described her as patient, but she *was* sensible and self-aware. She hadn't stayed single for thirty-six years without getting to know herself, and she'd never forgotten the lesson she had learned as a starry-eyed twenty-four-year-old legal secretary working for Paul Ziffren, back when he was still a young tax attorney at the Los Angeles law firm Loeb & Loeb. Helen was a lousy legal secretary, partly because she found the work so boring, but working for Mr. Ziffren had its perks. Namely, it kept her in meat and men. Meat, as Mr. Ziffren once gave her ten pounds of bacon as a gift (a client, Vons market, had given it to him) at the peak of rationing in the Forties, and she and her mother and sister had eaten it for eight days straight. And men, as the firm represented several wealthy entrepreneurs looking to buy or sell exclusive properties, and her job put her in close contact with all kinds of Possibles. When she wasn't typing up depositions, Helen fantasized about what it would be like to be the wife of Texan investor Joe Drown, who had just purchased the Hotel Bel-Air. Marrying into money wouldn't solve all of her problems—Mary would still be in a wheelchair, and Mother would still be depressed—but at least they wouldn't be poor.

One day, after Howard Hawks's wife, Slim, swanned into the office in Russian sable looking every inch the Best-Dressed Woman in the World, Helen approached her boss. Wouldn't it be something if *she* could marry rich and solve her family's problems?

Maybe Mr. Ziffren could send one of the firm's wealthy clients her way.

Mr. Ziffren studied her, a scrawny, needy little thing with a slight Arkie twang. "Helen, the kind of man you are thinking of, seriously rich, can marry anybody he wants to—a movie star, famous fashion model, heiress, somebody from a great family, her father a financial or political star," he explained. "He isn't necessarily going to want to marry *you*, whatever your inclinations!"

It was a cold but well-reasoned argument, and after Mr. Ziffren's little lecture, Helen put millionaires out of her sight—at least as potential husbands.

Instead, she took up with a wealthy builder—she later discreetly referred to him as "M."—who hired her to work at a movie studio that he had built in the heart of Hollywood. During her job interview, Helen gave an abbreviated version of her qualifications and her life story. After her father died in an elevator accident back in Arkansas, Mary had gotten polio and Mother had done everything she could to support them, but it wasn't enough. Even after moving back to Arkansas, they depended on *her* for money, Helen explained to this balding man with a limp who listened quietly before asking if she had a boyfriend.

He interviewed her on a Monday, and by the end of the week, they'd had sex on his office couch, all expensive buttery leather. In addition to a brand-new office, he set her up in a furnished apartment and began teaching her how to be a mistress. For starters, he said, she must buy some lingerie for herself and have cigars and alcohol on hand at all times. He soon sent over a fully stocked bar: more than three dozen bottles of liquor and liqueurs, from Chartreuse to crème de menthe.

It was a simple arrangement, and one in which they both had something to offer. He provided her with cash, a new wardrobe and wristwatch, a used car, and a stock portfolio; and she provided sex as well as constant entertainment with her funny-sad stories about Mother and Mary and all of their hillbilly relatives. She was Scheherazade of the Ozarks: charming, witty, somewhat well-read, and good in bed.

As long as she was with M., she didn't have to worry about money. He paid for Helen's first-ever airplane trip and sent her, alone, to explore places like Palm Springs and Catalina Island; but she soon grew lonely and unhappy. She had no office friends, no life outside of the affair. For a while she shared an apartment with a Jewish girl, her roommate Barbara, but M. was an anti-Semite and didn't want her associating with Jews. One day Helen was so bored in her little apartment that she polished off three bags of potato chips and a giant batch of clam dip all by herself before going downtown to watch three movies, one after another. She ultimately discovered that she wasn't very good at being a kept girl—eventually she started sleeping when she was with him instead of sleeping *with* him—but she milked M. for all she could.

It was M. who gave Helen the money to visit Cleo and Mary, and who found them an apartment in Los Angeles when they briefly moved back to California. Whatever the request—the plane fare to see her mother or some cash for new clothes—all Helen had to do was ask, providing a little something in return. "I was like a prostitute," she later told her friend Lyn. "I would sleep with him and get the $200." Despite her own waning interest in M., she was devastated when the affair ended; her security was gone.

Since then, Helen had gotten to know her share of the opposite sex. She continued to see men from the office, married men, and, occasionally, famous men like prizefighter Jack Dempsey. She discovered that what she lacked in natural beauty she could make up for in perseverance and a little skill she would later call "sinking in." No man ever tripped over himself when he saw Helen Gurley walking down the street, but over time, she found that if she could just get close enough to her target and turn on her own quiet charm, she could make an impression.

By her mid-thirties, Helen had had her heart broken several times, and with the help of her girlfriends and a few psychiatrists, she had glued it back together like a torn Valentine. Now David was the one who was recovering, and he would have to get starlets out of his system once and for all.

So, taking their mutual friend's recommendation, Helen waited. And then, one day nearly two years after his divorce from Wife No. 2 was finalized, David Brown liked the sound of Helen Gurley, too. According to Ruth's thumbnail sketch, she was a successful (but not aggressive) career girl who had:

- No debts
- No ex-husbands
- No kids
- No family nearby

At thirty-six, she had no history to hold her back, and everything she needed to be self-sufficient. Newly hired as a copywriter and account executive at the Hollywood ad agency Kenyon & Eckhardt, she lived in a cute little flat and was the owner of a Mercedes-Benz 190 SL and a small but sturdy portfolio of stocks.

One night in June 1958, Ruth hosted a small dinner party at her house for David and Helen. Slim and neat in a short blue shift, Helen felt chic but nervous. As they ate, she let David do most of the talking—after all, he was so good at talking, and she was rather shy. But when he walked her out to her little gray Benz, she mentioned that she had bought it the week before, paying $5,000 in cash. He was seriously impressed. Most of the women he knew wouldn't pay for a taxi, let alone their own Mercedes.

They began seeing each other somewhat regularly after that. Driving his beat-up Jaguar, David would pick Helen up at her little flat on Bonnie Brae Street downtown, a bit of a haul from his place in Pacific Palisades. Even though he wasn't wealthy himself (as it turned out, he didn't own the house overlooking the Pacific but rather rented it for three hundred dollars a month), David whisked Helen into a world of film premieres, dinner galas, and glamorous pool parties.

As accomplished as he was professionally, David had a painful past of his own. Born into a well-off family, he, too, had been abandoned by his father, Edward—but unlike Ira Gurley, who had died tragically, David's father had left by choice. An executive for the milk industry, he was a philanderer who abandoned his wife, Lillian, and their infant son in Brooklyn to marry his mistress. Raised by his mother and stepfather in Woodmere, Long Island, David met his father for the first time in seventeen years when an uncle arranged a visit. Edward later paid his way through Stanford and occasionally wined and dined him in Manhattan, along with whichever women joined them that night. But Edward's second family didn't know about David's existence until 1951, when he and his then-wife, Wayne, decided to make a spontaneous visit to his father's summer home in Southampton. In the moments before they arrived, Edward quickly brought his wife and grown children up to speed, divulging that he had a son in his thirties from a previous marriage, as well as a daughter-in-law and a grandson. "We were a secret. My father never listed me as his son in his *Who's Who in America* sketch until I was listed in *Who's Who in America* and included him in mine," David later recalled in his 1990 memoir, *Let Me Entertain You.* "He was the worst kind of snob."

David shared bits and pieces of his history with Helen early on, and sometimes, back at her typewriter, she wrote about his issues, which were starting to seem mixed up with her own. "He's only 42 but he feels he hasn't made an important contribution to the world," she mused after one of their dates in some notes to herself. (This particular document was a nearly six-page character study.) David was a bit of a dreamer, and not just when it came to the movies. Often when they were together, he would start telling Helen about his Ideal Girl, and that girl did not resemble her at all. "I feel more like a something with other people—smarter, cleverer, funnier and prettier," Helen wrote, "but feeling like that with other people just about equals feeling like nothing with David because he is so much smarter than *they* are."

After they had gone out a few times, David invited Helen over for dinner, giving her the perfect opportunity to investigate. His house was more run-down than she had expected, clearly in need of a woman's touch after his ex-wife's departure. Plaster was cracking throughout the house, the carpets were threadbare, and much of the furniture that David had been left with was old and mismatched; but again, Helen saw potential. Like David, the place had character. There was a large room lined with books—more than two thousand, Helen guessed. It was the first time she'd ever seen a real library in someone's home—clearly it wasn't just for show.

A few months into their courtship, when Helen's name came up for a charming garden apartment at the coveted Park La Brea complex, she turned it down, even though she had been on the waiting list for three years. Located in the Miracle Mile neighborhood of Los Angeles, within walking distance of the Farmers Market and

Wilshire Boulevard, the Park La Brea apartment was a fantastic deal with its two bedrooms, patio, and furnished kitchen for only eighty-nine dollars a month.

But in Brentwood, she found another apartment that had its advantages, too: It was newer, more modern, and best of all, only fifteen minutes away from David. Helen had learned from experience that if she wanted to have any chance of sinking into the man, she had to stay close.

GROUND RULES
1958–1959

"Don't you know that a man being rich is like a girl being pretty? You wouldn't marry a girl just because she's pretty, but my goodness, doesn't it help?

—Lorelei Lee (Marilyn Monroe) in *Gentlemen Prefer Blondes*, 1953

Sol Spiegel, Sam Siegel. Helen tried in vain to remember the difference. Or was it Sam Spiegel, Sol Siegel? Their last names were the same except for one letter, but the *p* was key. One of these two had produced *The Bridge on the River Kwai* for Columbia, while the other was the former head of production at Metro-Goldwyn-Mayer, but for the life of her Helen couldn't recall which was which. It wasn't the first time she'd had a problem remembering names. On one of her early visits to David's house, she met his son, Bruce, an awkward sixteen-year-old with glasses and a poor complexion, and their seven-year-old black-and-white collie, Duncan. At least to Helen's ears, both names sounded Scottish and vaguely aristocratic, and she hesitated to say either one out loud as they waited for his housekeeper, Mrs. Neale, to bring out the roast beef.

Eventually, she figured out a little mnemonic device: *D* was for Duncan and Dog, *B* was for Bruce and Boy. She never again got them confused, but she couldn't do the same for David's friends in Hollywood. There was no simple trick she could rely on to help her remember the names of all the important people she was supposed to know—and there was always so much she didn't know. For instance, what does one wear to a film premiere or the Academy Awards or a welcome-home-to-Hollywood party for Ingrid Bergman in the Crystal Room of the Beverly Hills Hotel? Helen spent at least half her salary buying black-tie dresses that she was beginning to see as dubious investments—if she and David ever broke up, she'd never have an occasion to wear them again. Not that she was getting much of a return on her investment in the present. She had felt sleek in a black dress slit down to her navel when she was introduced to the movie columnist Louella Parsons, but she might as well have been wearing a cloak of invisibility. Miss Parsons looked right through her and moved on to someone else, who mattered.

As nerve-racking as it could be to dress for one of David's events, what to wear was easier to figure out than what to talk about with his friends. What does one say to Ernest Lehman, the screenwriter extraordinaire who had written *Sweet Smell of Success* and *North by Northwest* and who happened to be one of David's closest friends? If you were Helen Gurley, you might rest your elbows on the marble table on his lanai, put on your most interested face, and say sweetly, "Tell me, Ernest, how do you write a screenplay?" If you were David Brown, you might choke on your gin and tonic and try to change the subject.

"You simply don't ask a screenwriter how he writes a screenplay," David informed Helen on the car ride home. "What would you think of somebody who asked *you* how you wrote copy?"

Nobody ever asked, but if someone had, Helen might have told that person how she wrote from life, drawing from her own experiences and observations and feelings. When she was a copywriter at Foote, Cone & Belding, she was the only woman present at meetings, and she used her instincts to her advantage. She knew what women wanted—things that the men in the room didn't know. She knew about tuna fish, which her girlfriends ate straight out of the can because they had just learned about the benefits of protein. She wasn't a mother, but she knew that the best way to sell Purex bleach was to speak to the woman at home, not as someone's mother or wife, but as an individual with her own agenda. "She's supposed to have a clean house for her husband and the children and everything, but I just have a *feeling* that she has some *feelings* of her own, which don't have to do with any of them," Helen might suggest at a meeting, before sharing the copy she had written from the mother's point of view.

"Nobody ever asks me," Helen told David now. "And I'd be delighted. Besides, I'm sure Mr. Lehman didn't mind talking about himself—he's human, isn't he?"

Helen prided herself on her ability to talk to anyone, but her charm didn't always work on the denizens of Hollywood. As much as she enjoyed rubbing shoulders with the rich and famous, it only left her feeling more self-conscious when the night was over.

"Look, you are not a Radcliffe undergraduate. You are a successful, mature businesswoman. Besides that, you're my girl, and when you're with me, you are not privileged to ask naïve schoolgirl questions about the movie industry," David said, not unkindly.

He was never unkind about the fact that she hadn't finished college beyond secretarial school, but it was clear to both of them that he possessed the superior intellect. "You must simply act," he told her, "as though you know more than you do."

(3)

SEX AND THE
NOT-SO-SINGLE GIRL
1961–1962

"It's useful being top banana in the shock department."
—Holly Golightly (Audrey Hepburn) in *Breakfast at Tiffany's*, 1961

Almost as soon as she walked into the rambling Spanish-style house at 515 Radcliffe Avenue in Pacific Palisades, Letty Cottin saw everything that Helen Gurley Brown was not.

She was not beautiful, or even pretty. Helen had admitted as much on the first page of *Sex and the Single Girl*, which Letty would be promoting as her book publicist, but this was their first meeting on Helen's home turf. Letty quickly assessed the tiny, wren-like woman standing before her. Just over five feet four in heels, Helen couldn't have weighed more than one hundred pounds. Everything about her seemed fragile; even her dull, Sanka-brown hair, which she worked into a sad bouffant or stiff flip when she didn't wear a wig. Except for her high forehead, there was nothing exceptional about her. Makeup could hide her wrinkles and acne scars to a point, but it didn't conceal the overall impression that she was, at the bottom of it all, painfully plain.

Sizing her up from under her own mane of long blond hair, Letty couldn't help but feel a twinge of disappointment. This was the woman she was supposed to sell to the public as the savior of single girls everywhere?

She was not sexy—and she wasn't single. As usual, David was standing nearby. With his sparse gray hair, sweet smile, and gentlemanly aspect, he didn't exactly seem like "the type who'd ravage females on leopard-skin rugs," as future gossip columnist Cindy Adams would soon write in an article about the Browns in *Pageant* magazine, but it was David who had come up with the idea for *Sex and the Single Girl* in the first place.

Letty took in the Technicolor sunset, panoramic views of the Pacific, and terraced gardens that cascaded down from the back of the house. Single girls didn't have haciendas—or housekeepers, for that matter. It was up to Mrs. Neale, the gray-haired British maid who had taken care of David after his second divorce, to get dinner ready, padding around in her crisp white uniform and ox-fords.

As she sat across from her new assignment, it dawned on Letty that the job of promoting Helen Gurley Brown would be trickier than she had anticipated. She had approximately three months to get Helen ready for the spring release of *Sex and the Single Girl* and the onslaught of TV, radio, and press promotion that they hoped would accompany it, and they had a lot of work to do. At forty, Helen was a well-respected account executive and copywriter at one of the biggest advertising agencies in Los Angeles, Kenyon & Eckhardt, where she went after leaving Foote, Cone & Belding. She could sell the fantasy behind any eye shadow, lipstick, or cake of makeup, but selling herself as a sexy, confident woman was another matter, and Letty was here to train her to act the part.

Letty's boss was Bernard Geis, better known as Berney around the New York offices of his publishing company, Bernard Geis

Associates, on East Fifty-Sixth Street. A natural showman with hooded eyes, a broad smile, and dark, deeply waved hair, Berney prided himself on turning books into sensations and authors into celebrities, if they weren't already. He got an early glimpse of the power of a good plug in 1957, while working as an editor at Prentice-Hall. When one of his authors, *House Party* TV host Art Linkletter, made an on-air mention of his new book— *Kids Say the Darndest Things!*— sales spiked, and a bestseller was born.

Realizing the potential of flashy promotion to sell books, Berney founded his own firm the following year, securing financial backing from several limited partners, including some of his top authors: Linkletter, "Dear Abby" columnist Abigail Van Buren, and Groucho Marx, to name a few. (Bernard Geis Associates' first list of five titles featured Linkletter's *The Secret World of Kids*, Van Buren's *Dear Teen-Ager*, and Marx's memoir, *Groucho and Me*.) Berney published books but left their distribution to other companies, and his particular genius was in advertising, promotion, and publicity. As Letty would later recall: "Berney Geis was an original. An innovator. Until he came along, publishing as a profession spoke in whispers and wore tweed. After Berney, it whooped and hollered. Dressed in neon. It made waves."

In the gentleman's world of publishing, Berney was considered to be a schemer and a spotlight-seeker. Around the office, he was a lovable scamp. He called women "dames" and wasn't above hiring a secretary because she had great legs. He razzed his underlings—"How many times a week do you have sex?" was a favorite question—and he kept them entertained. By the early Sixties, he had famously installed a fireman's pole in his office leading to the floor below. A modern dancer in college, Letty slid down it every day.

Letty had experienced Berney's salaciousness firsthand, but she also saw he was more bark than bite, and she knew he saw great promise in her. A lover of fine food and wine, Berney had given Letty her first taste of artichoke one day at lunch, teaching her how to eat it. He also gave Letty her first taste of real power. She was barely out of college when she was hired to be an assistant to a woman named Hilda Lindley, the director of publicity and subsidiary rights, and when Hilda left the company soon afterward, Letty begged Berney for the chance to step up to her job. He said yes, and she nearly passed out.

At twenty-two, Letty was running four departments at the company. She handled everything from subsidiary rights to advertising, and she soon discovered that she had a flair for promotion. Shortly before her trip to Los Angeles, Berney handed Letty the manuscript for *Sex and the Single Girl*, which Helen had been writing in stages and sending to Berney for his input. He thought it was going to be a "smasherino."

"I'd like to publish this," Berney told Letty. "What can you do for it?"

Letty took the pages home to her apartment in Greenwich Village and got to work. "Have you got it? Can you get it? Are you sexy? Let's see. What *is* a sexy woman?" Helen asked in one of Berney's favorite chapters, "How to Be Sexy." "Very simple. She is a woman who enjoys sex."

Reading Helen's dishy accounts of her own romances and romps, Letty was incredulous. She had just gotten her own prescription from her doctor for the Pill, two years after the Food and Drug Administration approved Enovid by G.D. Searle and Co. Delivered in a small brown medicine bottle, Enovid had already been on the market for a few years as a means of treating menstrual problems, but it was the first time the FDA had deemed a pill safe and effective for birth control purposes—on the condition that it was prescribed by a doctor. (In 1963, Ortho-Novum joined the market with its Dialpak dispenser, featuring a built-in memory aid, discreetly designed to resemble a makeup compact.)

Discreet as the packaging was, those tiny tablets changed everything. Single women no longer had to rely on their dates to provide a condom or, in the absence of one, wonder if the rhythm method really worked; their birth control was literally in their own hands. In Greenwich Village, where the Bitter End once displayed a sign that read "Folksingers Are Promiscuous; Don't Spoil the Image," sex between strangers became as common as a cold. People were definitely having it, but no one was talking about it casually, not out in the open, not like this: "The average man with an urge will charge like a Pampas bull, smear your lipstick, scatter your bobby pins, crush your rib cage and scare the living daylights out of you," Helen wrote in *Sex and the Single Girl*, working into her argument about why every woman should experience a Don Juan at least once. "Don Juan would curl his lip at such tactics. He never makes passes without first establishing desire. He will devote several nights to the project if necessary, which it rarely is."

Like a knowing older sister, Helen dished out cheeky advice on where to find men (the office, the tennis court, a wealthy chapter of Alcoholics Anonymous) and how to attract their attention ("Carry a controversial book at all times—like Karl Marx' *Das Kapital* or *Lady Chatterley's Lover*"). She gave tips on how to whip up crabmeat puffs, crash-diet on eggs and wine, mail-order a wig, and wear makeup. But there were also more substantial chapters on how to start a career, save money, find an apartment for one, and have an affair, from beginning to end. "A lady's love *should* pay for all trips, most restaurant tabs, and the liquor," Helen advised. "That's simply good affair etiquette." As for how to answer the age-old question, "Should a man think you are a virgin?" Helen was equally frank. "I can't imagine why, if you aren't. Is *he*? Is there anything particularly attractive about a thirty-four-year-old virgin?"

Helen's funny, forthright voice spoke to Letty immediately. She knew plenty of girls who'd slept with married men; one girl she knew scheduled her affairs for her lunch hour. Having seen *Breakfast at Tiffany's* the year before, Letty was modeling her life in part after Holly Golightly, her prototype for how a single woman could live in New York City in style. She didn't have a fish in a birdcage or a cat named Cat, but she did have, at various points, a duck, a rabbit, and a dog named Morpheus, God of Slumber. More important, she had her own apartment and her own mode of transportation. Miniskirted and zipping around town on her motor scooter, Letty was a vision of blond hair and bold independence. When Helen described the single woman as "the newest glamour girl of our times," something clicked. Who could be more glamorous than Holly Golightly, in her diamond tiara and little black dress? The difference was that Helen Gurley Brown wasn't at the whim of men who mistreated her. She had more than "mad money"; she made her own money. She was telling women they could give pleasure and *get* pleasure, without consequence. She was describing a lifestyle that Letty recognized as being real, if unspoken.

Back at the office, Letty cornered her boss. "Berney, you won't believe it. This is my life! This is true, this stuff is funny, it's shocking," Letty said. "We gotta do it!"

Not long after that, she was on a plane heading west to give Helen some media training in the comfort of her own home. "I want to see what you think of her as, you know, a talking head," Berney told her before she left.

What was she like as a talking head? Well, she had a head, and it was talking: "Letty dear," and "David dear." She had an odd (or ingenious) way of delivering her bold opinions in the same breath as little endearments and baby-talk phrases, like "pippy-poo" and "piffle-poofle." And then there was Helen's voice itself, soft and modulated, with little trace of her Arkansas roots. ("Listen to voices in movies. Most of them were willed into being by practice, practice, practice," she had written in her book. "If you squeak or squawk, are thin or reedy . . . or are decidedly nasal, consider a voice revise.")

In person, Helen came on as sweet as her recipe for chocolate soufflé with foamy vanilla sauce. But Letty knew from her exchanges with Helen that underneath the froth was a steeliness—and that she used flattery to get what she wanted. She was particularly ingratiating with Berney, whose thoughts were always *most* welcome, especially for a "girl writer" like herself. In the long letters that she regularly typed to Berney on her pink onionskin paper, she turned on the charm, and he responded to it. But it would be different when she was on TV with millions of viewers, a tough host, and just a few minutes of airtime to answer whatever questions he lobbed at her. Some people simply would not like her—some would even hate her for writing a book that threatened the very core of their beliefs and values, and Helen would have to learn how to deal with that without bursting into tears.

"Not everyone is going to be charmed by you," Letty said. "There are some people who are going to think that you are morally vapid, or worse."

The only way to get Helen past it was to practice—to put her through her paces. Letty made herself the interviewer in an impromptu press conference, right there in the living room. How would Helen respond when people blamed her for corrupting the minds of young girls? What would she say when they accused her of being a home wrecker? How would she answer when asked what kind of husband would let his wife write such a book in the first place? A girl like her didn't deserve a husband—she was a manipulator, a phony!

If all went according to plan, Helen and her book would be featured on the local and national news, on the *Today* show and the *Tonight Show*, and on every major radio station in every major city. She needed to have an answer for every question, or at least an out, and she needed to keep cool and stay focused. She had a job to do—and that was to sell as many copies of her book as humanly possible.

For now, they would start from the beginning. Most people tended to ask an unoriginal opening question, along the lines of, "How'd you come to write the book?" "Unless they've read the book—and most people will have only dipped in—you basically have to control the interview," Letty said. "If people aren't asking the questions that you want the reader to know the answers to, you have to answer no matter what the question."

She shouldn't answer too literally, though, Letty advised. No one would care about the technicalities. Readers would want the rags-to-riches story about a poor little girl from a nowhere town who thought she'd never get out. They would want to hear about the father who died young, the crippled older sister, and the poverty-stricken mother, all territory that Helen had covered in her book. Most of all, they would want to hear about how that poor little girl eventually made good, working her way through seventeen secretarial jobs and surviving countless broken hearts before becoming a successful career woman—and (at the ripe age of thirty-seven) landing the husband of her dreams. Because if Helen could do it, maybe they could, too.

From hillbilly to Hollywood: It was as exploitable a story as the hooker with the heart of gold, but Helen had to do more than tell her story. She had to *sell* her story. She had to do more than talk to her audience—she had to get people to talk among themselves. The most precious commodity would be word-of-mouth advertising.

"So, Helen," Letty asked, "how did you come to write this book?"

Once again, Letty was aware of David's presence in the room, and though it was distracting at first—not to mention a little weird—she soon saw the added benefit.

Long after Letty left, David would still be there to run Helen through whatever questions he had thought up, so she would not fall apart when the time came to step into the studio lights.

(4)

THE STORY EDITOR
1959–1962

"If you would please your woman, put her to work and help her succeed."

—David Brown, in an early interview with *Cavalier*

How did Helen come to write *Sex and the Single Girl*? The story the Browns decided to share with the public was Hollywood-simple. Helen was out of town visiting family when David came across carbon copies of letters she had written. In the press, Helen claimed the notes in question were to her former boss, Don Belding, when she was his executive secretary at the advertising agency Foote, Cone & Belding, but David also discovered some love letters she had sent to another man.

His name was Bill Peters, he was married, and he worked as an account executive at the Manhattan ad agency J. Walter Thompson. Helen met Bill on a flight from Los Angeles to New York in May 1949 (she was twenty-seven), and after that initial meeting, they wrote to each other for nearly two years. In letter after letter, Helen regaled Bill with engaging, funny stories—about a miserable party she threw for her girlfriends ("I kept thinking what an intolerable waste of gin it was"), a chic new haircut she got ("With a ukulele and a striped blazer, I could be a 1927 flapper"), and a visit home to Osage ("I swam and ate fried chicken and pondered the unprogressiveness of Arkansas"). He wrote back eagerly, always delighted to hear from her, and gradually, she fell deeply, madly in love. Nothing ever did come of their flirtation in the form of an actual relationship, but it yielded an unexpected result a decade later when, not long after they married, David stumbled upon the carbon copies in a storage room of their house. When Helen came home from her trip, he admitted that he had read her letters, which he thought were original, witty, and warm. She could really write, he told her. Maybe she should write something for publication, but what?

In many ways, David was essentially a talent scout by profession. Early in his career, after a stint as a freelance writer, he formed a company called David Brown Associates, tapping his longtime friend Ernest Lehman to be an associate. The goal of the company had been to find people with great stories to tell but without the ability to do them justice; David and Ernest would do the writing. In the late Thirties, one of their first clients was a journalist named Martin Proskauer (later Proctor), who had fled Germany as Hitler's attacks on Jews were escalating. Proctor had a story to tell about how Jews and other refugees had smuggled their wealth out of the country—diamonds were being hidden in snowballs and tossed over the Swiss border to catchers in carefully choreographed snowball fights—but he had difficulty writing in English. *Harper's* eventually ran the piece, "Black Money," with Martin Proctor's byline, but David and Ernest had ghosted it. Around the same time, they wrote about the aviatrix Jacqueline Cochran, who had grown up poor and orphaned in northern Florida before becoming a shampoo girl at a salon, eventually meeting Floyd B. Odlum, the successful businessman she would marry. It was a classic rags-to-riches story, and as those tales tend to be, it was also one of self-invention. After interviewing Cochran in Manhattan, David wrote up the piece and sold it to *Glamour*.

David had a nose for a good story, and he developed it first as the nonfiction editor at *Liberty* magazine, where he later edited fiction and eventually became editor-in-chief. By 1949 he was working as managing editor at *Cosmopolitan*; he was hired with the personal approval of William Randolph Hearst, known as "the Chief." While there, David reported to Herbert R. Mayes—the editor-in-chief of another Hearst title, *Good Housekeeping*—whom the company had put in charge of overseeing *Cosmopolitan* during a rough transition. Originally called *The Cosmopolitan* when it was started in 1886 by Paul Schlicht, a founding executive of Schlicht & Field Company, a Rochester, New York–based manufacturer and distributor of office products, the magazine had been through a few revamps already. It was conceived as a family magazine, featuring a mix of fiction and homemaking articles, but within a few years it was facing bankruptcy. Its next owner, a wealthy automobile entrepreneur named John Brisben Walker, reenergized the publication, introducing illustrations and attracting literary all-stars like Mark Twain and Willa Cather, before selling *Cosmopolitan* to William Randolph Hearst in 1905. A newspaper magnate with political ambitions, Hearst briefly turned *Cosmopolitan* into a muckraking magazine, before it became a literary magazine once again.

Over the years, *Cosmopolitan* published works by John Steinbeck, Edith Wharton, and Ernest Hemingway. Hollywood producers regularly mined it for material: Mary Orr's 1946 short story, "The Wisdom of Eve," became *All About Eve*, starring Bette Davis. For a while, *Cosmopolitan* enjoyed great success, but by the Fifties it began to suffer from a chronic identity crisis, along with other similarly broad-based, general-interest magazines, such as *Liberty*, *Collier's*, and *The Saturday Evening Post*. The more generalized *Cosmopolitan* became, the less impact it seemed to have. Was it upscale or popular? Targeting housewives or their husbands? What was the vision, and when it came to attracting both readers and advertisers, could it compete with television?

Herb Mayes was a legend, a Harlem-born high school dropout who had risen to become one of the most influential editors in the country. Over time, he became a mentor to David, who worked harder to impress Mayes than he had for almost anyone else, partly because Mayes was so hard to impress. Mayes got the best ideas out of David because that's what he demanded. Once a week, David and two other editors from *Cosmopolitan* would make the trek to Mayes's house in Stamford, Connecticut, to pitch story ideas for the magazine. The goal was to sell him on as many ideas as possible in one hour, while trying not to get blotto on gin, scotch, or bourbon; may the best man win. Mayes tried everything to save *Cosmopolitan*, but its circulation was plummeting. David had some ideas of his own about how to guide the magazine, but he wasn't going to hang around forever as the second in command, and it didn't seem likely that Hearst was going to hire him to be the next editor-in-chief of *Cosmopolitan*.

In the early Fifties, David was starting to get restless when Hollywood producer and studio executive Darryl F. Zanuck sent word that he wanted "the best editor in New York" to oversee 20th Century Fox's story department. Zanuck envisioned the studio operating more like a national magazine, and he wanted David Brown to be in charge of finding and acquiring material that could be made into movies. When David broke the news to Mayes that he was heading to Hollywood, Mayes was disappointed to see him go and suggested that he must have accepted the job because of the money, as David later recalled in his memoir, *Let Me Entertain You*: "I said, 'No, Herb, the truth is that I wasn't able to get the top job here. For whatever reason, it was denied me. And just as companies fire editors, editors can fire companies, and I'm firing this company because it was unable to give me the job of editor-in-chief.' "

In December 1951, Fox announced David's appointment as managing editor of its story department in California. A connoisseur of theater and literature, David soon built a reputation in Hollywood as a man who zealously encouraged writers to develop their craft. (*Three Coins in the Fountain*, *Peyton Place*, and *The Diary of Anne Frank* were among the stories he persuaded the studio to purchase.)

In fact, Helen suspected that he had wanted to turn his second wife, Wayne Clark, into a writer. They had met at Hearst, where Wayne, a leggy brunette with a Vassar education, was working as a senior editor at *Good Housekeeping*. When David brought her to live in Los Angeles, he also took her away from her career, and watched her become bored and unhappy in exile. They divorced after Wayne went back to work at an advertising agency, where she fell in love with her boss. Over time, it became David's firm belief that a woman's investment in her own career could save a marriage.

On September 25, 1959, after a year and a half of dating and one stern ultimatum by Helen, she and David finally married in a modest ceremony at Beverly Hills City Hall, surrounded by their mutual friend Ruth Schandorf, David's son Bruce, and David's secretary, Pamela Hedley. Wearing a conservative long-sleeve dress and holding a bouquet of flowers, Helen was the picture of primness, standing next to David in a dark suit and tie—which, presumably, he loosened a bit when they headed to Largo's nightclub on Sunset Boulevard to watch the bleach-blond stripper Candy Barr do her thing. (Originally from Texas, she was known to don a cowboy hat and six-shooters, along with her panties and pasties.)

Soon after, Helen moved into the rambling house at 515 Radcliffe Avenue, where she began the arduous process of making

David's bachelor's pad her home. By then she was already one of the most successful women working in advertising, but a few months into their marriage, she was miserable in her new job as an account executive at Kenyon & Eckhardt. At Foote, Cone & Belding, she had been something of a little mascot as the former secretary who had worked her way up to a copywriter—she was their status girl, their beloved pet.

At her new firm, there were quite a few girl copywriters, and competition was fierce. Working on the Max Factor account, Helen guessed that she personally dreamed up 9,274 names for various beauty products, but everyone else came up with just as many. Say they were trying to name a red lipstick. First, Helen wrote down every shade of red that came to mind. Next, she came up with a list of every wild animal, mineral, vegetable, fruit, flower, spice, emotion, and exclamation she could think of. Then she simply mixed and matched: WHIPPED CHERRY, WELL-BRED RED, WARNINGFLARE RED, WACK-A-DOO-RED! WOW! WHEEEEE! WHOOPEE! The exercise was fun, but frustratingly pointless. Before these brainstorm sessions, Max Factor had preselected the product name anyway. The goal was simply for the agency to come as close as possible to guessing it, proving how clever they were in the process. It was a battle of wits between client and agency, but the game was always rigged.

And then there were the commercials. Helen was terrible at writing for TV. She came up with one scenario where a girl took her hair to the shrink to see why it hated her, and another featuring a character named Mr. Acne who stalked schoolkids, looking for the perfect victim to attack. She doubted herself every time another girl's work was chosen over hers, and she worried that she was falling short of expectations. Worst of all, she was just another cog in the machine: Kenyon & Eckhardt had lured her in with one of the highest salaries ever paid to a woman copywriter, only to submit her ideas to the scrutiny of countless middlemen until they were totally leached of style. To add insult to injured ego, after she married David, the agency decided they were paying her too much and cut her $20,000 salary by almost half.

One Sunday, when Helen and David were out on their regular stroll in Will Rogers State Park, she vented about her job. "What am I going to do?" she asked David. "I don't know of any other jobs. I don't want to leave. They're not firing me but nobody is paying any attention to my work and I'm miserable." David had helped plenty of other people do some writing on the side, she pointed out. "How about me? Maybe I could write a book. Do you think so?"

As it turned out, David had just met with someone from a publishing company in New York, and he had given the man a one-page outline he had typed up for a guide on how to have an affair. He also had shared the idea with a woman writer he knew, but she seemed lukewarm about it. "There's a chapter on the apartment," he explained to Helen now. "There's one on cooking and one on how to clear the decks for action."

"David," Helen said, "that sounds like my book. I think I could do something with that. You've got to get that outline back from whomever you gave it to."

David did get it back, and Helen began to brainstorm, scrawling her thoughts in a shorthand book. At first it was just a borrowed idea on borrowed time: something to do when she got bored at the office, a way to keep her mind occupied. She took a stab at writing a few pages, showed them to David, and waited. "It won't work," he told her after that first read. "It's not yours. It's tight—it's not you." She showed David several other starts, which he promptly rejected for the same reason. Her writing was too structured, her tone impersonal—it wouldn't speak to people, it wouldn't sell.

David envisioned a cutesy manual for girls who wanted to get rid of the extra men in their lives so that they could home in on Mr. Right, but as Helen jotted down more and more notes about her days as a bachelorette, she realized that she was tapping into a much bigger theme: the stigma of the single woman. In July 1960, *Look* magazine had run a story titled "Women Without Men," which reported that 70 percent of American girls married before the age of twenty-four. "From then on," warned the writer, Eleanor Harris, "it's a downhill slide." In her piece, Harris portrayed singledom as a social illness worthy of psychiatric help. Single women generally felt that they weren't "getting much out of life," said one psychiatrist who was interviewed for the article. As a group, they were dissatisfied, anxious, and depressed. Those who weren't on a "frenzied man hunt," Harris added, possibly had a "sex problem" like Lesbianism (with a capital *L*). Others were content to settle for "a man-free life."

But what about all the women who weren't ready to get married and didn't want a man-free life? Did they really have to abide by the prissy advice in old-fashioned magazines like *Ladies' Home Journal*? "There are two sound ways for a girl to deal with a young man who is insistent," the *Journal* proclaimed in a May 1961 article about double standards. "She can marry him, or she can say 'No.'" Of course, a girl could say "yes" before marriage and often did—and Helen, for one, believed she would be better off for it. A woman who had taken the time to date around and develop herself as a full person would be more interesting and prepared for marriage when she finally did find the One.

Armed with new conviction, Helen sat down and wrote her opening lines—how she had managed to land a great man without being scintillating or all that pretty. She took it to David, and after reading it, he finally gave her the approval she craved. "I think you've got it," he said. It was a go.

Ideas came to her while she was in the shower, under the hair dryer, and at her desk at the agency. She developed her own outline, much more detailed than David's, and by the time she finished adding to it, she had a sheaf of papers—it was almost a book. She wrote and rewrote the sample chapters until they sounded as if they had simply written themselves.

David was her first reader and her connection to people who mattered. It was David's trail of friends from the publishing world that eventually led to Bernard Geis, after a series of other publishers had turned the book down, dashing her confidence. As hands-on as Berney was, David was Helen's live-in editor—and he was merciless. Sometimes he crossed out whole passages. He made her rewrite the big chapter, "The Affair," three times over before he accepted it.

It was David who told Helen to publish *Sex and the Single Girl* under her married name, even though he knew his own family would disapprove. For the book to be successful, he insisted, she needed to have authority, and in order to have authority, she had to be courageous enough to write about her own experiences and affairs.

As Mrs. Helen Gurley Brown, she was living proof that a nice girl could have sex, like it, and use it to her advantage.

5

A FUN SCAM
1962

> "An extra woman is a problem. . . . Extra women mean extra ex-
> pense, extra dinner-partners, extra bridge opponents, and, all
> too often, extra sympathy."
>
> —*Live Alone and Like It: A Guide for the Extra Woman,*
> by Marjorie Hillis, 1936

Back at the office in New York, Letty wrote to Helen to thank her for the visit, and for talking her up to Berney. "Your very kind, very superlative comments about me impelled Berney to ask if I had put you up to it," she joked. "I think that I have finally convinced him that no payola was involved and no pressure put upon you to rave about me to 'The Boss.'" After buttering up the Browns with some compliments of her own, Letty got down to business, mapping out the beginnings of a promotional and publicity plan. She knew that the success of *Sex and the Single Girl* depended largely on their ability to package the message with the messenger. But what was the message they wanted to get across?

It was the spring of 1962. The United States was intensifying its presence in Vietnam, while back home civil rights activists faced off against segregationists in the South. Politically, change was in the air, but socially, the early Sixties still felt more like the Fifties: John F. Kennedy was president, and the newspapers were saturated with photos of his perfect all-American family, including little Caroline riding her pony, Macaroni, on the White House grounds.

Against this backdrop of charmed domesticity, magazines written not for the single woman, but rather for the young suburban housewife who had everything, and nothing, to do. Acknowledging that "time is the housewife's great bugaboo" in its April 1962 issue, *Good Housekeeping* gave her time-saving tips on how to iron her husband's clothes, fix sandwiches for the children, shine the silver, wax the windows, dust the furniture (if she polished it at the same time, it could be fun, "like a game"), sponge-mop the floors, cook a Hungarian roast, whip up a Cherry Cinnamon Float, and still manage to put her face on and do her hair before *he* walked through the door. "When the clock says Charlie's due home, and I see something *must* be done, I twirl up a straggly wisp where necessary and plant a bow over it," as one housewife shared.

American society simply wasn't built for a woman on her own. In most parts of the country, a woman needed a husband to sign a lease, open a business, or apply for a credit card in her name. Looking through the help-wanted ads in a major metropolitan newspaper, such as the *New York Times*, she was limited to the "Female" section with its listings for sleep-in maids and housemothers, typists, secretaries, stenographers, clerks, switchboard operators, administrative assistants, and other Gal Fridays. (Listings for accountants, attorneys, and engineers were filed separately under "Help Wanted—Male.") Especially if she was applying to be a receptionist ("RECEPT 'NO SKILLS' Exciting ground flr opp for atr gal in glamorous midtown Mad Ave. office"), it helped if she had a pleasant phone voice and a pretty face and didn't wear glasses. If she got as far as the interview, her prospective employer might ask if she'd ever been pregnant or planned to be. Depending on her answer, she might not be hired, and if she got pregnant on the job, she could be fired. If she lived in a state where the Pill was a real option (many states restricted access to contraception), she might get a prescription if she felt brave enough to ask for it, but she still lived in fear of becoming pregnant and needing to have an illegal abortion. Her own family didn't know what to make of her. If she hadn't married by twenty-four, people became concerned. By thirty, she was considered a lost cause.

Everyone knew her, and yet sometimes she felt no one really understood her. But Helen Gurley Brown did. She understood her because she had been an "extra woman," until she married David Brown in 1959 at the age of thirty-seven.

The audience for *Sex and the Single Girl* was obvious. In 1960, there were an estimated 21 million "women without men" living in America—they outnumbered unattached men by nearly 4 million—but what would they make of the little biographical detail that the author of *Sex and the Single Girl* was now married and living in the lap of luxury? "I think marriage is insurance for the *worst* years of your life," Helen had written. "During your best years, you don't need a husband. You do need a man of course every step of the way, and they are often cheaper emotionally and a lot more fun by the dozen."

Helen's own status as a wife was a fact that couldn't be ignored but shouldn't be overtly advertised, either. And yet Letty saw that David as a husband was an undeniable part of the package; she sensed that his support could be a key to the book's success, and not just because of his Hollywood connections.

Over the course of her career as a book publicist, Letty would pull off a lot of stunts. To promote *Valley of the Dolls*, Jacqueline Susann's hugely popular novel about pill-popping starlets, she created fake prescriptions as teasers. At a party for another client,

Helen, thirty-seven, and David, forty-three, at Beverly Hills City Hall on their wedding day, September 25, 1959. (*Family photograph courtesy of Norma Lou Honderich.*)

Harpo Marx, she took over a room at the Algonquin, giving guests hard-boiled eggs, Harpo wigs, and harps to pluck on. Then there was her treatment for *The Exhibitionist*, a popular novel about an aging voyeur, published under the pen name Henry Sutton. Letty bought a Times Square billboard to advertise the book, an unheard-of move at the time, and hired a live model to dance in a bikini on the sign's scaffolding; she also gave the press body paint, along with instructions to decorate the girl as they pleased. (As anticipated, the model attracted lots of attention, especially when she removed her top in front of hundreds of gawkers; this led to Berney's arrest—and priceless publicity.)

The more outlandish the idea, the better; Berney loved a good

gimmick. But selling a mousy, married woman as the swinging patron saint of single girls when her own husband was standing by
her side, complicit in the whole presentation? That was truly a
master scheme.

"She worked very hard to create this package, which I always
felt she knew perfectly well was a put-on, a kind of a fun scam,"
Letty says. "We were selling the single girl experience through
the voice of a married woman. It was all very subliminal: 'What
you see is where you would end up if you wanted, but I'm not selling marriage. I'm selling singlehood.' If she had been single with
no trophy husband, I'm not sure that she would have carried the
authority that she did. The implicit message is: 'Do what I do, and
you get a David.'"

6

SINGLE WOMEN OF THE WORLD, UNITE!
1962

*Should Men Be Allowed
To Read This Woman's Book?*

"Is there any way possible to keep men from reading it? There's too much in it they shouldn't know!"—GYPSY ROSE LEE

"It should be put on every man's bed table—when he's free, that is."—JOAN CRAWFORD

—A press release for *Sex and the Single Girl*
from Letty Cottin, April 16, 1962

Several months had passed since Letty first read Helen's manuscript as it came to Berney's office, chapter by chapter. During that time, Joan Crawford had read it, too. She was Hollywood royalty, but she was also a friend of David and was happy to help Helen out by giving her a blurb. Letty used her endorsement, along with a quote from burlesque entertainer Gypsy Rose Lee, to run in daily teaser ads in newspapers across the country.

"It's the old '*Everybody* is talking about *Sex and the Single Girl*' approach," Letty told Helen, and they had to fulfill the hype. In three weeks they would have finished books, and Letty wanted to be ready to roll with their publicity campaign by the time the first shipment of books arrived at the office.

Berney was a firm believer in the old adage that there is no such thing as bad publicity, and *Sex and the Single Girl* was a perfect book for offbeat promotion. One of their more creative ideas was to get the book banned. To that end, Letty had sent an advance galley to the head librarian at the Little Rock public library, asking for a statement, but secretly hoping for a burst of fury.

"We're not getting too far in our attempt to get your book banned in Little Rock," Letty wrote in a letter to Helen after getting no response from the library. "A little bit of censorship in the right places won't hurt. Any suggestions?"

"Maybe a Catholic ban!" Helen wrote back. "Letty dear, I don't know *how* to get a public denunciation—a nice, strong, snarly, vocal one—from some religious leader, but it *is* a possibility. It's *such* an exploitable subject."

Letty promised to submit the book for review or advance comment to an editor at the *Catholic Digest*. If she had her number right, the woman would explode in a fit of moral indignation and call Helen Mary Magdalene, pre-salvation, she said.

The agency left no promotional stone unturned, but Helen was the one who would have to do the real digging, especially once the book was released. Her professional and personal contacts would be key, Letty added. Would she be willing to call up a few of her old boyfriends and enlist them in a wild promotional scheme?

No, Helen wrote back, her semi-famous exes were out, but not necessarily to protect their privacy. Her real concern was that, if she started name-dropping, she would seem like a show-off—and that would clash with her image as the humble and selfless savior of single women everywhere.

What about her contacts in the advertising world? Letty prodded. "I know you worked like a dog on the Max Factor account and I'm wondering how close you were with the big shots there. In other words, would it be conceivable that Max Factor would endorse your chapters on makeup while taking credit for the identification of you with their account. Perhaps co-op advertising lurks somewhere in the crystal ball."

Helen rejected that idea, too, since the company had recently fired her firm, Kenyon & Eckhardt. Not that Max Factor would have agreed anyway. When it came to other accounts, she added, "I just don't think there would be anything *in* it for them."

But Helen later reconsidered. If they sent along a book with a soft sell, pointing out the Max Factor connection, perhaps the company would think of *something*. After all, if Helen looked good, Max Factor would look good, too. She hadn't just been writing their copy; she was wearing their products. She was frequently buying what she was selling, and selling what she was buying. Max Factor's Hypnotique was in her top three for inexpensive perfumes, and she had been using Pan-Cake for twenty-two years to hide her acne scars. Naturally, she gave a nod to Hypnotique in her chapter on how to be sexy ("Douse the perfume on cotton, put another piece of cotton in front of it and tuck it inside your bra") and included beauty tips from the company's makeup director in her chapter on cosmetics.

It seemed only reasonable to let Max Factor know that she was touting their products in *Sex and the Single Girl*. On her pink paper, Helen drafted a note to the staff at Max Factor, explaining that someone who worked on their account had just written a book—and she personally wanted them to have a copy. By the way, they might consider turning to pages 80 and 216, where she wholeheartedly endorsed Hypnotique and Pan-Cake. Helen hammered out the rest of the message—part sales pitch and part bluff, suggesting that her success could be *theirs*, too—with directions for Letty to send it to Mr. Chester Firestein, the future heir to the throne of the Max Factor makeup empire.

Helen hadn't spent the better part of a decade working with advertisers for nothing: It was always about what's-in-it-for-them. The same was true of the consumer. They had to go after people who had something to gain, and no one had more to gain than the single working girls who could see themselves in Helen's image. On this point, Helen and Letty agreed.

"You are that *rara avis*, an agency copywriter turned author who draws her literary material from her personnel agency experience," Letty wrote to her. "If all the single girls now working in advertising agencies bought a copy of your book we'd be in the best seller strata without moving a finger. If even one-tenth of this group bought a copy we'd be well on our way!"

As an insider herself, Helen would know the best way to distribute the message of *Sex and the Single Girl* to the major ad agencies where single women were working as secretaries, clerks, and various Gal Fridays.

Of course, ad agencies were only a small slice of the promotional pie. They needed to find ways to make the book available to single girls where they gathered naturally, whether in a steno pool or a department store. "There are just too few single girls browsing through book stores," Helen pointed out.

They knew their audience: America's millions of single women, and working girls in particular. Now they just had to reach them.

IN MID-APRIL, HUNDREDS of book reviewers, newspaper and magazine editors, syndicated columnists, trade journalists, radio hosts, TV reporters, newscasters, and newsmakers around the country opened their mail to find an advance copy of *Sex and the Single Girl*, and an impassioned call to action.

DON'T KNOCK IT, GIRLS, SAYS AUTHOR—

BEING SINGLE IS SEXY

Single women of the world, unite! Here is your manifesto!

A daring new book that sheds no tears whatsoever for the unmarried female, "Sex and the Single Girl" (Bernard Geis Associates, May 23, $4.95) tells her instead how to be fascinatingly single. The author, Helen Gurley Brown (a single girl herself for 37 years) makes hash of the idea that all women must be married to achieve any degree of fulfillment. She points out that this is an arbitrary and ridiculously illogical notion—in view of the fact that there are four million too few single men in our country to go around.

In thirteen uninhibited and outspoken chapters, the single girl is told how to have a spectacular fling not by sublimating and substituting, but by living The Rich Full Life.

Letty spent the rest of the month canvassing the most influential readers in the country with promotional material for *Sex and the Single Girl*. She made sure that every major motion picture studio in Hollywood received a copy of the book. Often it came with her personal pitch, comparing Helen's book to Rona Jaffe's bestselling debut novel, *The Best of Everything*, published in 1958 by Simon & Schuster, where Letty had worked as a secretary the same year. One of David Brown's colleagues, a Fox producer named Jerry Wald, commissioned the book from Jaffe, a former associate editor at Fawcett Publications. He wanted to make a movie exploiting young women's appetites for sexually provocative stories (the previous year, he produced *Peyton Place*, starring Lana Turner), and, at twenty-five, Jaffe had the material to mine. Drawing from her own life, as well as her friends' experiences, she soon came back with a novel set in the steno pool at a fictional New York publishing company; it was a shockingly candid tale of three working girls trying to navigate the hazards of single life, from sexual advances in the office to an unwanted pregnancy. Two weeks later, the book was a bestseller. One year later, in 1959, it was a movie starring Hope Lange, Diane Baker, Suzy Parker, and Joan Crawford.

With any luck, *Sex and the Single Girl* would strike a similar chord with readers—and eventually moviegoers. "What *The Best of Everything* did to glamorize gals in publishing," Letty wrote in a letter to Jerry Wald himself, "this book does for single women the world over." Meanwhile, David quietly slipped the galleys to famous friends like Terry Melcher and his mother, Doris Day.

Bernard Geis Associates targeted bachelorettes themselves in a vigorous grassroots campaign. Responding to Helen's concern about the lack of single women browsing in bookstores, Letty sent personal missives to every conceivable place where they might congregate, from the YWCA to chapters of Parents Without Partners. In letters to resorts like Grossinger's in the Catskills, Letty directed hotel gift store managers to read Chapter Three, "Where to Find Them." Surely their clientele of working girls who saved all year long to vacation at YOUR HOTEL NAME HERE would consider their visit more successful if it resulted in a male liaison.

Around New York City, directors of the top secretarial schools received the book with specific instructions to read Chapter Five, "Nine to Five," with their students in mind. After all, Helen Brown herself traveled through seventeen different secretarial jobs before becoming one of the highest-paid female copywriters on the West Coast. "Naturally, not all of your girls will become the wife of a Hollywood producer or copywriter for one of the largest advertising agencies in the United States, or included in

Letty Cottin Pogrebin, photographed shortly after the publication of *Sex and the Single Girl*, in her office at Bernard Geis Associates. (*Collection of Letty Cottin Pogrebin.*)

'Who's Who of American Women,' but one can never tell!" Letty wrote. "That, I suppose, is the exciting part of the secretary's position: she has a close look at the important inside operations of a business. She can learn, advance and take initiatives."

Letty carefully tailored her letters to whomever she was addressing, but her main message always got through: "The book may shatter conventional shibboleths, it may offend self-styled moralists, it may delight liberal professional women, and infuriate many wives," she wrote, "but this is one book about which everyone will have an opinion."

7

The Decline of Western Civilization
1962

"As tasteless a book as I have read this year."

—Robert Kirsch reviewing *Sex and the Single Girl*
in the *Los Angeles Times*, July 6, 1962

O n the morning of May 23, 1962, Bernard Geis Associates sent Helen Gurley Brown a Western Union telegram, featuring an illustrated bouquet of roses and this message:

HEARTIEST CONGRATULATIONS ON THE BIRTH OF YOUR
LITERARY BABY
WE PREDICT A LONG AND LUSTY LIFE
ESPECIALLY THE LATTER

Staying at the Hotel Madison on East Fifty-Eighth Street in New York, Helen was only a short walk away from Berney's office, but the telegram was a nice welcome to New York—or, as he called it, Godless Gotham. Today was the day that *Sex and the Single Girl* would be hitting shelves in bookstores across the country. Helen's book tour had begun with a stop in Chicago, where she went tête-à-tête with the beloved gossip columnist Irv "Kup" Kupcinet on his weekly television show, *At Random*. She was in New York for a luncheon with Joan Crawford at the Gaslight

Club and various TV and radio interviews, including a spot on the *Tonight Show*. To celebrate the book's release, Berney and his wife wanted to throw a small dinner party for Helen and David. (Among the suggested guests in addition to Letty: David's old mentor Herb Mayes; the showbiz biographer Maurice Zolotow; the president of Bantam Books, Oscar Dystel; and their respective wives.) Unfortunately, David had had to cancel his trip east at the last minute—trouble was brewing at Fox over a multimillion-dollar adaptation of *Cleopatra*—but Letty had promised to meet Helen after another dinner for a late-night drink.

When the telegram arrived, it was before noon on Wednesday, and the city was at work. In offices throughout Midtown, everyone was still talking about the sultry birthday salute that Marilyn Monroe, sewn into a sheer, sparkly, flesh-colored gown, had given to President Kennedy four days earlier at Madison Square Garden. Outside Helen's window, vendors sold their last copies of the *New York Times* to businessmen in crew cuts and cordovan shoes wanting to read up on the Yankees' victory over the Angels, and what was happening in Vietnam. And in the boutiques along Fifth Avenue, salesmen fitted customers in seersucker suits as crisp as new banknotes, beckoning summer. Soon enough, people would be lining up in front of the Trans-Lux on Lexington Avenue and Fifty-Second Street to see *The Miracle Worker*, starring Patty Duke as Helen Keller and Anne Bancroft as her teacher, but the theaters were not yet open. And across the city, booksellers were still putting *Sex and the Single Girl* on the shelves, in time for the lunch crowd.

The book itself was far from showy. In fact, it looked more like a secret handbook. There was no picture on the front. Just a simple teal-blue cover, with the word *SEX* in light blue and the *i* in *Single* swapped out for the number 1 in the same shade. *The Unmarried*

Woman's Guide to Men, Career, the Apartment, Diet, Fashion, Money and Men, it read at the bottom under the author's name in all caps.

Long before it hit shelves, the distributors at Random House had insisted that the title be *Sex and the Single Girl* instead of *Sex for the Single Girl*, as was initially proposed—a subtle change that somehow seemed less crass. The jacket designers had been going for an equally understated, tasteful look that would titillate readers without going over the top and scaring them away. A single girl who was itching to get her hands on a copy of the book didn't have to feel conspicuous leafing through the pages. She only had to grab it before another girl did. When it was rightly in her hands, she turned to the back cover to get a good look at the black-and-white photo of the author, Helen Gurley Brown. Wearing a tailored jacket, pearls, and her hair in a prim flip, she looked like countless other agency girls who were just now typing on their IBM Selectrics at countless firms lining Madison Avenue. Or maybe she looked more like their boss. She had an authoritative air with her crossed arms, arched brows, level gaze, and small, bemused smile. "I dare you to read this book," she seemed to be saying to that girl.

Tens of thousands of girls accepted the dare.

By the time lunch rolled around, people were talking about *Sex and the Single Girl*. A week later, it was condensed in *The American Weekly*, reaching a nationwide audience and giving the book a flying start. It also landed on the bestseller lists of the *New York Times* and the *Los Angeles Times*, where on the latter it rose to No. 3, beating *Six Crises* by Richard M. Nixon. "How does it feel to be on top of Richard Nixon?" Letty quipped.

In millions of living rooms across America, Helen Gurley Brown was on TV talking about *Sex and the Single Girl*, though frequently the networks wouldn't allow her to actually utter the title. Instead, she displayed the book for the camera.

In hundreds of interviews with the press, she held her own, answering questions as Letty had instructed her to do—her way.

Where did she draw the line? Was she really suggesting that a single girl should pursue self-fulfillment at any cost, even if it meant having an affair with a married man?

"Now I don't have to go out and promote single women having affairs," Helen told a reporter from the *San Francisco Chronicle*, at a cocktail party in the St. Francis Hotel. "They have them all the time. . . . Far from wrecking a girl's life, it may make her a more interesting, womanly, compassionate human being."

But wasn't it ever terribly lonely being a single girl?

"Of course you feel alone sometimes, especially when all your friends are getting married around you," she told the Associated Press women's editor. "But if you want a husband, you'll get him— and a far better one at that—if you make it a secondary aim."

What kind of reaction to the book had she been getting so far?

Funny they should ask. Just a couple of weeks before, Helen's mother had sent her a furious letter, after reading a galley of *Sex and the Single Girl*. Scandalized by the subject matter, Cleo went so far as to urge Helen to stop publication altogether. Perhaps the book *would* be a sensation and stir up a lot of publicity, Cleo wrote: "So do murder and rape!"

Knowing a good hook, Helen trotted out the anecdote about her mother's angry response, furnishing one reporter's lead: "When Mrs. Cleo Bryan, 69, of Osage, Ark., picked up an advance copy of her daughter's first book, she was understandably proud," Art Berman wrote in the *Los Angeles Times*. "By the time she put the book down her pride had turned to horror."

Cleo, Helen's mother. (*Family photograph courtesy of Norma Lou Honderich.*)

Helen didn't mention that she thought her mother was being totally selfish, that all Cleo cared about was what a handful of busy-
bodies were gossiping about in the Ladies' Aid Circle in Osage.
Cleo's letter had in fact brought her to tears. (She'd read it while
sunning on the roof of her house—somehow, more than fifteen hundred miles away, Cleo could still bring her down.) She simply suggested that her book was meant for a hipper crowd. "My mother is
quite a dame," Helen told the *Times*, "but her day was different."

And what exactly did her husband make of it all?

"David put me up to writing the book, so to speak," Helen told
the *Times*, launching into their story of how he discovered copies
of old letters she had written to other men. The subtext was key:

Not only had he approved of *Sex and the Single Girl*, he had conceived of the idea and assigned it to her in the first place.

The day of her photo shoot for the *Times*, Helen put on a delicate sleeveless print dress cinched at the waist, round earrings, and what appears to be a glossy wig. Sitting on a sofa, she stroked the silky fur of her Siamese cat, Samantha, with one hand. In the other she held a single piece of paper several feet away from her face, so as not to obscure it—after all, a lot of effort had gone into those carefully drawn cat eyes and perfectly painted lips. In fact, she looked more like an actress reading for a role than a writer in the midst of her creative process, but she was going for glamour as she stared past the paper and typewriter placed in front of her, and somewhere into the middle distance.

As staged as it was, her pose was still better than the one that David, dressed in a jacket, starched shirt, and French cuffs, was experimenting with behind her. Leaning his elbows against the back cushion, he nestled his chin into his knuckles, framing his face like a heart, and pretended to read the page along with his wife.

POP! The scene was captured, and on the morning of Sunday, June 24, 1962, it ran in the *Los Angeles Times*. It was the perfect image, and it captured everything that the Browns and Bernard Geis Associates had worked so hard to engineer. Helen Gurley Brown was her own woman, with her own career, but she had her own man, too—not to mention a new book in the works. The article mirrored the image: Clearly Helen had found the right person in David, and he had found the right person in her. They were the picture of a new kind of couple, a husband and wife who were in business as well as in bed together, a team—that was the real message of the article, affixed with the headline "HUSBAND SAID 'WRITE.' Helen's Book Was a Shock to Her Mother."

As word of mouth spread, Helen Gurley Brown became the

topic du jour in offices and college dormitories, subways and living rooms, from the beaches of the Hamptons to the poolside lounges of Palm Springs.

In Los Angeles, bookstores couldn't hold on to their copies. For five weeks, Pickwick's in Hollywood devoted a window display entirely to copies of *Sex and the Single Girl*, opened to the more provocative chapters like "How to Be Sexy," and paired with a black bikini that the store owner had borrowed from a boutique across the street.

In Greenwich Village, hipsters mocked Mrs. Brown and her ludicrous guide for single girls over thirty. "There are no girls that age down here—only boys," a twenty-five-year-old Bronx-born reporter named Stephanie Gervis (later Harrington) wrote in the *Village Voice*, providing her own manhunting guide for readers. "Poets, writers, sculptors, and painters (unless they have galleries on Bleecker Street) are strictly for aesthetic nourishment and, of course, sex. Electricians are good for installing the hi fi set the stockbroker buys for you. . . . Radicals are good for nothing— they're always off making speeches." Folksingers could be found at the Café Wha? and the Bitter End, she added: "Be sure you arrive early, get a seat near the stage, and prostrate yourself at your idol's feet. Gaze at him adoringly."

Helen made an easy target, but spoofs and digs only carried the message further. People were talking about the book, and buying it, and that was what mattered. The religious bans that Letty and Helen were hoping for never happened—to their surprise, Helen was actually invited to speak at a Junior Catholic Woman's Club, whose single-girl members saw her book as their new bible. Meanwhile, newspapers published letters from incensed readers who shared the outrage Cleo had expressed to her daughter weeks before.

In the *San Francisco Chronicle*, one indignant man called Helen

Gurley Brown's messaging in *Sex and the Single Girl* "a libel against womanhood" that threatened the chastity of the nation's girls. "The breaking down of moral values . . . which this book indirectly advocates is leading Western civilization into a decline," he sputtered.

In the *Los Angeles Times*, book critic Robert Kirsch seemed personally offended by *Sex and the Single Girl*. "Miss Brown provides the blueprint of a female so phony that the man who cannot see through the mask and affectation deserves his fate," Kirsch spat. "Indeed, everything is a front. . . . She rushes breathlessly from punchy paragraph to compressed exposure, a creature of the advertising age, endorsing the phoniness and hard-soft-subliminal sell which substitutes for individuality, candor, sincerity. What she describes as sex is not sex at all but a kind of utility. Perhaps futility would be a better word."

Other critics agreed: Helen Gurley Brown was about as deep as a pillbox hat. But she also had her defenders. "At long last someone has written a book that says being single can be fun. Not only can be, but is fun—once unmarried ladies shake themselves free of the propaganda of wives' magazines," wrote Anne Steinert in the *New York Journal-American*. In the *San Francisco Examiner*, Mildred Schroeder predicted that the author's "sometimes shocking but always stimulating philosophy" would make *Sex and the Single Girl* "the most controversial topic on the cocktail circuit since Kinsey" and recommended it to every woman "over the age of consent," while the *Houston Chronicle* claimed it was as "racy and sassy" as its title suggested, but also full of "hard common sense." "Oh, you'll blush at a few of the paragraphs and ask yourself, 'Do I dare go on?'" wrote one reviewer in West Virginia's *Charleston Gazette*, before urging her readers to get past their embarrassment. "You'll bless her for her open frankness. . . . Honestly, you'll probably want to go out and try her 'secret formulas for success.'"

Just as the Browns had hoped, *Sex and the Single Girl* was a smash and Helen soon became a sensation. Reporters relished the chance to tell the tale of the poor little girl from Arkansas who made it big. Hers was a Horatio Alger story, and no one told it as vividly—or as frequently—as Helen herself.

Back at her typewriter, Helen fed in another sheet of onion-skin. "Brief Resume of What's Happened With the Book So Far," she typed at the top of the page, recapping her accomplishments through the month of June: *Sex and the Single Girl* would soon be on the *New York Times* bestseller list, having sold fifty thousand copies within a few weeks, and there was already a deal pending with Warner Bros., as well as talk of a Broadway show.

At the bottom of the page, she added a few more thoughts, her fingers tripping over the keys as she typed up her pitch for an article about the making of a bestseller—her own, of course. She imagined a picture story, illustrating her whirlwind tour through various autographing parties and TV appearances, all happening as she tried to hold on to her clients and her job at the ad agency. There would be a personal element as well. Thanks to her success with the book, David was benefiting in his career, too.

"David Brown in for new scrutiny at 20th Fox because described by me so often publicly and in print as brainy, charming and *sexy*," she pecked away.

Helen never got the allure of electric typewriters—the humming motor reminded her of a meter, measuring the minutes, as if to say, "Now it's time to get down to work." She didn't need a reminder. She was always working. She preferred her old-fashioned Royal 440 manual typewriter, a souvenir from her secretarial days. It was a different kind of reminder—a reminder of how far she had come.

8

SOMETHING'S GOT TO GIVE

1962

"Honey, nothing can live unless something dies."

—Gay Langland (Clark Gable) in *The Misfits*, 1961,
Marilyn Monroe's last completed film

In 1962, Helen Gurley Brown was David's most successful production to date, the one with the biggest payoff both personally and professionally, but he was having a much harder time producing movies. Toward the end of 1961, he had tried to make a comedy, *Something's Got to Give*, starring Dean Martin as a man who marries a blond bombshell after mistakenly thinking his first wife is dead. The film was troubled from the start, but it was nowhere near as troubled as its leading lady, Marilyn Monroe.

Like the rest of the world, David was smitten with Monroe. He never forgot the first time he laid eyes on her in Los Angeles, all smiles and sunshine, gently bouncing down the steps of Fox's Administration Building, along with a *Hollywood Reporter* columnist who introduced her as the new girl on the lot. David thought she was the most beautiful woman he had ever seen, and later, after watching her in *Gentlemen Prefer Blondes* and *How to Marry a Millionaire*, he discovered that she was funny, too.

When Norma Jeane Mortenson had her first screen test with Fox in 1946, she was just another ingenue in need of a new marquee name, but by the time David signed on to produce *Something's*

Got to Give, Marilyn Monroe was one of the most famous women on the planet. Her "Golden Dreams" calendar photo, featuring her fully nude and stretched out on red velvet, had long decorated the walls of barbershops and college dorms across the country. She already had divorced Joe DiMaggio and Arthur Miller, allegedly seduced President Kennedy, and pressed her hands into the wet cement in front of Grauman's Chinese Theatre. People knew about her troubles—the fractured childhood spent in orphanages and foster homes, the failed marriages, the miscarriages, the nervous breakdowns, the trips to psychiatric clinics—but they didn't know her. David didn't really know her, either, though he felt he occasionally caught glimpses of the scared little girl who lived just under her skin. "She used to come into my office and sit on my lap, sometimes tickling me," he later wrote in his memoir, *Let Me Entertain You*. "We'd talk a bit. Joke a bit. Yes, I got paid for that job."

Unfortunately, it didn't last, partly due to the meddling of Monroe's psychiatrist, Ralph Greenson, who supported the appointment of another producer whom he knew socially, Henry Weinstein. David was pushed out, and Monroe, who was working for a small fraction of her worth because of an old contract with Fox, derailed the production after she failed too many times to show up to the set, claiming that she was ill. Fox dismissed her, filed a $500,000 lawsuit against her (it was later upped to $750,000), and ultimately halted the production. In the meantime, David had committed to producing a historic drama about the Battle of Leyte Gulf, set to film in Hawaii and Hollywood.

There were many other films on Fox's list of upcoming movies, including an ambitious adaptation of James Joyce's *Ulysses*, as well as a project about World War II general George S. Patton that David had been working on for years. But the movie that everyone was talking about that summer was *Cleopatra*, which Fox's president, Spyros Skouras, prematurely had declared would be "the greatest grossing film of all times" as well as the greatest movie in the history of the motion picture.

It certainly was shaping up to be one of the most expensive. Costs for *Cleopatra*, originally budgeted at around $2 million, sky-rocketed thanks to a bungled production that began in London and later moved to Rome, where sets and costumes had to be re-created a second time. It was while in Rome that the film's two stars, Elizabeth Taylor and Richard Burton (cast as the Egyptian queen and her Roman lover Mark Antony)—married to other people—carried out an increasingly public and tumultuous af-fair that made Helen Gurley Brown's office romances seem junior league in comparison. Even before the gossip columnist Hedda Hopper broke the news of their tryst in her column in the *Los Angeles Herald-Examiner*, everybody knew about the couple, including Taylor's husband, the singer Eddie Fisher; and Burton's wife, the young actress Sybil Williams. Paparazzi stalked them, and pub-lications around the world wrote about them. In Italy, the news-paper *Il Tempo* described Taylor as an "intemperate vamp who destroys families and devours husbands." Even the pope chimed in, denouncing her as immoral.

No one could have predicted the colossal mess that *Cleopatra* would become—not even David Brown, who had pitched the idea for a remake in the first place. Five years earlier, in 1957, Skou-ras had asked David to come up with "a big picture" on "a big subject." It was while digging through some studio records that David learned *Cleopatra* was actually a Fox property. In 1917, Fox Film Corporation had made a film about the Egyptian queen star-ring the silent-screen star Theda Bara. Working for Paramount, the director Cecil B. DeMille later remade *Cleopatra* with Clau-dette Colbert in 1934.

More than twenty years later, this was the film David watched in a small screening room with Skouras and Fox's head of production, Buddy Adler. DeMille's version was in black-and-white, but if 20th Century Fox made their *Cleopatra* in full color with the right stars, it could be the Hollywood epic they needed.

Instead, in the otherwise capable hands of producer Walter Wanger, it became an epic disaster. After a year of production, two key original casting choices dropped out—Rex Harrison eventually replaced Peter Finch as Julius Caesar, and Richard Burton stepped in for Stephen Boyd as Mark Antony—and the original director, Rouben Mamoulian, was replaced by Joseph Mankiewicz. Elizabeth Taylor caught "the Asian flu," fell into a coma, and underwent a tracheotomy, further delaying the film. Scripts were written, rewritten, and discarded. Elaborate and expensive sets were built, destroyed, and rebuilt. ("Only the Romans left more ruins in Europe," David later quipped.) Meanwhile, forced to keep the cast and crew on salary through multiple shooting delays, Fox was hemorrhaging millions and having to answer to furious stockholders. The future of the company looked bleak.

Fortunately, David was having more success managing his wife's career than his own. After months of pitching an adaptation of *Sex and the Single Girl* around Hollywood, he finally got some good news.

EARLY ONE EVENING during the summer of 1962, the Browns sat in their sunroom with Helen's seventeen-year-old cousin from her mother's side, Norma Lou Pittman, and celebrated a deal that had been in the works for some time. *Sex and the Single Girl* was becoming a movie—and for the rights to the book, Warner Bros. was offering $200,000, the largest sum ever paid for a nonfiction work in Hollywood history. Even more incredible was the fact that the

studio was willing to hand over that much cash for a book with no
plot and no substantial character other than Helen Gurley Brown.
Word around town was that Warner's bought the book for its title alone. "Sex and . . ." was clearly a formula that worked, but
that wouldn't help the screenwriter. How was anyone supposed
to write a scene around making an omelet with leftovers from the
fridge, or wearing Band-Aids instead of a bra? The question of
how to adapt a seemingly unadaptable book would be left to the
film's producer, a friend of the Browns named Saul David. During
the negotiations with Warner's, David Brown insisted that Helen
be relieved of any responsibility to turn her book into a usable
screenplay so that she could focus on other projects, such as writing her next book and developing a syndicated newspaper column
aimed at the single girl.

Selling the rights to *Sex and the Single Girl* was a huge professional coup for David, who was also busy trying to sell the stage
rights to develop a musical based on the book, similar to *How to
Succeed in Business Without Really Trying*. For Helen, the victory was
personal. How many times had she been snubbed by celebrities
and patronized by studio executives and their wives, who were
nice to her simply because she was David's girl? And now, Warner's wanted to pay her to use her name and likeness in a movie
based on a book she had written. Out came the champagne. Pop!
Helen offered a flute to Norma Lou, whom she had started calling
"Lou" at the girl's request. "You're old enough, do you want a little sip?"

Lou was nervous, but didn't say it. She took a sip for Helen. It
was her first taste of alcohol.

No one back home would have believed it, but Helen actually
took time off work to spend with Lou, who would be staying with
the Browns for six days before visiting a girlfriend who lived in

the area. She had come a long way, flying from Tulsa, Oklahoma, where she still lived with her parents. The trip to California was her graduation present from Helen, who grew up playing with Lou's mother, Rosemary, who was her second cousin and four years older. When Helen described her Arkansas relatives as hillbillies who peed in the woods, she wasn't thinking of Rosemary, with her lush dark hair and dreamy hooded eyes. Helen called her the Beautiful Princess.

Lou also thought her mother was a natural beauty, but Helen was more glamorous. No one in the family understood why Helen considered herself unattractive, but Lou thought maybe it had something to do with living in California, the land of the gorgeous—all those girls with their blond hair and tans. Lou had blond hair and a bit of a tan herself from riding horses back home, but she also wore glasses. Her mother had bought her the frames, a pretty pale blue with tiny gemstones on the sides.

Norma Lou, photographed in 1962, the year she came to visit Helen and David in California. (*Family photograph courtesy of Norma Lou Honderich.*)

Lou was wearing her glasses and a new travel suit when Helen picked her up at the shuttle stop downtown. She had made sure to pack her Brownie box camera in preparation for her trip, but nothing could have prepared her for the culture shock. From the moment she stepped into Helen's Mercedes-Benz, she felt a long way from home, a feeling that further sank in as they drove to Pacific Palisades. Along the way, they stopped at an outdoor market so Helen could buy some big lemon leaves and flowers for the house, which to Lou's eyes seemed more like a European villa. Helen told her that an entire Asian family took care of the terraced garden.

And then there was Lou's room, next to the library downstairs. It was spectacular, with arched ceilings and huge windows forming a semicircle of glass. Lou looked out at her view and felt suddenly overwhelmed. She'd never seen the ocean before.

She didn't want to be a bad houseguest, but a couple of days into her trip, Lou began to tear up unexpectedly. She had a hard time hiding her puffy eyes from Helen, as much as she tried. She missed her parents and her home—the farthest she'd ever traveled alone before was to her grandmother's house and Girl Scouts camp, forty-five minutes away.

"Do you think you might possibly be homesick?" Helen asked her that weekend. "David and I have been talking, and we think you need to get out of the house."

Helen knew that Lou loved horses, so she and David took her to the Will Rogers Polo Club to see a polo match, and afterward they went out to eat. Helen also knew that Lou went to church on Sundays, so she brought her to a service at a beautiful Methodist church, even though David was Jewish and she never went. "I won't pretend that we go to church," Helen told Lou. "I know that *you* go to church, and it might be fun to go someplace different."

Now that she'd finalized the film rights to *Sex and the Single*

Girl, Helen wanted to celebrate, so she sought Lou out again one morning over breakfast.

"We're going to go shopping!" Helen said.

"What are you going to get?" Lou asked.

"Oh," Helen said, "let's shop for you."

Helen had seen Lou's clothes. Other than her travel suit, Lou had sewn almost every piece of clothing she'd packed in her suitcase. After breakfast, they drove to the village shopping district to look around. As Helen parked her Mercedes, she suggested that they find Lou a new dress.

"Well, I've got two dresses," Lou said, admiring the lacquered cars lining the streets. She had packed both of her homemade shirtwaists for the trip and had chosen the light blue one for their outing.

"You know, a girl can always have more than two dresses," Helen said, walking toward the stucco buildings.

They went into one shop, a small, minimalist boutique. Glancing around the store, Lou felt uneasy. There were no racks of clothes—just a dress here and there on a form. She wondered where they kept the rest. They left after about a minute, and Helen politely thanked the saleslady.

"How about a bathing suit?" Helen offered next. If anyone was prepared to help a girl find the right fit of bathing suit, it was Helen, who had worked on the account for Catalina Swimwear.

But Lou told her that she already had a bathing suit.

"A cover-up," Helen said as they continued past boutiques selling sundresses and swimwear. "A cover-up would be good."

"Well, I actually made a cover-up out of a towel," Lou said. "I made it with pockets, and I really like it."

Helen looked at her cousin. She was wearing loafers.

"How about some shoes?" she asked.

Lou was doubtful, looking at the sophisticated heels on display in the windows. She wore loafers to school, low flats to church, and cowboy boots to the stable. What was she supposed to do with a pair of strappy high-heeled sandals back in Oklahoma?

"WHERE ARE ALL the bags?" David asked when they got home. "When girls go shopping, you come home with lots of bags."

Lou showed David the copy of *The Good Earth* that Helen finally bought for her at the bookstore. "I like books better than clothes," she said.

He smiled at her. "You're my kind of girl."

It turned out that, even though she had just graduated from high school, Lou had read many of the same books that David had read, classics like *Les Misérables*, authors like Dickens. They talked about books a lot, and sometimes they talked about boys. Specifically, they talked about boys who were the same age as David's son, Bruce, who had been skipping school more and more—to do what? His father didn't really know.

"What do boys at your age do?" David asked Lou once.

"Well," Lou said, thinking of her boyfriend, her brother, and his friends. "They go to school, and on the weekends they might take their girlfriends to the movies, or they might work on their cars."

"How does it work when they skip school?" he asked.

"I don't know any boys who skip school," she said.

David said Bruce was so smart he could show up for tests and make an A without studying. But Lou could see that David was distressed about his son, and she felt sorry that he worried so much. Both David and Helen talked quite a bit about Bruce— his mother, Liberty LeGacy, was David's first wife—though Lou didn't meet him on that visit. She wasn't sure where he was, but he wasn't at their house.

Lou could tell that David liked her company, and she suspected that Helen enjoyed having a little "home person" around—someone to remind her of the Ozarks without actually having to *go* there. She knew that Helen appreciated her updates about the family, especially about her sister Mary, who was living in Shawnee, but it was hard for Lou to know what Helen liked about her, specifically. Helen just took an interest in her life. She always had. "You're going to college, right? You need to do that," Helen told her one day. Yes, Lou said, she had enrolled at the University of Tulsa. She was thinking of studying French, maybe becoming a translator. Helen looked pleased and emphasized how important it would be to stay in school and receive a degree.

When Helen gave advice, Lou listened. Her cousin had been her "glamorous go-to," the person she consulted with about all of her worries, since she was fourteen. It's not that Lou didn't get along with her mother—she did—but sometimes they crossed ways. Helen always knew just what to say to make her feel better. Lou first got to know her when she would come to stay at their house in Tulsa while on business. When Helen was a copywriter at Foote, Cone & Belding, working on the account for Catalina Inc., she used to visit department stores around the country. In Tulsa, Helen invited Lou to watch her sell swimsuits and help customers find their perfect fit. In her neat cardigan and high heels, Helen looked so sophisticated at work, Lou couldn't help but feel good when Helen sought her out back at the house. Helen used to ask Lou to wake her up in the mornings before school so that she could see her outfits. "Now turn around," she would say, admiring whatever was her choice. "You ironed and starched that blouse. Must have taken you all morning!"

During one of those visits, Lou stood in shorts in front of the full-length mirror to show Helen her legs. "They're deformed," she said despondently. Her skinny legs didn't touch at the places they were supposed to—thighs, knees, calves. Only her knees touched. Helen laughed and laughed. Then she told Lou that if her legs touched at age fourteen, she would be fat by the time she was twenty.

Lou's mother told her she was pretty, but her compliments seemed vague in comparison, reflecting a mother's love rather than the truth. Helen knew how to make you *believe* you were special. She found one feature that made you different and zeroed in on it. Looking past Lou's glasses, Helen told her that she had the prettiest hair in the family.

When they started writing letters to each other, Lou was still a kid who wore Peter Pan collars and loved nothing more than her parents, books, and horses. She and Helen were different in so many ways, but they both loved to write letters, and no one was better at it than Helen, who had a way of making any missive sound like a fan letter—and making you feel you were the most interesting and important person in the world. When Helen's letters arrived, Lou would pore over them. She always asked for details about Lou's life, rarely sharing any details of her own. "Helen's really busy," her mother would say; "don't write her *right* back because she's so good to write to you." But Lou couldn't help it; she just had so many questions. Sometimes she felt bad because she would lose her temper with her mother or she would tell a white lie about being at a friend's house when she was really going out. She was obsessed with making good grades. Helen was always so reassuring. "You don't have to be perfect," she'd say, or, "I think you need to quit worrying about being a good girl." Lou instantly felt better; if Helen said it was okay, it probably was.

Now the woman who had written her all those letters was the author of a bestselling book. Lou had learned what she could from family members. Other than Cleo and Mary, most of the family hadn't read it, because of the racy title alone; the friends and relatives who had read it were shocked. It wasn't just the sex: It was the fact that Helen had written about her own mother and sister, about their being poor and needy. One just didn't air dirty laundry in public like that, they said to each other; one didn't expose the family. Cleo, in particular, took offense at how Helen had portrayed them all as backwoods hillbillies. ("She sold her family down the river," she later vented to relatives at Mary's house.)

Since she had arrived, Lou had been eyeing the boxes of books in the den. One day, before she left, she asked Helen for her own copy of *Sex and the Single Girl*.

"Would your mother mind if you read it?" Helen asked her in return.

"No," Lou said. "I'm allowed to read what I want to read."

"Well, Cleo certainly wasn't happy about it," Helen said, giving Lou a copy.

Back in her room, Lou stayed up all night reading. She was riveted. But she couldn't help but wonder if Helen really believed everything she had written about life as a single girl—how it's okay to sleep with guys before you get married, or have affairs with married men.

"Do you really believe that?" Lou asked Helen the next morning.

"Absolutely," Helen said. "I believe the things I said. I just didn't talk about how lonely it can be."

(9)

THE WOIKING GIRL'S FRIEND
1962

"She's a phony. But she's a real phony. You know why? Because
she honestly believes all this phony junk that she believes."

—O. J. Berman (Martin Balsam) in *Breakfast at Tiffany's*, 1961

B y the end of the summer, Marilyn Monroe was dead, and
Helen Gurley Brown was a household name. Lou was no
longer the only young woman writing Helen letters and
hoping for some advice or reassurance in return. She was one of
hundreds, soon to be thousands. Across the country, Bettys and
Pattys and Donnas and Brendas were sending Helen bushels of
fan mail. Like Lou, they chose to confide in her, sharing their
most troubling concerns and insecurities with the one woman
they knew would understand. Sometimes they just wrote to say
thank you. "I've never been able to flirt before, and you made
it so easy I'm flirting like mad!" a secretary from Milwaukee
exclaimed. Five roommates sharing an apartment in Baltimore
wired to say that they were going out to lease five separate
apartments—they credited Helen for giving them the courage
to strike out on their own.

Helen received no shortage of passionate testimonials, but she
wasn't above faking the occasional fan letter. When *The Ameri-can Weekly* asked her to contribute an article, Berney reminded

Helen that no one could convey her message—that even a plain girl could attract men by following the guidelines in *Sex and the Single Girl*—better than Helen herself. "The best way to get this across would be by creating a few letters. If anyone has a talent for this it is you," Berney told her. "You might create one letter from a girl saying that she had just about resigned herself to life as a plain Jane when she read the condensation of your book," he suggested. "You have already received letters something like this, so it is just a question of making Nature follow Art a little more closely."

It's possible that Helen took Berney's advice, but she was busy enough trying to keep up with the demand for interviews. By the end of June, she had been on thirty radio and TV shows, including the *Today* show and *The Mike Wallace Show*. In the coming months, she'd be on dozens more. No station was too small, no amount of airtime too short—she did it all.

She brought the same frenzied work ethic to her promotional appearances. She said yes to all kinds of meet-and-greets, autograph sessions, press club dinners, and cocktail parties at posh hotels, but she never lost her focus on single working girls. She spoke to single mothers at Parents Without Partners, secretaries on Secretary's Day, and more secretaries and "female-type supervisors" on Female Day, a jokey luncheon organized for a group called Supervising Helpers in Television, otherwise known as S.H.I.T. "Once a year the dimly illuminated S.H.I.T. Society opens its creaky doors to the pretty side of the magic shadows business and invites GIRLS to gather together with us for lunch," the invitation read. "So, go in, swat yer secretary in the customary manner and place, and tell her she is going to lunch with you next Friday."

Our honored guest will be the woiking goil's friend—that
paragon of what to do til the preacher arrives—that tipper-
offer of how to pity the married wolf—that friend of the
compleat bachelor:
HELEN GURLEY BROWN
Nuf Sed?

This was an event not to be missed, the invitation noted. Mrs.
Brown was already working on another book and wouldn't be appearing in public again anytime soon.

DECIDING ON A second book hadn't been easy. In fact, Helen had
been trying to figure out what her follow-up would be as early as
January 1962, when she started sending pitches to Berney. Among
the ideas Helen and Berney discussed, over time:

- An autobiography focusing on life as a motion picture
  producer's wife
- *The Executive Wife's Handbook*, an elite wife's guide to
  negotiating the pressure and politics of being married to a
  successful husband
- A guide to California living
- A book about treating emotional problems through diet
- A book for men called *How to Love a Girl*
- A book for women titled *How to Love a Man*
- A book about lesbians (which Helen chronically misspelled
  lesbions)
- A book titled *The Second (or Third, Fourth, Fifth) Time
  Around*, about second (or third, fourth, fifth) marriages, and
  stepchildren

- A book called *Topic A*, about what *really* goes on between
  men and women—and men and men and women and
  women
- A book called *Sex and the Office*

At one point, Helen also submitted an idea for a novel, *The Girls of Beverly Hills*, featuring a familiar-sounding character named Cloe, a mousy former secretary at a soap company who uses wigs, clothes, men, and pure moxie to become a sex symbol and national television star. In a lengthy outline for the book, Helen explained that there could be some recapping of Cloe's affairs with other beaux, but a far more important character would be her husband, Kleinschmidt. A wealthy soap company tycoon, Kleinschmidt was "not too old nor too unattractive" and endlessly encouraging of her career. (Soap aside, Kleinschmidt seems to share quite a few traits with David.) Kleinschmidt and Cloe would do much of their plotting and scheming about her business (television) and his (soap) while lying in bed, *not* making love. "She is not the performer with her husband that she was with her previous lovers. Doesn't *have* to be and he doesn't mind," Helen wrote. "Privately she is a quiet, non-sexy, comfortable woman who knows the crazy fame might come to an end someday but she won't die."

Like Cloe, Helen knew that she wouldn't die if her fame came to an end, but she didn't want it to end. And yet, she was at a loss for what to do next. Her heart wasn't in the novel. The diet book went nowhere because she couldn't find a doctor to collaborate with her in the writing of it. "Lesbions" made a fascinating subject ("The doctors I've talked to tell me it is one of the most difficult human aberrations to treat—virtually impossible," Helen told Berney), but she just couldn't get into it. And *How to Love a Girl*, while in her comfort zone, wasn't the big mail-order book that Berney was hoping for. She wasn't very interested in reporting on other people's lives, but she had used up the juiciest of her own stories in *Sex and the Single Girl*. "The book I could write best would be for a woman who marries a man somewhat older, wealthier and wiser than she," Helen told Berney. Specifically, she envisioned an advice book about how to cope with an upper-class divorced man's ex-wives and children. "The wicked step-mother is now the *weary* step-mother, trying to make friends, learn to discipline an older child she didn't start out with," Helen said, perhaps thinking of David's son, Bruce.

Originally, Berney had been wary about a book titled *Sex and the Office*. He had wanted to wait to see if *Sex and the Single Girl* would be a success before getting on the "Sex and . . ." bandwagon. But by June, he was ready to jump aboard. "We are beginning to get fervent letters addressed to you . . . from single girls who consider your book the answer to a maiden's prayer," he told Helen. "While not all of your fans are office girls most of them are. We should strike while the ardor is hot."

Meanwhile, the letters kept pouring in. At one point, the volume was so great that the post office in Pacific Palisades refused to deliver the mail to the Browns' house; they had to pick it up themselves. Helen had tried to answer each letter personally, but there were just too many, and she couldn't keep up with the demand while traveling on a promotional tour that kept extending with trips to Chicago, Detroit, Cleveland, Pittsburgh, Philadelphia, Washington, D.C., and Boston. "Hold onto your lovely wig—this is just the beginning of the schedule," Berney wrote to Helen in a memo listing some of her October engagements on the East Coast, shortly before she kicked off the tour in Chicago with a well-oiled press conference at the Gaslight Club. The next two weeks were a blur of flights, taxis, hotels, handshakes, hair-and-makeup chairs, ten-second radio spots, late-night radio spots, early-morning TV calls, hurried departures to make the next booking, cancellations, near misses and just-made-its, interview lunches, outfit changes, press dinners, bookstore signings, fawning fans, fake smiles, cocktail parties, and quick exits—most of which she navigated by herself or with David.

In California, she'd had a publicist to shuttle her around to appointments, but lately Berney had been leaving her to deal with such logistics. And whatever happened to the flowers and champagne he used to send? "I am something of a little *star* now!" Helen reminded Berney, running on a low reserve of patience. "I make a lot of money for us." Speaking of money, she kept a running tab of her out-of-pocket expenses, noting every tip she gave to taxi drivers, baggage porters, doormen, bellmen, and elevator men; and she needed that money back, especially when she was already losing hundreds of dollars for every week of work she took off to do one of those trips.

By the fall, promoting *Sex and the Single Girl* had become something of a third job, the first being her work at Kenyon & Eckhardt and the second writing *Sex and the Office*. If she didn't get a break soon, she would simply break down.

IN NOVEMBER 1962, Helen finally quit her job at Kenyon & Eckhardt, and by December she had a firm offer from the Los Angeles Times Syndicate to write a newspaper column aimed at bachelorettes, divorcees, and widows. Eventually "Woman Alone" would reach more than one hundred newspapers around the country. It was a good solution: In addition to providing additional income for not much work, the column would give Helen a central place where she could answer her mounting fan mail.

It was auspicious for another reason. The column, like the book, was work Helen could do anywhere. That became an important consideration when 20th Century Fox crumbled down to its very foundation. To pay for *Cleopatra*, which ultimately cost around $44 million—the equivalent of more than $340 million today—the studio had to sell off most of its valuable 262-acre lot. (It eventually became Century City.) Before long, Fox president Spyros Skouras was out, and a new president was elected: Darryl F. Zanuck, the shrewd producer and kingpin who had cofounded the company in 1933 and now didn't waste any time rebuilding the studio. First, he finished its demolition: In short order, Zanuck canceled numerous productions, closed up studio buildings, and fired once-valued executives and other employees. Once again, David Brown was out of a job.

If David minded being known as "Mr. Helen Gurley Brown" after that, he certainly didn't show it. Was he riding on his wife's coattails? Absolutely! And why not? She had ridden on his. They were a team: a royal *We*.

"The 'We' explains why he oozes security, despite the demeaning fact that—as he candidly admits—'I never hear my own name being utilized in my own introductions,'" Cindy Adams wrote in *Pageant* magazine's December 1963 issue, after meeting the Browns at a Manhattan cocktail party. "It's because this is not HER book. It's THEIR book. He saw every scrap of paper. He edited every line. The idea was his. The title was his. It was his decision to tell all and not hold back. It was his decision to mention himself by name and not cheat the readers. He says quite plainly that there'd be no best seller, no forthcoming movie, and no syndicated column (in 70 newspapers) for his wife if it were not for him."

Shortly after that piece appeared, David was offered a

position as an executive vice president at New American Library, a medium-size publishing house known for its paperbacks and popular fiction, including Ian Fleming's James Bond novels. David accepted. After *Cleopatra*, taking a break from the movie business seemed like a good idea, and he, especially, welcomed a new start.

The Browns were moving to New York.

10

NEW YORK, NEW YORK
1963

"I was a country girl from Los Angeles and I [didn't] know about
New York addresses."

—Helen Gurley Brown, in 1993,
recalling her first days living in Manhattan.

There were no big headlines heralding the Browns' arrival in New York in March 1963, partly because they got there at the tail end of a massive newspaper strike that shut down seven of the city's major dailies. Led by a local printers' union in 1962, the strike was in retaliation against the automation of the newsroom. The computer was beginning to threaten the Linotype machine, along with thousands of jobs, and workers were demanding security and pay raises from newspaper owners. But the demonstration was much more than a battle over typesetting. It was a signal of changes to come as new technology infiltrated living rooms as well as newsrooms.

Over the course of 114 days, Linotypes, which depended on molten metal to set type, went silent and cold. No ink was spilled. Out of work, seventeen thousand newspaper employees took odd jobs driving taxis, shoveling coal, and busing tables to pay the rent. Jobless reporters, including Gay Talese and Tom Wolfe, experimented with new, more literary forms of journalistic writing, while another group of editors and writers used their time off to start the *New York Review of Books*. And across the city, New Yorkers remained in the dark about what was happening around the world and in their own neighborhoods. Without the benefit of printed ads and announcements, businesses suffered, and people missed everything from weddings to wakes.

By the time the strike ended on March 31—ultimately, workers won a slight pay raise, and both labor and management supported a plan to create a joint board to consider the future of newspapers—the industry had changed, and so had the city. People were still doing the Twist, but Chubby Checker no longer topped the charts, and a twenty-two-year-old folksinger named Bob Dylan would soon release his second album, featuring "Blowin' in the Wind," a protest song that would come to define a generation. In the art world, six painters were preparing to mount a show at the Guggenheim Museum that would solidify a new form, pop art, and help make the name Andy Warhol as familiar as Campbell's Soup. Central Park still hadn't fully thawed, but in department stores like Bergdorf Goodman and Bonwit Teller, buyers were watching Paris for spring fashions like Balenciaga's sporty capelets and brass-buttoned coats that flew in the face of coquetry. "These were costumes for women with energy to burn," the *New York Times* Western Edition declared, "and serious business to accomplish."

Spring was just around the corner, but it couldn't come soon enough for Helen. She barely left the apartment during her first few weeks in New York. To David she seemed almost catatonic with fear. She missed the sunniness of Southern California. Manhattan was dark and cold. On one of the first trips to New York that Helen and David had taken together, they were met at the airport by Bruce's mother and David's first wife, Liberty, who lived in the city. She had come to pick up Bruce, but she brought a wool scarf and mittens for Helen, who hadn't experienced a real winter since living in Little Rock as a little girl.

Finishing her lunch at Schrafft's one day in March, Helen understood that she would never get used to the cold. Manhattan was a black-and-white film when she had gotten used to color. Outside, it was gray, always gray. Gray skies, gray sidewalks, gray buildings, gray overcoats. Even the people were shades of the same bleakness—whitish, pinkish, brownish, but still gray. Once in a while, a woman in a red coat or a child in a yellow muffler would break the monotony, but the colorlessness always returned. And the crowds, they never left. All around her, people were lining up two deep at every chair. Businessmen schmoozed over steak lunches and oversize martinis, as secretaries nibbled on burger specials and touched up their lipstick.

Helen must have known Schrafft's would be packed when she walked in. It was as much of an institution as the three-martini lunch. Everyone from W. H. Auden to Mary McCarthy had written about the chain. In *The Best of Everything*, Schrafft's is the place where Rona Jaffe's heroine, Caroline, and her friends from the office order tomato surprise and strawberry soda. Helen knew that noon-to-two was the busiest time to be there—other than at twilight, when the Little Old Ladies started coming in for their blue-plate specials—but she was still surprised by the constant motion. She wondered how New Yorkers felt when they went out west, to a place like Arizona, which was relatively quiet and still. The silence would be deafening—all that time and space to think, alone with yourself, and really, wouldn't that just be terrible? Warming her hands around a cup of tea, she listened to the gray thrum of voices and yearned for California.

Helen and David had left Pacific Palisades shortly after his job offer came in. The decision had been a mutual one, and yet Helen

wasn't quite ready to say goodbye. Leaving California at the
height of her career was like breaking up with a steady boyfriend
to enter into an arranged marriage with a man she hardly knew.
The day they were supposed to leave 515 Radcliffe Avenue, Helen
couldn't find their cat Samantha. They would be boarding a train
headed east in less than two hours, followed by a huge moving van
packed with their furniture, and Helen started to panic. Roaming
the hillsides one last time, she hissed and whistled for Samantha,
who turned up just in time to be packed alongside the other cat,
Gregory, in a carrying cage. The Browns switched trains in Chicago, taking the Broadway Limited the rest of the way to New
York. Once in the city, they stayed at the Dorset hotel, near the
Museum of Modern Art, and started searching for an apartment.
They found it in a twenty-one-story, white-brick apartment
building at 605 Park Avenue, at the southeast corner of Sixty-Fifth
Street, for $550 a month.

In Pacific Palisades Samantha and Gregory had been outdoor
cats, stalking the hills for mice, snakes, and lizards. In New York
they became indoor cats, fed by the doorman when Helen and David went of town. They no longer hunted, but sat on the window-
sills, watching the snow fall over Park Avenue. Occasionally Helen
and David took the cats out on leashes to get some fresh air, but
they seemed unhappy. After a lifetime of being on the prowl, they
were suddenly housebound.

And Helen? The day David brought her to their five-room
rental, she stood in the doorway of No. 17C and cried. She had
gotten used to the twelve-room house in Pacific Palisades. Now,
in this small flat that didn't even fit their stuff, she had to deal
with neighbors. Some nights, the people who lived upstairs would
have parties, and Helen would knock on their door, barefoot in her
bathrobe, seeming older than she was. The noise bothered her at

night, but the quiet got to her during the day, when David went to the office. She didn't feel at home in the apartment with its white walls, neutral living room, and fussily arranged paintings. A decorator friend had lent her understated touch to the place, and the result was blanched of color and character. Helen tried to brighten her desk with lemon leaves and an ashtray that read "I'm sexy" in six different languages around the rim, but having spent twenty-plus years working in offices, she missed the feeling of having somewhere to *be*.

She had hoped that the coldness and the darkness would make her work harder on her column, which she planned to debut in a few weeks with the introductory headline: "CALLING ALL WID-OWS, DIVORCEES, BACHELOR GIRLS." But it wasn't turning out that way. In fact, "Woman Alone" was starting to seem like a fitting title for reasons she hadn't anticipated. Other than David and the cats, she had no family in the city and few friends. She was used to dressing for the office and spraying her hair with Satin Set, not roaming around her apartment with a bad case of bedhead.

When Helen dared to venture out, she found the city to be intimidating and exhausting. Her efforts to win over doormen, rental agents, and restaurant hostesses left her depleted. She could ooze compliments at a person until the air between them was sticky, but her attempts to charm rarely made a difference with New Yorkers. They didn't seem to like her any better for all her flattery, and more important, she noted after a few unsuccessful exchanges, they didn't seem to like themselves any better. What was the point? Knowing what made other people tick was one of Helen's talents, and in New York it seemed impossible.

Still, Helen noted that New York had at least a few redeeming factors. For one, men looked at her here. She could feel eyes on her when she was walking down the street or having lunch by herself.

Helen at home on Park Avenue in 1965, with her cats, Samantha and Gregory. (*Copyright © I. C. Rapoport.*)

In the absence of the California sunshine, she basked in their gazes and realized that their attention to her was due to another thing that she appreciated: In Manhattan, there were no streetcars teeming with starlets, big-breasted and tawny-skinned. "In many ways it's like Pittsburgh because there are some simply hideous people loping about on the streets," Helen observed in some of her early notes about the city. It was nothing like California, where pretty girls were "as plentiful as the palm situation," she added.

In New York, as in Paris, it was enough to be stylish and slender. And while it didn't hurt to be young, a woman of a certain age wasn't overlooked, partly because, in half of the city's restaurants, the lighting was so dim that she couldn't be fully seen in the first place. It was no wonder society ladies adored Longchamps, with its slick décor and dark corners—their wrinkles simply disappeared. And all that history . . . Hollywood was one giant facelift, but New York embraced its past.

"The west is for the babies . . . the sun goddesses . . . the *now's*," Helen wrote in another batch of notes about the city. "New York is far kinder to the old. . . . It's good to see because I'm not a baby either."

11

THE MEANING OF LUNCH
1963

"One of the lovely things that can happen to a girl in an office is lunch. Lunchtime is fraught with possibilities!"

—Helen Gurley Brown, *Sex and the Office*, 1964

New York was teeming with beautiful babies—they just didn't hang out anywhere near Helen Gurley Brown on Park Avenue. On weekends, bearded guys in berets and leggy girls with hair as straight as rain headed to MacDougal Street in Greenwich Village to check out new music at the Figaro or the Kettle and any number of coffeehouses offering a stage to anyone with a harmonica. On weekdays, Midtown blossomed with girls fresh out of college, wearing belted raincoats and sensible flats, and heading to their jobs at ad agencies, publishing houses, and magazine offices. "You see them every morning at a quarter to nine, rushing out of the maw of the subway tunnel, filing out of Grand Central Station, crossing Lexington and Park and Madison and Fifth avenues, the hundreds and hundreds of girls," Rona Jaffe had written in *The Best of Everything*.

Five years later, Helen had her eye trained on the real-life versions of those girls, and specifically on their lunchtime rituals. She was working on a series of chapters about lunch for *Sex and the Office*, and she had started observing the eating habits of office girls as closely as a mother hawk watches her chicks. When she saw a group of secretaries in the smudged window of a drab diner or lined up for a pale hot dog at a midtown catering truck, it occurred to her that girls who should be watching their wallets and their waistlines were buying lunch instead of bringing it from home. Since when had packing a lunch become a mark of shame? It's not as if they had to *wear* the brown bag—they just had to fill it with healthy food, as she had been doing for years. She would suggest two Brown Paper Bag Plans in *Sex and the Office*, including her own recipe for Mother Brown's Rich Dessert Tuna Salad with sweet pickles and raisins, which she used to eat every day of the week. When she was feeling really wicked, she allowed herself two Triscuits and four potato chips.

It was time to change the image of the Brown Bag Lunch, starting with the name. "American Beauty Lunches" would do. "Home-food can be delicious glamour girl fodder instead of junk," Helen wrote at her typewriter, addressing all those catering-truck-and-diner devotees. If they just packed their lunches, they could save enough money to spend Christmas in Jamaica *and* look better in a bikini.

Helen saw the importance of giving practical, everyday advice, and yet she knew that *Sex and the Office* was somehow missing the mark. She had managed to squeeze a lot of useful, and questionable, information into the book, such as how to give a firm handshake and how to cheat discreetly on an expense account. She had done her research, interviewing secretaries, businesswomen, and the occasional "tycooness" about their experiences in the working world.

Despite all the footwork that went into *Sex and the Office*, or perhaps because of it, the book felt forced. From the very start, Helen had warned Berney that she had no interest in getting into the technicalities of office work—how to type up neat carbons, for instance. "My idea is that a kind of secretarial handbook is *beneath* me," she said. She wanted *Sex and the Office* to be better than *Sex and the Single Girl*, but it just didn't have the same urgency. She had found that nothing was quite as motivating as the need to prove herself. "I'm best when I'm angry about something—and outrageous," she told Berney. The notion that a good girl shouldn't have a sex life—now *that* was something to rail against.

Lest *Sex and the Office* be as sexless as a stapler, she had to spice it up with titillating true stories, and the more taboo the better. Helen convinced Berney to let her write about the darker sides of the office, and he welcomed a chapter on call girls, who didn't work in offices per se but whose work largely depended on their existence. Having a call girl delivered to an office was about as common as ordering a new coffee machine: "The girl is sent as a bribe, payment for a favor expected or received," Helen explained to her readers. But not to worry: "The call girl, though enormously attractive to certain men, is not really competition for you. She's an entirely different thing."

Berney agreed to the chapter called "Some Girls Get Paid for It," but he and Helen had it out over several other case studies, which he felt were simply too hot to handle without getting burned. A story about a woman who gets raped on a date eventually got cut, but Berney allowed a reference to "office wolves" with predatory streaks. ("If your instinct goes 'sniff, sniff—peculiar, peculiar,' trust your instinct," Helen advised.) He okayed a story about an office girl who takes up with a man with a taste for S&M (who convinces her to ride in a convertible with her breasts exposed, and later whips her buttocks with a riding crop), but dropped an odd story about a secretary with a daddy complex who beds her much older, overweight boss. "I like that feeling of being squashed," the narrator confesses. "It makes me feel small and helpless."

During those long days alone with her typewriter in her New York apartment, Helen described sexual encounters in dripping detail, but no tale was quite as erotic as a story she wrote about two women who meet at work and end up in bed. Were they women she had known or simply imagined? Had she been in a similar situation herself or ever fantasized about it? It's hard to know, but she was very convincing in describing the slow-burning attraction between a young showroom model—the narrator of the tale—and a glamorous older designer named Claudia, who work at the same firm.

The story begins one day at the office when, after a fitting that lasts into the wee hours of the morning, Claudia suggests to the young model that they get a drink. The bars would be closed, so her apartment is the only option. Once they are at her pad, Claudia gives her a scotch and water, and they listen to records and talk about the new spring line she is designing. After Claudia gets up to mix another drink, she walks over to the model and kisses her on the mouth—and it's a kiss that is not so lustful as it is "full of sincerity and friendship," the model-narrator says.

An eternity seems to pass before Claudia carefully unbuttons the model's blouse, fondling her breasts and eventually removing her skirt. She is calm and confident. When Claudia touches her, she already knows how the touch will feel because she has experienced the same sensation. There is no question about what is wrong or right with another woman. It just feels natural, the model explains. There is no anxiety, not even when they are both naked on the bed and Claudia flips the girl on her back, kissing her mouth, her breasts, her stomach, "and then her mouth was THERE . . . really inside me with her tongue." When they entwine their legs like two pairs of scissors, the model orgasms for the second time. Usually, she's worn out after climaxing, but sex with another woman is softer, gentler, she confides: "you lack the final thrust . . . perhaps the final violence . . . there is a vague feeling of incompletion and you can go on."

It wasn't easy to shock Berney, but Helen sure caught him off guard. Though they had talked about her writing a chapter called "Boys Will Be Girls . . . and Vice Versa," about male and female homosexuality in the workplace, Berney assumed such accounts would be reported from a distance. "I thought it was going to be about how to handle temperamental homosexuals in the office," he wrote in a letter to Helen, after reading a draft of that chapter, which he later cut. Helen's detailed play-by-plays of actual sex acts between women was pushing the proverbial envelope too far. "I got a lot more than I bargained for," he admitted.

Helen reminded Berney that *she* had been dead set against a chapter called "The Matinee," which Letty suggested after hearing about a friend who sometimes used her lunch hour for sex. (Letty's friend eventually wrote a mini-essay on the subject, which Helen introduced as a special report in one of the book's three chapters on lunch.) Lesbianism was just part of office culture. It was the idea of a matinee that was truly "icky," Helen said, sounding suddenly Victorian in her prissiness, but she had gone ahead with it anyway.

Berney stood his ground. "No objection was made by me to the rape scene, the gal driving barechested in an open car, or the man beating the girl lightly with a whip. I just happen to feel that a literal description of a homosexual act between two girls would ruin your reputation if we were to publish it," he insisted. "There's no way of proving this except by publishing it. Then I could say I told you so—but it's much better to tell you so now."

SPRING FINALLY CAME, and along with the dogwoods and magnolias, a new club blossomed in New York. It had its roots in Chicago, but it soon found an outpost in a white, seven-story building at 5 East Fifty-Ninth Street near Madison Avenue. Tens of thousands of men bought keys to the club before it even opened, and when it finally did, it was packed. On an average day, 2,700 people entered the Playboy Club to eat, drink, and gawk at the scantily clad waitresses in Bunny ears and tails. Despite problems securing a cabaret license, the club was a total hit, grossing up to $90,000 a week, and to commemorate its success, *Playboy*'s April 1963 cover featured a Bunny in uniform serving cocktails. Inside the same issue was Helen Gurley Brown's *Playboy* interview.

Berney and Letty had groomed Helen to speak about *Sex and the Single Girl* in a respectable, acceptable manner—as the wifely Mrs. Brown—but in the pages of *Playboy*, she dropped the Sunday-morning-paper act and assumed the role of sex expert, sounding off on everything from extramarital affairs to abortion. When her interviewer asked what kind of response she had been getting from fans, she was blunt. "I get a lot of mail about how to keep from having a baby," she answered. "This mail I get is from girls who are quite sincerely interested in knowing. For some reason they feel they can't talk it over with their doctor. My inclination is to tell people exactly what I think they should do: They should get fitted for a diaphragm."

She didn't get her first diaphragm until the age of thirty-three, Helen added, but she had taken other precautions. Back when she was single, she knew plenty of girls who hadn't been as careful. One of her roommates tried to make herself miscarry before finally getting an abortion. The procedure itself wasn't as complicated as people thought. "There is some chance of becoming barren, but if the operation isn't performed by an idiot, it's quite simple," Helen said, grossly underestimating both the danger of illegal abortion and the difficulty of finding a reputable doctor.

The real problem was financial accessibility, she added. In most states, abortion was considered legal only if the mother's life was at risk, and illegal abortions were expensive, running up to one thousand dollars in cash. Most working girls couldn't afford one, and they either had to find a way to scrape up the money or travel to Mexico or Europe to terminate their pregnancies.

"It's outrageous that girls can't be aborted here," Helen continued. "Never mind that this little child doesn't have a father. And never mind that its mother is a flibbertigibbet who has no business having a baby. Abortion is just surrounded with all this hush-hush and horror, like insanity used to be."

Helen had tried to broach some of these subjects in *Sex and the Single Girl*, she told her interviewer, but her publisher, Bernard Geis, made her cut the parts about how to avoid getting pregnant. They butted heads about other cuts, too. In the chapter on affairs, Berney had tried changing "nymphomaniac" to "pushover" to describe a woman who feels secure only when she's in bed with a man. "I just hit the roof. I hate that word," Helen said.

"Pushover" made the woman sound like a weakling, a prude who didn't like sex. "*Au contraire*. She's asking for it. She needs it. She needs the reassurance. When a man is making love to you, the United Nations building could fall down and if he's really a man, he won't stop for a minute. . . . It does give you a feeling of power," Helen said. "I understand a nymphomaniac in that respect. Any girl who goes to bed with a man has a reason. I don't think one of them is that she doesn't know how to say no."

In fact, Helen wasn't describing a nymphomaniac—who, by definition, craves sex and struggles to control her desires—so much as a woman who craves control and gets it through sex. Either way, she saw sex as a powerful weapon, and a necessary one for any single girl who was fighting her way to a man when so few were available.

"I don't know of anything more ruthless, more deadly or more dedicated," Helen told *Playboy*, "than any normal, healthy American girl in search of a husband."

12

A STRANGE STIRRING
1963–1964

"The truth is that I've always been a bad-tempered bitch."
—Betty Friedan, *Life So Far*

A few months before *Playboy*'s April issue hit the stands, a young journalist from Ohio applied for one job that Helen Gurley Brown never could have landed, no matter how hard she tried: Playboy Bunny. Even with her wigs, false eyelashes, Pan-Cake, and padded bra, Helen simply didn't look the part. But Gloria Steinem did. Twenty-eight with dark brown hair, kohl eyes, and the killer legs of a Copa Girl, Steinem walked into Hugh Hefner's New York Playboy Club one brisk day in January 1963, carrying her leotard in a hatbox and a newspaper ad hyping the perks of being a Playboy Bunny: celebrity encounters, travel, and "top money."

Pretending to be a former waitress named Marie Catherine Ochs (a family name), Steinem told the woman who interviewed her that she had come to audition to work at the club. Indeed, she had, but her real mission was to go undercover as a Playboy Bunny and write about the seamy reality of the job for *Show*, a stylish monthly magazine covering the arts.

Steinem ended up training and working as a Bunny for about three weeks. Like the other women on her shift, she donned her cleavage-baring costume with its collar, cuffs, and tail, perfecting her Bunny dip. Unlike the other Bunnies, she also took notes about the job's not-so-glamorous demands: grueling working conditions, a demerits system that left many girls broke, and the disturbing requirement that all Bunnies get a gynecological exam by a *Playboy* doctor.

The first installment of her witty, groundbreaking two-part series, "A Bunny's Tale," ran in *Show* that May, followed by the second installment in June. And while the exposé was an instant sensation, it also created lasting problems for Steinem. Hours upon hours of wearing high heels and carrying heavy trays permanently enlarged her feet by half a size. Long after she turned in her costume, *Playboy* continued running her employee photograph out of spite. (In 1984, *Playboy* ran a different photo of Steinem, at age fifty, in which her breast was accidentally exposed.) In some circles, she became known as just another Playboy Bunny rather than as a serious journalist who had gone undercover for an assignment. It would be years before she felt proud of the article, realizing that, as she put it, "all women are Bunnies."

While Gloria's star was rising in New York, another journalist was igniting a new movement among women. Barely over five feet with salt-and-pepper hair, heavy-lidded brown eyes, and a nose that got her teased as a kid, Betty Friedan might as well have strapped a ton of dynamite under her housecoat: Her book *The Feminine Mystique* exploded onto the scene in February 1963, blasting a hole in the image of the happy housewife. Millions of women had fallen victim to an empty notion of femininity propagated by companies selling everything from washing machines to face creams, she argued. Marrying and having kids younger, they felt trapped in their homes, in their sex lives, and in their own bodies; and they grappled with an existential dread that she called The Problem That Has No Name.

"It was a strange stirring, a sense of dissatisfaction, a yearning that women suffered in the middle of the twentieth century in the United States," she wrote. "Each suburban wife struggled with it alone. As she made the beds, shopped for groceries, matched slip-cover material, ate peanut butter sandwiches with her children, chauffeured Cub Scouts and Brownies, lay beside her husband at night—she was afraid to ask even of herself the silent question—'Is this all?'"

It was a question that Betty Friedan, a mother of three, had asked herself. Originally from Peoria, Illinois, Betty Goldstein (her maiden name) graduated summa cum laude from Smith College in 1942 and won a fellowship to the University of California, Berkeley, to study psychology. Instead of pursuing her Ph.D. in California, she moved to New York City, where she started writing for leftist publications and eventually met her husband, Carl Friedan, a summer-theater producer who later went into advertising. They married in 1947 and soon began building their family in Parkway Village, Queens. To friends they appeared to be a happy couple, but Carl was cheating on her. When Betty became pregnant with their second child—a condition that cost Friedan her job at a union newspaper—he began calling home from the office to say that he would be staying late. "I later learned he was having an affair with a former girlfriend," Betty Friedan wrote in her memoir, *Life So Far*. "I knew who she was. I sensed they'd been seeing each other and I felt desolate, deserted, betrayed, all those things."

Carl was also abusive. In 1956 they moved to Rockland County, New York, for Carl's job (he eventually established his own advertising and public relations firm), settling into a beautiful but isolated old stone barn that they rented. In this rural setting with two kids and a third on the way, Betty became dependent on Carl for adult companionship, and he depended on her to help out with expenses by taking on freelance writing assignments. "I must have gotten sharper with Carl about his deals, when we were so behind on our bills, or his not getting home for dinner," she wrote in her memoir. "I seem to remember a sense of unspeakable horror; fear; I felt numb, until, one night, he hit me. And he cried afterward, that first time." (Carl later refuted her charges of physical abuse.)

It was around this difficult time that, in 1957, Betty was asked to conduct a survey of her Smith classmates leading up to their fifteen-year reunion. Though she was hesitant at first—she felt guilty that she hadn't done more with her Smith education— Betty agreed to do the survey, largely because of a controversial book that had just come out called *Modern Women: The Lost Sex*. The authors, Freudian psychoanalyst Marynia Farnham and journalist Ferdinand Lundberg, argued that too much education was making American women unhappy at home. Fired up, Betty decided to use her Smith questionnaire findings to write a feature article for a major women's magazine—and *McCall's* wanted to run it.

Drawing on her background in both psychology and journalism, Betty threw herself into developing the questionnaire with Marion "Mario" Ingersoll Howell, the vice president of the Class of 1942, and another Smith classmate, Anne Mather Montero. After several brainstorming sessions, they came up with a list of questions that voiced many of Betty's own personal doubts and disappointments. The final survey asked about marriage, sex, children, household chores, finances, reading habits, and religious and political beliefs, but it also featured more ambiguous categories, such as "The Other Part of Your Life" ("Did you have career ambitions?" "If your main occupation is homemaker, do you find it totally fulfilling?") and one tellingly called "You, Personal" ("In what ways have you changed inside as a person?" "What difficulties have you found in working out your role as a woman?").

They eventually received two hundred responses from Betty's classmates. While they appeared to have picture-perfect lives with nice homes, husbands, and children, many of the interviewees said they felt depressed and trapped—they just didn't know why. Betty tried to publish an article about her findings, suggesting that it wasn't too much education that was making women unhappy, but rather their limited roles in society, but *McCall's* no longer wanted it. After a year of rewrites and rejections, Betty decided to write a book exposing the truth that no women's magazine dared to print. She had a much easier time finding a book publisher: Her agent sent her to Norton to meet an editor named George Brockway, who listened intently to her proposal for a book about American women's disillusionment with domestic life. As it happened, Brockway's wife, a graduate of Bryn Mawr, had just given birth to their thirteenth child. (A few years later, she went back to school and earned her Ph.D.) After that meeting, Betty got a $3,000 book advance and began writing her book, which would take her several years to complete.

By the spring of 1963, dog-eared copies of *The Feminine Mystique* had made their way into suburban living rooms from Schenectady to Salt Lake City. Housewives recognized themselves in the book's portraits of women who didn't know the cause of their mysterious blisters or bouts of depression. "Sometimes a woman would tell me that the feeling gets so strong she runs out of the house and walks through the streets. Or she stays inside of her house and cries. Or her children tell her a joke, and she doesn't laugh because she doesn't hear it," Friedan wrote. "I talked to women who had spent years on the analyst's couch, working out their 'adjustment to the feminine role,' their blocks to 'fulfillment as a wife and mother.'

But the desperate tone in these women's voices, and the look in their eyes, was the same as the tone and the look of other women, who were sure they had no problem, even though they did have a strange feeling of desperation."

The Feminine Mystique began with a question—"Is this all?"—and ended with a plan of action. The last chapter was titled "A New Life Plan for Women." Women needed to stop pretending that housework was a career. "The only way for a woman, as for a man, to find herself, to know herself as a person, is by creative work of her own," Friedan wrote. "There is no other way."

SEVERAL MONTHS LATER, Friedan's message embedded itself into Helen Gurley Brown's consciousness as she was writing and revising *Sex and the Office*. "I'll tell you *this*," Helen typed, addressing the legions of unhappy housewives, newly outed. "Women in offices never have to wonder who *they* are. They *know* who they are, and nobody lets them forget it!" A career girl didn't have to search for her identity, she argued: She was the secretary, the actress, or the executive. People needed her and depended on her.

But they also judged her. In 1963 the career woman was as maligned as the single girl had been two years before when Helen started writing *Sex and the Single Girl*. Helen had been looking for something to rail against, and she found it in the advice of Dr. Benjamin Spock, who suggested that working mothers were doing a disservice to their children; in the housewife who snarled over the career girl's success; in the working girl who dropped her job as soon as she found a husband; and in the blatant misogyny of writers like Philip Wylie, who authored a vicious article, "The Career Woman," for *Playboy*'s January 1963 issue. "They call her brilliant, this highly paid Circe," Wylie wrote. "If she is, however, she is also, outside her career, more ignorant than institutionalized Mongoloids. . . . On her throne she sits, this skirt-girt squid, the she-tycoon, caring only about herself and heedless of the damage she is doing to the national psyche." (Two decades earlier, in his 1942 book, *Generation of Vipers*, the woman-bashing Wylie blamed society's ills on "momism," a term he coined to describe the phenomenon of American mothers smothering and emasculating their sons.)

The realization that the career girl was the new single girl hit Helen like a rolling metal filing cabinet. The working woman was just the outcast du jour. Helen felt her plight deeply, the unfairness and the injustice of it, but she knew she had to be careful not to sound scolding, or else another Philip Wylie would come along and lump her in with the rest of the shrieking she-wolves. She had to be subtle. And witty. She had to make people laugh before they would listen. So, she wrote a little riddle.

"We haven't been introduced though I may have been pointed out to you at parties," she began. It's likely that she was talking to a group of men, and that the person doing the pointing was a woman, gossiping with a gaggle of other women. "I might as well stop playing 'I've Got a Secret' and tell you who I am!" Helen wrote. "I'm one of those driven, compulsive, man-eating, penis-envying, emasculating, lacquered, female wolverines known as a career woman. Frankly . . . I've been about as much in vogue in recent years as rattan bedroom furniture. Rosalind Russell *used* to play me in movies of the Forties, but *nobody* wants to play me anymore."

In her signature, snappy style, Helen went on to list twenty-four reasons why women should work, suggesting that instead of becoming professional housewives they consider becoming psychiatrists, nurses, schoolteachers, social workers, and medical professionals, as well as entering fields monopolized by men, like physics and engineering. The chapter "Come with Me to the Office" was a clear invitation to women to follow her up the ladder, one rung at a time. Helen wanted it to be her first chapter, but it landed on Berney's desk with a thud. He was all for the sections on how to catch a man in the office, but for the most part he thought Helen was wasting space encouraging girls to get ahead in their careers. One day, he suggested, she could write a separate manual for the really ambitious girls.

"Most girls—probably 90 per cent—who work in an office are *not* pyramid-climbers," he told Helen in a letter. "You happened to belong to the 10 per cent."

But Helen argued right back. She was willing to tone down that chapter, not to lose it entirely. The book needed a cause beyond instructing office girls how to flirt—she wanted them to soar. The typical working girl felt sorry for herself, just as the single girl had before, she pointed out to Berney. She was all of eighteen when she took her first job at radio station KHJ in Hollywood to pay off her tuition for secretarial school. She worked because she had to, because she didn't have a choice, and at first it felt like just another punishment that poor girls had to endure. It wasn't until she landed at Foote, Cone & Belding that she found her calling and a boss who was willing to take a chance on her as a copywriter. And where would she be now if not for that chance?

"Tell her she not only isn't *unfortunate* to be working but has the best of all possible worlds," Helen pleaded with Berney. If he insisted on cutting all the getting-ahead-in-a-career stuff, the book would lose its mission, and she would be stuck as a crusader without a cause.

Maybe it had something to do with the phenomenal success of Betty Friedan's bestseller, but more and more, Helen Gurley Brown, champion of the single woman, began to set her sights on attracting the married woman she had once mocked. It was time to stamp out the idea that the career girl suffered from some incurable illness that would derail Mother Nature's plan for her to procreate. A woman's fulfillment outside of the home was good news for the whole family.

In a chapter called "Come Back Little Wives, Widows, Divorcees," Helen made a special plea to the Little Wives to join the working world: "Explain to your husband, if he doesn't already understand, that you will be a better companion, a more adoring wife and loving mother if you are allowed to take a job," she advised. "Don't you see that by working you could have it *all*?"

IT WAS ONE thing to try to change the image of the Brown Bag Lunch, and quite another to change the image of the working woman in America. But Helen wanted no less, and she didn't have to look far to find a poster girl for the glamorous career woman. In the spring of 1963, newly pregnant and still as chic as ever, she was on TV almost as frequently as her husband, whom she might not have met if not for her job.

Jacqueline Bouvier was twenty-three years old when she began working for the *Washington Times-Herald* newspaper as "The Inquiring Camera Girl," a reporting gig that paid her $42.50 a week to interview and photograph notable people around the city, including Richard Nixon. Granted, her questions weren't exactly hard-hitting. In 1952 she asked six housewives if they thought that Mamie Eisenhower's bangs would become a nationwide fad. Shortly thereafter, she met a soon-to-be senator named John F. Kennedy, whom she featured in her 1953 column and married the same year. Ten years and two kids later, she had one of the most important jobs in the world as first lady of the United States. How was that for having it all?

13

WOMEN ALONE
1963–1964

"No matter how accustomed to your own community you may become, never grow to feel safe in it. Feel threatened. You *are* threatened. You are *never* safe."

—Max Wylie, *Career Girl, Watch Your Step!* 1964

On August 28, 1963, all eyes were on the nation's capital, where a massive crowd of 250,000 people gathered for the March on Washington for Jobs and Freedom. It was a Wednesday, and thousands of New Yorkers had decided to skip work to head south to Washington, D.C., instead. Those who stayed in the city congregated—in boardrooms, barbershops, bars, living rooms, dorm rooms, and newsrooms—to watch a live, black-and-white broadcast of the procession toward the Lincoln Memorial and to hear the melodious but mournful voice of the Rev. Dr. Martin Luther King as he cried out his vision for equality. "I have a dream that my four little children will one day live in a nation where they will not be judged by the color of their skin but by the content of their character," he told the crowd in a speech invoking the Constitution and the Bible, the spirit of Lincoln and of America itself. As the sun dropped lower in the sky, King's voice crescendoed, keeping a nation in thrall. But just as the final words of "I Have a Dream" echoed through Washington, a nightmare was unfolding in New York City.

That same day, two young women were brutally stabbed with kitchen knives in their third-floor apartment at 57 East Eighty-Eighth Street near Madison Avenue, an exclusive address in an affluent neighborhood. The victims were unlikely targets for violence in their doorman-protected building. Janice Wylie was a twenty-one-year-old copy girl at *Newsweek* who came from a prominent family. Emily Hoffert was a twenty-three-year-old Smith College graduate with a teaching assignment lined up on Long Island.

A third roommate, Patricia Tolles, later came home to a wrecked flat and called the local precinct before investigating any further herself. Then she called Janice's parents. By the time the cops showed up, the Wylies were already waiting inside the apartment. Janice's father, an author and advertising executive named Max Wylie, led the detectives to a shared bedroom, where blood spattered the walls. On the floor, the bodies of the two roommates lay under a blue blanket. One was nude and had been disemboweled; her ankles were bound together by strips of white cloth, curlers still in her hair. That was his daughter, Janice Wylie.

Less than twenty-four hours later, the news broke: "2 Career Girls Savagely Slain," trumpeted the *New York Daily News*, coining a catchy moniker for the double homicide that would soon turn into a citywide obsession. Adding to the drama was a cast of already well-known characters, including Janice's father, Max, and her uncle, the author Philip Wylie, whose venomous screed on career women Helen Gurley Brown had referenced in an early draft of *Sex and the Office*. "The Career Girls Murders lit up the city like a hit Broadway show," T. J. English wrote in his 2011 book, *The Savage City: Race, Murder, and a Generation on the Edge*. "The case had innocent female victims, shocking brutality, and the makings of a classic whodunit. . . . The race of the victims, the savagery of the killings, and the social standing of the Wylie family all conspired to make the story a keeper," what cops and crime reporters called "a good murder at a good address."

In the days that followed, the March on Washington receded into the back pages, while tabloids found new ways to package the stories of the dead Career Girls. With both pity and morbid curiosity, New Yorkers read about Janice Wylie, who actually had planned on going to the March on Washington the day she was killed; her father, worried about her safety at such a mass demonstration, convinced her to stay home. The prettier of the two roommates, with blond hair, a Marilyn Monroe mole, and arched eyebrows, Janice quickly became an object of gossipy speculation, thanks to her good looks and once active dating life. Was she promiscuous? A swinger? A sleep-around girl who finally slept with the wrong guy? Or just a nice girl who liked to have a little fun?

The entire city was on edge about the slayings, but especially single women, who saw themselves in the victims, reported Gay Talese, who headed uptown to capture the mood among East Side residents shortly after the story first broke. "Throughout the day, girls were asking superintendents about double locks, or were going to hardware stores to buy door chains," Talese wrote in the *New York Times*. "Residents at The Barbizon were telling Oscar, the doorman, how lucky they are. Many of those who live alone, such as the blonde social worker in an East Seventy-third Street walkup, were moving out and staying with friends."

It wasn't just the Upper East Side. From midtown Manhattan to Crown Heights, Brooklyn, girls began to change the locks on their doors and install peepholes. Some vacated their apartments altogether, seeking refuge back home with Mom and Dad. "All I remember is that a wave of fear ran through single women in New York. That's all we talked about," Jane Maas says now. Back then, she was a married thirty-one-year-old mother, who would go on to become a creative director at the advertising agency Ogilvy & Mather. "I went home to a Marine Corps husband every night, and yet I was super aware of how worried all my single, apartment-living friends were: *Are we safe going on dates? Or are we taking our lives into our hands? Are blind dates now not to be had? Maybe I should get a roommate.* . . . Our mothers called us and said, 'I think you should give up this wild notion about living in the city.'"

Fleeing New York might seem like an overreaction now, but it didn't seem like such a crazy idea then—especially because the killer was still on the loose. By late September 1963, the New York City Police Department hadn't found a likely suspect after canvassing the city and questioning almost five hundred people. "The police [are] under intense pressure to solve the crime and remove from the streets a killer whose act has frightened thousands of lonely women," the *New York Times* reported.

Inside of her apartment on Sixty-Fifth and Park, Helen Gurley Brown tracked the case along with the rest of the city. Never one to back away from a sensationalist story or a controversial subject, she also wrote about the Career Girl Murders in her column, "Woman Alone." The headline was . . . not subtle: HOW DO YOU KEEP FROM GETTING MURDERED? it blared. Despite the fearmongering title, however, the article itself was quietly and calmly informative. Its advertised purpose was to give girls tips on how to stay safe in the city, and Helen dutifully interviewed the NYPD's deputy commissioner for his advice on defense tactics. (For instance, what to do if a man is following you on the street: "Scream," he advised.) She published other tips from a self-defense booklet that he gave her, but she had another agenda in writing about the Career Girl Murders, one that wasn't advertised but was still obvious. As frightening as the city could be, she didn't want one freakishly horrible story to scare off her readers; many were small-town girls who dreamed of pursuing their careers in the big city, just as she had. In writing her column, she was always talking to a version of herself, the little girl from Little Rock. If she could make it in a city like Los Angeles or New York, so could they—and they shouldn't let anything stop them, not even a terrifying double homicide.

"Is there so much more crime in New York City that girls should stay away from here?" Helen asked the deputy commissioner.

Not at all. Of the twenty-five major American cities, she learned, New York ranked eighteenth in murders, seventeenth in rape, and tenth in aggravated assaults.

"Well, maybe girls alone should stay away from all big cities entirely?" she asked. Wrong again. In fact, crime was going up in suburban areas, she reported back. It was simply impossible to predict when and where a woman might end up in the grip of a psychopath, the deputy commissioner said, adding that "it will have nothing to do with where she lives."

At least one person strongly disagreed with that assessment. A few months after his daughter's murder, Max Wylie was researching a new book, *Career Girl, Watch Your Step!*— a 125-page safety manual aimed at unmarried women who were thinking of leaving home to go to big cities in search of a dream job or husband, or both. In a somber, fatherly tone, he advised would-be career girls to first live in a temporary residence with other women, such as the YWCA, and to avoid "the fringe element . . . the beatniks, the Bohemians, the far-out group with a distorted sense of values."

"Don't think of yourself as being safe," Wylie cautioned.

"Think of yourself as being in danger all the time. This will make you wary. There is no better protection than an awareness of the dangers that *might* engulf you."

Wylie's safety manual was written in response to the gruesome murder of his daughter, but in a broader sense it was also a reaction against the philosophies espoused by Helen Gurley Brown in *Sex and the Single Girl* and "Woman Alone."

Helen had built a career on encouraging single, working girls to leave the nest, strike out on their own, find an apartment, get a job, meet new men, date around, sleep around if they wished—and, above all, embrace their independence.

Just beware, Wylie warned those same girls: Your independence could get you killed.

HAD HELEN BEEN single during that time, perhaps she would have wanted to stay locked inside her apartment forever, but as the leaves changed and the air turned crisp, the city's fears began to dissipate along with the summer heat. It was impossible to step outside without discovering something or someone new. One cold sunny day, she was heading west across Park Avenue when a tall, striking woman heading east with her husband stopped her. "You're Helen Gurley Brown," she said. "I'm Jacqueline Susann."

At first Helen didn't recognize her—all lips and eyelashes, with a thick slab of black hair and a deep widow's peak. Truman Capote hadn't yet called her "a truck driver in drag" on national television, and Helen hadn't seen the commercials that Jackie, once an aspiring actress, had done for Schiffli embroidery machines, along with her beloved French poodle, Josephine. (They wore matching mother-and-mutt outfits.) But as they started talking, Helen realized she knew exactly who she was. She had heard about Jackie from the team over at Bernard Geis Associates, who soon would be publishing her novel, *Every Night, Josephine*, a larky account of life with her now famous poodle. In time the two authors would become close friends. Jackie knew all about Helen's *Sex and the Single Girl* tour and would use it as a model for future promotion of her own books. Helen studied Jackie herself—how she walked, talked, dressed, and demanded star treatment long before she was actually a star. "I loved the way she looked because it was always showbizzy," Helen told the author Barbara Seaman in the latter's biography of Susann, *Lovely Me*. "It was sequins, it was chiffon, it was high heels and ankle straps and lots of jewelry and the beautiful dark hair. I adored her. She was like a role model."

Of course, Helen also had David, the best tour guide New York City could offer. Through David she saw the New York that Sinatra later sang about, a city of new starts that could melt away little-town blues—and, best of all, her own husband was top of the list. He had taken her here shortly after they married in 1959. Seeing Rodgers and Hammerstein on Broadway, dining at Le Pavillon, waiting arm-in-arm for a taxi outside the "21" Club, drinking champagne at the Dorset hotel as the snow fell on Fifty-Fourth Street, so pretty it seemed staged, like something out of a Christmas scene in a Saks window display . . . New York was wonderful, but it was his. She needed to make it hers.

New York intimidated her with its piercing skyscrapers and medieval churches, its grand hotels and four-star restaurants, its army of doormen and maître d's—but it also made her want to belong. Some nights in her apartment, she wondered about the scenes unfolding in the other buildings up and down Park Avenue. More than a few of her neighbors were famous, like Helena Rubinstein, the multimillionaire cosmetics manufacturer, now a widow who lived alone at 625 Park in a twenty-six-room triplex with a circular marble staircase, forty closets, and surrealistic murals by

Salvador Dalí. And then there were all the lit windows of apartments whose tenants she would never know or know of. All the marriage proposals, domestic spats, makeup sex, extramarital affairs. The sheer number of lives being lived out in such close proximity amazed her, and she grew to marvel at her place in it all.

Los Angeles was for the young, but New York wasn't interested in little girls. A girl couldn't pull off a sharp knitted suit with a smart leather hat, or a black satin peignoir. A girl couldn't hail a cab or a man's attention in this city, but a woman could—and, in her early forties, Helen was determined to become a sophisticated New York woman. Slowly but surely, she started walking like she knew where she was going, and when she took cabs, a rare occurrence because she hated spending the fare, she gave directions to the drivers. In L.A. she had dressed like a baby doll, but in New York she smartened up in designer dresses and watched the windows at department stores like Saks, where the world's most fashionable women shopped for floor-length evening coats, twill trenches, mohair jackets, and fur stoles.

Like every other woman who cared about style, Helen also watched the first lady, who had been a constant presence in *Women's Wear Daily* ever since 1960, when the fashion trade trumpeted the news that Jacqueline (then a senator's wife) and her mother-in-law spent a combined $30,000 per year on Parisian clothes and hats. "Jacqueline Kennedy orders mostly from sketches like a mail order catalogue—at Cardin, Grès, Givenchy, Balenciaga, Chanel and Bugnand. Each house has a well-shaped Jacqueline Kennedy dummy," wrote *WWD*'s new editor, John Fairchild, who soon turned the formerly staid industry publication into a gossipy, must-read rag. As first lady, Jacqueline had cut down on her public shopping sprees, but she never failed to give *WWD* something to buzz about, donning endless varieties of A-line coats, pillbox hats, streamlined suits, and candy-colored silk dresses confected by her personal designer, Oleg Cassini.

Of course, nothing would be quite so memorable as the Chanel-inspired pink bouclé suit and matching pillbox hat that Jacqueline Kennedy wore the day her husband was assassinated in Dallas, Texas, on November 22, 1963. Hours later, when she boarded the plane back to Washington, she still wore the bloodstained suit for the world to see.

While the rest of the country grieved, Jacqueline Susann charged into the offices of Bernard Geis Associates, which had published her novel *Every Night, Josephine*, the week before Kennedy's assassination. When she saw the publicity team watching television in tearful silence, instead of preparing for a meeting about her poodle book, she blew up, giving them an early forecast of the ego storm to come.

"Why the fuck does this have to happen to me?" she moaned. "This is gonna ruin my tour!"

Helen had her own books to promote—she was almost finished with *Sex and the Office*—but where Jackie saw an inconvenience, she saw a great opportunity.

Shortly after the president's death, Helen took it upon herself to rebrand the first lady in her newspaper column. "As we have seen through our tears these last few weeks, the most beloved man is mortal," she wrote from her perch over Park Avenue. "The most beloved wife can become a woman alone."

14

PEACE THROUGH UNDERSTANDING
1964

> "It was the perfect time to think silver. Silver was the future,
> it was spacy."
>
> —Andy Warhol, reflecting on his Silver Factory
> in *POPism: The Warhol Sixties*

In April 1964, more than half a year after the slayings of Janice Wylie and Emily Hoffert, the NYPD finally arrested a suspect: a mild-mannered, black nineteen-year-old named George Whitmore Jr., who confessed to the murders of both Wylie and Hoffert. A grade-school dropout who had been described in the press as "possibly mentally retarded," Whitmore soon recanted his confession, saying that he falsely admitted to a number of brutal crimes, including the double homicide, after being beaten and coerced by detectives. On the day Wylie and Hoffert were murdered, Whitmore said, he actually had been in Wildwood, New Jersey, watching the Rev. Dr. Martin Luther King Jr. deliver his "I Have a Dream" speech on television. Despite Whitmore's apparent innocence, he was indicted and sent to prison, only later becoming a tragic symbol of a corrupt and racist system. The real killer, a white heroin addict turned burglar named Richard Robles, was still out there and wouldn't be apprehended until January 1965, after confessing to friends. Convicted of the double homicide, eventually he was sentenced to twenty years to life.

Wrongly believing a madman to be off the streets, the city resumed its normal rhythms. Once again single girls started apartment-hunting in Yorkville and going on blind dates with oxford-shirt-wearing friends of friends, but their hearts belonged to John, Paul, Ringo, and George, who landed in America that February, and were taking over the charts by spring. Another British import, the James Bond film *From Russia with Love*, was playing in New York, and across the country, throngs of men poured into theaters to see soft-core comedies like *3 Nuts in Search of a Bolt*, starring blond bombshell Mamie Van Doren as a stripper named Saxie Symbol, and *Dr. Sex*, following the exploits of three sex researchers working on a follow-up to the Kinsey Report. "In Flaming COLOR and SKIN-A-RAMA," the posters promised.

The movies mirrored the runways, where the look was all about mesh, flesh, and sexual freedom. As Andy Warhol was transforming an industrial loft on East Forty-Seventh Street into the Silver Factory, a soft-spoken Vienna-born fashion designer named Rudi Gernreich was tinkering with new ideas for old forms, like the see-through shirt and the No-Bra Bra, a sheer nylon garment that promised to free the breast from centuries of bondage. A no-sides bra, no-front bra, and no-back bra would soon follow, as would a tank suit paired with thigh-high plastic boots and a visored helmet to block out the sun.

Gernreich's topless bathing suit made the biggest splash of all. In many high-end department stores, it wasn't advertised or displayed; interested customers had to ask for it by name. Only then did salesclerks sneak into some back room to find the one-piece with its sleek bottom and bosom-baring straps. Also called a monokini, the suit made the bare breast the fashion statement of the year. By June, the nation's first topless bar was born when a nineteen-year-old go-go dancer named Carol Doda wore the monokini to perform at the Condor Club in San Francisco's bo-hemian North Beach neighborhood. The future of sex had been ushered in, and Helen Gurley Brown helped open the door.

Everybody was thinking about the future in 1964, especially or-ganizers of the World's Fair, which was bringing innovations from every sphere of art and industry under one giant Unisphere in Queens. The World's Fair beckoned progress, but for Helen it also dragged up a painful past: As a girl, she had been to the World's Fair in Chicago, twice; her mother had taken her in the years after her father died, and it was a bittersweet chapter in both of their lives.

Thirty years later, when Cleo came to visit Helen in New York, it seemed only fitting that they go to the Queens fairgrounds, now that one of the biggest events of the decade was happening in her backyard. But that didn't mean it would be easy. A million trips around the giant tire Ferris wheel in Flushing Meadows–Corona Park couldn't throw Helen off the way Cleo did. With her gray schoolmarm bun, wrinkle-etched face, and tiny four-eleven frame, she couldn't have looked smaller or more vulnerable standing amid all the behemoth buildings of Manhattan, and yet she made Helen feel like the vulnerable one, the visitor in town. The tension between them had been building up for years, and it rose to the surface now.

Helen had wanted to show Cleo a good time at the World's Fair, but the mood spoiled seconds after they stepped into a cab heading for Queens. As soon as Helen started giving directions to the driver, Cleo began undercutting her, belittling her as usual.

"Don't pay any attention to her," Cleo told the driver, ignoring Helen's protests. "She has a nasty disposition."

Helen snapped. She hit Cleo right there in the taxi. Not very hard; she just cuffed her. But still. She couldn't believe she had struck her mother, a little old lady who never even spanked her as a child. She considered herself a gentle person, but Cleo brought out something wild in her, something wounded.

WHEN CLEO TOOK Helen to the World's Fair in 1934, the theme was "A Century of Progress." Three decades later, in Queens, the motto "Peace Through Understanding" might have seemed like a taunt to Helen and Cleo, the difference between them simply too wide to be bridged. Did they make it to the fair? Did they turn back after their fight? It's unclear: Helen's account of that day stops with her hitting her mother in the cab. The frame freezes.

In a sense, the frame froze for millions of visitors, but especially for baby boomers, who would remember the World's Fair as a more optimistic time, when moms wearing pastel capris, dads smoking cigars, and suntanned kids carrying Brownie cameras gawked over modern miracles like the electric toothbrush and got their first glimpse of a computer system at the space-age IBM Pavilion. With Watergate still in the far distance, it was a small world—just as the Disney ride said—and everyone was welcomed to a piece of it. "Practically everybody in the world is coming to the fair!" trumpeted an early promotional film, To the Fair! "The Wilson family is driving in from out West. . . . They're coming from the four corners of the earth, and from Five Corners, Idaho. They come down from New Athens, Maine, and from Athens, Greece. And from Tokyo, and Kokomo, and Rome. Down from Frisco, and down from Troy . . . from Aurora, Illinois."

For a ticket price of two dollars, fairgoers could visit pavilions representing more than thirty foreign countries, traveling from Hong Kong to the Hashemite Kingdom of Jordan. Or they could go to more far-flung places, thanks to a "time tunnel" designed to bring people into the prehistoric past, complete with dinosaurs, all while sitting in the comfort of a 1964-model Ford. General Motors offered trips to the moon in Futurama, a lunar landscape complete with "lunar crawlers" for getting to the space market. In the shadow of the giant Unisphere—the fairgrounds' 140-foot high, 900,000-pound, stainless steel centerpiece—titans of industry unveiled the future . . . Picture-phones! Belgian waffles! Moving sidewalks! Underwater apartment-pods for humans who wanted to live on the seafloor! And heralding it all was a new president, Lyndon B. Johnson, who cut the ribbon at the U.S. Pavilion.

It was a season of possibility and a summer of resistance. On July 2, 1964, almost eight months after President Kennedy's assassination, President Johnson signed into law the Civil Rights Act. In states throughout the South, blacks tested their new rights, eating steak and mashed potatoes in restaurants side by side with white families, and slowly stepping into swimming pools where WHITES ONLY signs still hung. In Kansas City, Missouri, what should have been a simple haircut became a national event when Gene Young, a thirteen-year-old black boy and delegate of the Congress of Racial Equality (CORE), walked into the Muehlebach Hotel barbershop for a trim. When he was denied service, several other black delegates staged a sit-in, forcing the shop to close its doors. The next day, Young was photographed, with knitted brows and a somber expression, while getting his head shaved by a white barber.

Frequently, the testing met strong, sometimes violent resistance from white segregationists. In places like Jackson, Mississippi, and Atlanta, Georgia, business owners chased blacks off their property, wielding pistols and ax handles. And in Charlottesville, Virginia, a restaurant owner named Buddy Glover closed the doors of Buddy's Restaurant minutes after the bill's passage, opting to lose business rather than serve black patrons.

The signing of the Civil Rights Act was a landmark moment,

but the fight was far from over, and it was a fight that was starting to gain many supporters among women. A key part of the legislation, Title VII, prohibited employment discrimination on the basis of race, color, religion, national origin, and sex.

Shortly after the bill was signed in July, the Washington, D.C.–based advocacy group National Association of Manufacturers launched a series of seminars across the country to educate business owners and managers about what to expect when the Civil Rights Act went into effect. "When these slick woman's magazines start telling their readers about 'your new rights,' why, the emancipation proclamation will be a pygmy by comparison," NAM's vice president of industrial relations said at a seminar in Baltimore. "This could be a headache to employers long after the last of the race complications have been solved." Very soon, he told his audience, everyone in the room would be living in a very different world, one where "Help Wanted—Female" ads would no longer exist. The new law forbade them. "That secretary that you advertised for to sit in your lap," he warned, "may wind up being a man."

And the boss might wind up being a woman. At least, that was the message that Helen had wanted to get across in *Sex and the Office*, which Letty—now married to a lawyer named Bert Pogrebin—would be broadcasting. Around the same time that NAM was schooling businessmen in Baltimore, Letty launched another huge publicity and promotional campaign. This time she sent briefcases filled with copies of *Sex and the Office* to secretarial schools around the city, with her pitch to administrators: "Despite the thoroughness of your course program, there are other procedures that no school can begin to teach. . . . *SEX AND THE OFFICE* gives instructions on how to dress 'Up to Here and Down to There,' how to survive 'Jungle Warfare' (office politics) and how to move onward and upward, where 'the money, the men, and the spoils are even greater.'" It was as much an invitation as it was a challenge: Was a school like the Washington Business Institute on Seventh Avenue training its female students to become secretaries or was it preparing them to be businesswomen, possibly executives themselves someday?

Read this book, and this briefcase could be yours, the package seemed to say. And yet the briefcase spoke louder than the book itself. Berney had made his cuts.

Sex and the Office was successful, but it didn't have the impact of Helen's first book, which spawned other imitations—among them, *Saucepans and the Single Girl, Sex and the Single Man,* and *Sex and the Single Cat.* "A publisher asked me to write a 'me-too' book—about sex and the college girl," says Gloria Steinem, who was more interested in critiquing Helen Gurley Brown's new book. Writing for the *New York Herald Tribune,* Steinem put *Sex and the Office* into a political context, comparing the recent spate of books about the problems facing women to books about the problems facing blacks.

"Both have suffered allegations of smaller brain and other natural inferiorities," Steinem began. "Both have gone (or are going) through periods of imitating the former master—in the case of women, being more masculine than men; in the case of Negroes, of being more middle-class-white than the whites." The common wisdom was that women, like blacks, were supposed to have some kind of deeply ingrained expertise on the problems of their kind, Steinem argued, but "knowledge by nature" could take a person only so far. Who had appointed Helen Gurley Brown as the spokesperson for the American woman?

Certainly not Steinem. She dismissed Helen Gurley Brown's writing style as "an ingenious combination of woman's-magazine-bad and advertising-agency-bad," before likening Helen to another famous mogul whom she respected even less.

"*Sex and the Office* doesn't quite fit into George Orwell's category of 'good-bad-books,'" Steinem wrote, "but, like Hugh Hefner's '*Playboy* Philosophy,' it is worth studying as an unusual example of a standard American mashed potato mind at work—unusual, because it is not the sort of mind that frequently produces books. Future governmental commissions on American Goals may read it and weep."

15

IN THE MAIL
1964–1965

"What is it like to be the little princess, the woman who has ful-
filled the whispered promise of her own books and of all the advertisements, the girl to whom things happen? It is hard work."

—Joan Didion, "Bosses Make Lousy Lovers,"
Saturday Evening Post, January 30, 1965

Helen looked ten years younger on television, and she was
the first to admit why. On TV, she wore a wig, false eyelashes, powder, two kinds of rouge, lipstick, eyeliner,
pencil, and shadow. The great thing about radio was that it was all
about the voice, and Helen's voice was made for radio—or rather,
she remade it for radio. Soft and silky, it glided across the airwaves
like aural lube. Callers could rant about her ruining American
morals, hosts could call her names, but they never got her to raise
her voice. "I'm kind of outspoken and *controverseeyal*," she would
coo in agreement.

When Joe Pyne, a former marine turned talk show host known
for his confrontational interviewing style, called her a "terrible woman" for giving girls explicit instructions on how to have
a lunchtime affair with a married man, including advice on what
kind of lingerie to wear, Helen didn't flinch.

"Well, Joe, it's just that I think if a girl is going to be involved
in a matinee relationship, she should do it in style, that's all."

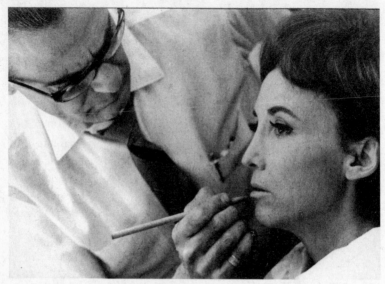

A rare behind-the-scenes glimpse at all the hard work (and makeup) that went into being the public Helen Gurley Brown. (*Copyright © Ann Zane Shanks.*)

"You know, I expect that you're soon going to have a book on murder! You're going to say, 'Now, If you're going to murder someone—which I don't recommend, but if you do murder somebody—pick somebody who really deserves it!'" Pyne fumed.

"Oh, Joe Pyne," Helen purred, "you really can't equate murder with girls having affairs. I think you have a kind of puritanical, funny, rigid attitude about things."

As 1964 came to an end, so did Helen's twenty-eight-city promotional tour for *Sex and the Office*. One day she climbed into a white, two-door Volkswagen Beetle with no air-conditioning that would be her chariot around Southern California. Her driver was Skip Ferderber, a twenty-three-year-old press agent who worked for an independent publicity company hired by Bernard Geis Associates to promote *Sex and the Office* in Los Angeles, and whose mission was to bring Helen to as many TV and radio interviews as possible in seventy-two hours.

There was another passenger in the car, too. Sitting in the backseat of the White Angel, as Helen dubbed her ride, was a diminutive young novelist who was quietly scribbling notes about Helen Gurley Brown for a profile of her in an upcoming issue of *The Saturday Evening Post*. Finishing up the final stretch of a thirteen-week promotional tour of England and the United States, Helen was hanging on, but just barely. In Los Angeles, Joan Didion found "a very tired woman indeed, a woman weary of flirting with disc jockeys, tired of parrying insults and charming interviewers and fighting for a five-minute spot here and a guest appearance there."

Didion kept herself in the background; she was inscrutable even then. Still, she was clearly charmed by Helen's gumption and impressed by her work ethic—if somewhat disparaging of her actual work. At the time of the interview, Helen had sold nearly two and a half million copies of her two books, combined, and Didion attributed the sales partly to various daytime and late-night radio talk shows, like *Long John Nebel*, that featured Helen as a guest and reached "a twilight world of the lonely, the subliterate, the culturally deprived."

She also noted that a good number of the night owls who called in to shows to sound off on Helen Gurley Brown's depravity hadn't actually read her books, which were actually quite sweet and sincere. In fact, those listeners weren't responding to her books at all, but rather to the idea of them; just as they were responding to the idea of *her*, a woman whose studied, seductive voice had been transmitted via hundreds of radio and TV shows over the past year, and, with any luck, would soon be on hundreds more.

But then a funny thing happened. After being shuttled around to countless tapings in Los Angeles, Helen suddenly had a hard time booking TV and radio interviews back home in New York. In November, Letty and a colleague wrote a memo to the Browns warning them that they were getting "over exposure signals on HGB." Bookers at some of the biggest shows like *The Tonight Show* simply felt that Helen had been on too many times. Their audiences just weren't interested in her at the moment, Letty reported: "No amount of idea suggesting, controversy proposals, or cajoling can change their minds it seems."

Letty suggested putting Helen under wraps for a while, but Helen and David had another idea—they *always* had another idea. This was hardly the first time they had run into rejection. After *Sex and the Single Girl* first hit shelves, they churned out countless proposals for TV shows, some of which they pitched through the talent agent Lucy Kroll.

Among their ideas that never made it to screen: a food-themed quiz show (sample challenge: taste five types of milk, from skim to evaporated, and identify each); a game show in which ordinary people would present their ideas for new inventions in front of an audience (nearly forty-five years later, ABC's *Shark Tank* would be based on a similar premise); and a cheeky talk show, *Frankly Female*, which Helen would host. Though aimed primarily at women, the show would also feature a male cohost to attract some men. In one proposed segment titled "EXPLAIN PLEASE!" the idea was that Helen would ask an expert a ridiculously basic question about a subject that the Browns deemed long had eluded women—such as the names of the seven continents—only they were too ashamed to admit it. A man from the Internal Revenue Service could break down a tax form to Helen on the air, for instance. Other experts could explain how to count using Roman numerals, or why World War I started in the first place. In answering, the expert would speak very simply as if to a child, using props if necessary. Easy enough for "how to change a tire," though "How it started with the Jews and the Arabs and who's right?" could prove more challenging.

The Browns never did convince a network to green-light *Frankly Female.* Nor did they have success with a comedy-drama series, *Sandra (The Single Girl)*, about the adventures of a somewhat plain, but charming, single girl who works as a copywriter in an advertising agency. ABC rejected the idea for what were then obvious reasons. No one wanted to watch a TV show set in the world of Mad Men—especially not one that focused on a woman. "It is a series built around a female lead, and the unfortunate history of television indicates that this has been uniformly unsuccessful," wrote the network's bearer of bad news. (In 1966, Marlo Thomas would star as a struggling actress trying to make it in New York City in ABC's *That Girl*, one of the first sitcoms to focus on a single, working woman who didn't live with her parents. The Browns had been a bit *too* ahead of the curve.)

Sooner or later, something had to stick, but it sure as hell wasn't going to be *The Unwind Up*, a show that promised to feature a psychotherapist named Charles Edward Cooke, coauthor of the 1956 guide *Hypnotism Handbook* with sci-fi writer A. E. Van Vogt. Cooke would actually hypnotize viewers into a near-sleep state—with the help of soothing music and somnolent readings of telephone directories, Teamsters union bylaws, and *The Communist Manifesto*. Keeping the viewer in a hypnotic state, Helen pointed out, would be ideal for sponsors wanting to soft-sell their products. Not so ideal for the viewer, perhaps. "The only possible harm that could come to anyone from this kind of hypnosis," Helen noted, "is that they might have left something on the stove before they fell asleep, failed to put out a cigarette, or left a child unattended."

Although most of their ideas never panned out, the Browns didn't stay discouraged for long. If anything, they saw rejection as a kind of creative fuel—a reason to keep trying. David had lost his job enough times to know the importance of having something "in the mail," whether it was a book proposal or a new concept for a column. Whatever it was, he always had some idea floating around—something that might lead to the Next Big Thing. All it took was one great idea landing in the right hands at the right time.

As it happened, by the fall of 1964, there *was* something in the mail that was beginning to spark some interest.

16

FEMME

1964–1965

"Here's a proposal for you from Helen Gurley Brown. While it *is*
a marriage proposal, I'm afraid it's your magazine she suggests
living with happily ever after, not the boss."

—1964 letter from Bernard Geis to Richard Deems,
the president of Hearst Magazines

In December 1964, Helen's epic tour finally slowed to a halt
with a few last stops, including one in Miami, where she visited Tropical Park Race Track, appeared on Larry King's TV
show *Miami Undercover*, and signed autographs at Burdine's department store. There were worse ways to spend a few days in
winter than staying at the Doral Beach Hotel, a brand-new tower
in Miami Beach with ocean views on Collins Avenue's famous Millionaire's Row, but Helen didn't stick around. She was eager to
get back home for a few reasons, not the least of which was that,
on Christmas Day, the movie adaptation of *Sex and the Single Girl*,
cowritten by Joseph Heller, whose novel *Catch-22* had come out
three years before, would be hitting theaters.

Sex and the Single Girl's journey to screen had been fraught with
its own catches and conundrums, starting with how to adapt a
plotless how-to guide into a feasible film. Along the way, the original producer, Saul David, dropped out, but with director Richard Quine at the helm, the production attracted an all-star cast,
including Tony Curtis, Henry Fonda, Lauren Bacall, and Mel

Ferrer. The film's star was Natalie Wood, who played a character named Dr. Helen Gurley Brown, a doe-eyed twenty-three-year-old research psychologist and author of the titular bestseller advocating sexual freedom for unmarried women. Other than those surface details, *Sex and the Single Girl* the movie had almost nothing to do with *Sex and the Single Girl* the book. But that didn't stop single girls from lining up to see the film at the Rivoli Theater on Broadway and the Trans-Lux 52d Street, or the occasional critic from enjoying the Technicolor romp with its suggestive one-liners and jazzy score. "It's not the worst picture ever made, girls and boys," A. H. Weiler wrote in the *New York Times* the next day.

Sex and the Single Girl didn't exactly get glowing reviews—"It was ridiculous, a horrible movie," says Rex Reed, who claims that "even Natalie, who became one of my best friends, wouldn't talk about that film"—but it did get Helen's name out there once again, quite literally, along with the title of her bestselling book, which was featured as a recurring prop in the movie.

The timing couldn't have been better. In the weeks leading up to the film's release, Berney had been circulating a proposal for a new magazine concocted by the Browns. A self-help magazine aimed at single, working women, it was called *Femme*.

THE CONCEPT FOR *Femme* wasn't exactly the result of a flash of inspiration—it was simply another idea in a chain of dozens that Helen and David had discussed. By the summer of 1964, she had been getting fan mail for two years thanks to her books. She still tried to answer letters individually when she could—a staggering number of girls wrote to her about being in love with married men, a subject she considered to be one of her specialties—but it was impossible to keep up with the demand. One day, after a new bag of mail arrived, David brought up the idea.

"You know, Helen, you really ought to have a magazine for these girls," he said. "Most of the magazines are only talking about married girls. It's motherhood and home and God. You ought to have a book for good-citizen swingers like you were."

It was as simple as that. Not long after that conversation, Helen and David sat down at the kitchen table and started brainstorming. (At a certain point, Charlotte Kelly, a close friend of Helen's from her advertising days, also pitched in.) Between them, they had two pads of paper, two pencils, and a gazillion ideas for new features and departments. Helen focused on the beauty pages, jotting down all the concepts she had tried and failed to sell to Max Factor, while David came up with eye-catching headlines and wrote a preamble about *Femme*'s enormous advertising potential. Once they had gotten everything down on paper, Helen typed up the keepers.

Among their ideas for monthly departmental features: a dating column in which Helen would dole out advice, a health column in which a medical professional would answer women's pressing questions about everything from diaphragms to male impotence, a financial column in which a female economist such as Sylvia Porter would advise readers on budgeting and investing, and a photo spread titled "However Do You Do *That*?" in which a model would simulate performing "masculine" household repairs that often eluded the woman on her own. (How to fix a leaky faucet, for example.)

Among their suggested headlines for major articles: U.S. PRESIDENTS WHO LIKED GIRLS (a look back at the last ten presidents and their taste in women), SEXUAL PROWESS IN MEN (asking the age-old question, "Is size important?"), ABORTION! (in which the following line was written and crossed out: "Femme is for it in many instances"), I'M NOT MARRIED TO THE BABY'S FATHER . . .

AND NEVER WAS (written anonymously), THE NOSE JOB (a step-by-step account), BABY-BRAIN ASTROLOGY (men love girls who can tell them about their signs!), "IF YOU COMMIT SUICIDE I'LL KILL YOU!" (or, "How to help a suicidal person"), I LOVE GIRLS LIKE YOU LOVE MEN ("Article by a ~~lesbion~~ Lesbian"), THE WORLD OF FALSIES (with before-and-after pics), and perhaps the best-worst fashion spread ever imagined in the history of magazines, THE POODLE AND THE SINGLE GIRL, featuring "various costumes girls wear with poodles (and various poodles)."

Over time, Helen and David would go through several versions of the proposal, tweaking ideas for features and smaller, departmental articles. But from the very start, they imagined a magazine that looked as sexy as it read, with hot, color-saturated images that could compete with photo-heavy books like *Look* and *Life*. To get that vision across, they put together a crude editorial dummy, with "FEMME" written in black marker on a scrap of paper taped to the cover.

The girl on the cover was not famous; she was just a girl. Like *Femme*, which was only a temporary title, she was a placeholder. "The bathing-suit girl," Helen called her—a nobody who looked like a somebody because she was beautiful, and clearly comfortable in her body.

But before you picture her, picture what came before her—close-up shots of serenely smiling faces belonging to housewives and celebrity spouses who regularly graced the covers of women's magazines like *Good Housekeeping* wearing turtlenecks and tidy flips.

Now see the supple bathing-suit girl in her teeny, flowery bikini, her blond hair on the verge of looking unkempt. Her face is in profile, nuzzled against her bare shoulder smelling, you imagine, of summer and the slightest hint of sweat. Gaze at her for a few seconds and you begin to notice her sooty eyelashes, manicured nails, the way a small smile is just beginning to spread on her lips. You wonder why she is smiling, and whether she's at the beach or perhaps basking in the sun on some swimming rock, her boyfriend just out of frame. But those thoughts come later, because at first glance, here's what you see: chest, flesh, and navel. Soft skin in soft focus.

Look just to the right of her armpit, at another scrap of paper taped onto the page: "For the woman on her own," reads the subtitle in black type. Closer to her breast, you'll find the teasers for this sample issue: "U.S. Presidents Who Liked Girls" and "Where the Men Are." (Compare those lines with the far more somber ones that ran on the covers of *Cosmopolitan* around the same time: "Do Religious Schools Teach Prejudice?" and "Diabetes: Will Your Children Inherit It?")

The tour continues as you goose the bathing-suit girl's thigh at the lower right-hand corner of the page and turn it to find the letterhead of Bernard Geis Associates, trumpeting the arrival of a proposal for a new magazine. Now that the gorgeous girl on the cover has gotten you this far, Helen and David will take over, telling you all about their discovery of a new audience and a new market, as a result of the phenomenon that is *Sex and the Single Girl*. They will tell you that, in an era of specialized magazines, there is one unique group that has been ignored: smart, financially sound women. They will tell you that Helen Gurley Brown, champion of single girls everywhere, recognizes the unmarried woman "as a first class citizen," as opposed to a societal outcast, and has commanded a loyal audience practically overnight. After sharing some figures to illustrate the astronomical success of *Sex and the Single Girl*, the Browns will then guide you through a few more relevant statistics, pulled from recent census records, and show you just how America's unmarried women, divorcees, widows, and other

women on their own add up to a grand total of 27,381,000 potential readers—more, if you count married women who have an "independent attitude."

But the statistics don't tell the whole story. They don't capture
the essence of the reader—her wants, her needs, her insecurities,
her goals and dreams. Again, before you imagine who this woman
is, remember who she is not. She is not a housewife interested in
reading about how to make the perfect jelly roll for the holidays
or how to banish mildew from the basement, in traditional wom-
en's magazines like *Ladies' Home Journal* and *Good Housekeeping*. She
is not the urban sophisticate targeted by upmarket fashion magazines like *Vogue* and *Harper's Bazaar* or even the collegiate girl
next door reflected in the pages of *Mademoiselle* and *Glamour*. She is
too old for *Seventeen*.

Now imagine a single, working-class woman; let's say she's
twenty-nine. It's possible that she never got a chance to go to college
and never will. She might be looking for a husband, but then again
she might enjoy being on her own. *Femme* is for the woman who likes
men—and, more important, who likes herself. She may *seem* shy and
ladylike, but she is actually quite frank, and if you scratch the surface, you might find that she is as ambitious, cutthroat, and egocen-
tric as any man. She is tired of reading women's magazines edited by
men who assume that she is a sweet, sheltered, easily shocked little
cream puff unable to talk about real subjects, like sex. She is weary
of being force-fed the message that women love serving everyone
else. And she's not the only one. Don't forget the Betty Friedan disciples: married women who had good educations and inquisitive
minds that were no longer sated by articles about cookie swaps and
easy ways to save time in the kitchen.

"This woman's magazine will *never* deal with the problems of
school lunches, PTA, laundromats and making over the attic," the

Browns wrote. It *would* start frank discussions about sex, money, careers, apartments, fashion, and beauty—oh, and men, men, men. "It will view the woman on her own as potentially, if not actually, the most desirable, affluent and interesting segment of our female population," they added.

Now, just for a moment, pretend you are a magazine publisher in desperate need of a circulation boost and advertising revenue. What if the Browns could promise that this new audience of career-minded women on their own would also have money of their own? What if the Browns told you that they would do everything in their editorial power to ensure that those women spent their hard-earned cash on advertisers' products? That this new readership would also be a distinct, largely untapped market for companies looking to hawk makeup, swimsuits, shoes, bras, jewelry, home appliances and décor, soda, liquor, cigarettes, cars, airlines, travel resorts, TVs, candy, banks, brokerage firms, drugs, stationery, and slenderizing products?

Not sold yet? What if they told you that the editor of this prospective magazine, Helen Gurley Brown, was such a valuable commodity herself that it would cost a fortune to create and promote such a spokeswoman, starting from scratch? And what if they told you that, in hiring her, you'd also be getting former *Cosmopolitan* managing editor David Brown's editorial insight and expertise as a bonus?

Would it matter that his wife had never worked at a magazine before, let alone edited one?

FROM THE BEGINNING, the Browns pitched Helen as *Femme*'s editor-in-chief. That variable never changed. But this one did: In an early draft of the proposal, David pitched himself as the magazine's publisher, highlighting his early editorships at both *Liberty* and *Cosmopolitan* as well as his role in originating the *Sex and the Single Girl* franchise and managing his wife's career. Once again, he was restless at work, and in the short biography of himself that David included in their packet, he announced he would be leaving his post at New American Library in order to focus on *Femme*.

By the time Bernard Geis was circulating the prospectus to various publishers in the winter of 1964, David had renamed himself as an editorial consultant. Geis was also listed as a consultant, someone who could bring a considerable amount of promotion and publicity to the magazine. But first, he had to get the proposal to the right people, which proved to be more difficult than he had anticipated. *Esquire* had seemed like a natural ally—Berney once worked at the magazine as an assistant editor—but he was having a hard time convincing anyone there to even look at the outline. By November he was still waiting to hear from *Look*, although he finally heard back from *Playboy*, where he knew the editorial director, A. C. Spectorsky, or "Spec."

"Spec said that he and Hefner would be glad to look at the prospectus," Berney wrote to David Brown. "He said that they already have more projects than they can handle, but you never can tell."

After reviewing the prospectus, Hefner turned the Browns down. He was too busy managing the *Playboy* empire and the failing *Show Business Illustrated* magazine. He wasn't interested in starting a new magazine—not this one, not now.

Despite the tepid reaction *Femme* was getting, Berney refused to be daunted, playing a never-ending game of who-do-you-know. Meanwhile, David personally brought the magazine prospectus around town to try to sell it. He pitched executives at Macfadden-Bartell, and he called on an old friend, George T. Delacorte, the extremely wealthy founder of the Dell Publishing Company. More rejection.

Then David went to lunch with his friend John O'Connell, also known as Jack. Back in the day, they had worked together at *Cosmopolitan*, and in 1950 O'Connell had gone on to be the editor-in-chief, a position he kept for nine years. While they were waiting for a table, O'Connell mentioned that Hearst didn't know what to do about *Cosmopolitan*, which was flailing. "It looks as though they may fold it. But they're taking one more shot," O'Connell said, adding that Hearst wanted to turn *Cosmopolitan* into a women's magazine, targeting single career women. David just listened, but after lunch, he called Berney with an urgent question: "Don't you know the president of Hearst Magazines, Richard Deems?"

Berney knew everyone. Yes, he knew Dick Deems. They had worked together at *Esquire*. David asked Berney to send their magazine dummy over to Deems, which he did, after negotiating a finder's fee.

A few hours later, Berney called David back. "You're to telephone Deems," he said. "He's very interested in *Femme* as a replacement for *Cosmopolitan*."

The Browns met with Deems shortly after Berney's call, and he explained that Hearst didn't want to replace *Cosmopolitan*. The company wanted to graft a new format onto it, and the outline for *Femme* was a good place to start. Following their talk, Helen began to think more about what her idea of a perfect issue of *Cosmopolitan* would look like, before submitting a second presentation to Deems. In a new proposal for *Cosmopolitan*, she critiqued the previous eight issues of the magazine under the current editor, Robert C. Atherton, and, with David's help, solidified her own ideas for how to improve it. She began with a close analysis of *Cosmopolitan* cover lines: "How many copies does 'Our Unadoptable Children' sell, whether you put that line in eighteen point type

or twenty-four point type?" she asked. "Compare that with 'The
ONE Diet You Can Live With.'"

At the request of Hearst, the Browns also included detailed
mock-ups of several future issues, fleshing out ideas for new departments and features, as well as listing potential writers and
what they would cost. Still, there was some concern that, in editing *Cosmopolitan*, Helen Gurley Brown would be a one-hit wonder. Despite her impressive track record with the "Sex and . . ."
franchise, Hearst wasn't convinced that she could keep up the mo-
mentum needed to sustain a monthly magazine. And then there
was the looming question of what *Cosmopolitan*'s more conservative
readers would make of her racy single-girl slant.

Looking for another opinion, Richard Deems asked Ruth
Manton, a valued Hearst employee who worked in marketing at
Harper's Bazaar, to get to know Helen a bit and report back on
what she thought. Ruth set up a lunch, and it was a meeting she
wouldn't soon forget. Shortly after they sat down, Helen explained
her theory that any girl, no matter how plain, can get the man she
wants—if she knows what *he* wants.

"One of the first things Helen said to me was, 'I'm completely
flat-chested, and I wear falsies because that's what men are looking
for,'" Manton says. "I nearly fell off my chair! I'm not a prude in
any way, but in the Sixties, a woman didn't say this the first time
you met her, not normally anyhow. I liked her immediately because she was so direct and honest. And she believed passionately
in what she wanted to do."

When Deems later asked Manton what she thought of their
new candidate, she was blunt. "I said I liked her, I was intrigued
by her: 'She's got a whole new viewpoint for the magazine. I don't
know whether women are ready for it. How will they respond to
an exploration of their sexuality? I can't say.' That's how I left it,"

Manton says, "and the next thing I knew, Helen Gurley Brown was the editor-in-chief of *Cosmopolitan*."

Though David initially planned to be Helen's publisher, he abandoned his bid in December, when Darryl and Richard Zanuck asked him to return to 20th Century Fox and fill a newly created position as head of story operations. (After the *Cleopatra* debacle, the studio was back on its feet thanks to the success of 1965's *The Sound of Music*.) David accepted the job, and while his name never again appeared on the *Cosmopolitan* masthead, he played an instrumental part in its production, and in the continued advancement of Helen's career.

One wintry night in Deems's apartment in the Waldorf Towers, it was David who negotiated a deal for Helen to edit *Cosmopolitan*.

"I think Helen was cowering in a corner somewhere," David later recalled, rendering the scene with a raconteur's sense of irony. "She had never edited a magazine. I don't think I had ever seen her read one."

While it's possible Helen would have felt like hiding out, it's doubtful that she actually cowered in the corner during the negotiations. Even more dubious is David's implication that she didn't read magazines before she was hired to edit one. But like Helen's rags-to-riches rise, the tale of how she went from a meek wallflower to one of the most powerful editors in the world isn't her story alone. It's also David's—and what good is a story editor who doesn't set the stage for a dramatic journey?

17

FOR THE GIRL WITH A JOB
1953

"Helen Gurley got browner, browner, and browner—where else
but on the beach at Waikiki?"

—"Helen Gurley Wins a Holiday in Hawaii," *Glamour*, May 1953

Growing up, Helen inhaled magazines. She and her sister Mary pored over pictures of Carole Lombard, Joan Crawford, and Jean Harlow in *Photoplay* and *Silver Screen*, though as she got older, Helen didn't read for leisure so much as she did for escape, literally. In June 1949, she was still working as an executive secretary at Foote, Cone & Belding when she was one of thirteen women featured in *Glamour* after attending a job seminar hosted by the magazine. The next year, she was spotlighted again in an article about ambitious secretaries. *Glamour* was her bible, and in the years after World War II, a woman like Helen Gurley was the magazine's target reader, to judge by its new tagline: "For the girl with a job."

Though she would have been attracted to any number of lifestyle articles, Helen took particular interest in *Glamour*'s annual competition, "Ten Girls with Taste," which recognized ten women with modest incomes who still managed to show impeccable taste, whether hosting or dressing or decorating. After a friend of hers won the contest and its prizes—a trip to Europe and a new wardrobe—Helen entered for the first time in 1951, filling out a questionnaire that asked about everything from what she typically wore to work to how she would entertain guests for an evening to what she considered her life's philosophy. *Glamour* chose her as one of twelve finalists and flew her to New York, but she never made it past the next round. In 1953, at the age of thirty-one, she entered again. This time she was one of thirty-nine thousand hopefuls—including receptionists, switchboard operators, and "home economists"—who answered a similar questionnaire.

Helen gave it her all. Her typical work outfit hadn't changed much since the first time she filled out the form, so she made up a new-and-improved one. She wasn't much of a cook, so in response to a question about how she would entertain friends for dinner, she lifted ideas from the food section of *Ladies' Home Journal*. As for her philosophy of life, it borrowed heavily from Edward R. Murrow's radio show *This I Believe*, which broadcast the voices of famous public figures and everyday Americans, sharing their heartfelt, personal philosophies for the common good.

In her final application, Helen Gurley painted herself as a hardworking but fun-loving California girl who enjoyed having friends over for Sunday brunch or for an evening of casual conversation and listening to records. While loyal to her boss, she also slipped in a little mention of the fact that she hoped to someday have a career in copywriting. But she really must have won the judges over with her generous heart, or at least the suggestion of it, cornily declaring that good taste "starts with that most basic commodity—one's own self—and extends outward to speech, clothes and possessions. It reaches its supreme station . . . in kindness to another human being."

Helen submitted her application, and to her delight, *Glamour* chose her as one of seventeen semifinalists. After surviving the next round of cuts, she was named one of the ten winners and invited to collect her prizes: a new vacation wardrobe to go with a two-week vacation to Hawaii, where she would sightsee, sunbathe, and sip pineapple punch on the terrace of the Royal Hawaiian Hotel, all while being photographed for a feature slated for the magazine's May issue.

Fine as it was to hang out on the beach, her victory afforded her much more than travel. In the weeks after her win, the name Helen Gurley appeared in newspapers around the country. The magazine made her a mini-celebrity, the "Ideal Career Girl," as one women's editor christened her in the *Hollywood Citizen-News*. It also made her true ambitions known. Had she not confessed her desire to become a copywriter on the magazine's contest form, she might have remained a secretary. Don Belding assigned Helen to her first account, Sunkist, after being hounded by Mary Campbell, the soon-to-be-legendary head of Condé Nast's personnel office, who wanted to know why Belding hadn't given her a chance to write copy of her own.

Glamour was Helen's passport into a more sophisticated world. Long before David brought Helen to Manhattan, her favorite magazine did, putting her up at the ritzy Waldorf-Astoria when she won. While in town, she also visited *Glamour*'s headquarters in Midtown—it was her first time in a magazine office.

The second time was in March 1965, when she entered *Cosmopolitan*'s offices at 1775 Broadway as the magazine's new editor-in-chief.

18

THE MOST EXCITING WOMAN
IN THE WORLD
1965

"She has no intention of turning the rather bland magazine
into something racy."

—*Time* on new *Cosmopolitan* editor Helen Gurley Brown,
March 26, 1965

In the beginning of 1965, Helen got a new appointment book, a stiff red vinyl diary with gold writing that looked more like a motel Bible. She cracked it open to Tuesday, March 16. "FIRST DAY AT HEARST," she wrote in blue pencil, under the small print on the upper right-hand corner of the page: "290 days follow." And so the countdown began.

David's old mentor Herb Mayes was the first to call and officially congratulate Helen. The contract had been signed (David negotiated for a total annual compensation package of $35,000 for the first year of her contract, the equivalent of approximately $264,000 in 2015), and the public relations department at Hearst had written up a press release, calling Helen Gurley Brown "a spokeswoman for single women and girls with jobs." "A lot of people will think we hired her because she wrote *Sex and the Single Girl*," Deems would soon tell *Newsweek*, scrambling the message, "but actually we hired her in spite of those books."

It was too late to back out even if she had wanted to—and she had thought about it. Over the weekend, after having dinner at Christ Cella in Midtown with David and the author Irving Wallace, Helen put on a bit of a show, shedding tears over her new position while simultaneously using the moment to flatter their friend. "I don't want to be a magazine editor!" she cried, as they walked past the Waldorf-Astoria. "I just want to be a bestselling author like Irving!" For what must have been the twelfth time that night, David reminded her that the job was temporary, and she could decide how she felt about it later. All she had to do was show up and try her best, like she always did.

Despite David's confidence in her ability to succeed, Helen sensed that Hearst was waiting for her to fail. Just in case, her contract included a stipulation that if her editorship didn't work out, she could use up the rest of her term writing articles for other Hearst magazines. It wasn't so much a matter of *if* but *when*, they seemed to be saying, and she wrestled with her own insecurities. Being handed a magazine to edit without the benefit of any previous editorial experience was daunting, to say the least—she felt like someone had told her to suddenly become an astronaut or a brain surgeon. She didn't have the slightest notion of what to *do* when she got to the office. "Ask the managing editor to have lunch with you," David suggested. The managing editor would be able to tell her what articles had been assigned so far, and she could start by taking a look and seeing if she liked any of them.

David's reassurance gave her some relief, but she still went to bed feeling like she would be starting a prison term in the morning. At least she could get out after a year.

IN 1965, WHAT is known today as the Hearst Tower wasn't yet a tower, but rather an imposing six-story sand-colored building that took up a full block along the west side of Eighth Avenue between Fifty-Sixth and Fifty-Seventh Streets. In 1926, William Randolph Hearst, the founder of the Hearst Corporation, commissioned the virtuoso architect Joseph Urban to design the structure, soon to be known as the International Magazine Building, to house the twelve publications he owned at the time. Though it was intended to be a skyscraper, the Great Depression intervened, and the builders never saw their vision fully realized.

Born in Vienna, Urban had built his reputation in the theater as a stage designer, working on countless plays, musicals, operas, and other productions throughout Europe, before coming to America in 1911. A few years later, in New York, he met Florenz Ziegfeld Jr. and began designing sets for the legendary producer's Follies. When Ziegfeld later introduced Urban to Hearst, the designer and the publishing giant found a shared love of spectacle—which explains why the Hearst headquarters turned out the way it did. Urban pulled out all the stops, drawing from Art Deco, Secessionist, and Baroque influences. Built from cast limestone, the building features an arching main entrance flanked by tall fluted columns and statues representing the arts. On one side: Music and Art. On the other: Comedy and Tragedy. (Today, the cast-stone structure of the original International Magazine Building serves as the base for the new Hearst Tower, a geometric, glass-paneled forty-six-story skyscraper, which was completed in 2006.)

When Helen reported for her first day of work, *Cosmopolitan* wasn't located in the main Hearst headquarters. It was about a block away in the General Motors Building, at the corner of Fifty-Seventh Street and Broadway. Walking into the lobby, she wasn't completely sure how she had gotten this far, but here she was, preparing to meet her staff. It was a fair, blue-skied day, and she had chosen a look to match, wearing a simple light blue jersey dress with a ruffle around the neck.

Helen had little idea of what to expect, and her staff knew even less. A few days earlier, a rumor pinballed around the offices of *Cosmopolitan*. By Monday, Atherton would be out, replaced by a new editor-in-chief, a semi-celebrity. For the rest of the day, the halls buzzed with anticipation and uncertainty about the fate of the office. "Who do you think it is?" secretaries asked each other. "Well, who's around?" "Who's been making headlines?"

Vene Spencer, a petite brunette with big brown eyes, dimples, and bangs, was the unofficial leader of the pack, having worked at *Cosmopolitan* for longer than most of the other secretaries. As the assistant to the fiction editor, she even had her own office, but it was impossible to ignore the chatter of Les Girls, which is what she called *Cosmopolitan*'s secretaries, herself included. (An aspiring actress, Vene chose the name in honor of the Gene Kelly movie *Les Girls*.) Each of the major editors had a well-coiffed office girl to fetch coffee, type up line edits, or sort through the slush pile of unsolicited manuscripts. They had names like Robin and Diane and wore belted dresses and brooches, nylons and pumps, just as Helen had worn in her day as a secretary, but it never occurred to them that their new boss would be a former secretary herself—or a woman, for that matter. Standing outside Vene's office, they might as well have been trying to guess the Mystery Guest on *What's My Line?* Was Mr. X a controversial figure? Someone who had written for *Cosmopolitan* in the past? George Plimpton, maybe? Tom Wolfe?

Hearst didn't officially announce Helen Gurley Brown's appointment to the press until she showed up for work. Many of *Cosmopolitan*'s staffers learned the news along with the Associated Press, which also reported that Robert Atherton would be named international editor of Hearst Magazines. Les Girls, for one, couldn't believe it. "It came as a complete shock," Vene says. "We, the younger women, thought, 'Oh, boy! This is going to be fun!' We knew her now by reputation: 'Sex and . . .' We'd all read it. But she was the furthest thing in our minds because no one had ever talked about changing the direction of the magazine."

Within hours, Helen's red vinyl diary filled up with lunches and interviews with reporters from *Time* and *Newsweek*, but her top priority was to meet the staff, and she started by inviting her new employees into her office. Over the weekend, Atherton had moved out and Helen Gurley Brown had moved in, or at least some of her stuff had. (It was only right to set up a lunch with Atherton for the following Tuesday at the Lotus Club.) Fresh flowers filled the spacious corner office, with its brown-and-orange color scheme, neat bookshelves, and bulletin board. Window blinds and heavy drapes obstructed an otherwise clear view of Huntington Hartford's newly erected Gallery of Modern Art, a ten-story, white-marble monstrosity with Venetian-style pillars. In the center of the room was a large and rather manly desk, and Helen made a point of standing in front of it, not behind it, as she welcomed the staff into her office one by one.

Earlier that morning, Vene had been filled with apprehension about meeting her new boss. She had dressed extra nicely, but she couldn't quite quell the flurries of nervous energy as she stood in a sort of reception line to meet Helen. To Vene's surprise, Helen knew all about her.

"You're Vene—Vene Spencer," she cooed, extending a delicate hand. "You live in Brooklyn Heights. Your husband's an actor." Vene beamed. She was bowled over. How did Helen Gurley Brown know so much about her life? This woman is a marvel, she thought, as she walked away. She did her homework.

Helen had indeed been researching, including learning and memorizing a few personal details about every employee she met that morning. But some things she just couldn't have anticipated. Just as David suggested, Helen asked her managing editor, Betty Hannah Hoffman (who was actually listed as "Executive Editor" on the masthead), out to lunch. She had hoped to glean important information about the production schedule and future editorial material, but Betty promptly turned her down. She already had lunch plans, she said.

Instead of dining at the Russian Tea Room, one of her favorite spots to see and be seen, Helen ate a sandwich that someone had brought her. She knew that people didn't take her seriously—talk was already getting back to her. Along with a failing magazine, she had inherited a relatively small staff, including the previous editor's assistant, Robin Wagner, and gossip spread quickly. She knew that her underlings had more magazine experience than she did, not to mention bachelor's and graduate degrees from elite colleges and universities.

In the opinion of more than a few people on staff, Helen Gurley Brown was an impostor and a hack, just an ad woman who had written a sex book—and overnight she had become the editor-in-chief of *Cosmopolitan*. "The magazine is bubbling with enthusiasm over its new editor, even though she has no editing experience," *Time* reported in late March, quoting *Cosmopolitan*'s publisher, Frank Dupuy Jr., who churned out the hype: "She is the most exciting woman in the world!"

What was Hearst thinking? Almost instantly there was mutiny in the ranks. Much of the staff began job-hunting, using their expense accounts to treat well-connected friends to lunch, hoping for a phone call on their behalf in return. A few editors considered quitting—a better option than being fired or, worse, having to report to some pseudo-celebrity who didn't know the first thing about how to run a magazine. Someone started a rumor that Helen Gurley Brown was going to take over *Cosmopolitan* and clean house, picking off longtime employees one by one, but she had no such plans. At this stage it was more important to find allies.

She started by announcing that she didn't intend to fire a soul (at least not yet). When she asked to see what was scheduled for future issues, she was surprised to learn that there wasn't a formal schedule—nothing in writing unless you counted Betty's chicken scratch. April was on stands, and May was almost finished, so there was no use in complaining about "Dental Reciprocity," a mind-numbingly dull feature about the national shortage of dentists. Helen looked over the stories for June. Wary of alienating her single, working-girl readers, she might have done without a beauty story on bridal makeup and a political article about female protestors titled "Women Dissenters: The New Breed," but it was too late to make any major cuts, and it was more pressing that she not anger her staff by trashing their hard work. What else did they have planned? Not much, she was told. Nothing that was ready, anyway.

Helen was still getting a feel for the layout of the offices and the different departments, but there was no shortage of article manuscripts. They were everywhere: stacked on top of desks, pouring through the slush pile. In the coming days she would go through them, hoping to find something she could salvage. To her disappointment, many of the submissions were months old and outdated. She could have assigned a junior editor the chore of reading through the manuscripts, but she couldn't rely on someone else to enforce her editorial vision for *Cosmopolitan*. So she began the Sisyphean task of reading each and every manuscript herself.

The bulk of the material was boring and bland: stuffy,

self-conscious writers writing to impress instead of to communicate. It wouldn't suit her girls. Disappointment dawned, then fear. If these articles were unusable, how was she supposed to fill the July issue, her first?

By the time she left the office, she was exhausted. If Betty had said yes to lunch, Helen might have been able to ask her about how to fill holes in future issues, stick to the budget for articles and art, find freelance writers, turn ideas into assignments, or how to delegate at least some of the above to her staff, but Betty made no accommodation, no attempt to reschedule her lunch date and help Helen out.

At least she had David. "You don't need literary people," he told her that night over dinner at the Russian Tea Room. She needed writers who could deliver the types of pieces she wanted, and she had a few contacts already, he added. "Just get those articles assigned. Don't pay attention to what people are saying. The only people who matter are the ones who are going to read your magazine."

After dinner, he offered more reassurance, and they went to bed. As Helen later recalled in David's memoir, *Let Me Entertain You*: "I went to sleep but it didn't take. About four in the morning, David came and found me under my desk in the den. There was just room enough to get into a fetal position and I don't know exactly how long I had been there. Maybe hours. He brought me back to bed and for the first time, among many times in subsequent years (about three a year) told me this job wasn't the end of the world; that, of course, I could *do* it but if I didn't *want* to, I didn't *have* to—I could leave."

Helen would tell the story of this night countless times over the years. Like her story about how she wept in front of the Waldorf ("I don't want to be a magazine editor!"), it became a part of her repertoire of charming, comical little scenes in the madcap movie of her life. She cast herself as the smart but sometimes silly working girl who was always getting in over her head, and David as the charming gentleman who was always bailing her out.

Frequently, she *was* in over her head—and David did bail her out—but as with some of her other stories, the details of this tale changed slightly with each telling, and people who knew Helen well cast doubt on such scenes. She wouldn't have crawled under her desk or gotten down on the floor (unless she was doing exercises).

"That wasn't her," says Walter Meade (he now goes by Walker Meade), who worked with Helen for many years, first as an articles editor and later as a managing editor, her second in command. "She may have *felt* like she was threatened, and that's how she rendered it, but she would never have done that."

It's more likely that she would have had a Joan Crawford moment, standing by a window and *wanting* to curl into a little ball at the thought of what lay ahead. Of course, that's not nearly as fun to imagine. As Meade puts it: "When it seems to you as though she's being a storyteller, she is."

THE JULY ISSUE
1965

"I hope to have a magazine that reflects life as it is lived, and that does indeed include sex. But nothing will be dragged in. It'll just come along naturally."

—Helen Gurley Brown in *Newsweek*, March 29, 1965

A former secretary herself, Helen couldn't believe the incompetence of a couple of the assistants who worked for her. Her own secretary didn't take dictation, at least not up to snuff. Occasionally Helen got so swamped she borrowed another editor's assistant to do it, paying her extra. Sometimes after she finished dictating, Helen passed by the girl's desk and saw all of her letters stamped and neatly stacked on a ledge, as if waiting for an invisible wind to carry them to their destinations. Apparently mailroom runs were beneath her.

It wasn't just that secretary. Half of *Cosmopolitan*'s staff seemed to be against her. Some people had been there for decades, and they resented the sudden change of guard, as Helen's assistant Robin explained to her one day.

"Mrs. Brown," Robin said, "it just seems to me that it would have been more fair if they'd brought you in as a managing editor so everybody could get used to the idea—and *then* you took over."

Helen looked at the pretty girl standing before her and bit her tongue. Robin was only trying to help, to tell her in the *nicest* possible way that people thought she didn't belong here, and they wanted her out.

At some point every day, Helen picked up the phone and called David, anxious to talk, and she was particularly desperate on the day her executive editor, Betty Hannah Hoffman, quit. It was only Helen's first week as editor-in-chief, and suddenly she was left without a second in command. She needed to find a replacement, fast. She had told the staff that she would get back to them on important decisions, so they expected answers.

David always came to the rescue. Early on, he gave her advice about everything from budgeting to personnel issues, and he committed to reading all of *Cosmopolitan*'s fiction. Even though she had a fiction editor, William Carrington Guy—better known as Bill—David was ultimately the one who decided which short stories to snatch up and which novels to excerpt. He also reviewed articles. A few times when she was really desperate, David met Helen at work in the middle of the day so that they could hail a cab together and just drive around Central Park. As they drove past still-bare cherry and dogwood trees and the first of the ice-cream vendors with their yellow-canopied carts, he told her what material to buy, what not to buy, what to edit, and what to throw out.

After work the conversation continued at their apartment. In those chilly evenings of early spring, Helen brought home as many articles and stories as she could possibly stuff into her briefcase, as well as the production schedule. She read manuscripts at the office, and in bed, and by the end of her first week she had a clearer sense of the material she could salvage and what she still needed to assign. Maybe it was because she was a writer herself, but she got a real rush out of assigning stories to other writers and promising big money—$1,000 to $1,500 for a major piece.

For the July issue, she asked Doris Lilly, the society columnist and author of *How to Marry a Millionaire*, to update her strategy on winning a rich man in an article offering concrete tips. Ever aware of the marketing angle, she also slated a fashion feature all about the clothing brand Jax, essentially creating a giant advertisement disguised as a trend story.

Helen wanted the pictures to be sexy, and she got what she wanted from the artist and photographer J. Frederick Smith, whose illustrations of pert-breasted pinup girls she had clipped from the pages of *Esquire* as a younger woman. For his first *Cosmopolitan* assignment under Helen, he photographed models who personified her idea of the Jax girl: slender and small-waisted with "a bosom she doesn't make much of a fuss about but everybody else does," as the display copy read.

It was while going through Smith's images from the Jax shoot with the fashion editor Harriet La Barre that Helen spotted The Girl: a honey-blond bursting out of her red-and-white gingham cotton dress (legend has it that the photographer turned the dress backward to show off her cleavage), her substantial breasts looking like the main dish on a picnic table. Staring straight at the camera with bedroom eyes and pale lips parted just enough to reveal her top teeth, she looks like she was caught by surprise.

"What's this one?" Helen asked when she saw her.

"Oh, that's just one of the rejects," Harriet said.

"That's *it*," Helen said.

"That's what?"

"That's the cover," Helen said.

"You're kidding," Harriet said. "My God, the bust is all hanging out."

Helen smiled to herself. "What better thing could a bust do?"

HER NAME WAS Renata. Renata Boeck, when she was in the tabloids, but she had decided to not use her last name as a model since no one could pronounce it anyway. She was among the first German models to make it big in America, part of what *Life* magazine dubbed "The Fraulein Fad." She was one of the first models to become known by her given name alone, years before Vera Gottliebe Anna Gräfin von Lehndorff-Steinort became, simply, Veruschka. And she was the first *Cosmo* cover girl under Helen Gurley Brown.

The truth is, Renata never really cared about modeling. Growing up in Hamburg, she considered it to be low-class. Instead, right after high school, she became a stewardess for a charter airline, a calling that eventually led her to America, where she intended to start a job with another airline, Flying Tigers, in San Francisco. The plan was to take a ship from Hamburg to New York, where she would stay for the week at the Barbizon Hotel for Women, before flying to San Francisco, but she never made it that far. In March 1961, her ship docked in Manhattan. Renata disembarked, and a cluster of photographers from various daily newspapers around the city spotted her right away. "They were looking for someone famous. There was nobody famous, so they all zoomed in on me," Boeck says. "A few hours later, in three papers, I was on the front cover. It was really weird. I couldn't believe it. I still don't!"

Modeling agencies courted her, and movie moguls called her. Famous men on both coasts made a point of meeting her. She began seeing the producer Robert Evans, and after they broke up, she started going out with singer Eddie Fisher, who was in the midst of a divorce from Elizabeth Taylor. She was also spotted around town with Warren Beatty, who once brought her to a dinner with the Kennedys. Everyone noticed Renata, including "Jack," who excused himself from the table and said goodbye. "Ten minutes later, I got a call," Boeck says. "I went to the phone, and that's when he said, 'Hello, this is Jack Kennedy.' He wanted me to leave the party and meet him. I said, 'I'm here with Warren, I couldn't possibly!' He was married. I said that to him, too. I wouldn't see a married man, no matter what he was the president of.'"

In 1964 Renata became one of photographer Slim Aarons's "attractive people doing attractive things in attractive places," when he shot her wearing a monocle and reading the paper in bed at the Regency Hotel, a photograph he titled *Monocled Miss*.

By 1965, Renata was a Girl of the Moment in a decade full of them—Twiggy with her little boy's body and pixie haircut, Jean Shrimpton with her cute snub nose and blue eyes as big as Tiffany's boxes—but she stood out among the rest. She was a solid C-cup, so busty that Eileen Ford used to tell her to strap her breasts down. Fashion editors wanted flat-chested girls, but Helen wasn't a fashion editor, and she didn't really care about clothes. She cared about what was underneath them.

"She wanted cleavage, and she told me that I was the sexiest of all," Boeck says. "I was the only one with breasts in those days. That's why Helen Gurley Brown chose me."

WITH HER COVER girl chosen, Helen could zero in on putting together the rest of the issue. She eventually dumped dozens of articles that just wouldn't fit the new format, but she decided to snatch a piece about estrogen therapy that had been commissioned for an earlier issue and slate it for July.

In the piece, the writer, Lin Root, focused on the work of a New York City gynecologist, Robert A. Wilson, who was about to release what would become a bestselling book, *Feminine Forever*, in which he pushed hormone therapy as a natural cure-all for menopausal women. ("It is the case of the untreated woman—the prematurely aging castrate—that is unnatural," he claimed.) The estrogen pill, Premarin, had been around since 1942, but Wilson popularized the idea that hormone therapy could be a continuous, lifelong treatment for women of all ages, "from puberty to the grave." If taken regularly, he promised, estrogen would make the average woman feel younger, look more beautiful, and take greater pleasure in the act of sex—no matter what her age.

Now *that* was information worth sharing with *Cosmopolitan* readers—and Helen intended to. She rewrote the article, describing the "femininity index" that Wilson had devised with a colleague to measure a woman's level of estrogen, and explaining exactly what this "honey of a hormone" could do: In addition to ending period pain and the worst effects of menopause, it could act as a contraceptive or increase a woman's chances of getting pregnant, all depending on how and when it was used. Perhaps best of all, the women who used it found that they had gotten their youthful glows, figures, and sex drives back. "My skin is fresher, my hair has more shine; the pill makes me feel and look more attractive!" one excited pill-popper shared.

To this day, a misunderstanding about this article persists, and Helen is applauded for publishing a protofeminist piece about "the Pill," one of the first to run in a mainstream women's magazine. But read past the cutesy headline "Oh What a Lovely Pill!" and you'll find that the story itself doesn't promote sexual freedom so much as it is sells the scary and sexist idea that hormone therapy is a magic bullet for any woman wanting to feel "forever feminine"—not old and dried up like the "castrate" Wilson later described in his book.

As it turned out, many of the millions of women who took "the youth pill" after reading about it would be forever damaged; years later, studies showed that some hormone replacement drugs increased the risk of cancer and strokes. It's possible that Helen later regretted the role she played in spreading the gospel of hormone therapy, that she would have scrapped the story altogether if she had known about the long-term effects sooner. "I mainlined Premarin for years because I wanted to stay sexy and juicy and young," she told *New York* magazine in 2002, fifteen years after being diagnosed with breast cancer at the age of sixty-five. "If not for all those hormones, maybe this wouldn't have happened to me."

FALSEHOODS AND PSEUDOSCIENCE aside, "Oh What a Lovely Pill!" encapsulated Helen's vision for the new *Cosmopolitan* as a magazine that talked about sex openly and frankly. Above all, she wanted *Cosmopolitan* to feel personal, a magazine edited for a specific woman by a specific woman—much like a frank and sophisticated older sister. For the magazine to succeed, it was crucial to communicate this vision to her staff, and in the weeks and months ahead she would have more success with some of her editors than others. In a rush to fill the position of managing editor, she offered the job to the fashion editor, Harriet La Barre, who turned it down. The fiction editor, Bill Guy, rejected it next. Who was left? Just *Cosmopolitan*'s books editor, George Walsh, whom Atherton had planned to let go. A Catholic family man with the lean physique of a basketball player and the serious mind of an academic, Walsh brought considerable gravitas to the magazine, but he was hardly an ideal fit for the new *Cosmopolitan*, and over time, Helen would come to resent how he made her feel intellectually inferior.

In addition to Walsh, several other editors had worked at the magazine for years, and she knew they knew more than she did, at least when it came to the technicalities of putting out a magazine. There were the two Tonys: *Cosmopolitan*'s production manager,

Anthony Guzzardo, had been at the magazine for more than three decades, while *Cosmopolitan*'s Sicilian art director, Anthony C. La Sala, was approaching two, having started as a paste-up assistant. La Sala would be Helen's guide through the portfolios of fashion photographers, designers, and cartoonists. He would communicate her preferences back to contributors: more color, humor, bosoms, and depictions of men and women together. No pictures of kids. ("For information on children," Helen told *Writer's Digest* the following year, "read Doctor Spock.")

Harriet La Barre, soon to be listed as fashion *and* features editor on the masthead, would help show Helen around the editorial side of the operation. A stylish, slender woman who was as hardworking as she was tightly wound (Helen used to call her "a white-knuckle girl"), Harriet had been at *Cosmopolitan* for more than a dozen years, covering a range of subjects including beauty and travel. Going forward, Helen would make sure that Harriet geared travel articles toward the single girl on a budget, but not *too* small a budget. "Don't come at me with the inexpensive, off-season vacation story," Harriet would tell potential freelancers. "Sure there are a lot of them, but who's there? We like to talk about places where women can meet men."

Helen would get a similar message across to Bill Guy, a dark-haired, soft-spoken Virginian and former English instructor at the University of Richmond. Helen appreciated that *Cosmopolitan* had a rich history as a literary magazine—more recently, it had been publishing popular mysteries and thrillers—but now that it was a magazine for single girls, she wanted the fiction to reflect this new demographic. That meant more stories about girls in the city—no rustic or rural settings—and the girls should be unmarried. For the July issue, Bill brought her a titillating thriller about a secretary who gets strangled, and another tale about a plain sister who gets the upper hand over a pretty one. (Helen had a preference for stories with happy endings.)

With his connections to established writers and his passion for finding new talent, Bill was a powerful asset. So was *Cosmopolitan*'s entertainment editor, Liz Smith, whose job included writing film reviews, assigning celebrity profiles, and finding freelancers to work for the magazine. Months before Helen walked into the offices at 1775 Broadway, Liz had been writing about movies and movie stars for *Cosmopolitan*'s previous editor. She had cut her teeth as an editor for *Modern Screen* when the magazine was at its peak and she had experience on her side, but in many ways she was still the same tomboy who had grown up riding horses and watching movies in Texas, where her father was in the cotton business. Having been raised in Fort Worth during the Depression, she was as starstruck as Helen. "She was just a little girl from Arkansas like I was just a little girl from Texas," Liz says. "We had a lot in common: poor upbringing; nice people, but no money; living through the Depression. We had left home, shaken the dust off our feet, and we were living the high life. I mean, I was in Paris with the Burtons—it doesn't get any better than that for a writer."

Before Helen's appointment, Liz had written the magazine's cover story about Richard Burton and Elizabeth Taylor—a feat in itself, considering that the most famous couple in the world were trying to avoid the press. Liz eventually tracked them down in Europe, where they were filming *The Sandpiper*, and embedded herself in their entourage. She turned in a profile of Mr. and Mrs. Burton, whom she described as being "like icebergs—only partly visible to mortals," that melted off some of those layers, at once humanizing and flattering the famous lovers. "As always, she was breathtakingly implausible in the flesh," Liz wrote of Taylor. "A cloud of long black hair, the *ultra*violet eyes, the famous face, and she was quite petite—much slighter than screen size. She was wearing cream-colored flat shoes, tight khaki slacks, a purple top that covered her waistline. But she wasn't fat. I knew everybody would ask."

Like many of her colleagues, Liz Smith had come in to work expecting to be fired by her new boss. After getting a glimpse of Helen, who seemed so helpless in her new position, she even considered doing her a favor by simply resigning. Instead Helen invited Liz into her large office, which she was in the process of redecorating into a ladylike drawing room with pillows, candles, and scarves draped over lights to create a soft glow. She soon added personal touches wherever she could, bringing in potted houseplants; framed pictures of herself with David; assorted crystal vases and ceramic dishes to hold flowers, pens, and paper clips; a Japanese-style hand fan that she tacked up to the bulletin board along with pages from the magazine; and a large, plush tiger that sat on the floor.

"Well, Lizzie, what shall we do with you?" Helen asked sweetly, making Liz think of the actress Billie Burke, who played Glinda the Good Witch in *The Wizard of Oz*.

Before Liz could respond, Helen told her exactly what she wanted to do with her. In her soft, breathy voice, she told Liz that she loved her writing and asked if she would consider staying on to help her turn *Cosmopolitan* into what it should be—"a glorious unfettered, sexy and seductive paean for aspiring young women who wanted to unleash their ambitions, have sex with the same careless abandon as men, make silk purses out of sow's ears that we all mistake for romance, marry millionaires, etc.," as Liz recalled in her memoir, *Natural Blonde*.

Liz leaped at the opportunity. Little did she know that Helen Gurley Brown, the first and only woman she would ever work for, would be the toughest, most demanding editor she ever had.

"I'll never forget—she was so shy and deferential, like she wouldn't *dream* of succeeding," Liz says now. "Of course, we were all taken in by that innocent act."

20

TECHNIQUES
1965

"In an ideal world, we might move onward and upward by using
only our brains and talent but, since this is an imperfect world,
a certain amount of listening, giggling, wriggling, smiling,
winking, flirting and fainting is required."

—Helen Gurley Brown, *Sex and the Office*, 1964

In her first month, Helen made a few hiring decisions that
would impact the magazine, and her personally, for years to
come. One was promoting George Walsh to managing editor.
Another was hiring Walter Meade.

A copy chief at the ad agency Batten, Barton, Durstine & Os-
born (BBDO), Walter was already known around *Cosmopolitan*'s
fiction department as a talented writer who had published short
stories in the magazine, and Bill Guy thought he would be good at
dealing with other writers and making assignments.

"We need an articles editor," Bill told Walter around the same
time that Helen started. "Why don't you come and do it?"

Walter was interested in the job, but not in pretending he was
qualified for it. "I don't know anything about it," he said.

"We have a new editor, Helen Brown, and she doesn't know
anything about it either," Bill replied, "so why don't I tell her
about you, and we'll go from there?"

Walter considered his options. He wasn't long for the advertising world. Before he got the call from Bill, Walter had just been

through a somewhat life-altering experience. He had been walking down Forty-Fifth Street with his boss, a workaholic who was also a husband and father in his mid-forties, when his boss said, "Oh my God, Walter," grabbed his arm, and then dropped dead. Unsure of what to do, Walter chose the most practical route: He went into a nearby store, asked for a furniture blanket, and put it over his boss's limp body before the cops came. When the shock of what had happened subsided, he realized that he had to get out of the advertising business.

That was the mind-set Walter was in when Bill called and said that *Cosmopolitan* was looking for a new articles editor. After Bill described the position in more detail, Walter thought, Yeah, I can do that.

And that's how he found himself sitting across from Helen Gurley Brown in her office. Right away, he told Helen that he had never been an editor before. "I don't know what I'm doing either," she said, "and I don't really know how I got this job."

Then she told Walter the story of how David had essentially gotten it for her, encouraging her to apply in the first place. Listening to Helen recount the whole process, Walter thought she was the most direct person he'd ever met, and possibly the most flirtatious.

It certainly didn't hurt that Walter, thirty-five years old to her forty-three, was good-looking: dark-haired, tall, and cool in a tan poplin suit. Helen soon began her process of sinking in. She did not sit behind her desk, but rather joined Walter on her sofa. As they talked about a starting salary, he couldn't help but notice how she didn't so much sit as curl like a kitten, despite the fact that she was wearing a short, slinky dress. "Her gestures were extremely feminine," Meade says. "She talked very quickly and very smartly. She was never at a loss for words. And she called me 'Pussycat.'"

Over the years, Helen would call countless people Pussycat, her favorite term of endearment. (Later, an illustrated pussycat became something of a mascot for *Cosmo*, similar to *Playboy*'s Bunny.) And yet, sitting in her office on that spring day, Walter Meade may as well have been the only man in her world. He had come in for what was essentially a job interview, but now that he was here it felt more like having a drink with an old girlfriend. Walter wasn't sure how she did it. She was not a beautiful woman, not by a stretch, and yet he felt drawn to her—physically attracted to this petite, plain woman with her kittenish purr. And that was really something because Walter was gay.

In fact, Walter knew he would like Helen before he even met her. He had heard the rumors that she was just a silly dumb broad who couldn't possibly edit a magazine if her life depended on it, and who would fall on her face; it was only a matter of time. He hadn't read her books, but he knew she was adored by single girls and ridiculed by the press, and he admired her because the press was often wrong. Bill Guy, for one, thought she was a natural. Even with her lack of experience, he believed she had a strong vision and that she could turn *Cosmopolitan* into a success.

As Bill and Walter would soon learn, Helen was very feminine in her manner, and she wanted a similar feel for the magazine: sexy but respectable, with a certain patina of properness. But she was also Machiavellian, and to get to her ladylike ends she had no problem resorting to unladylike means.

Before the meeting in Helen's office, Bill showed Walter a written response that Helen had given to a short story he had submitted to her—about a young couple who were deeply in love. "They went to a Tunnel of Love thing in an amusement park and the tunnel had its way with them—in an erotic way," Meade says.

"The Tunnel of Love itself became an erotic experience, and they had sort of a threesome with it."

Meade never forgot the memo that Helen sent back with the manuscript. "The note was all in lowercase, and it said, 'bill, dear, i do think we have to draw the line somewhere—and being fucked by a machine is it.'"

EVEN AS SHE brought on new people, Helen lived with the constant threat of losing her staff to other jobs. But at least one former staffer wished she had never left in the first place when she heard that Helen Gurley Brown was *Cosmopolitan*'s new editor.

Before Liz Smith took over her position, Lyn Tornabene had been the magazine's entertainment editor under Robert C. Atherton, and she witnessed its decline firsthand.

At a low point in circulation and staff morale, a few of the editors got so desperate that they started assigning each other freelance articles just to subsidize their meager salaries. They tried to be sneaky about it, writing under assumed names—Harriet La Barre wrote under "EMD Watson" for "Elementary, my dear"—but management eventually found out about it. Dick Deems called Lyn into his office, slapped her on the wrist, and told her that she'd just have to stick with her salary of thirty-eight dollars a week. Lyn quit, moved to Connecticut with her husband and daughter, and started freelancing. But when she heard that the author of *Sex and the Single Girl* had replaced her old boss, she felt compelled to write to her. "If I had known you were coming," Lyn told her, "I'd have stayed."

Shortly after getting that note, Helen invited Lyn into the office to chat about freelance assignments. She needed strong, reliable writers, and Lyn had experience and insight on her side, having worked at the magazine for years. When Liz Smith took over the entertainment section and asked her predecessor for some advice about how to run it, Lyn answered with her characteristic candor. "Why should I do that? Why help you succeed? I don't want you to do a good job. I want to be remembered as the best."

A cute brunette with a brassy sense of humor, Lyn would become Helen's go-to person for funny social commentary, like an essay she wrote under a pseudonym called "What It's Like to Be a Jewish Girl," as well as her friend and confidante. But that day in Helen's office, she wasn't sure what to expect.

"It was a very strange meeting," Lyn says now. "One of the things she believed was that talking to someone across a big mahogany desk was intimidating, so she curled up on the couch in the corner—she weighed, you know, two pounds—and then gestured, 'Darling you sit here,' on the other end of the sofa. So I sat. The very first thing she said to me was, 'You know these aren't my cheekbones.' Dr. [Norman] Orentreich, he was silicon-ing everybody. Then she said, 'This isn't my hair. It's a Kenneth fall.' She went over all the parts of her body that were not original.

"Also by the end of that meeting," Tornabene adds, "I knew that she had slept with one hundred and seventy-eight men."

OVER THE YEARS, Lyn would hear a lot more about Helen's conquests during their hours of interviews and conversations. At a certain point, she stopped counting the number of times Helen used the word *mistress* when talking about all the men she had slept with to get ahead, but she witnessed her seduction skills firsthand when Helen and David, headed to a restaurant in Bedford, New York, made a last-minute visit to her house in Greenwich, Connecticut, one November night in the mid-Sixties.

"She called on Thanksgiving, whispering, 'Darling, David and I are on our way to Bedford, and we're going to go right past your place. Can we stop in and say hello?'" Tornabene says. "I said, 'Look honey, there are twenty insane people here. Both families. You're very welcome, but I have no idea what's doing.'

"So here comes the stretch limo up the driveway, and I have no recollection whatsoever where David was because I was fixated on Helen. She had discovered my father-in-law, who was a very handsome man, a Sicilian: a tall, tweedy sort of guy. He was actually a baron and couldn't ever earn a living. Anyway, Dad is sitting at the far end of the sofa, alone. Helen spots him, sits on the arm of the sofa, and then realizes she's looking down on him, so she slides to the floor so she can look up at him.

"Like [Anna and] the King of Siam, she would never sit higher than a man she was talking to. Of course, in the kitchen is my wonderful Sicilian mother-in-law, who is calling for my husband, 'Get the *putana* off your father! Get the *putana* outta here, outta here!'

"I don't think Helen needed to see how far she could get. She *knew* how far she could get. It was just her. That's how she functioned," Lyn says. "She was scared to death all the time, and she managed to dispel any possible fears with her various techniques that she'd worked out over the years."

21

PIPPY-POO COPY
1965

"What was so marvelous about Helen is that she was entirely self-created. She invented herself, and then spread the message. What I love about those early years is that she never published anything she didn't believe in. She was like Billy Graham. This was her religion."

—Lyn Tornabene

The week the July issue was scheduled to hit stands, an affable reporter named Dick Schaap sat across from Helen and asked what she made of the fact that some people still resented her sudden ascent to editor of *Cosmopolitan*, considering her lack of experience.

"You don't just fall into a job like this," Helen said silkily, explaining how she worked her tail off at the ad agency during the week, while writing *Sex and the Single Girl* on weekends. "It was a best seller. It may not be literature, but it certainly didn't *bore* anybody to death. I got into scoring position so I could get into the magazine. I possibly will fall on my face and the minute I do they will have a new editor."

Schaap scribbled down her response. A reporter for the *New York Herald Tribune*, he was more accustomed to profiling athletes—five years before, he interviewed a young Cassius Clay before Clay became the heavyweight champion of the world. Helen Gurley Brown wasn't typical as an interview subject, and not just because Schaap frequently covered sports. She was different even among her kind.

In between glances at the July cover girl, a juicy-looking blonde in a low-cut Jax dress, the sportswriter studied the new editor. She wore a light blue suit by Marquise and white mesh stockings. A demure black bow was affixed to her hair. As Schaap asked about her plans for the new *Cosmopolitan*, Helen lounged on her sofa, occasionally stretching her arms like a cat rousing from a nap. "She did not look like most editors I have seen," Schaap later observed. "She did not act like most editors I have seen."

That Helen Gurley Brown was not like any other editor—any other boss, really—seemed to be the consensus among the staffers and freelancers who found themselves in her office, but they still didn't know *what* to make of her. "I always thought I was smarter than she was," says Liz Smith, "but I found out later she was smarter than I was."

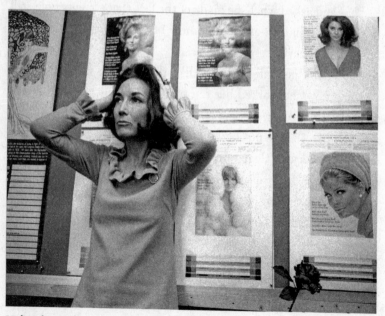

Helen during her first year as editor, 1965. (*Copyright © I. C. Rapoport.*)

Despite *Cosmopolitan*'s abysmal circulation figures in recent months, editors still took pride in the magazine's rich history as a forum for intellectual thought—"the magazine for people who can read," as David Brown once nicknamed it. Suddenly Helen seemed to be editing the magazine for people who were reading-*impaired*. She wanted articles to be "baby simple" with no unnecessary big words. "We don't want very many cosmic pieces—about space, war on poverty, civil rights, etc., etc., but will leave those to more serious general magazines," Helen told *The Writer*. She wanted fun pieces, nothing too heavy. Most important, she wanted her girls to feel happier after reading an issue of *Cosmopolitan*. Articles needed to be optimistic and upbeat. That meant no bad reviews of books, records, and movies, but especially movies. (She was married to a movie producer, after all.)

Helen's rules drove Liz Smith crazy. Whatever chance she once had to become a respected movie critic, Helen sabotaged: What use was a critic who couldn't write an unkind word? "You are censoring me!" Liz yelled. Helen dealt with Liz the way she had learned to deal with men: She listened to her, fussed over her, petted her ego, and eventually cajoled her into doing things her way. As for a certain young movie critic whom Liz had been mentoring, he clashed with Helen even more.

A few months earlier, Liz found in her mail an unsolicited review of *Lilith*, starring Warren Beatty, Jean Seberg, and Peter Fonda. The writer of the review was a dark-haired, long-lashed, and dimpled twentysomething named Rex Reed. Having come to New York after college at Louisiana State University, Rex was working as a press agent at a public relations office when he really wanted to spend his time watching movies. He hadn't expected much to come of his submission to the entertainment editor at *Cosmopolitan*, but Liz was impressed. As it happened, he had been born in Fort Worth, her hometown, and she liked the idea of having another southerner around.

A few days later, Liz called Rex to say that *Cosmopolitan*'s editor-in-chief, Robert Atherton, wanted to meet with him. Not only did Atherton want to publish his review of *Lilith* for a nice sum of fifty dollars—his first byline in a national magazine—he wanted Rex to be *Cosmopolitan*'s new movie critic. Rex was ecstatic.

And then Atherton was out, and Helen Gurley Brown was in. Even if Helen hadn't been familiarizing herself with old issues of *Cosmopolitan* all along, she certainly would have read Reed's negative review of *The Yellow Rolls-Royce*, starring Rex Harrison and Jeanne Moreau, in the June issue. "Car lovers will drool over *The Yellow Rolls-Royce*. Movie buffs, however, may appraise it as a motorless vehicle for some 24-karat stars who find themselves hijacked in chromium-plated material," he had written.

When Helen called Rex in for a meeting, he found the new editor-in-chief sitting on top of her desk wearing a skirt so short it showed off the tops of her thighs, netted in Bonnie Doon stockings. He wasn't sure how old she was, but too old to be dressing like *that*—and those fake eyelashes and that false hair! Was she wearing a wig? It was only noon! He was interrupting her lunch, in fact—he noticed a little container of yogurt next to a perfectly sculpted salmon-colored rose.

"My dear," Helen said after they exchanged hellos, "you write pippy-poo copy. I'm afraid I can't use you because you're upsetting my girls."

What? Rex had no idea what "pippy-poo" meant. And which girls was she talking about, exactly? He didn't know about the legions of young women from the middle of the country who wrote to Helen looking for advice on what to wear on a first date or on a first job interview. He didn't worry himself over their menstrual cramps and acne scars, their broken hearts and battered egos—but Helen did, and she felt that Rex's opinions were too critical for the new, upbeat, optimistic *Cosmopolitan*.

"My girls have never heard of Mike Nichols," she explained. "They don't want opinion. They just want to know a good movie to go to on a Saturday night at the drive-in."

"How do you know such a girl exists?" Rex asked.

"Because, my dear," Helen cooed, "I *was* that girl."

22

DADDY'S LITTLE GIRL
1920S—1930S

"Have *you* a rotten family, bad health, nowhere looks, serious
money problems, a minority background, nobody to help you?
Early-in-life problems can be the yeast that makes you rise
into *bread*!"

—Helen Gurley Brown, *Having It All*, 1982

Helen often told the press that, in editing *Cosmopolitan*,
she was essentially aiming the magazine at the girl she
was twenty years before, "the girl with her nose pressed
against the glass." In 1965, she was forty-three, and in many ways
a very different woman from the person she was at twenty-three,
when she was still working her way through secretarial jobs. But
to understand who she was then, you have to go back even further, back to her childhood in Arkansas.

You have to start in Carroll County, in the northwestern part
of the state, near a town called Blue Eye (current population
30)—not to be confused with Blue Eye, Missouri (pop. 167).
Head south from the Missouri border on AR 21, toward a town
called Berryville, and take in the sights along the way. Go past
Snake World, a roadside "attraction" featuring a collection of
seventy-some snakes, including rattlesnakes and pythons, kept
inside one man's trailer, along with their prey. To the west is
Eureka Springs, an artsy hippie town that's also known for its
sixty-seven-foot statue, Christ of the Ozarks—worth a visit,

maybe another time. Instead head east on U.S. 62, passing the occasional Confederate flag and signs for livestock auctions, Home Style Cookin', and Cowboy Church, which hosts "Come as You Are" services every Sunday, until you reach the center of a small town called Green Forest.

Welcome to the birthplace of Helen Gurley Brown. (Not a fact that the town chooses to advertise, by the way.) These days, Green Forest is better known for chicken—it's home to a Tyson poultry processing plant and a large Hispanic population. Most people who would have known the Gurley family when they lived here in the early 1920s are no longer alive, and the few who remain don't have much to say. At Mercy Thrift Shop, near a flower and gift store on Main Street, the white-haired woman behind the register looks as though she has been sitting in the same chair for decades. If anyone is still around who knows about Helen Gurley Brown's connection to this place, she would be a likely candidate, but she is impassive. Either she doesn't remember the Gurley name, or she doesn't care to.

Strolling through the public square—past brick buildings blanched by the sun, boarded-up windows, and the occasional empty storefront—you have to squint and imagine a time when Main Street was in its prime, when people rode horses into town. This was the Green Forest where Helen Gurley Brown was born on February 18, 1922, when some of her more affluent relatives owned a good portion of Main Street, including the Mercantile, the dry-goods store in town.

Helen described her family as hillbilly and poor, but her parents were hardly uneducated (her father, Ira, had a law degree from Cumberland University in Tennessee), and they weren't always poor. "That's sort of a misconception a lot of people have—that everybody was desperately poor," says Helen's cousin Lou (now

Main Street in Green Forest, Arkansas—where Helen was born on February 18, 1922—as it looks today. (*Photo by author.*)

Honderich). "Helen's grandparents indeed lived in the country, and they had outdoor plumbing; but that was rural Arkansas." When Helen was still a baby, the Gurleys moved to Little Rock, where they were "solidly middle class," Lou adds. "They had a really nice house in a nice neighborhood. Mom had been a teacher, Dad worked in the Capitol. I would think that was about as ordinary and as stable as it could be, but things did get very, very hard when her sister got sick and her father was gone."

Later, when she was in her seventies, Helen would tell a much more accurate and nuanced version of her family history in a memoir she wrote, "Memories of Mother and Early Life in Little Rock," but it was never published. Apparently, the truth about where she really came from wasn't nearly as interesting as the first rags-to-riches story she ever told. "I think it helped sell books,"

Lou says. "I think her shtick kind of took over. There was not any other side—just the poor-little-girl side."

FROM GREEN FOREST, take U.S. 412 to downtown Osage (a pinpoint on the map with a population of 418 in the whole township, at last count). You'll know you're in the right place when you see the sign for Osage Clayworks, a mammoth, multilevel old stone building with a wooden frame and large arched windows, standing to the south.

The roads are dustier here, the sky flatter and bluer, but the hills are gentle and sloping, and those are ancient cedars and black walnut trees in the distance. It's beautiful, but it's also remote and, for a certain kind of person, it would be impossibly lonely.

Not for Helen's mother, Cleo. Born in 1893 in the tiny nearby village of Alpena, Cleo moved back to Arkansas from Los Angeles in the 1950s, eventually settling in Osage, where she lived for many years in a simple, one-story house that no longer exists. When it still stood, Helen visited her here—but rarely.

Helen did write to Cleo frequently, and Cleo used to pick up her letters at her mail slot at Stamps General Store—now converted into the Clayworks space, filled with stoneware mugs, vases, and pinch pots in various states of completion. When the potter Newton Lale bought the place, he made a deal with the family selling it that he would preserve the heritage of the general store, including old ledgers dating back to the early 1900s, when people bought everything from eggs to overalls here.

Newt has assumed the role of unofficial town historian ever since. He never met Cleo, but when he first came to town, he bought her house—it once stood across the street, where a pavilion is now—which was known as the Cat House, on account of the dozens of cats that Cleo used to have prowling around the property. Newt didn't know her, but he knows her type: an Ozarks woman.

"Our mothers and our grandmothers grew up, and there was a no-nonsense attitude," he says. "You didn't have time to fool around. You were trying to survive, you were trying to feed your family."

He never met Helen, but he knows her type, too: a small-town girl who wanted to see if she could make it in a bigger world. "My understanding was that she wasn't real proud of Arkansas," he says. "It was a poor place, she came from a poor condition, and she had to do what it took to get out of here."

Cleo had wanted to get out once herself, but by the time Helen was born, four years after Mary, she was tethered to a long line of disappointments. Abandoning her college education because of family obligations was one. Marrying Ira Gurley was another. Even as a young woman, Cleo was plain to the point of homely—especially when compared with a sister who was beautiful and courted by several men—so her parents were thrilled when they found her a suitable match.

Smart and charismatic, Ira was a golden boy who hunted and fished with Cleo's brothers and impressed her parents. Everyone loved Ira, except for Cleo, who was enamored of a poor, soft-spoken young man named Leigh Bryan. As for what Ira saw in Cleo, Helen didn't really elaborate on it in her writings, but her cousin Lou speculates that perhaps he valued her education, which would be useful in raising children, even though he later insisted she give up her career. As the eldest of nine children, Cleo had been the rare girl who attended high school, going on to spend one semester at college at the University of Arkansas at Fayetteville, before becoming a teacher at a rural, one-room schoolhouse "I think Ira was smart, and I think he wanted a smart wife. She was solid, she had a nice family—her parents were wonderful. Maybe he saw the whole thing as being a good package," Lou says. "I don't know what else would make sense for a good-looking, going-places guy to marry a plain girl. I think it had to be rational, practical."

Leigh was Cleo's first love, and he would remain her only love, long after she married Ira. Ira was her husband, a "devout male chauvinist" who had voted against women's suffrage, as Helen later recalled. Ira wanted Cleo to quit teaching, so she did, even though she loved it. And then she got pregnant. Giving birth to her first daughter, Mary Eloine, Cleo suffered painful tearing and almost died—she had needed a cesarean, a procedure that the simple country doctor attending her knew little about and couldn't perform. Four years later, Helen Marie Gurley was born after another difficult labor.

Eventually, Ira took Cleo to the Mayo Clinic in Rochester, Minnesota, where some of the physical damage was repaired, but Cleo never forgot the pain of childbirth. She lived with those scars for the rest of her life.

"Having babies isn't everything," Cleo told Helen from the time she was a little girl. "Not that I don't love you and Mary, but having babies isn't all there is."

CLEO'S FAMILY ALWAYS knew that Ira Gurley would become a *somebody*, and the year after Helen was born, he was already on his way, heading for a career in politics. In 1923 the Gurleys moved to Little Rock, where Ira won election to the state legislature.

The Gurleys were comfortable, but they weren't wealthy. To bring in extra money, Cleo worked as a seamstress, setting up a small dressmaking service at home, where she fitted the occasional wealthy customer. One of Helen's early memories was of seeing a striking, red-haired woman dressed in fur pull up to the house in a shiny Pierce-Arrow, driven by a chauffeur. Ira and Cleo never talked to their daughters about people being rich or poor, but growing up in the suburb of Pulaski Heights (now Hillcrest), Helen gradually became aware of the difference. "It was before the depression when money didn't *consume* people so, anybody but *me* that is," she later recalled.

Her obsession with money followed her through first grade, where she befriended wealthy little girls with names like Mary Louise and Mildred. Again, she wasn't exactly sure how she *knew* they were well off—they all went to public school and played with the same Patsy Dolls and clipped the same pictures of movie stars out of magazines like *Photoplay*. She only knew that she gravitated toward those girls and would say or do anything to gain their favor. When one of the rich girls wanted to play make-believe, Helen always humbly accepted the role of the respectably dressed gentleman, while her friend pretended to wear pink satin dresses and diamond-buckled pumps. Why did she put up with those rotten little creeps and their unfair rules? Simple: They were rich, and she wanted to be friends with them.

Soon enough, with the onset of the Great Depression, some of Little Rock's wealthiest families would lose their fortunes, but the Gurleys avoided the first major disaster. On the October morning in 1929 when the stock market crashed and banks closed around the country, Ira and Cleo brought the girls into the living room to say they had managed to salvage most of their savings. Not long after he was elected to the state legislature, Ira had secured a job with the Arkansas State Game and Fish Commission, which was headquartered in the State Capitol Building, and it paid well. They always had food on the table, even if it was just the usual mashed potatoes, canned peas, and overcooked meat.

At church, Helen always had fifteen cents to put in the

collection envelope, and once, when she was falling behind, Ira gave her a five-dollar bill. After church, when they went to Franke's Cafeteria to eat roast beef, she got seconds *and* thirds.

Helen adored her father. Most people did. Stocky and sure of himself, he was a man's man who played cards but didn't smoke or drink. (It was the Prohibition era.) When Ira Gurley was home, neighborhood kids found reasons to stop by. On hot summer evenings he would hold court on the front porch with the lights off. When he laughed, everyone laughed. When he told a story—he loved unspooling long, pointless tales, like the one he sometimes told about mosquitos moving grains of sand across the Sahara Desert—they joined in. When everyone left, Helen kissed Ira on the forehead or cheek. She was Daddy's little girl.

Cleo was the homemaker, the caretaker. Ira was the fun-maker, the thrill-seeker. Every fall he took Helen and Mary to the state fair to enjoy the Ferris wheels and clouds of cotton candy. On Sunday afternoons he brought the girls to a local airport to watch single-engine airplanes take off and land. Thanks to a connection in the statehouse, one Sunday Ira was invited to ride in a plane himself. Helen beamed with pride at the sight of her daddy, wearing goggles and a helmet, ready for flight.

Ira had the power to call in favors, and if things went according to plan, soon he would have the ability to grant them. By 1932 he was preparing to run for secretary of state, a position that would launch the family into the upper strata of Little Rock society. The family had moved to a nicer house, and for a while it seemed as though the stars were aligned. Over the summer, however, everything changed.

Helen was ten years old and in the fifth grade when Ira was killed in an elevator accident in the State Capitol Building. One of the Gurleys' neighbors, a man who also worked at the State

Helen (*left*) and Mary as young children. (*Family photograph courtesy of Norma Lou Honderich.*)

Capitol Building, rushed home to tell Cleo the news. They weren't sure how the accident happened, but most likely the elevator operator had shut the gate and begun going up before noticing that someone was trying to jump on. Ira's body was crushed between the elevator floor and the door frame. He was forty years old. Cleo was thirty-eight, and that summer she mourned for the husband she never loved with a well of grief that ran as deep as love. As Helen came to see it later, Cleo felt responsible—she thought that, in withholding her love, she somehow caused Ira's death.

Ira died on June 18, a Friday. That night, people flooded the Gurleys' house. They brought heartfelt condolences, food, and flowers, and in the following days, newspapers ran front-page stories celebrating the life of Ira Marvin Gurley. Helen almost forgot to mourn her father—she was too distracted by the attention and drama. Overnight, her family had become important, famous even, and she realized that her father must have been a great man. Seeing him fixed up in a suit and laid out in his gray-velvet-lined coffin, Helen thought he looked handsome.

The next day, they drove Ira's body to Green Forest for the funeral. It was at the graveside, along with relatives from both Cleo's and Ira's sides, that Helen truly understood that her daddy was gone.

The sun began to set, casting a soft pink glow on the fields in the distance. It was time to go home, but Helen wasn't ready. On the walk back to the car, she kept breaking away from Cleo and Mary and a couple of aunts to run back to Ira's grave and talk to her father one last time. "One last time" happened a few times: They walked, she ran, they let her. Eventually, they got the grieving little girl into the car.

✦   ✦   ✦

HELEN AND MARY spent the next week in Osage with Cleo's parents. Surrounded by woods and fields cleared for cattle, the one-story white farmhouse was simple but comfortable, with wide wooden floors and a main room with a big, round cast-iron wood-stove that had warmed Helen through many winter days. In the summer their grandmother set up fans to stir the breeze.

The Gurleys had spent summers here before, but this one was unlike any other. For Helen and Mary, it was a time of escape. When they returned to Little Rock, Cleo let the girls do what they pleased—anything to get through their loneliness and loss. They went to the movies several times a week, taking in double bills and single, serial features like *Tarzan of the Apes* and *Mandrake the Magician*.

In the darkness of the theater, Helen watched Fred Astaire dance with Ginger Rogers and worshipped sophisticated movie stars like Carole Lombard and Claudette Colbert. Matinee showings came with a free candy bar, which Helen loved almost as much as the movies themselves.

That summer, Cleo let the girls eat more sweets than usual. At home, Mary and Helen whipped up batches of fudge and divinity, a lumpy white confection bursting with pecans. Measuring, mixing, and pouring the mixtures out to cool kept their minds occupied and their hands busy.

Cleo tried to keep her own hands busy, too. She sewed as she always had, but with new intensity, concentrating her efforts on her two daughters. Hers were no mere cookie-cutter creations: Knowing how much Helen loved Hollywood glamour, Cleo made her an evening dress that was a near replica of Colbert's wedding gown in *It Happened One Night*. She also made her a brown wool coat with a beaver-fur collar and a pink taffeta dress with a blue velvet sash. Working feverishly, she sewed baby-doll dresses for Helen—and for her baby dolls. She made ruffles and ribbons, flowers and frills. She sewed to fill the time, and to mend her mind, but her husband's sudden death had left a gaping hole in their lives that couldn't be stitched back together.

He was here, and then he was gone, and no one really knew what happened that day in the Capitol Building. Looking for some answers later that summer, Cleo drove her gray Chevy to the south part of town, where the elevator operator lived. Helen waited in the car while Cleo talked to the man, perhaps hoping for a confession, or at least an explanation. She never got one, though she heard some theories. A pretty woman had been inside the elevator when Ira jumped—perhaps he had been trying to get her attention.

Later, Cleo found out that the legislature had set aside funding for a new, safe elevator, and a cheaper, outdated one had been purchased instead to the benefit of corrupt state officials. The state of Arkansas eventually paid a settlement, claiming at least some responsibility for the accident, but even with money that she would get from the settlement, Cleo had little security for the long term: no job, no prospects, and no plan for how she would raise two children on her own.

23

GOING WEST

1930S

"Helen may have come to the false conclusion about her looks after moving to California. She really wasn't like the starlets she saw there. Maybe that was it? A small, pretty fish in a big pond of spectacular mermaids."

—Lou Honderich

Before Ira died, there were a million things that Cleo did and did well. In the winter she made hot cocoa and toasted cheese sandwiches, warming the house. She dutifully tended to her home, her husband, and her children. She spent hundreds of hours taking Helen to dance classes and friends' houses, helping with homework and Sunday school assignments, and made all of her clothes. Even after Ira died, Cleo found ways to give her daughters little luxuries, but laughter was one luxury she could not afford. A serious woman by nature, Cleo turned more inward every day. Sometimes her melancholy shrouded the house like a veil.

Helen grew up during some of the worst years of the Great Depression in Arkansas, and yet, for a girl of ten whose father had just been ripped out of her life, perhaps her mother's great depression was the harder one to bear. After the attention brought on by Ira's death faded, the Gurleys had few visitors. Once in a while, a relative came by, but for the most part Cleo distrusted people outside her small circle. She lived in a constant state of anxiety, much of it centered squarely on her daughters. Scared that they, too, could be snatched away at any moment, she dressed Helen in long underwear through April and seemed to hold her own breath every time her daughters waded into the water at one of the local swimming holes. Coming up for air, Helen would spot Cleo, hand on her brow to shield her eyes from the sun, frantically searching the water. "The days were somewhat pleasant, despite our being daddyless," Helen would write many years later, "except for the deep sadness that had enveloped Cleo and made passes at Mary and me . . . 'poor little fatherless children.'"

Helen found a happier home nearby in the house of her new friend, Elizabeth Jessup. Not only was Elizabeth prettier and more popular than Helen; she was charming and so was everything around her. She had the best dollhouse in town; no flimsy baby doll furniture, but sturdy pieces that really functioned.

And then there was the house she lived in: It was always filled with laughter, friends, and music. Elizabeth's mother, Mrs. Jessup, was the junior choir conductor at a local Methodist church, where she played the organ. At home she played the piano and invited Elizabeth's friends from choir practice to come over and sing along. Helen had been baptized in a Presbyterian church, but Elizabeth's church was far more fun, and she soon became a regular at choir practice as well as at Mrs. Jessup's sing-alongs. Everyone got to choose a solo, and Helen's song was "Smoke Gets in Your Eyes."

Even when Mrs. Jessup wasn't around, Helen and Elizabeth sang their hearts out to songs like "Love Is Just Around the Corner," "You're Getting to Be a Habit with Me," and "Blue Moon." But Helen liked it when Mrs. Jessup was there. She had a warm, welcoming way about her, and she treated all the kids who came to her house like they were her own. Helen was at Elizabeth's house listening to the radio the day Franklin Delano Roosevelt was elected in November 1932. When Roosevelt visited Little Rock the next year, Mrs. Jessup played the organ for the welcoming assembly, and lucky Elizabeth got to sit on the bench.

Elizabeth had everything that Helen wished she had—a cheerful home, good looks, a certain star quality—and yet somehow Helen didn't envy her. She just felt fortunate to know her. Elizabeth had other friends, too, of course, but she and Helen were best friends. They walked to grammar school together, rode their bikes together, climbed trees together, and starred in a school operetta together. (Elizabeth played the lead, Helen her maid.) At Mrs. Jessup's weekly choir rehearsals, they also discovered boys together. Writing about her Little Rock childhood years later, Helen wouldn't remember the church hymns she sang so much as the sexual undercurrent she felt, being tightly packed into the choir loft with the other sweaty prepubescent girls and boys.

Surrounded by velvet-lined pews and stained glass, Helen nurtured a giddy crush on a boy named Dick Anderson, who, as it turned out, had a crush on Elizabeth, who wasn't particularly interested. Helen didn't mind being overlooked by Dick, as long as she had Elizabeth to talk to about it. Giggling hysterically, they sang the lyrics to Pinky Lee's hit, "The Object of My Affection," which became their code theme song for Dick. Ever the loyal friend, Elizabeth devoted herself to helping Helen plot ways to get the object of her affection alone in the room with her. Not that Helen would have known what to do with Dick back then, had she gotten the chance. These were innocent times, when the naughtiest thing Helen did was pass notes with Elizabeth in class. Day after day, they would write in a small brown spiral notebook, confessing their crushes and assessing each boy for each other's amusement. Knowing that the entries were for their eyes only, they could fantasize about being touched and kissed when, in real life, they had experienced nothing of the sort.

In junior high, Helen and Elizabeth continued to confide in each other, though there were certain subjects that they didn't broach. Elizabeth had always been the pretty one, and as a teenager she only became prettier, with her curly dark blond hair and curvy figure. With both pride and horror, Helen watched as her friend evolved from a flat-chested girl, like herself, into the fortunate owner of a substantial bosom. The transformation seemed to have happened overnight. One day after swimming together at a public pool, Helen saw Elizabeth scooping her breasts into her bra as she got dressed. Helen wasn't jealous—she was simply incredulous that in the span of just a few years, she and her best friend had become so different.

The fact that Helen didn't like her own body very much didn't stop her from appreciating Elizabeth's. On the contrary, she thought Elizabeth had been blessed with "the most beautiful breasts anybody ever aspired to," as she would put it in her memoir. She came to associate "loving Elizabeth" with "loving *boys* in the yeasty, sensuous, long simmering summers of Little Rock."

Over one of those summers, Helen and Elizabeth fell for the same boy, Freed Matthews, a dark-haired teenager from a poor family who wouldn't survive Little Rock's imminent polio epidemic. But while he was alive, he was so *very* alive, managing to convince both girls that he wanted them equally. Nothing happened—unless one counts what happened between the dolls in Elizabeth's dollhouse.

Helen knew that they were too old to be playing with dolls, and yet they were too young and inexperienced to be playing this game any other way. Lying on the floor of Elizabeth's bedroom, they took turns being the girl doll and putting her in various positions with the boy doll—Freed Matthews. They weren't *sexual* positions; the dolls were just talking, very closely.

It was a fleeting and very friendly threesome. "If Elizabeth and I were going through a homosexual phase, we didn't know it," Helen later wrote, "but we were surely as much in love with each other as we were with Freed Matthews."

AROUND THE TIME of Helen's sexual awakening, her mother was having an awakening of her own. In 1933, Cleo took Helen to the Chicago World's Fair, while Mary stayed behind with relatives. Helen, eleven years old, was enthralled. Going to Chicago was the most thrilling adventure, and she soaked in the sights: the skyscrapers and double-decker buses, Marshall Field and the Shedd Aquarium. Riding up and down the escalators as many times as Cleo would allow, Helen was oblivious to the real reason for their trip: Cleo was trying to track down her first love, Leigh Bryan.

Cleo found Leigh the following year, in 1934, not in Chicago, but in Cleveland. Once again she told Helen that they were going to Chicago for the World's Fair, but as they approached the city, Cleo suggested that they continue on to Cleveland instead. Helen, unsuspecting, went along with the change in plan that, very likely, had been Cleo's mission from the beginning. Later that night, staying at the Cleveland Hotel, Helen woke up to find herself alone in the room. Terrified, she eventually found a note Cleo had left saying she would be back in an hour. When Cleo returned, she confessed that she had been out with an old acquaintance. She never said who he was, but quietly Cleo and Leigh continued to keep in touch.

By the summer of 1935, Cleo was becoming restless in Little Rock and agitating for a new start somewhere else. "It's been three years since we lost your daddy," she used to say. "We didn't *lose* him," Mary would retort. "He's not out in the parking lot." Despite a small sum of insurance money and the settlement Cleo had gotten from the state of Arkansas, there wasn't enough to pay off the mortgage and maintain the lifestyle that she and the girls had grown accustomed to. Very soon the money was going to run out, and when it did, they might as well be far away from friends and neighbors who could bear witness. So Cleo started making plans to head west, joining the hundreds of thousands of people before her who had led the exodus to California. John Steinbeck wrote about the pilgrimage of the Joad family in *The Grapes of Wrath*, and Woody Guthrie sang about the "garden of Eden" in his song "Do Re Mi." Of course, not all of these Eden-bound migrants had lived in the Dust Bowl or worked in the fields. Even among the have-nots, some had more than others. There were Gurleys as well as Joads.

In 1936, Cleo took the girls on a road trip. As far as Mary and Helen knew, they were going to visit one of Ira's brothers, Uncle John, in Los Angeles, and they would stop at the Texas Centennial Exposition, in Dallas, along the way. They did stop at the fair, just as Cleo had promised. As they enjoyed themselves, they had no clue that, back home in Little Rock, their house and all their furniture had been sold or that Cleo was moving the family to Los Angeles. When Cleo finally broke the news, Mary revolted, hopping onto the first bus she could get back to Little Rock, where she stayed with some girlfriends and tried to find a job. Cleo let Mary do what she wanted, but her independence didn't last long. Not having much luck finding a job or a social life for herself in Little Rock, she soon joined her mother and younger sister in Los Angeles.

During summers at their grandmother's house in Osage, Helen and Mary had spent plenty of hours dreaming about Hollywood. Sitting on the porch, they would watch the stars and read about them in *Photoplay*, *Movie Mirror*, and *Silver Screen*. Still, as much as Helen loved the idea of Hollywood, she didn't actually want to live there, and she didn't understand why they had to move so far away from everyone and everything they knew. (Cleo continued to keep her daughters in the dark about Leigh Bryan, who was living in Cleveland, but would join them in Los Angeles soon enough.)

Other than Uncle John and his family, they didn't have anyone else to depend on in L.A., and Uncle John couldn't offer much. A mechanic who was in and out of work, he wasn't much better off than they were. At the very least, Cleo hoped that he would be able to provide some moral support, but that was before they got the phone call that changed their lives once again.

24

GOOD TIME GURLEY

1930–1940s

"'Guppie' likes having her back scratched and frosted cokes and
dislikes being called 'Good Time.' . . . Her ambition is to become a successful businesswoman."

—from a profile of senior Helen Gurley
in her high school newspaper, May 1939

O
n a Sunday afternoon in April 1937, the Gurleys got the
news that Mary had polio. At first the doctor thought it
was influenza, but then they got the real diagnosis, and it
was devastating. Mary's legs would be paralyzed, and she would
be in a wheelchair for the rest of her life. She was nineteen.

Sometimes Helen wondered why polio picked Mary, a sweet-
natured girl with cat-eye glasses and dark curls—the prettier
of the two sisters, some people thought. Helen could have fallen
victim to the disease just as easily. "[We] were formed from the
same gene pool, ate the same food, lived in the same apartment,
slept in the same bedroom, breathed the same air, were accessible to the same floating germs out in the street," Helen wrote
in her 2000 memoir, *I'm Wild Again*. As a girl, she knew that
she had been spared, and yet the fact that Mary was paralyzed
and wheelchair-bound, and she was healthy and mobile, didn't
make her own adolescence feel much easier. She was still dealing
with the death of her father—she would always feel that loss—
and getting used to their new life in California. In Little Rock,

she had envied her friends with more money, but soon she would know what being "poor" really felt like.

Shortly after getting the diagnosis, Cleo and Helen relocated to the East Side of Los Angeles, moving into a small bungalow across from the Los Angeles Orthopaedic Hospital, a clinic that specialized in treating children with crippling disorders including polio, knock-knees, bowlegs, and spinal curvatures. Mary lived at the clinic, where she was treated by the founding doctor, Charles LeRoy Lowman, who was experimenting with new treatments for polio, like turning a fishpond on the hospital grounds into a therapy pool. Her doctors tried everything—pool treatments, massage therapy, two muscle transplants—but nothing worked. Hoping to cheer Mary up, Helen wrote one of her first fan letters, addressed to President Franklin Delano Roosevelt at the White House. "Dear Mr. President, my sister Mary has polio just like you," she began, before asking if he would send her a letter. When Roosevelt later wrote to Mary, wishing her a full recovery, Helen marveled at her own power. She was all of fifteen, but with a little pluck and a three-cent stamp, she had gotten the attention of the president of the United States.

In the meantime, Mary's medical bills were putting a serious dent in their finances, and they were all feeling the strain. Starting classes at John H. Francis Polytechnic High School, Helen acclimated to the idea that she was going to school with other poor kids now: blacks and whites under one roof. If she wanted to see rich people, she would just have to go to the movies.

ANXIOUS THAT SOMETHING would happen to her, Cleo insisted on walking Helen to school throughout her freshman year. For a teenage girl who was the new kid in class, being escorted to high school was embarrassing, but nothing close to the humiliation she felt whenever she looked in the mirror. Helen recoiled at her own reflection—pimples studded her face like braille. For the next two years, Cleo spent much of her time taking care of Mary, who had returned from the hospital, but she also arranged for Helen to see a doctor about her acne. And so Helen's treatments began: Twice a week after school, she went to see a family doctor who didn't know much about dermatology but popped her pustules for no charge, leaving her face red and blotchy.

Perhaps if she had been born beautiful like her friend Elizabeth Jessup, Helen could have coasted through high school on her looks. Partly because of Cleo's criticisms of her, Helen recognized what she lacked, and knew she had to make up for it in other ways. She had to be smarter, wittier, and more memorable than other girls. She simply had to try harder.

Helen with her sister, Mary, who in 1937 was diagnosed with polio that left her paralyzed from the waist down. (*Family photograph courtesy of Norma Lou Honderich.*)

At home, Helen became a part-time caretaker to Mary. She learned how to negotiate her wheelchair over curbs as they went window-shopping or to the movies, and while she took pride in giving her sister a smooth ride, she was relieved when Mary eventually found other friends. Their next-door neighbor was also a polio victim and had gotten past the hardest times with the help of her husband. Together, the couple zipped Mary all over town.

At school, Helen was determined to become more social, performing in class skits and talent shows, joining school clubs, and even running for office. At home she chafed under Cleo's control. They loved and infuriated each other. They were as "close as stitches," as Helen later put it, and they both wielded the power to wound. As overprotective as Cleo was, she could chip away at Helen's confidence like no one else. And there were times when Helen hurt her mother so deeply that Cleo would crawl into bed, weeping with her face to the wall.

At school Helen became someone kinder, softer, and sweeter. She was elected president of the Scholarship Society and of the World Friendship Society, hosting events like "Hello Day," an after-school mixer that was held in the gym. As a senior, she worked on the school yearbook and joined the prom committee as chairman to help plan the St. Patrick's Day–themed dance—and to get a little closer to her crush, Hal Holker, the student body president and the most popular boy in the twelfth grade.

Spending all that time planning with the committee eventually paid off. The day of the senior prom, Hal didn't have a date, so he asked Helen to go at the last minute; he figured she could take care of herself. Dancing together in the gym, decorated with shamrocks and streamers in green and white, they had such a good time that Hal asked her out again, the following week.

"Good Luck" was the theme of prom that year, but luck had little to do with Helen's high school success. It wasn't luck that secured her a spot in the Ephebian Society, a coed club made up of students who demonstrated outstanding scholarship, leadership, character, and citizenship. It wasn't luck that made her popular (her classmates voted her the *third* most popular girl) or the second most likely to succeed or the fifth best dancer. She didn't place for "prettiest girl," though she corralled third-place honors for "biggest apple polisher" in the graduating class of 375 seniors. Pluck, not luck, got her into the final round of tryouts to be the commencement speaker at graduation, and into the school paper, *The Optimist*.

Student reporters made it a point to interview Helen Gurley (alternately nicknamed Guppie and Good Time) about everything from extracurricular activities to her thoughts on whether girls should be able to wear pants to school. "It lowers the respect of other fellows and girls for the one who comes to school in slacks," she told her interviewer. "It is just as out of place as a playsuit at a formal affair."

In the spring of 1939, she even commanded her own mini-profile in the school paper, thanks in part to her membership in the Ephebian Society. "I've dreamed of being an Ephebian for so long that I just can't believe it's true," she gushed, ever the apple polisher. "It's just about the grandest thing that ever happened to me."

On graduation day, Helen delivered her commencement address. At least among her friends, she had made a name for herself. No one doubted that Helen Gurley was college material, and she soon lined up big plans to go to Texas State College for Women in Denton.

Shortly after Helen's high school graduation, the Gurleys moved again. This time Cleo went to Warm Springs, Georgia, where Mary could receive care at a polio treatment center established by Franklin Roosevelt.

Helen sitting for a portrait as a young woman. (*Family photograph courtesy of Norma Lou Honderich.*)

Meanwhile, Helen began life as a freshman all over again in Texas, but like her mother, she stayed in college for only one semester. Cleo and Mary returned to Los Angeles and needed her back home.

EVEN AS SHE made other friends in L.A., Helen never stopped idolizing her old friend Elizabeth Jessup. They confided in each other through letters, signing off with their nicknames for each other: Helen was "Kitten" and Elizabeth was "Buzzie," "Sassafras," or "Sassy" for short. Helen loved getting updates about her friend's life in Little Rock. Throughout their high school years, Helen had rooted for Elizabeth when she nabbed the lead in a class play or got elected as student body president at Little Rock Central High School.

Over time, Elizabeth also had become a sort of barometer. Simply by living out her own life in Little Rock, Elizabeth allowed Helen to gauge just how much she herself had changed since leaving. As much as Helen was evolving, her living situation was not. After Mary's treatment in Georgia, she and Cleo came back to Los Angeles, and they all moved into a little stucco house in South-Central. From her backyard Helen could see railroad tracks and hear the freight trains that passed by. Some nights she would be necking in the car with a boy, and a train would suddenly come crashing past. As bad as the noise was, at least it was outside. Inside the house, sharing a room with Mary and her wheelchair, Helen became attuned to the clawing sounds of the gophers that would tunnel their way up under the floorboards. *Scratch, scratch, scratch.* Once, in desperation, she and Mary ran a long hose down one of the gopher holes to flush the rodents out. They got one—a wet, drowning ball of brown fur that they didn't try to revive.

Maybe it was cruel to kill the gopher, Helen thought later; he was only trying to survive, to hoard some food while he had the chance. Born blind and helpless, he was hardwired to tunnel up into a better place. The gopher was just doing what gophers do— any creature trying to make it would do the same.

Helen had managed to tunnel her way up at high school, but it was over now. She would have to start tunneling again. She had been the shining example of a well-rounded student, the epitome of "college material," and had she not been poor and applying to schools at the end of the Depression, perhaps she would have found herself reading Shakespeare at Smith or some other elite college. Instead, she was heading to secretarial school at Woodbury Business College in downtown Los Angeles. At the very least, learning shorthand and typing would guarantee her a job when she got out.

In the meantime, she was stuck living with her mother and her new stepfather. In 1939, almost seven years after Ira's death, Cleo married her high school beau, Leigh Bryan, who moved from Cleveland, where he had been working as a Good Humor ice-cream salesman, to live in Los Angeles with his new wife and two grown stepdaughters. Helen, who was seventeen when Cleo remarried, knew Leigh cared for her mother, but she found him to be embarrassing, especially when a date came to the house to pick her up. Outside the house, Leigh's ice-cream cart sat idly by the front door, and on many evenings when he was home, the living room reeked of whatever he was cooking for dinner with Cleo. (Sadly, Leigh soon became ill and would die of stomach cancer five years into their marriage.) .

Still, they were managing to get by. Cleo had gotten a job pricing merchandise at Sears, Roebuck, and despite the pain and discomfort she experienced daily, Mary never complained. But just shy of eighteen, Helen was getting fidgety. She knew that she was changing, and growing, and soon she wouldn't fit into the little life that her mother and sister had created for themselves.

In the back room she shared with Mary, Helen wrote long letters to Elizabeth about the changes she had already witnessed in herself. Lately, she had begun to think a lot about God. To obsess over God, really. She still said her prayers at night, but she wasn't sure she believed in a higher power. Sometimes it felt like believing in Santa Claus—when she prayed, she basically listed everything she wanted to accomplish, hoping to see some improvement the next day. Granted, she was no great student of the Bible, but wasn't it more rational, more reasonable, more productive, to believe in oneself?

Helen and Mary outside of their house near the railroad tracks in South-Central Los Angeles, circa 1945. (*Family photograph courtesy of Norma Lou Honderich.*)

Helen knew Elizabeth had different views and aspirations. Within a couple of years, Buzzie would be headed down the aisle. She wanted a husband, a house, and children—she wanted what women were supposed to want.

Helen wanted something other than the life of duty and sacrifice that had been prescribed for her. She couldn't just settle for the boy who bagged groceries, not with Cleo and Mary depending on her for help. She needed to marry up, up, and away—out of her sad little life and into something bigger and grander. She could relate to Scarlett O'Hara; they shared a selfish streak, a yearning to be free at whatever cost.

"If I'd been beautiful I might be a gold digger," Helen confided in Elizabeth, "but I'd rather die than be poor all my life. I have a hideous, disgusting, but sincere ambition to have a great deal of money someday."

IN 1946, WHEN Helen was twenty-four, Cleo, widowed again, took Mary back to Osage. Cleo said they'd have a better life there, living with her parents and surrounded by family, but Helen suspected that, characteristically, her mother had another motive. "She really did it because she saw me being a semi-nurse-companion to my sister, too deeply involved in Mary's life (and problems) perhaps to have a life of my own," Helen later wrote in *I'm Wild Again*.

Finally, she was free to live life on her own terms.

25

TURNING POINTS

1950S

*"The world that shaped Helen had two drivers:
Poverty and movies."*

—Walter Meade

In the early 1970s, while working on her musical with Lyn Tornabene, Helen created a tape on the theme of turning points in her life. Generally, Lyn interviewed Helen, but in this instance, Helen recorded herself, talking about moments that had formed her. Many of those moments had to do with her family and upbringing—Mary getting polio, for instance—but others were far more fleeting.

Here is Helen Gurley, thirty years old, at a photo shoot for Rheingold Beer in Beverly Hills, in the early Fifties. She has come with her beau, the head of the Rheingold account and a top executive at Foote, Cone & Belding's New York office. He is in town for the shoot, and to see her, but they stand at a professional distance so no one will suspect that they are having an affair. At this particular session, the famous Hollywood photographer Paul Hesse is getting ready to shoot the beautiful winner of this year's "Miss Rheingold" contest. The setting is a party scene, and a couple of guys and one girl have been hired as extras in the background. The two male models walk in, but the female model still hasn't shown, and time is money, so Helen's lover suggests the obvious: They should just use Helen as the girl. All she has to do is blend into the background—pretend to mix a martini or put on a record. Easy fix. But it's a no-go. Hesse won't use her. He would rather wait for the model. So they wait, and she still doesn't show, and he still won't use Helen. "That nearly killed me," Helen confided in Lyn nearly twenty years later. "I wasn't even presentable enough to fill in as a background girl."

Helen wanted a lot out of life, but what she wanted most of all—to be beautiful—was unattainable. She never cared about being the next Marie Curie; she wanted to be Lana Turner, the blond goddess who conquered Hollywood and three husbands. Of course, she was about as far away from being a blond goddess as one could be, but she did have something else going for her. "I learned very early to be good in bed," Helen told Lyn. "Nobody ever told me. I just knew."

She never slept with a man on the first date (she *was* from the South, after all), and the pursuit was a big part of the fun. In the Forties and Fifties, there was no end to the tactics a man would try to get her into bed, and when he finally succeeded, Helen didn't have to *pretend* to like it. She didn't lose her virginity until she was twenty, but she had known the feelings of lust and desire ever since she was a girl.

So she didn't look like Jane Russell—she didn't need to once she got a man alone with her. She liked to talk dirty, a bit of a novelty in those days, and her orgasms were usually real. Nothing was more exciting or flattering to the ego than being in the tight grip of a man who wanted her. Even when she didn't climax, she loved the power she wielded—and she enjoyed watching the effect she had on her lover. "It was the most *marvelous* feeling because, my goodness, he was looking at me, at *me*, and there wasn't anyone else 100,000 miles away," she told Lyn during one of their marathon interview sessions. "I was incandescent. I was fantastic. I was the star."

A young Helen posing playfully for the camera. (*Family photograph courtesy of Norma Lou Honderich.*)

Her enthusiasm kept men coming back for more. In no particular order, there were the commercial artist she met through an ad account, the U.S. general who chased her around a hotel, the young doctor who seduced her in a car, the treasurer for Rheingold Brewing Company who wooed her in Paris, and there were "the boys in the band" who played on the radio station KHJ, where she landed her first job. In addition to the occasional aging athlete or entertainer, like Jack Dempsey (whom she met while working on a commercial for Bulldog Beer), onetime teen idol Rudy Vallee, and the actor Walter Pidgeon, she also enjoyed a few foreigners, including a French painter, a mustachioed Englishman who struck her as "devastating" and happened to be the head of Revlon (hence the Rolls-Royce), and a bearded skier from Zurich who brought her Swiss chocolates and spoke German to her when they made love. She learned something from each of her exploits, but along the way, she also had her heart crushed and her confidence shredded. That's where therapy came in.

Psychoanalysis, hypnosis, touch therapy—Helen tried it all. As a single girl in Los Angeles, she had seen good therapists and bad ones, like the Beverly Hills shrink who asked her what she wished to be in life. When she answered that she wanted to be a famous actress, he told her she didn't have the right looks—a sharp blow. A Pasadena psychiatrist who came highly recommended turned out to be a total creep. When Helen confessed how many men she had slept with, he looked at her with disgust. "What about your mother?" he asked. "Did she put out, too?"

Helen had never heard the term "put out" before, but she left the session feeling unnerved. It wasn't until she went to group therapy that she found a man who really listened to her and seemed to understand her. Charles Cooke wasn't actually a doctor. (Presumably, he was the same "Charles Cooke" who Helen would later suggest as the hypnotist-host for her proposed TV show, *The Unwind Up*. By then, he had coauthored the *Hypnotism Handbook*, offending the famous psychiatrist and hypnotist Milton H. Erickson, M.D., who regarded Cooke as somewhat of an impostor.) Still, in Helen's opinion, he did more to help her heal than any M.D., using some far-out techniques, including hypnosis and psychodrama. Week after week, individual members acted out whatever problem they were having, with another member of the "cast" playing the role of mother/father/sister/brother/boss/lover. Helen tended to drift off during other people's reenactments—she frequently brought along a dress to hem because time was money—and then, one day, it was her turn. The first time Charles invited Helen to sit on his lap like he was the Daddy and she was Daddy's little girl, she felt safe and cared for in a way she hadn't experienced since she was small. Another woman might have seen him as a lecher, or a fraud, but he had a way of getting through to her—he stripped away the shame.

With Charles she was willing to try almost anything, including nude therapy. In 1958, good girls didn't take their clothes off in front of their own boyfriends, let alone a group of strangers, but Helen let the group see her. Standing there, naked and vulnerable, she cataloged each part of her body that she hated. Her small bosom. Her large hips, much too wide for her otherwise narrow frame. Her "poochy" tummy.

Another time, when Charles brought a "potty" to a session, Helen made herself use it in front of everybody. The point was that people felt ashamed of their bodies and their bodily functions. Shame wasn't unique; it was universal.

26

SELF-PORTRAIT
1965

"God damn it, Helen, you aren't a mouseburger anymore and
maybe . . . never were. Distorted image!"

—letter from Lyn Tornabene to Helen Gurley Brown

Helen worked on her issues, but she never worked them
out. Her insecurity was cellular, so much a part of her
that it was practically its own organ. Helen Marie Gurley was a straight-A student, but she saw herself as average. Her
friends thought she was cute, but she thought she was nothing
special. Growing up, she was firmly middle class, but she felt
poor—even before she actually *was* poor. She wasn't from "hillbilly stock," as she claimed, but she believed that she was. Her
self-portrait mattered. Because of it, she understood at some deep
level that in order for *Cosmopolitan* to work, she not only had to
change society's image of the single, working girl—but also had to
change that girl's image of herself.

She started by writing that girl a letter. One day in the spring of
1965, Helen sat down at her Royal manual typewriter and started
composing her first column as the editor of *Cosmopolitan*. She had
written hundreds if not thousands of letters before this moment,
using this same typewriter, but this letter was different—this
one meant everything. It was where she would announce herself
and what she stood for: her beliefs, convictions, and ideas for the

magazine going forward. The challenge was to package it in a way that felt fun and breezy, not too serious, not forced. Many readers already knew her from her books and her "Woman Alone" column, so she introduced herself as an old friend before explaining how she personally selected the articles in the July issue: "I thought they'd *interest* you . . . knowing that you're a grown-up girl, interested in whatever can give you a richer, more exciting, fun-filled, friend-filled, man-loved kind of life!"

The column bore all the signature stylings she would become known for: italics, exclamation points, fawning assessments of *Cosmopolitan*'s featured writers. Once the letter was finished, Helen gave it to David to read, and he left his marks as usual. Of course, the real judge wouldn't be David or her Hearst bosses, but the reader, the person Helen simply referred to as *you*.

EVEN THOUGH HUGH Hefner had turned down the Browns' early proposal for *Femme*, Helen continued to look at *Playboy* as a prime example of how to mold a magazine with a specific reader in mind. Hearst avoided the comparisons, but not Helen. "A guy reading *Playboy* can say, 'Hey, that's me.' I want my girl to be able to say the same thing," she once said. She admitted that she admired *Playboy* "to the point of ridiculousness" and thought Hefner was "a bona-fide genius." With *Playboy*, Hefner hadn't just created a magazine. He had created a lifestyle and a philosophy—literally, "The *Playboy* Philosophy," a monthly feature that broke down his vision not just for the magazine, but for the future of the modern American male.

Who was he? In the inaugural December 1953 issue, featuring Marilyn Monroe on the cover, Hefner began by describing the *Playboy* man in terms of who he wasn't. He wasn't necessarily the family breadwinner or the Father of the Year type featured in popular family magazines, nor was he the rugged outdoorsman portrayed in traditional men's magazines. He didn't care much for camping or fly-fishing or do-it-yourself projects. In fact, the *Playboy* man preferred to stay indoors, where he could satisfy his appetite for "the good life" more easily. "We like our apartment," Hefner wrote. "We enjoy mixing up cocktails and an *hors d'oeuvre* or two, putting a little mood music on the phonograph, and inviting a female acquaintance for a quiet discussion on Picasso, Nietzsche, jazz, sex. . . ."

The single girl Helen wrote about could also mix a good cocktail and talk about sex without blushing. And while Hefner wasn't ready to invest in a new magazine for women, he liked the idea of there being "a female version of *Playboy*," and he took a keen interest in Helen's vision for a sexually liberated *Cosmopolitan*.

"It was the beginning of the sexual revolution. *Playboy* played a major part in igniting that, and I felt that there was more than a little room for the same thing for women," Hefner says today. "I thought that, if she hired the right people—and we helped her hire the right people—she should do very well. There was a waiting audience for what she had in mind; it really made sense.

"What I did personally was align her with and introduce her to my own editors so that she had contact with the agents and the writers that we were using," Hefner continues. "We gave her a frame of reference in terms of the marketplace and what we paid for various kinds of pieces."

Early on, Helen commissioned writers whose work had appeared in *Playboy* to pen pieces for her, and *Cosmopolitan* soon adopted a similarly frank tone. Both magazines advocated for sexual freedom and expression, featuring photos of beautiful girls in seductive poses. But while the two editors had many convictions in common, their target readers were, at the core, far more different than they were alike. The *Playboy* man was handsome, successful, and sophisticated; he not only knew how to make an hors d'oeuvre, he knew how to spell it. He was at ease with himself and seemingly free of insecurities.

The *Cosmopolitan* Girl, on the other hand, was full of hang-ups. She might want to date the *Playboy* man, but he didn't necessarily want to date her—too much baggage. While he was busy adding to his wine collection, she was worrying about paying her rent, financing her car, dealing with her overbearing mother, asking her boss for a raise or promotion, and trying to manage the feelings of helplessness and rage that she occasionally felt when she thought about all of the above.

Had they met in the real world, these two might have had a fling, but eventually they would have gone their separate ways, realizing that they were incompatible. (If anything, the *Cosmopolitan* Girl had more in common with the working-class Playmate. "Playmates," Hefner says, "were often *Cosmo* Girls with their clothes off.")

And yet, the *Playboy* man and the *Cosmopolitan* Girl shared one essential trait. Both characters seemed like much more than figments of their creators' imaginations—they seemed real. "I think magazines are the most personal form of mass communication, and the best magazines have a personality that is almost human," Hefner says. "Both *Playboy* and *Cosmo* defined their readership in a very clear way, and that was part of the reason for their success."

Before Helen Gurley Brown took over, *Cosmopolitan* had no editor's letter, only a roundup of what was in the issue. Just as Hefner had done in *Playboy*, Helen wrote directly to the reader she imagined. Hers was one specific girl—essentially the girl she had been.

At seventeen she was the scared high school graduate, soon to be a secretarial student, who had confessed that she would rather die than be poor all her life.

By the age of thirty-five she was the loveless career girl at Foote, Cone & Belding, the odd specimen who conveyed an ambition so intense it fascinated an observer from an outside consulting company, Runner Associates, studying her for a job evaluation that read more like pages from a psychoanalyst's notebook:

"She seems constantly aware of her lack of fulfillment. . . . She is as intrigued by it as if it were an aching tooth that she keeps worrying with her tongue," the report pronounced. "She doesn't want to have to work out her long-range problems. She wants both to be cared for, and to feel exquisitely needed. She wants proof of romance, and glamour, and ease."

Eight years later, when a forty-three-year-old Helen began typing up her first editor's letter for *Cosmopolitan*, she was addressing the girl who wanted it all. Other people might have seen that girl as someone's bored secretary, unmarried daughter, insecure friend, or dissatisfied wife, but Helen spoke to the person she was on the inside. She saw her for who she truly was—a woman with desires as strong as a man's.

Helen's first-ever editor's letter was a page long, squeezed in next to an ad for a powdered deodorant promising to end "a woman's 3 worst odor problems" (odorous sanitary napkins and perspiration under bras and girdles). The mostly black-and-white layout could have been more inviting, but the name of the column welcomed readers right in: "Step Into My Parlour."

Her first picture showed her multitasking with the phone at her ear and a manuscript in her hand. Over time, Helen's vision for her column would continue to take shape—she tried never to be photographed in the same dress or pose, and she liked to be shown in far-flung locations with fabulous people—but from the start, she made it clear that everything in the issue was in service of her imaginary girl, who had very real problems to deal with and dreams to pursue.

She personally selected articles about how to avoid a disastrous divorce, how to find a good psychiatrist on a budget, and how to travel in style when single. Equally important were the countless advertisements curated for this specific young woman, who, in fact, *was* horrified by the sweat that collected under her bra and girdle—and also needed a cure for her period cramps (Midol), a tampon with a slimmer applicator (Kotams by Kotex), and a quick fix for getting rid of her calluses and corns (Pretty Feet).

At the same time, Helen acknowledged this girl's need for some kind of proof that more was out there—romance, glamour, and ease: "You also want to be inspired, entertained and sometimes whisked away into somebody *else's* world," she wrote.

The girl reading could start by stepping into Helen's parlor, if only for a moment.

27

PARLOUR GAMES
1965

"Desk accessories should be female . . . sharpened pencils in
a blue Delft jar, a Can Can dancer's bronze boot for a paper-
weight, a cigarette box that is glass and gilt."

—Helen Gurley Brown, *Sex and the Office*, 1964

Helen's real parlor appeared to be as welcoming as her
theoretical one. Over the decades, she would redecorate
it several times, though most people would remember
the chintzy pink-and-green version featured on the cover of her
1982 book, *Having It All*. By then she had traded in her desk for a
gilded console table, opting for floral wallpaper, a matching couch,
a collection of antique dolls, and needlepoint pillows bearing messages like "I love champagne, caviar and cash." Toward the end of
her reign, it looked more like the cluttered living room of a sassy
grandmother than the office of one of the most influential editors
in the world.

Through all of the transformations, Helen's office would always
feel homey. And yet, like so much about her, the soft surface was
misleading. Like her column, her office was a kind of a stage, and
she was a great entertainer, regaling readers and staffers alike with
stories about visiting Mother and Mary or attending some glamorous premiere party with David. "I always thought that when
Helen decided to call her column 'Step Into My Parlour,' that told

everything about how she operated," Walter Meade says. "Although she was not a cold person, she was incapable of real empathy, and if you started talking about personal stuff to her, her eyes would glaze over in about two seconds."

Just because she invited you into her parlor didn't mean she cared to step into yours, not for long anyway. In the Seventies, *Cosmopolitan*'s longtime art director, Linda Cox, came to expect Helen's brisk monthly check-ins. "About every four weeks, she would come into my office to ask how my son was. She didn't *really* want to know. She probably ticked it off in her monthly calendar: 'Ask Linda about her son.' She was very programmed that way," Cox says, adding that, as soon as she began to answer, Helen would start backing out of the office, loath to get caught in a conversation about nursery school. "She was just trying to keep me happy and be a good boss." Despite her impatience for small talk, Helen was a great listener when she wanted to be. "Or," adds Meade, "when she wanted something from you."

From the start, David edited "Step Into My Parlour." He also went over page proofs, read captions, and wrote cover lines. He and Helen were a great sales and marketing team. There was just one problem: Hearst wasn't quite ready for what they were selling and marketing.

Around the same time she was putting the finishing touches on her column, Helen got a call from the Hearst Corporation's president, Richard Emmett Berlin, concerning the July issue, which was about to go to press. Berlin didn't mince words: He wanted her to cut a risqué cover line that David had written for the big estrogen feature.

Like the company itself, Berlin was conservative: a broad-shouldered Roman Catholic from Omaha, Nebraska, who had served in the navy during World War I, before joining Hearst as an advertising trainee and working his way up to a business manager. He had a reputation for being tough and unsentimental, the pragmatist to William Randolph Hearst's idealist. During a period of financial floundering in the 1940s, Hearst himself had given Berlin the Herculean job of reorganizing the company. Berlin proved to be a fearsome leader, firing executives who weren't meeting profit goals, and selling and merging properties, always with an eye on the bottom line. He was largely credited with staving off bankruptcy and turning the company into a profitable entity once again. Hearst was the visionary, but Berlin was captain of the ship, the man credited with rescuing it and keeping it afloat.

Helen had every reason to want to impress Berlin, but when he told her to cut the cover line, "The new pill that makes women more responsive to men," she stood her ground. The estrogen piece epitomized *Cosmopolitan*'s new direction and demographic. It had to be advertised boldly on the cover, not hidden deep inside the issue. It was important that her girls *know* about this pill, which could make the very act of sex more pleasurable, but it was just as important, if not more, that they buy the magazine, and she and David both knew that this was the line that would sell it.

Sitting in her new office, Helen argued with Berlin until he finally hung up on her, but not before telling her that he expected to see a different cover line that they could run instead.

After crying at her desk, she next called David. "Why don't you try this on Mr. Berlin?" he asked. "Take off the last two words." They didn't really need to say "to men." What else would women be responsive to? Wallpaper?

Berlin approved the new blurb, and Helen learned something about power that day. In the future, she would make her points more swiftly. It was better to hang up early than to be hung up on.

◆   ◆   ◆

ON JUNE 24, the July issue hit newsstands with the edited blurb, "The new pill that promises to make women more responsive," right under *Cosmopolitan*'s title in calamine lotion pink. True to form, David wrote several eye-catching cover lines, but the main attraction was the cover girl herself. Overnight, the old *Cosmopolitan* had been carried out on a gurney, and the new *Cosmopolitan* had arrived flaunting blond hair, a flimsy gingham dress, and big breasts.

When Helen got the sales figures, she went to find Walter Meade, who was in Bill Guy's office.

Like the rest of the staff, Walter and Bill had been living on tenterhooks. Helen's takeover had been so sudden, longtime readers were bound to be confused. Some of the editors had worried that the new *Cosmopolitan* would scare away loyal readers or, worse, that people would just pass it by.

Helen, for one, never underestimated the power of a sexy woman, but the figures blew her away. The July issue sold approximately 954,000 newsstand copies, almost 260,000 more copies than June. The new *Cosmopolitan* was an instant success.

Walter heard her before he saw her two-stepping down the hall to Bill's office.

"Guess how much?" she asked, breathless with excitement.

Walter and Bill exchanged a look. They didn't know that the sales figures had come in, until Helen showed them the proof.

"I think she said, 'We're on the Yellow Brick Road,'" Meade says. "She was the way you get when you've been validated. She wasn't silly about it, she was just sort of: 'I told you so.'"

ONE SUMMER DAY in Winter Park, Florida, a *Cosmopolitan* reader picked up the July issue and stared in shock at the busty blonde on the cover. Flipping through the pages, she only became more incensed when she saw an excerpt from *Aly*, Leonard Slater's biography of the late Prince Aly Khan, who had been Pakistan's United Nations representative and who also happened to have been a notorious womanizer and the third husband of Rita Hayworth. When she had read enough about Aly's art of lovemaking, the mother of four sat down and wrote a furious letter to *Cosmopolitan*'s new editor, declaring that she planned to throw the July issue into the garbage, where it belonged. "I will not have it in my home where my children might possibly read it," she huffed, before signing off, "A former *COSMOPOLITAN* reader."

Helen Gurley Brown published her letter along with many others, from readers who alternately praised the magazine and denounced it. There was the woman from Philadelphia who blasted the decision to put such a "whorish" model on the cover, and the anonymous reader who accused the magazine of reducing a woman to "nothing but a stupid, idiotic *cow* of a sexpot."

Hate mail poured in. Readers canceled subscriptions, newsstand vendors refused to sell the new *Cosmopolitan*, and advertising giants like AT&T and Coca-Cola backed away or bailed, pulling pages. But for every reader who dropped a subscription, there were countless new ones who felt as though, finally, someone was talking directly to them. "The July issue of *COSMO* is alive and right up to the minute in its point of view about life as we modern women really know it to be," wrote a reader from New York, notably shortening the magazine's name.

"I feel that you have given career girls a 'laughing look' at themselves—and let's face it, everybody needs a good chuckle once in a while," wrote a woman from Winnipeg, Manitoba. "I am looking forward to the next issues and will recommend them to my friends."

As *Cosmopolitan* gained the attention of readers across the country, in New York, editorial teams at major national magazines took note of the new girl in town, trying to figure out just how a sex book author with no previous editing experience had managed to turn a failing magazine into an overnight success.

One of those magazines was *Look*, a photo-driven general-interest magazine founded by an Iowan entrepreneur named Gardner "Mike" Cowles Jr. in 1937, one year after Henry Luce started *Life*. A seasoned veteran of the magazine industry, Cowles was no stranger to failure, having launched several magazines with life spans as short as their titles, such as *Flair*, a magazine for the moneyed elite, conceived of and edited by his third wife, Fleur Fenton Cowles. He ultimately struck gold with *Look*, a tabloid-style picture magazine that, under the influence of Fleur's sophisticated sensibility, evolved into a hugely influential biweekly with a focus on entertainment and politics, including early in-depth reporting on the civil rights movement. In the mid-Sixties, *Look* boasted a circulation of 8.5 million, thanks in no small part to Samuel O. "Shap" Shapiro, the magazine's vice president and circulation director.

Shapiro was a powerhouse in the world of circulation, a man who was brimming with ideas on how to sell magazines, but even he had never seen anything quite like the newsstand sales figures for *Cosmopolitan*'s July issue, which he addressed at a weekly management meeting with Cowles and a handful of *Look*'s top editors and department heads.

A young editor named Patricia Carbine (Pat, for short) was in the magazine's conference room when conversation turned to *Cosmopolitan*, Hearst, and Helen Gurley Brown. Like the others in the room, Carbine was familiar with *Sex and the Single Girl*, which she had skimmed enough to know that she wasn't a fan.

"I thought she was talking about somebody I didn't know and didn't want to be," says Carbine, who was then the highest-ranking female editor at a national general-interest magazine. "I

remember an emphasis of hers was that if one knew how to manipulate men in the business setting, then your life would work
out more happily because you would be more desirable and attractive, and that would be *wonderful* for your career. My existence in
my working world bore virtually no resemblance to what she was
talking about, and I was working in a world of men."

Despite her personal ambivalence about reading *Cosmopolitan*,
Carbine was intrigued by the idea of a magazine for single women,
and so were her male colleagues. When Cowles asked Shapiro if he
had any insight to offer on Helen Gurley Brown's impressive debut, Shapiro wondered aloud if the success of her first issue wasn't
simply a fluke—she had ridden in on the coattails of *Sex and the
Single Girl*, but she couldn't exploit that formula forever.

"What she had managed to do was turn her book into a
magazine—into her first issue of the magazine," Carbine says.
"She had done it, and she had done it very successfully, but what
else did she have to say?"

How did she do it? Cowles had asked.

Shapiro's question was more to the point: Could she do it again?

28

JAMES BOND ON A BUDGET
1965

> "She had flattery down to a high art, and I learned a lot from
> her about getting ahead. She would never openly fight with
> people like the rest of us, throwing our egos around. She gave
> me a positive philosophy for getting along—and it really
> worked for me."
>
> —Liz Smith

A few weeks into her appointment as editor, Helen walked as
if she knew where she was going. Watching her float down
the hallway in one of her eye-popping Puccis, shoulders
back and chest out, one realized how poorly other women carried
themselves in comparison, how clumsily and inelegantly. The hallway might as well have been a runway. Helen strutted like a model
channeling a movie star, maybe Barbara Stanwyck. She didn't swing
her arms idly like the younger girls on staff, partly because she was
always holding something, a manuscript or a layout. But it was also
just how she was: deliberate. She walked with purpose, and as her
staff got to know her, they learned to watch her walk for clues.

"You could tell where she was going when she was about half-
way down the hall because she had different looks for different
people," says Walter Meade. "She was always very flirty with me."
On her way to Walter's office, Helen often stopped and said hello
to his assistant, Barbara Hustedt, a college student who would be

heading back to school in the fall. "How's your summer going?" Helen might ask Barbara, who went by Bobbie. "Are you enjoying New York?" She made it a point to be welcoming, but Bobbie sensed that she didn't really care about her answers. It was as if an egg-timer were ticking in Helen's mind, about to ding. "She always made me nervous. Not nervous in the way that I was tongue-tied, just, 'Let this be over so I don't overstay my welcome,'" says Barbara (now Hustedt Crook), who also kept her chitchat to a minimum in the restroom, where Helen frequently sang in the stalls. "She really had a great ladies' room alto," Barbara adds. "I guess she didn't feel self-conscious. I mean, she had a perfect sense of pitch. If she was in the john, she was humming."

On the outside, Helen seemed to be taking everything in stride, but that summer and fall, failure was still a very real possibility. She had inherited a legendary magazine with legendary problems, and the cards were stacked against her, just as they had been stacked against her predecessor—maybe even more so now.

Richard Berlin had been reluctant to hire Helen in the first place, wary that her racy ideas would turn off regular readers of *Cosmopolitan*. But recognizing her marketability, Richard Deems, president of Hearst's magazine division, and Frank Dupuy Jr., *Cosmopolitan*'s publisher, convinced Berlin to give her a go on the conditions that there be little money spent to promote the new *Cosmopolitan* and that she produce the magazine adhering to its current editorial budget—one that hadn't changed since World War II.

Deems monitored *Cosmopolitan*'s editorial content and reviewed its cover designs and blurbs, determining what was appropriate and what crossed the line. Dupuy advised Helen on business matters, including budgeting and advertising, and oversaw the physical production of the magazine: contracts with the printer, page counts, and pricing.

Early on, Helen decided to raise the cover price of the magazine from thirty-five to fifty cents, but she was just scratching the surface. For *Cosmopolitan* to sustain its success, she needed more support from Hearst: not just a bigger budget, but the force of a major ad campaign. She also needed to cut costs, drastically. That meant penny-pinching on expense accounts for work-related meals and travel—not exactly the way into her staff's good graces. It also meant finding affordable writers and photographers.

From the start, she sacrificed some big literary stars and had to deal with the fallout. How could she pass over a story by Isaac Bashevis Singer? asked the old guard on staff. "Well, I don't understand it," Helen said, after reading the story herself. She started seeking out writers on her own, without dealing with the big literary agencies. She didn't care to talk to agents anyway.

Back at the office, people hurled names of writers and photographers at her. Half the time she found herself asking, "Who's that?" She needed answers before she could give them to her staff, but the phone never stopped ringing. Agents called wanting assignments for their writers; writers called wanting to know what was happening with their articles.

One day, George Walsh and Harriet La Barre came in complaining about a freelancer who'd turned in a poorly written profile of the actress Julie Christie. It was garbage, unprintable, they insisted, but Helen overruled them. They should fix it, not nix it—it was too valuable as a cover blurb. "Well," they huffed, "if Herb Mayes were here, he wouldn't be doing it that way."

At least George and Harriet had the guts to challenge her directly. The night she went to a Writers Guild dinner, freelancers fawned over her, asking what they could write for her, but she found out that later they flayed her behind her back. "Those two-faced bitches—all they wanted to do was criticize me," Helen told Lyn. "Betty Friedan led the pack."

Meanwhile, submissions kept coming in over the transom, and manuscripts and mail piled up on her desk. Many nights she stayed in her office until eleven o'clock, poring and picking over every single word, her copy of Strunk and White's *Elements of Style* nearby. With surgical precision, she nipped here and tucked there, sanded down and reconstructed whole paragraphs, streamlining syntax and turning flaccid prose perky.

It was amazing how sloppy writers could be—how lazy! Using "this" and "that" to refer to a subject that the reader had long forgotten. She counted up repetitious words and bloodied manuscripts with her cuts and line edits, split one never-ending sentence into two sentences, sometimes three. She cast out clichés. Slash, slash, slash. Circle, circle. She added *italics* and (!!!) and(. . .) and CAPS.

There were still countless improvements to make, and new people she wanted to hire, but at least some of her editors and writers were working out. Privately, Liz Smith was stewing about her new boss's mandate that she write only upbeat, accessible reviews, but she did as she was asked: So long, art-house films by the likes of Godard and Truffaut. The only New Wave her new readers cared about was the kind they could set under the dryer.

"One thing I decided," Smith wrote in the August issue: "it is simply impossible for the average girl, who has to do her own nails, keep her clothes in order, fool with her hair, work eight hours a day, or keep a house and kids in line, to be *au courant* and a member of the cinema avant-garde." Heaven knows she *tried* to understand the French filmmakers' "*nouvelle vague*," but, she concluded, "I guess I'm just too earthbound."

For better or worse, she sounded just like Helen Gurley Brown.

✦   ✦   ✦

EVERY WEEK BROUGHT countless drafts to edit, deadlines to meet, and calls to make—in her appointment diary, Helen penciled in Clairol, Shirley MacLaine, Eileen Ford. When she wasn't on the phone, staffers constantly came by for her input. Harriet needed her to sign off on a fashion story about scanty lingerie. George, the managing editor, needed to go over the schedule. Tony, the art director, needed to show her pictures for October's article about nose jobs. Helen assumed he would illustrate the piece with before-and-after photos, but Tony refused. He wanted something more tasteful. He showed her a black-and-white shot of a pretty blond girl in profile, her nose straight and smooth. People wanted to see only the "after," he said.

Typically there might be around thirty articles running in an issue, but on any given day, they were working on one hundred different pieces in different stages, and three months of issues at once: closing the current issue, putting the next issue up on the layout board in the art department, and planning the month after that.

After getting a sense of all of the different material that was coming in or being generated in-house, George made up a schedule for an upcoming issue several months in advance, selecting a mix of different articles: say, an emotional feature, a health article, a how-to-get-ahead-in-your-career story, a first-person narrative, and a couple of celebrity profiles, along with whatever subjects *Cosmopolitan*'s regular columns and departments were covering that month. The editors overseeing beauty and fashion, for instance, worked on their schedules months ahead of time. Meanwhile, the fiction editor was thinking about which short stories and novels to buy, and the art director was reading all of the above and deciding how to illustrate each component.

Helen tried to keep up with the status of every single item by checking in regularly with her art director, managing editor, and production manager, but there were mistakes and oversights. Filling a single issue of a magazine with fresh material was hard enough. Managing three issues at once was almost impossible.

One day, George came bearing bad news: There was a hole in the August issue. "How can you have a hole when trunkloads of manuscripts arrive at a magazine every day?" Helen asked. But there they were . . . two blank pages staring back at her.

In a near panic, Helen called on her new friend, Jacqueline Susann. Helen had taken to Jackie at first sight, ever since they met on Park Avenue, and in the months since, her book *Every Night, Josephine!* had become a bestseller.

"Have you written anything recently?" Helen asked.

It turned out she had: Jackie had just finished "Zelda Was a Peach," a whimsical short story about a rather naïve woman who learns about the birds and the bees, quite literally, through her indoor peach tree, named Zelda.

Helen slated "Zelda" for the summer fiction issue, along with a short story and poem from John Lennon's new book, *A Spaniard in the Works*, and an excerpt from Edna O'Brien's novel *August Is a Wicked Month*; a high-protein diet for girls with low willpower; a guide to "Swimnastics," exercises anyone could do in the pool; and a fashion feature pegged to the new James Bond movie, *Thunderball*.

She was pleased with the photos of the Bond girls wearing various furs over various bikinis posing in front of various Bahamian scenes (a yacht, a palm tree, a white Bentley), but the real showstopper was the cover, featuring a hairy-chested Sean Connery nuzzling noses with his shirtless and slick-haired French costar, Claudine Auger. They were on the beach, but they might as well have been in bed.

29

MR. RIGHT IS DEAD

1965

"The girl of the fifties would stay home waiting for Mr. Right.
But the girl of the sixties will date three or four rats at once."

—Rona Jaffe, in an interview with the Associated Press, 1965

In the fall of 1965, ABC debuted a new game show that the Browns never pitched to the network. Hosted by Jim Lange in a jacket and tie, *The Dating Game* invited viewers to play the voyeur as a series of career-girl types hidden behind a stage partition asked questions of three eligible bachelors who tried to score a date and a laugh from the studio audience. Sample question: "How would you go about telling your date that she had a dress that was maybe too short or too tight?" Answer: "They can't make a dress that's too short or too tight."

On national TV, a single girl had to play by the rules and pick just one boy for an all-expenses-paid night on the town, but across the country girls were dating Bachelors One, Two, *and* Three. Why choose? Marriage was no longer the only option, and going steady had gone out of style. Rona Jaffe, newly appointed as a contributing editor at *Cosmopolitan*, put it best with the title of her latest book: *Mr. Right Is Dead*. Like her first book, *The Best of Everything*, her "sextet" of stories about bachelorette life arrived at just the right moment, aimed at just the right market: young, single, working women.

In New York they colonized the streets of the Upper East Side, filling up brownstones and slick apartment buildings from Sixty-Fifth Street all the way up to the Eighties, from Park Avenue to the East River, a swath of real estate that *Cosmopolitan* later dubbed "The Girl Ghetto." Around 8:30 a.m. on weekdays, they stalked the sidewalks in pencil skirts and strappy heels, wearing head scarves, headbands, and hair bows the size of chinchillas. At night they gathered at singles bars like T.G.I. Friday's and Malachy's. From the time it opened in 1958, Malachy's welcomed men and women, a revolutionary and brilliant business plan considering that, located on Third Avenue between Sixty-Third and Sixty-Fourth Streets, it was around the corner from the Barbizon Hotel for Women. Pan Am stewardesses, Madison Avenue secretaries, and sweater-clad coeds piled in for burgers, beer, and bachelors.

And in Southern California, a girl could do worse than rent a furnished apartment at one of the area's brand-new coed singles housing complexes—also known as "passion pads"—a place like Torrance's South Bay Club, with its tennis matches, sauna sessions, late-night dance parties, and endless opportunities to score with the opposite sex. It didn't hurt that a typical party attracted three guys for every girl.

ACROSS THE COUNTRY, entrepreneurs were targeting bachelors and bachelorettes, and the writer Thomas Meehan was investigating the singles market for a two-part series in *Cosmopolitan* called "New Industry Built Around Boy Meets Girl." Considering the population's abundance of unmarried women and shortage of eligible men, it was no wonder so many girls were going on coed vacations like Puerto Rico Fiesta House Party, sponsored by the Singles Travel Center (part of Liberty Travel Service), and signing up with programs like Bachelor Party Tours Inc., which offered a twenty-one-day European adventure complete with gondola rides, Swiss yodeling, dinner at the Eiffel Tower, and the possibility of a marriage proposal.

Not that finding a spouse was the industry's only raison d'être. "Many single women take cruises or head alone to resort hotels so that even if they fail to corral a husband they can at least find a man interested in having a no-strings-attached affair," Meehan reported in his first dispatch for the September issue. "In short, it's the sex drive of America's forty-two million unmarried adults that has helped to create the booming Singles Industry."

In addition to Meehan's first dispatch, *Cosmopolitan*'s September issue included a book excerpt called "How Yoga Can Change Your Life," complete with suggested stretches and poses; an illustrated feature teaching novices how to play the guitar; and an optimistic article by Lyn Tornabene about the entertainment industry called "Do Be an Actress" ("Don't listen to the pessimists. You can do it!"), featuring the inspirational personal stories of six young stars. "What's new this month, pussycat?" Helen wrote in September's "Step Into My Parlour," and the answer was *everything*. The September issue was essentially a 140-page self-improvement manual filled with articles that not only spoke directly to the reader, but also told her that she could do anything and be anyone . . . with a little help from *Cosmopolitan*, of course.

Helen was a believer in "experts," and she rounded up advice from the best she could find. She asked Huntington Hartford to write a primer on how to start an art collection, and she tapped William Pahlmann, an interior designer known for his eclectic tastes, to help a career girl spiff up her apartment, using second-hand furniture, bargain finds, and buckets of paint.

Many a career girl also had a cat or dog waiting for her at home and needed some good advice about housebreaking—like the kind dispensed in "Pets and the Working Girl." Mia Farrow wasn't the only one taking her pet to work. (Her fluffy white cat, Mr. Malcolm, was a regular on the set of *Peyton Place*.) The writer reported that many bosses were allowing their employees to bring pets into the office.

After hearing about the pet piece, Bill Guy brought in his Yorkshire and Maltese terriers, Ginger and George. George barked a lot, but otherwise they didn't create too much of a disturbance—and now Helen had a cute story to tell in "Step Into My Parlour." "If you hate being away from *your* darlings all day," she wrote, "you might show the article to your boss."

Helen asked her own staffers to dream up alcoholic health drinks, promising a prize to whoever came up with the best one. They gave her forty-seven recipes, and after experimenting at home with her electric blender, she chose nine to publish alongside photos of boozy beverages garnished with strawberry and cinnamon sticks.

"Husband-Coming-Home Clothes," the big fashion spread that Harriet had edited, also got the color treatment. The idea was that, even if a woman worked, she could still get home before her husband, mix up an iced martini, and change into a sexy outfit: say, frilly white knickers, a "rumple-proof" sari, or a slinky catsuit in leopard print. ("Of course I'm purring, pet," read the caption for the catsuit. "You're home early. Do I detect you're purring *too* because I'm wearing such a pretty nylon and Lycra stretch tricot 'Scat Suit'? By Vanity Fair, $30.")

Inspired by the colorful op art of Richard Anuszkiewicz, the photographer Melvin Sokolsky wanted to experiment with patterns, layering mod fashions with mad prints and fur rugs for a trippy effect. The merchandising editor had brought in sixty-seven garments, from which they selected ten hot looks for the models for the shoot. One blond, the other brunette, they lounged and rolled around on the floor, clinging lustily to a couple of male models in suits—the husbands coming home. "I never paid much attention to them, to be honest—they're foils," Sokolsky says of the men. "The girls needed a male stimulus."

Their blatant sexuality pushed the bounds of propriety, and yet, leopard print aside, these wives really weren't so different from the housewife featured in traditional women's magazines who managed to cook dinner, clean the house, and pretty herself up before her man walked through the door, with one major exception: They were as eager to *be* pleased as they were to please.

Mr. Right wasn't dead, after all—he was just repurposed.

30

THAT *COSMOPOLITAN* GIRL
1965 On

"A color photograph of a pretty brunette with a deep V, bo-somy neckline has helped sell lots of Cosmopolitan magazines this month."

—Eugenia Sheppard, *New York Herald Tribune*, September 9, 1965

In late August, the September issue flew off the stands, thanks partly to Melvin Sokolsky's cover shot of a young model named Paula Pritchett—the sultry brunette featured in the "Husband-Coming-Home Clothes" fashion spread. The same month, *Vogue* hit the stands with a head shot of a fresh-faced inge-nue in sparkly earrings and a pale blue boa, and *Mademoiselle* ran a close-up of a model in a turtleneck and coat. Pretty as they were, anyone with a pulse would have been drawn to Pritchett with her bed-tumbled hair and deep cleavage. The stretchy, red-jersey wraparound dress she filled out so effortlessly actually belonged to Sokolsky's wife, who had worn it as a maternity outfit, but it was incidental, merely a delivery system for Pritchett's curves.

"Basically, that red dress is selling the most beautiful set of breasts you've ever seen," says Sokolsky, who first began shooting for high-end fashion magazines like *Harper's Bazaar* when models posed like upper-class women "with their noses turned up," and sex was still a taboo subject. "Then the Sixties came around, Helen came around, . . . and gestures changed. Put a pair of beautiful tits on the front of the magazine to knock people's heads off? That could never have *been* before."

Sokolsky shot other covers for *Cosmopolitan*, but one photographer soon became Helen's favorite, at least when it came to shooting the magazine's covers. Small and slight with thinning black hair, a deep tan, and a nervous energy, Francesco Scavullo wasn't the picture of glamour, but he produced thousands of glamorous pictures that defined an era and a brand. Helen invented the idea of That *Cosmopolitan* Girl to describe her target reader. Scavullo created the fantasy of her, with the help of bright lights, hairspray, makeup, push-up bras, and lots and lots of tape.

Scavullo shot many beautiful girls for many magazines, but no relationship was quite like the one he had with *Cosmopolitan*—it lasted for more than three decades. Working in a spotless, white-walled studio that took up the first floor of a four-story carriage house on East Sixty-Third Street, he approached *Cosmopolitan*'s cover shoots with the eye of a film director, controlling each element to capture the image he had in mind. He managed every decision made about hair, makeup, and clothes, and had many outfits custom made by fashion designer friends like Halston, but it always came down to the look of the girl—and he often handpicked her, too.

Scavullo's first cover for Helen was of a blond, Finnish model named Kecia Nyman. She had been featured in an earlier issue of *Cosmopolitan* in an article called "The Bittersweet Lives of Fashion Models," talking about the pressure she felt as a model to always appear beautiful no matter how tired or sick she felt. "I don't know what other models ate, I just know that I starved a lot," Nyman says now.

When she showed up at Scavullo's studio in New York, Kecia had just come from another booking overseas and felt exhausted and weak. Not long into her session with Scavullo, her stomach began to hurt. Her cramps were so horrible that at one point Scavullo stopped shooting and ordered her a hamburger from a nearby restaurant, which she barely touched. She finished the job, but rushed out of the studio and into a taxi back to her apartment, where she started vomiting blood. Somehow she managed to get herself to the emergency room at a nearby Catholic hospital. Suffering from a bleeding ulcer, she stayed in the hospital for two weeks.

Kecia appeared on more than two thousand magazine covers over the course of her career, but she always appreciated Scavullo's kindness in an industry that could be very cruel. "We all loved Scavullo. He was understanding, he was generous," she says. "He always equipped the studio with food because he knew that models were on the run and starving."

In the image that ran on the October 1965 cover, Kecia wore a cotton-candy-pink hat by Halston, pearl earrings, thick mascara, and pale peach lipstick. Set against an off-white background, the conservative, close-up beauty shot looked more like a cosmetic ad than the type of sexy covers that Scavullo would become known for—but then, the look of the *Cosmopolitan* cover girl was still a work in progress, too.

NOT LONG AFTER she started at *Cosmopolitan*, Helen began hosting weekly advertising luncheons at the "21" Club. A former speakeasy at 21 West Fifty-Second Street, "21" boasted a history as colorful as the lawn jockeys on the iron gates that guarded the entrance. It was a place of legend and extraordinary leverage. "21" was where Humphrey Bogart proposed to Lauren Bacall at table 30, otherwise known as "Bogie's Corner," and where Cary Grant came for peanut butter and jelly sandwiches because he could, although the restaurant also served antelope and black bear when they were in season.

It was easy to spend a fortune at "21," but for some it was just as easy to make one. Salvador Dalí, known to show up with a pet ocelot on a leash, rarely left without getting a new commission from a fellow diner. Sitting under the toy trucks and planes hanging from the ceiling in the front room, the rich sometimes grew richer over their power lunches—a term that didn't yet exist. Everybody else got seated in Siberia, the restaurant's least desirable room, if they got seated at all.

When Helen first started going to "21," she was "just another 102-pound nobody in a Pucci dress," as the writer Gael Greene later put it in *New York*, but before long, she began dropping three hundred dollars or more a week there on business lunches, and soon she had her own table. She was joined by her publisher, Frank Dupuy Jr., and over time they developed a routine. Every Thursday they would head over to "21," where they reserved a private dining room to seduce advertisers and agency representatives with cocktails, wine, brandy, and cigars.

The group changed from week to week, but generally there were about twenty people present, including the president and vice president of the company (say, Revlon) and their advertising agency executives. Select *Cosmopolitan* editors and the occasional assistant were also invited on a rotating basis. Playing the hostess, Helen used her charms to her advantage, flattering and flirting with her mostly male prey. She made sure that the head of the company was seated beside her, and while they ate, she homed in on her target.

"She would go through the dummy of the upcoming issue, page by page, giving a little précis of what this story's about, just a few lines for each," says former *Cosmopolitan* beauty editor Mallen De

Santis, who went along as backup during lunches with cosmetics companies. "All these ad people were just dumbfounded, gazing at this magazine, which of course was not out yet. I mean, that was a brilliant stroke."

From the start, Helen understood that the market was just one part of it; companies worried about *Cosmopolitan*'s new message. Not to worry, she assured advertisers in a statement she prepared in 1965. During her career in advertising, she had seen too much change come too soon whenever new management came in. Change didn't necessarily mean improvement, but she *was* a bestselling author, and after all the book tours and lectures and letters and face-to-face meetings with single women around the country, well, she knew a thing or two about what her girls wanted, and she felt that she could funnel all that knowledge into the pages of *Cosmopolitan*. As for any concerns about risqué content, just because she wrote a couple of books with *sex* in the title didn't mean that *Cosmopolitan* was going to become "prurient." Heavens, no! Her books, by the way, were filled with practical, positive advice for the average girl.

As cigar smoke filled the room, Helen described the typical *Cosmopolitan* reader, a woman between the ages of eighteen and thirty-four. She knew what her girl liked to eat, drink, smoke, wear, and drive; where she liked to vacation; and how much she was willing to pay for her hotel. Market research showed as much, but Helen also knew what was going on inside her girl's head: She might seem like a delicate flower, but she was stronger, bolder, and more ambitious than people realized. In a voice soft but sure, Helen drew a portrait so complete, it was as if she knew this girl personally, and by the time she was done, the executive knew her, too: Helen could have been describing his wife, girlfriend, daughter, or secretary.

For advertisers, part of the beauty of the *Cosmopolitan* reader was that she was always trying to improve herself by dyeing her hair or losing weight, increasing her bust size or contouring her makeup to make her nose look smaller. The *Cosmopolitan* cover girl was a different species altogether, and nowhere was the disconnect between the real girl and the fantasy girl more obvious (or ingenious) than in the newspaper ads that Helen soon began writing for *Cosmopolitan*. Frequently, the ad pictured the face of a glamorous model (shot by Scavullo), but the voice of a less sophisticated woman who confessed her goals and dreams (everything from mastering a headstand to conquering dating as a divorcée) in an inner monologue that ended with her loyalty to the one magazine that truly understood her.

Over the years, Helen perfected her pitch to an art. She might have been trying to get a cosmetics company to advertise their latest lipstick in *Cosmopolitan*, but by the time the executives went home to tell their wives about meeting Helen Gurley Brown, they were ready to buy much more than a quarter page of ad space. They were ready to buy into the very idea of the girl she described—not just any girl, but That *Cosmopolitan* Girl.

31

THE IRON BUTTERFLY
1965

"The U.S. Weather Bureau did *not* track the course of a Hurricane Helen last spring, but there was one."

—Chris Welles, *Life*, November 19, 1965

Helen didn't have much patience for parties, but one fall day she broke out champagne and glasses for the staff to celebrate an exciting milestone: selling one million copies of *Cosmopolitan*. (By November, the magazine would average about a million copies per issue.) Clutching the bottle in hand, Helen closed her eyes, threw up an arm, and cheered. Somewhere nearby a camera clicked, capturing her in the ecstasy of the moment for an upcoming feature in *Life*. As a couple of secretaries topped off their glasses and lit up their cigarettes, George Walsh made his way through the small crowd and handed her a gift from the *Cosmopolitan* staff: a gold record, mounted and framed. "Congratulations, Chieftess," it said.

Reaching the million-copy mark was a huge coup for Helen. Even her biggest critics on staff couldn't deny that she was a success. Once again, she was also a national story. Shortly after penciling "Life Mag" into her red journal, Helen welcomed the writer Chris Welles into her office. As usual, she launched into her poor-little-me routine. Every whispery utterance brought a new confession of helplessness—for instance, how she wore a padded bra and Pan-Cake makeup to compensate for what she didn't have naturally. The fact that she, an average girl, could land someone like David Brown as a husband was testament to the fact that her advice worked—and it was advice that could work for other women, too.

"It's just a half-baked crusading idea, I guess," Helen said, smiling bashfully.

Welles glimpsed the steel under the smile, and so did Helen's staffers, he soon found out. Just as Liz Smith had been fooled, at first, by her innocent act, other editors soon saw that "Helen's terribly polite, terribly innocent, terribly quiet exterior was a convenient and effective cover for a terribly determined and terribly ambitious interior," Welles wrote, noting that one staffer compared her to a butterfly wrought of iron.

"She had a nickname: the Iron Butterfly," Vene Spencer says now. "We knew she had that moxie in her. She'd come across very sweet and timid and delicate, but she had the fighter in her. She was fierce."

When *Life* ran the article in November, it was with the headline "Soaring Success of the Iron Butterfly," and it was a major PR coup for both Helen and Hearst. In the article, Welles corrected a persisting misconception that the company was bleeding money. On the contrary, earnings were up, and the company was reportedly worth more than $100 million.

As for *Cosmopolitan*, which had been aimless and unprofitable under the direction of its former editor, it was making publishing history, thanks to Helen Gurley Brown, who, in addition to hitting the million-copy mark in circulation, had brought in a torrent of new advertising, raising the third-quarter ad revenue 50 percent over 1964. In just a few months, she had managed to turn the magazine into a flashy, phenomenal success. When Welles asked Frank Dupuy Jr. for a comment, the publisher was ecstatic, but not everyone was so supportive. A former freelancer for *Cosmopol-itan*, Betty Friedan, called *Cosmo*'s new outlook "quite obscene," showing "utter contempt for women."

"It an immature teenage-level sexual fantasy," she grumbled to Welles. "It is the idea that woman is nothing but a sex object, that she is nothing without a man, that there is nothing in life but bed, bed, bed."

32

RESOLUTIONS
1966–1967

"This is it. The turning point. Black, white and gray are out of
the living room. Red, green, blue, yellow, vermillion, fuchsia,
magenta and company are in—very, very in."

—"TV Set Buyers Guide," *TV Guide*, 1966

In the beginning of 1966, President Johnson ordered U.S. war-
planes to resume air strikes in North Vietnam after a thirty-
seven-day pause in bombing failed to bring about a peaceful
settlement with Hanoi. A few days later, the Soviet spacecraft
Luna 9 landed on the moon. Across the country, Americans tuned
in to brand-new RCA Victors and Westinghouse Jet Sets to watch
grainy footage of soldiers fighting their way through rice fields,
and images of the lunar landscape, which turned out to be hard
and rocky, not blanketed with dust, as scientists previously believed.

There was another force battling the war and the moon for airtime. Her name was Jacqueline Susann, and she burst into living
rooms in full color: a vision of bronzed skin, glossy dark-brown
hair, Day-Glo eye shadow, and loud Pucci dresses. She was made
for color TV, and in a sense, so was her new book, *Valley of the
Dolls*, the salacious saga of three fame-seeking friends who become
addicted to pills, or "dolls," while attempting to make it big in
showbiz. Long before she touted her novel on talk shows and game

shows, her husband, the movie producer and former press agent Irving Mansfield, screen-tested potential book covers to make sure that the title would read clearly when Jackie held it up for the camera. They eventually went with a crisp white jacket, scattered with brightly colored pills. "A new book is just like any new product, like a new detergent," as Jackie would put it. "You have to acquaint people with it. They have to know it's there."

In February, *Valley of the Dolls* exploded onto the scene like a supernova. Bantam published the book, but the team at Bernard Geis Associates nurtured, edited, and publicized it. As usual, Letty Cottin Pogrebin launched the publicity campaign in style, mailing out teasers written on faux prescription pads: "Take 3 yellow 'dolls' before bedtime for a broken love affair; take 2 red dolls and a shot of scotch for a shattered career; take *Valley of the Dolls* in heavy doses for the truth about the glamour set on the pill kick."

Using *Sex and the Single Girl* as a model, Irving and Jackie embarked on a promotional tour that would go down as legend. Jackie went everywhere, and so did *Dolls*. It sold in bookstores and in delicatessens, to suburban housewives and the Hollywood elite. Soon everyone was talking about Jackie's pill-popping heroines, Anne, Jennifer, and Neely, while gossip columnists speculated about their similarities to real-life celebrities. (Was troubled Neely based on Judy Garland?) In early May, *Dolls* took the number-one slot on the *New York Times* bestseller list, where it stayed for twenty-eight weeks.

Even after extensive edits, the book itself wasn't exactly great literature, but it was a game-changer in terms of marketability and mass appeal. As Jackie told *Life*, she had no interest in turning a phrase like Henry James. "What matters to *me* is telling a *story* that *involves* people. The hell with what critics say. I've made characters live, so that people talk about them at cocktail parties, and that, to me, is what counts."

Critical reaction to *Sex and the Single Girl* had been brutal, but it was nothing compared with the reception of *Dolls*. Most reviewers simply dismissed the book as trash, not bothering to review it, even as it sold out in stores.

The Browns thought *Valley of the Dolls* was a near-perfect novel. Months before it was published, David bought the movie rights for 20th Century Fox and asked Gloria Steinem, by then a well-known name in New York media circles, to write the screenplay.

"He must have gotten very far down the list because I'd never written a script in my life," Steinem says. "I read it, and I said no—this is one of the worst books ever written by a human hand."

The Browns remained undeterred. David cast around for another screenwriter, while Helen secured an excerpt for her readers in *Cosmo*'s June issue, later giving Jackie a blurb for the paperback edition of her book. "MADDENINGLY SEXY," she raved. "I wish I had written it."

In fact, Helen was at work on a new book with Bernard Geis Associates, *Outrageous Opinions*, a collection of her columns for "Woman Alone." She was also developing a new TV talk show by the same name and appearing in panels and talks around the country on subjects ranging from blush to age to the new tide of women in advertising. Helen titled the last talk "What Business Men Should Know About Girls."

"Women are interested in everything men are interested in," she told the Adcraft Club of Detroit. "In fact, women are much like men—more than you think. Their emotions are the same. They have massive egos. They love publicity. They're vain." More and more, women were entering the man's world, she continued, and they had a lot to offer. "Let the girls into your agencies. Not just that one gal you have for status. Let them all in."

Life was busy, but that's how the Browns liked it. Toward the end of 1966, they went to Europe on a whirlwind tour. The first-class pampering began the moment they stepped onto TWA's overnight flight to London, where they both had business meetings. It was an eventful week, filled with breakfasts with writers, lunches with British agents and magazine editors, cocktails at the Savoy, and post-dinner plays.

Walking with David past pubs in the early evenings of fall, Helen thrilled to the sight of so many men, spilling out onto the streets in their suits. London was such a *male* city, and it made her feel so *female*, switching along in one of her favorite Rudi Gernreich dresses, in tiger or zebra print. In New York she felt as though her hemlines were usually two inches shorter than anyone else's— anything longer would have drawn attention to her wide hips— but on Carnaby Street, she fit right in. Almost. She was about twenty years older than the kids in their thigh-high space boots, cropped tops, and Mary Quant miniskirts.

From London they continued on to Sutton Place, in Surrey, for a tête-à-tête with the World's Richest Man, Jean Paul Getty, who solicited Helen's advice on women as they drank tea. From there, they went to Palma, Majorca, where they spent one day with Fox's president and David's boss, Darryl F. Zanuck, and another with the travel guide scribe Temple Fielding, who literally wrote the book on Europe, and served up an eight-hour lunch with pink sangria at his villa overlooking the glittering water. Next up: Athens and then Rome. One mustn't appear unkempt while touring the Acropolis, and Helen didn't. She came equipped with dark sunglasses, silk scarves, false eyelashes, and several chic dresses. When she traveled, she traveled in style, and it always cost her.

In 1966 alone, Helen spent \$3,343.30—the equivalent of nearly \$25,000 today—on dresses, shoes, suits, coats, purses, jewelry, lingerie, and one luxurious lynx coat. The same year, she meticulously recorded her measurements. On March 1, 1966, her bust was 34; her waist was 24½; and her hips were 38½. Shortly after Thanksgiving, she had plumped up to 35-26-40.

Helen was obsessive about her weight, and she had a will of steel, which friends who ate with her witnessed firsthand. "We lunched at the Tea Room," says Lyn Tornabene. "I would be eating blini or something enormously fattening, and Helen would be eating a lettuce leaf, staring at my food, saying, 'Oh, that looks so good. Is that good? It looks good.' I wanted her to take a bite, but she wouldn't. In my presence, in all the years that I knew her, she probably never consumed at one meal more than 150 calories."

For Helen, staying thin was a lifelong vow, and it was one that she honored. In her January 1967 editor's letter, she wrote down some of her other resolutions for the new year. In addition to buying "fewer but better clothes," she resolved to try to keep her face relaxed, no matter how stressed she felt; buy some nice stationery (no more typing paper); and monitor David's diet, which also affected hers. "There's no use resolving anything major, of course," she wrote. She could tinker around, but it was too late for a total overhaul: For better or worse, she was stuck with herself.

HELEN WASN'T ALWAYS the best listener, but she did take an interest in some of *Cosmo*'s young secretaries, whose adult lives were just beginning. Sometimes she treated editors and assistants to lunch for their birthdays. Once, she even brought Les Girls to the famous "21" Club. "None of us had ever been there or would have dreamed in a million years of ever gaining entry to a place so posh," Vene Spencer says. The club opened its doors for presidents and movie stars, not secretaries, but Helen knew the staff, and they treated Les Girls like *la crème de la crème*. Without her there they never would have gotten past the wrought-iron gate, let alone the brick wall that hid the secret wine cellar. Watching the steady parade of waiters carrying silver wine buckets and preparing steak Diane tableside, Vene felt grateful to Helen, even though she didn't stick around. She had work to do back at the office. "But you ladies stay," Helen said, waving her hand like a wand. "I've arranged for you to have a private tour of the wine cellar."

As a rule, Helen couldn't stand the loud girls who took up her time with long-winded stories about their roommates or their noisy neighbors. She gravitated toward the shy girls who watched her, just as she once had watched her bosses. The quiet ones were often the smartest, and she liked to draw them out with questions: "Where do you live?" "Do you have a boyfriend?" "Do you want to get married?"

Vene Spencer (*middle, in white collar*) and her friends, photographed on the town in the 1960s. (*Courtesy of Vene Spencer.*)

If one of those assistants had a dream and the will to make it happen, Helen helped her. If a girl wanted to get her nose done, she recommended the plastic surgeon. (Helen had her nose done at age forty.) "Both Robin and I got our noses fixed, and it was Helen Gurley Brown's doctor," says Vene, who was going through a divorce at the time. "She would feature an article about how to move on after a divorce—move on, don't grieve—and there was something in one of the articles that said, 'If there's something you don't like about yourself, get it fixed.'" When *Cosmo* published articles like "Do Be an Actress," they spoke directly to Vene, who lived for doing summer stock and dinner theater and the occasional TV interview, but felt self-conscious about her profile. So, she got her nose fixed—no more bump, no more slump, and she had Helen to thank for it all.

Not that her support was totally selfless. In recognizing their individual talents, Helen got the most out of her assistants, like the time she summoned Vene into her office for an impromptu rehearsal. They rarely spoke one-on-one, and Vene worried that she had done something wrong as she walked down the hall, but Helen quickly explained what she needed. She had been invited back as a guest panelist on the game show *What's My Line?* (In December 1966, along with show mainstays Arlene Francis, Steve Allen, and Bennett Cerf, she had to guess the identities of a tour guide to the Egyptian pyramids, a maker of billiard balls, and Steve McQueen.) Everyone in America would be watching, and she had to be prepared. She wanted Vene to run lines with her—a practice session, a trial run before the taping.

For the next couple of hours in Helen's office, they played *What's My Line?* Vene took on different identities, and each time Helen asked questions trying to uncover her occupation. Once in a while, Helen broke in to compliment Vene's responses, but she didn't appear to be having fun. It wasn't just a game; it was a test, and one she had to win. "She wasn't taking any chances," Vene says. "She didn't want to go on and make a fool of herself. It was work. This was her public image that she had to maintain."

At the end of their session, Vene got up to go back to her office, and Helen opened her desk drawer.

"I hope you will accept this as a little token of my apprecia- tion. You were *wonderful*," she said, handing Vene a small package. "You're still young. You can get away with this."

"Thank you so much," Vene said, opening the package to find a pair of sequined false eyelashes. "They are lovely."

"I was laughing to myself, thinking, Where am I going to go with these?" Vene says now. "But it was so typical of her. She was very feminine. Everything about her—except her work ethic."

VENE WAS A valuable assistant, but she proved herself to be indis- pensable after Bill Guy had a heart attack in the office. One min- ute, everything was fine, and the next he was panting: "Loosen my tie! Loosen my tie!"

Unsure of what to do next, Vene went screaming down the hall. Somebody called an ambulance, and suddenly her boss was being carted off on a stretcher. Over the next few days, Vene visited Bill at the hospital and kept him up to date about what was happening at the office. As the days of his recovery turned into weeks, she started doing his job in addition to her own. "I was buying the fiction, nego- tiating with the agents," she says. "Actually, when he was sick in the hospital, we got submissions that really interested me. Among them was Joyce Carol Oates." Bill never liked her style—too downbeat and dark—but Vene loved it, and she pushed one of her short stories through to Helen's desk while Bill was laid up.

Bill eventually came back to the office and worked a couple of hours at a time, but his *Cosmo* days were almost over. When he resigned, Vene quit to fully devote herself to acting. Around the same time, Walter Meade turned in his notice to take a job as managing editor at the *Reader's Digest* Condensed Book Club.

In a matter of months, Helen had lost her fiction editor, her articles editor, and a resourceful assistant. She was sorry to see Vene go, but she was also proud of her. Vene was a true *Cosmopolitan* Girl, seizing the day and the spotlight. When she started landing lead roles in musical theater productions in New Hampshire, Helen was the first to congratulate her on a glowing review and put it up on the bulletin board. Not many people managed to do what they really loved to do *and* get paid for it—and the office couldn't stop talking about her, Helen wrote to Vene, who held on to her letter for nearly fifty years.

33

THE 92 PERCENT

1967

"Everyone has an identity. One of their own,
and one for the show."

—Jacqueline Susann, *Valley of the Dolls*

In 1967, Helen made her TV debut with *Outrageous Opinions*, a half-hour talk show syndicated in eighteen cities. Every weekday at 2 p.m., New Yorkers could tune in to Channel 9 to watch Helen ask famous people about their sex lives. *Casino Royale*'s blond bombshell Joanna Pettet gamely dished about her first real-life girl-on-girl encounter, but more than a few guests were unlikely interview subjects, to say the least. Woody Allen confessed his perverse attraction to mailmen ("Probably the uniform and the leather pouch get me," he joked), while Norman Mailer fielded Helen's questions about his masculinity. "You're the first lady analyst I've ever seen in pink," he fired back.

Canceled after one season, *Outrageous Opinions* was a failure, one of the few Helen ever had. She was faring better at the office, playing Masthead Musical Chairs. In addition to hiring a new art director, a Danish woman named Lene Bernbom, she found a new articles editor, Junius Adams (he later became the fiction and features editor), and she soon hired back Barbara Hustedt, who had graduated from college, to fill Vene's old post as assistant in the fiction department. She let Harriet La Barre focus on editing the travel pages, now that Mallen De Santis was in charge of beauty.

A tall and striking woman with the understated elegance of a *Vogue* editor, Mallen came to *Cosmo* from *Brides* magazine, where she served as editor for one year, after editing beauty features for the teen magazine *Ingenue*. She was also a published author: Her 1963 book, *Bubble Baths & Hair Bows: A Little Girl's Guide to Grooming*, dispensed tips for the eager-to-please child on everything from how to brush her hair to how to wash her little white gloves. Under Mallen, *Cosmopolitan*'s beauty section soon became a grown-up version of *Bubble Baths & Hair Bows*, only unlike the little girl featured in the book, the *Cosmo* Girl wanted to please a man, not her mother.

A graduate of Bennington College in Vermont, Mallen not only knew the latest Coty perfume or cure for stretch marks, but she was well-read in many other areas, and Helen consulted her on matters far beyond the beauty section. "I did what Helen referred to as 'material evaluation,'" Mallen says. In addition to planning her own section six months ahead, Mallen read *Cosmo*'s major stories—the territory of the feature editors—and sent her notes back to Helen, who welcomed the extra set of eyes. ("She really relied on Mallen being her guidepost," says Eileen Stukane, a former features editor, sounding sympathetic toward Helen rather than begrudging of the beauty editor. "She thought Mallen was the staff intellectual. Mallen would sort of make pronouncements, and Helen would rely on her as being the smart one.")

Like Helen herself, the magazine was in a constant state of improvement, and soon she developed a system. *Cosmo* came out once a month, and each issue used up a few dozen ideas, which meant that they needed a fresh crop of articles to assign to writers every week.

Editors were responsible for generating story ideas, which they shared once a week during a meeting in Helen's office. Every four weeks, they reviewed the *last* issue of *Cosmo* to determine what they could have done differently. Looking over a feature on swimsuits slated for May, Helen wished that all of the models had been shot underwater, instead of one on a rock and another in a hammock— but the photographer wanted to vary the scenes, and he had gotten his way. She'd had more success with a writer whom she made revise an article about polygamy—too historical the first time around— but she found plenty of other examples to pick apart.

"Every time an editor sees a new issue of her magazine (unlike the mother who believes her child is perfect), she's apt to decide, 'Oh dear, we really could have been a little more amusing here,' or 'How did we get so boring *there*?'" Helen confided in her readers in her May editor's letter. "She always thinks it could be *better*."

Helen leading a staff meeting in the mid-1960s. She often stood in front of her desk, instead of sitting behind it. (*Copyright © Ann Zane Shanks.*)

◆   ◆   ◆

In January 1967, Helen typed up her first memo to the staff on the subject of writing and editing. It was thirty-five pages. "Everybody—and especially me—needs editing!" she began. Recently, she had seen too many mistakes in okayed manuscripts that editors had passed on to her desk for approval. Rather than sigh and stew in her irritation, she decided to teach her staff to do things her way. She started by laying out twenty-four editing rules to live by. "RULE 1. <u>WRITING SHOULD BE CLEAR:</u> Nobody should read a sentence in *Cosmopolitan* and say *whaaaaaaat?*" It was imperative that *Cosmo*'s articles be accessible to the average girl.

A select few writers could muse on whatever they pleased. To amp up *Cosmo*'s music coverage, Helen hired Nat Hentoff, a music critic known for writing eloquently and eruditely about jazz in publications like the *Wall Street Journal*. Working from home, he had complete control over his column, "*Cosmo* Listens to Records," and he liked the idea of reaching an audience he might not have found otherwise: young women. On a single page, Hentoff wrote about chamber music, bluegrass, flamenco, and Donovan, the latest singer-songwriter to join the scene, with his album *Sunshine Superman*. But even Hentoff, whom Helen admired and personally edited, still had to follow the golden rule.

"She was always interested in clarity. If I used a multisyllabic word, she might say, 'Maybe you could make that shorter,' " Hentoff says now, adding that he once received a similar piece of wisdom about composition from Dizzy Gillespie. "He said it took him most of his life to learn what notes *not* to play."

For Helen, the point was to reach as many people as possible—to enlighten, not to frighten away. Editors of food and decorating features shouldn't assume that *Cosmo* readers owned a soufflé pan or knew what it meant to cut something on the bias. "All instructions for making *anything* should be understandable to a ten-year-old girl," she reminded them. Articles should be inspiring and entertaining, but above all they had to be in service to the reader, and, as always, Helen used herself as a model.

"She edited the magazine for three Helens," Walter Meade says. "For instance, she kept all the how-to stuff, the decorating in particular, really dumb. She would read 'How to Make Your Window Shades out of Wallpaper' very closely, and she would not print something she herself could not do.

"Then there were the super-sexy covers, which was what Helen the party girl *wanted* to be," he continues. "She was ashamed of her small breasts and insisted that her cover girls have ample 'bosoms,' as she always called them. The sexy articles and advice columns were written for that girl.

"The interior well of the book had serious pieces, usually written by very good writers—and that fed her need to be intelligent and wise."

Helen was acutely aware of her lack of a formal college education, and through *Cosmo*, she educated herself and her girls. She gravitated toward erudite people, chief among them David, who sometimes used his own intellectual prowess to school her. ("I just didn't get David in his boutonnière," says Lyn Tornabene. "I thought he was the most pretentious man.") Helen didn't necessarily share her husband's taste for great literature, but thanks to David, she knew enough about the classics to drop the occasional literary reference—and to appreciate one that was well placed in an article. Some writers needed to be studied a little, which was fine as long as the story was worth the time put into reading it. Whether she was writing about marriage or the Maharishi, *Cosmo* contributor Gail Sheehy could do no wrong.

But most writers could do wrong and did. In an article about drinking, for example, a writer might insult an advertiser whose ads ran in *Cosmo*'s pages—they lost several pages of liquor ads that way. ("RULE 22. *DON'T ATTACK THE ADVERTISER!*") In celebrity profiles, too many writers gushed over their subjects—a sure sign of amateurism—instead of really getting to know the person by talking to their friends, family, colleagues, and lovers. In self-help articles proffering advice, they made girlish promises they couldn't keep—"25 men will follow you down the street," for instance—when the point was to give practical tips and set realistic goals that regular girls could accomplish. Worst of all, many freelancers were just lazy, turning in flabby sentences. "Show no mercy toward sloppiness," Helen exhorted, citing some examples of mistakes made in the past. "Edit ruthlessly."

Helen edited ruthlessly, just as she had been edited by David. She liked her sentences as she liked her figure—tight and taut. She commanded the editors to cut sentences in half, to watch out for repeating words, to use complete sentences with subjects and predicates, and to banish clichés. Why not aspire to be a little more like the ad copywriter who had to grab people on their way to work by saying something in a new and surprising way?

Speaking of which, some words were just out: *groovy*, *fun* as an adjective, *gizmo*, and *gals*. Dirty words were another no-no. Calling someone a bastard? Fine. Calling someone a good lay? Not fine. *Cosmopolitan* was a sexy magazine, but its articles had to be tasteful for it to survive. A man could go to bed with a woman, but he could not put his hand up her skirt. They could "make love," but they couldn't have "sexual intercourse," and the writer mustn't use anatomical parts.

Some of these rules might as well have been written on a blackboard in a high school English class. Helen was a stickler about grammar and syntax, and she honored other rules to keep the peace with Hearst management and outside advertisers. When it came to actual editorial content, she took a slightly different tack. On her watch, *Cosmo* published more than a few phony diets and faked letters to the editor.

"It wasn't that we didn't get letters—just that they weren't necessarily as punchy as we might have liked," says Barbara Hustedt Crook, who edited the letters section for years and wrote many of them herself. "I can't remember Helen specifically writing any letters, but have no doubt she did—especially at the beginning, when I wouldn't have been around."

"We made up things all the time!" adds Mallen De Santis, who dreamed up nonsense regimens like the Grapefruit and Hard-Boiled Egg Diet. "In our articles, a lot of the quotes were made up, fictional people. You know, we never really thought much about that. We didn't have to observe time-wasting rules."

HELEN NOT ONLY allowed writers to make up material; she encouraged them, particularly when it came to *Cosmo*'s case histories. "It's pretty tough, as you know, to make 'fake case histories' sound *real*," she told her staff in the same January 1967 memo. While some writers used *only* authentic sources in their articles, she conceded that not everyone had the time or the research skills to "ferret out the 'realies.'" But this was nothing that a little creative reporting couldn't solve. To make her point, she relayed a recent conversation she'd had with George Walsh about a feature on widows. Helen had wanted George to call up the writer, Jane Howard, to ask how long one of the widows had waited to go back to work after the death of her husband. But it would be difficult to get the answer she wanted—the widow in question was a composite of five different girls. "Very good!" Helen wrote. "I hadn't realized she was a 'fake.' The challenge is always to *try* to supply enough details to make the men and women sound real."

Likewise, writers should feel free to change the subject's background—fewer case histories should be set in New York City. Say they were writing about a secretary from Manhattan. Why not make her be from Reno or Raleigh? "Only 8 per cent of our readers live in New York City," Helen reminded her editors. They needed to focus on reaching the other 92 percent.

Who were the 92 percent? They were the girls living in small towns and suburbs across the country, riding buses to work, and blowing their hard-earned money on lunch when they should have been saving up for their first apartments. They were the girls who called *Cosmo*'s offices, looking for some answers and tying up the receptionists with their urgent questions, because they didn't know who *else* to ask about what dress they should wear for a date on Friday night or whether it was okay to call a guy who hadn't phoned for three days. They were the girls who depended on *Cosmo* for advice on how to survive a job interview or an affair.

They were mostly white, but not all. Some were black women who might have been pleasantly surprised to see an article called "The Negro Girl Goes Job Hunting," about the bigotry dark-skinned women regularly encountered while looking for employment. "Hey, beautiful dark girl," wrote Ruth Ross, then an assistant editor at *Newsweek*, "go on out there and get your job!" (Despite this rallying cry, Helen's own staff at *Cosmopolitan* was overwhelmingly white in the late Sixties, a black woman named Mary being the exception. She was known as "the mailroom girl," though she appeared on the masthead as an editorial assistant and took on many other responsibilities, growing close with Helen in later years.)

Other women recognized themselves in *Cosmo*'s first-person essays like "I Didn't Have the Baby, I Had the Abortion," described as "a true story, told by a young woman for whom you cannot help but have sympathy." "I'm still shaking! That girl is me—two years ago," a reader from Boston wrote in. "Everything she said, her innermost thoughts—they were mine." Helen rarely gravitated toward political articles, but certain issues directly affected the lives of her 92 percent, and none more so than the war. Every month, the draft claimed thousands more of America's men—many of them young, white, and middle class.

Helen regularly ran articles about where to find eligible bachelors, and in 1967, Vietnam was an obvious, if ludicrous, place to look. Shortly after more than one hundred thousand antiwar protestors gathered in Central Park to demand a stop to the bombing that April, Helen published a shockingly tone-deaf article selling the glamorous side of Saigon, where a girl could soak up the sun and lap up the attention of so many single young men. What was a little artillery fire in the background compared with the bachelorette's battleground back home?

"COULD <u>YOU</u> WORK IN VIETNAM?" *Cosmo* asked readers in the July 1967 issue. Reporting from Saigon, the writer, Iris George, interviewed several career girls. One was an American Red Cross recreation aide whose responsibilities included going on coffee runs and entertaining the troops with games of charades and tic-tac-toe.

"The boys think we're pretty special," she confided. "You have to watch it. The constant attention can go to your head."

"A stateside girl in Vietnam feels like Miss America," added a program director for the USO. "It's not that we're all beautiful, but there are so many of our men here and so few women."

It wasn't the first time Helen promoted the benefits of looking for men off the beaten path. In *Sex and the Single Girl*, she had recommended taking up sailing, going to AA, or joining a political club (Democratic, Republican, or both) to get a little closer to the opposite sex. She could be shameless, but she really topped herself when she sold the pluses of manhunting in a war zone.

34

NOBODY OVER THIRTY
1967

"The trouble with most teen magazines is that they're too parental. They always seem to be talking down and teaching. *Eye* won't be that way because we're all nearly the same age."

—Susan Szekely, "Nobody over Thirty,"
Women's Wear Daily, December 11, 1967

They came by thumb and by Greyhound bus, braless and barefoot, with feathers and flowers in their hair. Some came because they were disillusioned with the war or with the fight for civil rights or with their parents, and they wanted to be with other people who understood their ideals. Others came because it sounded like fun. They came for free food and free love and free drugs and free music. They came to be free. In 1967, spring break turned into the Summer of Love as tens of thousands of high school kids and college students from all over the country flocked to San Francisco's Haight-Ashbury district, home to Jefferson Airplane, the Grateful Dead, and a new breed of young hipsters who called themselves hippies.

That May, Hunter S. Thompson explained their kind to readers of the *New York Times*—"The word 'hip' translates roughly as 'wise' or 'tuned in.' A hippy is somebody who 'knows' what's really happening, and who adjusts or grooves with it," he wrote—but by then, images of flower children saturated the media, beckoning more than 75,000 young people to join a revolution that started long before they got there.

They'd read about the Human Be-In in Golden Gate Park, where Timothy Leary told a crowd of thousands to "turn on, tune in, drop out," poet Allen Ginsberg led a Hindu chant, and the Grateful Dead expanded minds and the future of music in a cloud of incense and marijuana smoke. They had heard about the Diggers, a group of anarchists and guerrilla theater performers who spread their anticapitalist message by salvaging other people's trash to provide the masses with everything from free stew to Free Stores, where nothing was for sale and everything was for the taking.

By July, the Haight was overrun with gawking tourists and television crews wanting to catch a glimpse of "Hippieland" and the thousands of runaways, many of them barely into their teens, who slept in the park and loitered in the streets, hungry and half-conscious. By October, the same month that *Hair* premiered off-Broadway, the hippie was dead—symbolically, at least. As a final protest, the Diggers led a mock funeral through the streets to mourn "Hippie, devoted son of Mass Media." They rejected the commercialization of their culture, but more important, as one of their members, Mary Kasper, later explained, "We wanted to signal that this was the end of it, don't come out. Stay where you are! Bring the revolution to where you live."

The revolution spread with every joint passed, every postage stamp laced with LSD, every thumb lifted, and every subscription to a new rock magazine that promised to document and celebrate both the music and the movement it spawned. In his editor's letter for the debut issue of *Rolling Stone*, which featured John Lennon on the cover, the young publisher Jann Wenner captured the cynical idealism of a generation: "We hope that we have something here for the artists and the industry, and every person who 'believes in the magic that can set you free,'" he wrote, wary of "sounding like bullshit" should he explain its mission much further.

As promised, *Rolling Stone* spread the magic around the country—along with the message of a movement and a generation that advertisers wanted to reach. In some ways, selling anything to hippies was counterintuitive, but that didn't stop the biggest corporations in the world from trying to cash in on their culture. "If you want to swing college, come to the type-in," Smith-Corona quipped in an ad for its new electric portable typewriters. "Pick a flower. Power. Do a daisy. Crazy. Plant your stems in panty hose," read an ad for Hanes nylons in daisy-printed, fluorescent colors. Canada Dry winked at Timothy Leary with its slogan for Wink, "Join the cola dropouts," while Diet Rite Cola invited everyone to "Join the Youth Quake," not just kids.

At Hearst, Helen Gurley Brown was busy creating a new glossy aimed at the bearded-and-braided set, when she wasn't working on *Cosmo*. A kind of *Life* for college kids, *Eye* would target young men and women between the ages of sixteen and twenty, part of the booming youth market that Richard Deems estimated to be about 26 million strong. He appointed Helen as *Eye*'s supervising editor, until they got the magazine off the ground.

One of their first hires was a thirty-year-old art director named Judith (or Judy) Parker, who had overseen the design of *New York* magazine when it still appeared in the *World Journal Tribune*. Tall and thin with translucent white skin and her long, black hair parted and plaited in twin braids, she was beloved by artists and musicians in New York's counterculture scene. Soon after hiring Judy, Helen found *Eye*'s editor in Susan Szekely, a twenty-seven-year-old Bryn Mawr graduate who would soon change all of her stationery to reflect her married name, Susan Edmiston. When

Hearst plucked her from the *New York Post*, Susan had been writing her own nationally syndicated column, called "Teen Talk." (Around one hundred pounds with dirty-blond bangs, she could have passed as a teenager herself.) Like her supervisor, Susan had no prior editing experience when she took the helm, but she had established herself as a national authority on all things teen, from the mods to the Monkees, and Helen desperately needed a guide.

In September, Hearst announced its plans for *Eye* to the press, and soon afterward, Susan was featured in a big write-up by Eugenia Sheppard in *Women's Wear Daily*, along with a taste of her plans to reach the Now Generation, with the help of "a dozen girls and men all under 30," as Sheppard reported, making no mention of their much older supervising editor. Around the same time, the young staff moved into their new offices, located in an old art gallery just south of Washington Square Park on LaGuardia Place.

Over the next few weeks, Susan threw herself into the epic adventure of editing a magazine for teens, rounding up material for the March issue, *Eye*'s debut. Pete Hamill made a provocative case for drafting women into war, Warren Beatty pondered the pros and cons of the Pill, Lisa Wilson (daughter of Sloan Wilson, who wrote *The Man in the Gray Flannel Suit*) wrote about why she dropped out of college in the States to study abroad in Europe, and *Eye*'s advice columnist answered questions from young readers, hungry for independence.

Unlike *Cosmo*, which sounded like a single person with a singular voice, *Eye* sounded like the generation that created it—and this was a generation that had absolutely nothing to do with Helen Gurley Brown. Then again, she never claimed to be an expert on this crowd. Other than offering some line edits, Helen gave Susan free rein to assign and edit the features she wanted.

Her real issue was with the look of the magazine. Helen wanted it to be slicker and sexier—like *Rolling Stone* meets young *Cosmo*. From the start, she butted heads with the art director, who wanted the design and photography in the magazine to be as experimental as the culture it would be covering. For the first issue, Judy planned a pullout psychedelic poster—perfect for tacking on a dorm room wall—and color-saturated photos capturing the trippy, battery-powered electric dresses of designer Diana Dew. (Among other moody settings, she sent the photographer to shoot models "in the quiet setting of Woodstock, an artists' colony in New York State." The music festival named for the town was still almost two years away.)

Judy also worked on a profile of the model Cathee Dahmen, who was known for her kooky, curly black hair—the result of a permanent that made her look like a cross between Harpo Marx and Betty Boop. On the day of her shoot for *Eye*, Dahmen wore a men's dress shirt with a tie—and at one point, no makeup. Judy loved how she looked naturally and wanted to run the "before" picture of her bigger than the "after," but Helen wouldn't hear of it. "Helen and Richard Deems would come down in the limousine and would look at the layouts," Susan Edmiston says, "and they would *insist* that she use the photo with the makeup as the full-page photo."

Susan stayed out of it. She had her work cut out for her conceiving, assigning, and editing so many articles, but sometimes she heard Helen and Judy arguing in the art department. "I was not really directly involved with the conflict, and, in fact, Judy maybe didn't feel that I supported her enough," she says now. "I believe that Deems and Helen wanted me to oppose Judith, and Judy wanted me to stand with her against them. I was not directly involved in the conflict. I just kept my head down and did my work."

◆   ◆   ◆

UNLIKE *Cosmo*, *Eye* didn't have a prototypical girl. The only constant in the models' looks from month to month was a shot of irreverence. Headlines were flip: "Should a Proper Young Woman of Impeccable Upbringing Wear an Ankle Bracelet?" read an April feature on hippie anklets. In fashion stories, beautiful people modeled irony and an anything-goes mentality as much as the clothes. Girls wore ties and military fatigues, their hair loose and free. Guys wore necklaces and pink-lensed glasses. Occasionally the magazine ran a beauty feature like "Follow the Dots," a guide to painting on faux beauty marks and freckles, but for the most part the emphasis was on being made-down instead of being made-up. Trying too hard, an overabundance of hairspray, and skintight dresses were on the way out. Authenticity and earthiness were in. "You could call it cosmetics of the soul—the art of being as beautiful inside as outside," the rock critic Lillian Roxon wrote of the latest beauty trend.

Eye's fashion editor, Donna Lawson (now Donna Lawson Wolff), wanted her section to reflect the counterculture, not the *Cosmo* culture—Janis Joplin was her idea of a style icon—but Helen wasn't having it.

"I had a meeting with her once—I think Judith was there—and she told me how wrong she felt the beauty and the fashion was," Donna says now. "She tried to explain, and I held fast to my point of view, because I was young and pretty obstinate, but I really felt it should express the kids at the time, and she disagreed: They looked poor, they looked unkempt.

"She was from another generation, and she just didn't get it," Donna adds. "It was beyond her comprehension what we were trying to do."

✦　✦　✦

TWO YEARS INTO her reign, Helen knew exactly what the ideal *Cosmo* Girl looked like—unfortunately, her art department did not. Many afternoons at *Cosmopolitan*, she held a new layout in her hands, crumpled it up, and hurled it into the trash can. If she didn't like a photo, she didn't ever want to see it again, and her photo editors learned not to try to show her the rest of the take. If she didn't like the look of the girl or the style of the dress, it was out.

Nothing angered her more than a failed attempt that she actually had to run, like the August 1967 cover featuring Raquel Welch, who emerged as the sex symbol of the decade after starring in the 1966 adventure film *One Million Years B.C.* Playing a curvaceous cavewoman named Loana, Welch uttered only a few lines, but no one cared what she was saying. Audiences cared about what she was wearing: a teeny-weeny doeskin bikini that clung to all the right places.

With her new role as "Lust" in the campy British comedy *Bedazzled*, Welch was an obvious choice for a *Cosmo* cover girl, but the images from her session with William Connors left Helen cold: He'd given her head shots when what she really wanted to see was Raquel's great body. Wild-haired and wearing nothing more than a patterned orange Fieldcrest towel, Raquel oozed sex appeal from the waist up, but the whole reason for dressing her in a short towel was to show her off from the waist down. "Raquel Welch was to have been shot in full figure," Helen wrote in a memo to her art department after the issue went to press. "This was an opportunity to do something *different* on the cover."

Unfortunately, against the yellow background, the orange towel looked washed out. Plus, they already did bright yellow for April's cover, and they had another yellow one planned for the fall. "From lack of communication and because so many people were involved, I didn't get what I asked for," Helen fumed. She didn't care that some of their regular photographers complained about matching the models' outfits to the no-seam background paper used on set. She wanted hot models in hot "costumes" posing against hot colors—red-on-red, orange-on-orange, pink-on-pink—a different one every month so that readers would know instantly that a brand-new issue of *Cosmopolitan* was out.

On weekends, David tried to lead Helen away from her typewriter, but it was no use—she never stopped working. She went to bed thinking about the magazine and woke up with new ideas about how to make it better, more visually stimulating.

She wanted more color, more optimism, more energy. She wanted more smiling girls who looked, as she wrote in another memo, "*SOFTLY SEXY*," as opposed to *Playboy* girls who looked " 'chippily' sexy" or *Glamour* girls who sometimes looked like tomboys. She wanted more originality in the styling of models—bare arms were sexy, but so were furs and feather boas—and in the magazine overall. Instead of hiring professional models for lifestyle stories, why not use more real-life girls? Instead of letting the article dictate the artwork, why not try it the other way around? A stunning nude photo, a sexy picture of two people kissing, a bold psychedelic design—anything could be a potential launching pad for a story idea.

In general, she wanted "more boy-and-girl-*together*-pictures" showing couples kissing, hugging, and holding hands—and she wanted the chemistry to feel real. Why use a homosexual male model when they could hire a heterosexual one? The point was for the models to look like they enjoyed sex—and like they were about two seconds away from having it. "We are the one magazine for women which can show so much love," she reminded her staff. And while men were an important part of the package, she also wanted to picture beautiful women with a sexual identity and de-sire that were all their own.

Perhaps she explained what she wanted best to the photogra-pher David McCabe, who walked into *Cosmo*'s offices right around this time to hear about his first assignment for the magazine—a lingerie shoot—straight from Helen herself.

The fact that she, and not the art director, would be the one briefing him about the assignment was the first surprise. In his years working for magazines like *Vogue* and *Mademoiselle*, Mc-Cabe almost never met the editors-in-chief—"they were always off somewhere in an office being treated like gods," he says—but Helen was hands-on. And she was very clear about what she wanted for the shoot.

"David," she said silkily, after they had sat down, "I want you to make these girls look, you know, really . . . wet."

McCabe stared at the prim woman before him, unsure if he had heard her correctly.

"You mean, you want me to shoot them in the shower?" he asked.

"No, silly boy," she purred. "I want you to make them look *excited*."

35

THE WORLD'S
MOST BEAUTIFUL BYLINE
1968

"We just wanted *one* cover with somebody with small breasts.
It was sort of chic at the time because we all went braless, but
Helen wanted her bosoms. And man, we never got one sock
thrown to us."

—Barbara Hustedt Crook

By 1968, everyone knew the ideal image of That *Cosmopolitan* Girl. On covers, she wore very little clothing—an orange boa and nothing else, or green crocheted pajamas with peekaboo holes—but whatever she wore was bright. Her style was sexy. Given a blouse, she might lose the top button. Given a tunic-and-trousers combo, she might lose the trousers. Her smile was sultry, not innocent. Her stance was confident, and her gaze was direct. As a rule, her breasts were big, and her hair was long and tousled, though occasionally she wore it in a doorstopper bee-hive or a heap of sausage curls or a quirkily askew updo studded with tiny pink bows. Styles shifted, but Helen remained adamant about one rule. As she later told her art department: "Girls must ALWAYS look man-loving."

For the cover Helen used only professional models, but inside the book she wanted to picture more "civilian girls," at least one a month, especially for beauty stories and lifestyle features on subjects like food and decorating. In general, civilian girls were great for trend stories and career roundups, but no matter the subject, they had to look like the *Cosmo* Girl, attractive and ambitious. After *Valley of the Dolls* came out, Helen ran such a story about girls in publishing. Rex Reed wrote the piece (after firing him as a film critic, Helen hired him on a freelance basis to write other features), which spotlighted Helen's former book publicist at Bernard Geis Associates, Letty Cottin Pogrebin, who posed in a photo alongside her bestselling author Jacqueline Susann. "For a jazzy company, which BGA is acknowledged by competitors to be, Letty is perfect," Reed wrote. "She projects the right image, gives the feeling of *now*."

In 1968, Helen reached out to another young woman who projected the right image and gave the feeling of now: Gloria Steinem. A few years before in *Newsday*, Harvey Aronson anointed her the World's Most Beautiful Byline. "That's it, that's her, that's who. That's Gloria Steinem, the sweet belle of success, the queen of the slicks, and the sweetheart of the slickers," he wrote breathlessly. "That's Gloria Steinem, a career girl who has conquered New York in print and in person." For the July issue, Helen asked Gloria to conquer the subject of her hair for a larger feature all about brunettes. *Cosmo* would illustrate the package with photos of famous brunettes throughout history, including Gloria herself.

Despite her initial misgivings about writing for *Cosmo*, Gloria took the assignment for one simple reason—she needed the cash. She and her roommate had just moved from a cramped midtown studio into a more expensive apartment in the Lenox Hill neighborhood of the Upper East Side. It was a beautiful space, occupying the parlor floor of a nineteenth-century brownstone on a leafy street off Park Avenue, but the rent was high, and Gloria was tired of worrying about money. "I used to get up in the morning and think, Oh, God, we spent ten dollars. Where are we going to get ten dollars?" Steinem says.

Cosmo paid well, so she took the job, sat down at her Olivetti, and pounded out the deepest thoughts she could muster about her hair. She liked it long and loose, and the previous summer, she had bleached two sections of it blond to frame her face.

"I *always* wear a center part," read the final article, which bore Helen's signature italics; "it's my trademark."

GLORIA WASN'T THE first of her friends to appear in *Cosmopolitan*. A few months before, the magazine had profiled her roommate, Barbara Nessim, in an article about working girls with irregular hours. (Barbara, an artist, was featured alongside a professional bassoon player and an owner of a pop-art necktie business.) But unlike other "civilian girls" whose pictures ran in *Cosmo*, Gloria was a semi-celebrity—she had been a recognizable name ever since she went undercover as a Playboy Bunny for *Show*. It wasn't the first time she would be posing as a model, either.

In the early Sixties, working as a contributing editor for *Glamour*, Gloria frequently posed as the girl model, or model girl. In 1964, when *Glamour* sent her to London to interview an emerging star named Vidal Sassoon in his Bond Street salon, she wasn't just the reporter, but the girl in the hairdresser's chair—she was photographed with a sleek new bob. When *Glamour* decided to do a story on how to throw a swinging holiday party, a writer and photographer followed Gloria home to the cramped midtown studio she and Barbara shared at the time and captured their effortless cool. "Gloria and Barbara didn't try to make their apartment into something it isn't," *Glamour* reported. They simply strung up some twinkly white lights, served their guests hot dogs and champagne, put on the Beatles, and frugged their hearts out. "Dear Gloria Steinem," wrote one reader from Atlanta, "How do I get to be Gloria Steinem?"

While working for *Glamour*, Gloria wrote witty articles offering readers advice on how to put up with a difficult man, how to pick up a man on the beach, and how to identify their own personality type and then change it. (When asked about *her* type, she quipped that she aspired to be "Audrey Hepburn in the CIA . . . with bosoms.") She also landed assignments for *Vogue* and the *New York Times*, but the truth was that the career she had cobbled together for herself bore little resemblance to the kind of important writing she once envisioned doing after graduating from Smith magna cum laude. By day she might be writing about textured stockings or tropical vacations, but after hours she was volunteering for political campaigns, attending antiwar demonstrations, and fund-raising for the United Farm Workers Organizing Committee, a group of migrant farmers led by Cesar Chavez and Dolores Huerta.

Gloria Steinem during her days as a "girl reporter," interviewing Michael Caine, the star of the 1966 film *Alfie*, for the *New York Times*. (*Copyright © Ann Zane Shanks.*)

It wasn't until she started writing for *New York*, a magazine that she helped found with editor Clay Felker, that her life and her lifework truly began to merge in her column, "The City Politic." By the summer of 1968, she would be covering the upcoming elections as well as fund-raising and campaigning for presidential candidate Senator George McGovern, whom she would soon join at the Democratic National Convention. But all of that was still a few months away when *Cosmo* came calling.

When she originally agreed to do the *Cosmo* shoot, Gloria thought it would be with the former Cleveland Browns fullback Jim Brown, who had retired the previous year to start an acting career. (One of her first assignments for *New York* would be to profile Brown, who later claimed that they had an affair, in his memoir, *Out of Bounds*.)

"I *knew* him," Gloria says now. "Also, nobody told me that I had to wear anything except my own clothes."

Gloria found a scenario completely different from the one she had agreed to when she arrived at the studio of a young British photographer named Gordon Munro, who worked out of a building at 100th Street and Fifth Avenue. Instead of the football player, *Cosmo* wanted her to pose with the TV actor Vince Edwards, who showed up sporting dark sideburns and a shamrock-green turtleneck, which he would wear for the photo. Though Gloria was under the impression she, too, would be wearing her own clothes, the magazine had another plan for her, and it involved "some truly ridiculous costume with, like, snakes around your breasts or something like that," she says.

Gloria refused to wear the first outfit, but she grudgingly put on the second: a low-cut purple romper with bloomer-style shorts, black stockings, and a bejeweled serpent arm cuff. "I remember her saying, 'You mean I really got to do this?'" says Munro, who ultimately had to satisfy *Cosmo*'s beauty editor, and Helen herself. "I had to say, 'Yeah, you do,' even though it was the editors who were standing over me with the ax. Once she sort of realized that she was going to do it, she did it, and she was great."

Looking back now, Gloria realizes she could have refused the whole setup. She could have walked out, but she stayed. Why? "I'm trying to think of an analogy where the whole thing is wrong and you try to fight for details, when actually you should just forget the whole thing?" she offers. "But it was very difficult. The whole thing was set up, and, you know . . . It was a case in which I was a mouseburger, I think. I just went along with it."

If it had been even a year later, she probably would have done things differently. For that matter, the photographer might have done things differently, too. "I didn't really know who Gloria Steinem was at the time, to be honest," says Munro; he was more familiar with Edwards, who played a doctor on TV's *Ben Casey*. His biggest concern was figuring out how to create an interesting composition using a white set, two models, and a cluster of green grapes—*Cosmo*'s nod to Cleopatra. "They had this idea that Gloria was supposed to be this brunette bombshell, and she was enticing this famous man," Munro says. "She was supposed to be feeding the grapes to him, but [Edwards] didn't like that idea, so luckily it didn't happen."

Munro appeased Edwards, but this picture wasn't about him. It was all about her. Helen wanted a story about a brunette bombshell whose power to entice men rivaled any blonde's. Egypt had Cleopatra. Hollywood had Elizabeth Taylor. New York had Gloria Steinem.

Munro tried to pose her so that she would be comfortable, but the setup wasn't working. "She needed to be able to sit comfortably, which meant she needed a chair to sit in. So, Vince Edwards, I turned him into that chair," Munro says. He told Edwards to bend one knee and to put his arm over it, and Gloria nestled in. Leaning back into her actor-chair, she gazed into the camera. "Chin down," Munro instructed her. "A little bit more. Now look up at me." POP!

When Gloria first walked into the studio in her coat and large sunglasses, Munro thought she was attractive, though he wasn't crazy about long hair. But under the lights, he began to appreciate her beauty: how her blond highlights perfectly framed her face and the feminine way her wrist bent to hold those stupid grapes by Edwards's ear. He felt a familiar stirring, which he experienced when he connected deeply with a subject he was photographing.

"I tend to fall in love for a moment. I definitely was able to form a relationship with her," Munro says nearly fifty years later. "How two-way a street it was, I don't know, but I started to see all the parts of her, the attributes, the shape of her face . . . it began to appeal to me more and more until the picture happened. And then she left."

A FEW MONTHS later, the July issue hit stands, featuring the beauty story, "Brunettes: A Touch of Evil Is Required . . ."

Seeing herself in that horrid purple romper dress cuddled up with Edwards, Gloria was aghast. Then she read the display copy, which introduced her as a "onetime Playboy bunny." "It was a nightmare," Gloria says now. "I remember not going out of the house when those photographs were in. The whole time it was on the newsstands, I thought, Oh, my God, somebody I know is going to see this."

Munro felt so bad about the whole shoot that he offered to take a simple, black-and-white portrait of Gloria shortly before she left his studio that day. "I wanted to make amends for being the guilty party—taking this picture that made her feel so awkward. I thought she was such a beautiful woman, and after I learned about her, I realized how incongruous it was—what my picture was all about," he says.

That picture mortified Gloria. It baffled Munro. But to Helen, it must have made perfect sense. Gloria was everything she admired in a woman: beautiful, brainy, and beloved by men. What better role model for That *Cosmopolitan* Girl?

36

FAKE PICTURES
1968

"That's the whole enchilada, darling. The will to please. That's
the difference between good whores and bad whores—good
wives and bad wives."

—from "The Park Avenue Call Girl"
by Liz Smith in *Cosmo*, July 1968

Around the same time Gloria posed for her photo spread,
Liz Smith was working on a story for *Cosmo* that turned
out to be much more involved than she ever imagined.
Helen wanted her to get an exclusive interview with a high-class
prostitute for a profile, but Liz was having troubled finding girls
who wanted to go on the record. Desperate, she even tried paying
the going rate just to talk, but no one took her up on the offer. The
only person she found who *was* willing to talk wasn't a call girl,
but a faux socialite from the Hamptons named "Nicky." As they
chatted, it occurred to Liz that Nicky knew quite a bit about this
particular line of work, even if she didn't actually do it herself.
During one of their conversations, Liz floated an idea. They could
role-play, just for fun. Nicky could pretend she was a call girl, and
Liz would ask her questions about her life—*the* life. "We'll tape
it," Liz said.

Nicky proved to be the perfect source. Over the course of
the interview, she gave Liz the lowdown on everything from
how much she charged to what kind of birth control she used (a

diaphragm). She also told her how she dealt with johns, got dates with millionaires, passed as a socialite in polite company, and handled her competition: not other call girls, but sweet "civilian girls" who were willing to hop into bed with any smooth guy in exchange for a night of dinner and dancing. "Too much free stuff around competing with us," Nicky whined. "How can you make an honest dollar these days?"

Back at her desk, Liz went for high drama, waxing poetic about Nicky's sun-streaked blond hair, as luxurious as anything coming out of Kenneth's hair salon. Nicky wasn't just any prostitute—she was a prostitute who lived on Park Avenue and made $40,000 in a year, not counting gifts. Sure, she *seemed* tough. She smoked Pall Mall golds, cursed the cops, and delivered brassy bad-girl lines, but it was all an act: An escort didn't spend all that time around the rich without learning a thing or two about how to operate in high society. "The day before at lunch," Liz wrote, "she had toyed with her Dover sole and then smoothly asked the waiter for a bottle of Pouilly-Fuissé."

When Liz turned in her story, Helen went crazy for it. She called it "The Park Avenue Call Girl" and published it in the July 1968 issue, alongside a sexy photograph of the model Heather Hewitt, just a few page-flips away from Steinem's photo spread. The article was a hit, and much later, Liz got a call from the director Alan Pakula. Over lunch, he took out her piece and explained that he was making a new movie with Jane Fonda, *Klute*. Clearly, Liz was an expert on call girls. Would she be an adviser on the film?

Liz turned down the offer and admitted to him that the interview was a fake. Nicky may or may not have been an actual call girl. She just couldn't be sure. "It was the one thing I ever did for Helen that wasn't entirely kosher, and I don't think that she cared," Liz says now. "It was a great feat of imagination on my part—and desperation. I spent a lot of money trying to find a call girl. I offered everybody I knew! I remember I went to a guy who was running Le Club, an early discotheque, and I said, 'I'll pay whatever the call girl wants,' but he was afraid, you know." She laughs. "I was never a good investigative reporter."

THE PARK AVENUE call girl story wasn't exactly Pulitzer-worthy, but to Helen it was *Cosmo*-worthy—whether it was made up or not. Hundreds of thousands of single girls across the country were buying *Cosmopolitan*, and it wasn't for its literary prestige or political coverage. In April, Martin Luther King Jr. was shot in Memphis and cities across America burned. In June, Robert Kennedy was killed in Los Angeles, and a nation mourned the loss of another beloved leader. In August, during protests against the Democratic National Convention in Chicago, police used rifle butts, billy clubs, and tear gas to assault thousands of young antiwar demonstrators and innocent bystanders in a brutal and seemingly orchestrated attack that left blood on the streets. No year came close to the violence of 1968, but to look at a copy of *Cosmopolitan*, one would assume that the most pressing issues in life were cleaning your closet and mastering a recipe for Korean-style chicken.

Helen knew that many of her own editors wouldn't have read *Cosmo* if they didn't actually work there, but the magazine wasn't meant for them—it was meant for simple, small-town girls who might have gotten through a year or two of college at most. These were the girls her editors needed to consider when they brought story ideas to the weekly editorial meetings in Helen's office. For the September 1968 issue, the food and decorating editor was working on that story about clutter-free closets and had found some good tips to share, like how to create the illusion of order by covering everything—walls, shelves, shoeboxes, hatboxes—with red patent-leather plastic, the shinier the better. Meanwhile, Harriet La Barre was following up on a couple of leads for her column, "The Travel Bug." She had heard about a new kind of cruise for single girls who wanted to shed some pounds while they sailed the high seas. American Export–Isbrandtsen Lines was offering the 7-Day Caribbean Cruise, which cost only ninety-eight dollars and included lots of fun-in-the-sun activities, but zero meals—ideal for the budget-and-calorie-conscious *Cosmopolitan* Girl, she explained: "On *this* cruise, you can even board ship with twenty-one cans of Metrecal and a jar of instant coffee; diet your way back through the Caribbean . . . arrive back home sleek, sun-bronzed—and seven pounds lighter!"

Sitting on the love seat in Helen's office, Mallen De Santis contributed some of the tawdriest ideas, all the more surprising coming from someone so elegant. How many ideas did she bring over the years? "Oh, hundreds! Hundreds!" Mallen says now, and laughs. " 'I had an affair with my mother's stepfather.' I mean, you get to the point where you're really scraping the bottom." George Walsh brought the fewest, and Helen brought the best and worst. Over the decades, she contributed thousands. Yes, there were tons of stories about sex, but many of Helen's ideas came directly from her own life, like "FAMILY FISTICUFFS," about the day she hit Cleo in the cab going to the World's Fair in Queens. "One day I found myself taking a swipe at my <u>mother</u> . . . my dear, sweet, little grey-haired <u>MOTHER</u>, for God's sake!" Helen wrote in a memo titled "NOTES ON GIRLS WHO GET HIT OR VISA VERSA." And then there was that time with David. They had been having one of their usual squabbles over tipping—he had given a cabdriver a ten-dollar bill for a six-dollar ride—and Helen blew up. She screamed until he shook her and gave her a light cuff on the cheek. What exactly was it that drove men and women to hit each other?

In later years, editors typed up their story ideas on blue sheets, which were filed in huge loose-leaf binders labeled "major emo" or "major non-emo," depending on their emotional content. Writers who came to the office to meet with an editor could leaf through the blue sheets in the "major emo" binder, reading endless ideas about jealousy, envy, guilt, bottled-up rage, and existential long-ing. Stories like "THOSE <u>OTHER</u> PEOPLE . . . the ones who <u>be-long</u>," a dreamlike meditation on loneliness that Helen considered assigning to one of *Cosmo*'s regular writers or else someone who was "more intellectual," as she wrote at the top of the memo. Wasn't it strange how a person could eat at the poshest restaurants, attend the hottest fashion shows, admire spectacular views from one's own apartment, and still feel like all of those wonders belonged to *other people*? "even when you <u>belong</u> at them . . . or can afford them . . . or have every reason to be there," she wrote, "you feel like one of the people looking <u>in</u> . . ."

Or maybe a better take on a similar idea would be "THE YOU NOBODY KNOWS," a probing piece about people's secret sides. Some girls led double lives. She knew the type: a woman who acted one way around the rich and powerful and another, com-pletely different way around people without money; or a girl who fooled everyone at the office into thinking she was sweet and innocent when, on her own time, she swore a blue streak and slept around. She was a special sort: sneaky, complex, and able to keep up appearances. "now, the reason all this is occurring to me is that *i* am one of the kinky ones," Helen confessed. People in different areas of her life had completely different impressions of her, probably because she encouraged them to see her as they *wanted* her to be—not as she really was. "i just somehow fail to mention to them that they're getting a fake picture," she wrote.

At least one person saw her for who she really was: an actress. "She grew up in an age when movie stars were Joan Crawford, Bette Davis, Barbara Stanwyck . . . women who used guile and seduction to get what they wanted in films," Walter Meade says. "She never struck me as having the personal characteristics of any of the great women stars of her day. It was their techniques she emulated: the crying, the fabricating, the willfulness and egocentricity."

Like Anne Baxter's Eve in *All About Eve*, Helen was willing to do whatever it took to get her way, but she had a vulnerability that reminded Walter of another famous heroine: Scarlett O'Hara. "I think Scarlett is closer to Helen than almost any other image. Except she was beautiful and Helen was not," Meade says. "The point is that, to HGB, life itself was an invention. People made themselves into images that spoke to them so there was nothing amiss in molding a magazine the same way."

37

THE ACTRESS

1968

"To be a woman is to be an actress.
Being feminine is a kind of theater."

—Susan Sontag

In the spring of 1968, a twenty-year-old Barnard sophomore named Linda LeClair made national news for doing something totally mundane—living with her boyfriend. Thousands of college kids had similar arrangements, but Linda also did something they did not: She publicly admitted it. A couple of years after moving into an apartment on the West Side with her boyfriend, a Columbia junior named Peter Behr, Linda was interviewed by a *New York Times* reporter working on a story about the increasingly visible phenomenon of coeds shacking up on campuses around the country.

In her article "An Arrangement: Living Together for Convenience," which ran that March, Judy Klemesrud wrote in depth about three couples, including Linda and Peter, who explained that they were living together because marriage was "too serious a step." They shared a bank account, divided household chores, and didn't bother buying a bed—instead, they had six mattresses on the floor, crash pads for their friends and for themselves. Their parents knew that they were living together, and disapproved, but they may not have been aware of the fact that, shortly after moving in, Linda became pregnant and traveled to Puerto Rico for an abortion. Linda also admitted that, in order to sidestep Barnard's strict housing regulations, she lied on her housing form, claiming that she had taken a job as a live-in caretaker off-campus.

Klemesrud changed Linda's name to "Susan" in the article, but she provided more than enough personal information for college officials to identify Linda and track her down. The college president called for LeClair to be expelled, but angry students protested on her behalf, attracting the attention of the national media. No one was more vocal than Linda and Peter themselves; they handed out leaflets calling their case "a Victorian drama" and distributed surveys asking other Barnard students whether they too had broken housing rules. Three hundred girls answered yes. Many Barnard women resented the double standard—why did they have a curfew, while Columbia men could come and go as they pleased?

Under pressure, Barnard granted Linda a hearing open to both students and faculty, and in April, before the Judicial Council of Barnard College and her peers, she copped to lying on her housing form and living out of wedlock with a Columbia student. But she also read a statement of her own, accusing the college of discriminating against students on the basis of sex, among other factors, and challenging the idea that a school should be able to govern a student's private life. She was old enough to marry without her parents' consent—she should be able to live wherever and with whomever she wanted.

A Barnard philosophy professor took Linda's side, along with two religious counselors, a rabbi and a minister. After deliberating, the council proposed a revision of the housing rules. They also issued a statement against her expulsion, letting her go with a slap on the wrist: She would be banned from using the campus snack bar and cafeteria.

Over the next few weeks, the story of "the LeClair Affair" continued to attract a media maelstrom. Letters poured into the president's office at Barnard. Strangers accused Linda of being a whore and a blight on society, but thousands of students revered her as a hero, someone who finally was exposing the truth about double standards on college campuses—and in society at large.

"A sexual anthropologist of some future century, analyzing the pill, the drive-in, the works of Harold Robbins, the Tween-Bra and all the other artifacts of the American Sexual Revolution, may consider the case of Linda LeClair and her boyfriend, Peter Behr, as a moment in which the morality of an era changed," wrote William A. McWhirter in *Life*. McWhirter marveled at how a girl as "unalluring" as Linda LeClair, with her lank hair and ruddy complexion, could ignite such a firestorm.

The press appointed Linda as an unlikely poster girl for the sexual revolution (her boyfriend, Peter, later became a poster boy for resisting the draft), while others saw her as a radical and a champion of women's rights. To others still, her story symbolized the divide between old and young, the Establishment and those challenging it—a power dynamic that was playing out in the pages of *Eye*, with articles like "Are Your Parents Making You Drop Out?" and "Who's Who in Student Power," a guide to ten students leading the revolt on campuses around the country.

What connection did Helen have to these articles or to the counterculture movement in general? "*None*," says Susan Edmiston, *Eye*'s former editor-in-chief. "I just can't remember any way in which her values were oriented toward young people."

When Berkeley student activist Jack Weinberg said never to trust anyone over thirty, he might as well have been talking about Helen Gurley Brown, but it wasn't only her age that set her apart.

It was everything about her, from the clothes she wore to the four-year college degree she never earned. She was the antithesis of the young idealists who made up *Eye*'s editorial staff.

In June, Susan received a newsletter titled "Notes from the First Year" from a friend who was a member of the women's liberation group New York Radical Women. Growing out of a young but powerful radical feminist movement, the explosive manifesto soon gained notoriety, along with its founding editor, Shulamith Firestone, a twenty-three-year-old rabble-rouser with long black hair, Yoko Ono–style specs, and a fierceness that could border on madness. (She was later diagnosed as paranoid schizophrenic.) One of six children raised by Orthodox Jewish parents, Firestone would become best known for her landmark 1970 book, *The Dialectic of Sex: The Case for Feminist Revolution*, in which she argued that the patriarchal family structure was at the root of women's oppression. (She also called pregnancy "barbaric" and shared a sister's grievance that giving birth was like "shitting a pumpkin.") But in 1968, Firestone was still just warming up. In addition to her primer on the women's rights movement and Anne Koedt's essay "The Myth of the Vaginal Orgasm," the newsletter featured a page devoted to causes and people they supported and rejected. Linda LeClair was filed under "WE SUPPORT." Helen Gurley Brown was filed under "AUNT TOM OF THE MONTH."

Susan didn't especially like Helen, but she got along with her. *Eye*'s art director, Judy Parker, did not. She boldly opposed Helen's ideas and didn't hesitate to take a stand against her. *Eye* had a small staff, and it was no secret that Helen and Judy were a bad match, or that the magazine was struggling. In May, *Women's Wear Daily* caught wind of a rumor that *Eye* was "on the blink." Around the same time, Judy was fired, less than a year after she was hired. The way it happened was especially brutal.

Shortly after the firing, Susan got a call that Hearst was changing the locks on the doors, presumably so that Judy and her boyfriend, *Eye*'s chief photographer, Michael Soldan, couldn't get into the office and steal valuable artwork—a concern that struck Susan as insulting and unfounded. It was a Friday, and they left. That was the last time anyone heard from them. Tragedy struck over the weekend, when Judy, Michael, and another photographer went sailing on Long Island Sound in the middle of a storm, and drowned. Susan got the news from a friend of a friend who called her before information about the accident went public, but it spread soon enough. "I remember hearing that they were on acid, and that the waters were rough," says then–fashion editor Donna Lawson Wolff. "We were all really heartsick about it."

It's possible that drugs played a role in the accident. "Perhaps they were handicapped in handling the boat, or high on the storm experience, and that affected their ability to function," Susan says now. But at least a couple of *Eye*'s young staffers also questioned Helen's involvement, as they grappled with the sudden loss of their friends. If she hadn't been so stifling, if Judy hadn't been fired so coldly, if the locks hadn't been changed . . . maybe Judy and Michael wouldn't have gotten on that boat that day.

In retrospect, it seems unfair to suggest that Helen was somehow responsible for the sad turn of events—people get fired all the time and survive—but all these years later, the theory that she wasn't exactly blameless is still hard to shake.

ONCE THE SHOCK of Judy's and Michael's deaths subsided, the reality settled in, and it was disturbing. Susan already felt disillusioned when she heard that Hearst was interviewing other people for *her* job. When her lawyer advised her to start looking for work elsewhere, she took his counsel and quit.

Along with Richard Deems, Helen personally interviewed thirty-five people, searching for *Eye*'s next art director and editor-in-chief. Meanwhile, at *Cosmo*, she had just managed to hire a replacement for her former features editor Harriet La Barre. She found a star in Jeanette Sarkisian Wagner, who became *Cosmo*'s new articles editor, but with Susan's sudden exit, Helen felt she had no choice but to send Jeanette downtown to edit *Eye*.

She had solved one crisis, but there were countless others, and by August, Helen was close to hysterical. Sitting at her desk one night at seven thirty, she felt sorry for herself for still being at work when everyone else was at home or on vacation.

Usually Helen consulted David about her problems, but he was in California until tomorrow. She needed someone to talk to *tonight*, but she couldn't go to Dick Deems. He was the one who had asked her to get involved with *Eye* in the first place. She didn't want to let him down, but the fact was, she couldn't stand it anymore. Now that Judy and Susan were gone, Helen estimated that *Eye* was taking up nearly a third of her time—time that she desperately needed to spend on *Cosmo*.

At one point Helen tried seeing her publisher, Frank Dupuy, but he was away. So she fed a piece of typing paper into her typewriter and began writing a letter to the vice president of Hearst Magazines, John R. Miller.

"Dear John, I'm in trouble," she began. But where to begin, really? She was so overwhelmed, she wasn't even sure what she needed from him—or so she said. "I seem to be snap-crackle-popping under the strain and it's *not* a case of $5.00 more for this one or add one more secretary or get the fiction editor a raise . . . it seems to be the TOTAL EDITORIAL PICTURE."

Her staff at *Cosmo* was falling apart at the seams. Two secretaries had left just a week before. Another girl had turned in her notice even after getting a raise. They'd also lost an assistant art director and a paste-up girl, and they were about to lose someone else in the copy department who was leaving to have a baby.

Every other day, it seemed, another staffer left *Cosmo* and someone new and green came in. Helen had been searching for months for a decorating editor who could write *and* spiff up a room on a shoestring budget, but she was most upset about losing Wagner to *Eye*, even though she was the one who recommended her for the position in the first place.

Just the other day, she had finally hired a promising text editor for *Cosmo*. Well, it turned out *he* was an alcoholic! Joanne Hearst was another disaster. Helen hired the young heiress to help out in the fashion department, and all the other girls resented her, probably with good reason. Most days, Helen couldn't even find her, and she wasn't paying her $175 a week to disappear. And speaking of vanishing acts, her managing editor was MIA. "Where is George Walsh, my strong right arm?" she asked Miller, before supplying the answer: He'd left at lunch to head to Cape Cod.

George's weekly jaunts to Cape Cod were hardly her biggest concern, but, she confessed, she was beginning to think about replacing him with someone who cared more about the job—and about her sanity. There was always some looming catastrophe keeping her at her desk until 10 p.m. She worked in the office when other people were at home sleeping. She worked at home when *she* should have been sleeping.

She simply couldn't handle it all.

"John, I have told you before I am someone who has to be SAVED from herself," Helen wrote, making sure to mention a couple of job offers she'd had recently. Norman Cousins had asked her to edit *McCall's*, and Mary Campbell from *Glamour* had also approached her. She was bringing it up simply to emphasize her point that good editors were hard to find—and she desperately needed some backup. Something was wrong, and if it didn't get righted soon, she wouldn't last another six months.

As it turned out, it was *Eye* that wouldn't last. Hearst suspended publication after the May 1969 issue. Once again, Helen would be able to focus her attention on *Cosmo*.

38

A Groovy Day on the Boardwalk
1968

"As they glide back and forth across your television set, you can't
help but wonder for a moment if Mary Quant, John Lennon,
Vidal Sassoon and Dr. Timothy Leary ever did happen."

—from "There She Is . . . Miss America," *Eye*, April 1968

Having so winsomely put Miller on notice about her unhappiness—and those other job offers—Helen eventually used *Cosmo*'s newsstand success as a bartering chip for a bonus, while negotiating for a pay raise and a new-and-improved contract. She had no problem playing the damsel in distress, if it helped her get what she wanted from a man, but a new movement was brewing, and its members didn't pretend to need rescuing. They needed a revolution.

In 1968, a civil rights activist named Carol Hanisch came up with the idea of protesting the Miss America Pageant to call attention to the women's liberation movement. Robin Morgan, a poet and member of New York Radical Women who was well versed in guerrilla theater tactics, joined her in crafting a plan and a press release titled "NO MORE MISS AMERICA!"

All were invited to join in a daylong demonstration on the boardwalk, in front of Atlantic City, New Jersey's Convention Hall, where the pageant was being held that September. "The Annual Miss America Pageant will again crown 'your ideal,'"

Morgan wrote. "But this year, reality will liberate the contest auction-block in the guise of 'genyooine' de-plasticized, breathing women. . . . We will protest the image of Miss America, an image that oppresses women in every area in which it purports to represent us."

Interested participants were encouraged to bring any bras, girdles, and other "woman-garbage" they had around the house to throw into a giant Freedom Trash Can. "Lots of other surprises are being planned (come and add your own!)" the release read, "but we do not plan heavy disruptive tactics and so do not expect a bad police scene. It should be a groovy day on the Boardwalk in the sun with our sisters."

The organizers discouraged men from joining the demonstration, but invited sympathetic husbands and boyfriends to volunteer as drivers. Other women coming from New York City took a bus. By 1 p.m., more than one hundred women had gathered on the boardwalk. Some sang the lyrics of a new protest song written by the folksinger Bev Grant: "Ain't she sweet, making profits off her meat. Beauty sells she's told so she's out pluggin' it." A few of the demonstrators were already famous or would be soon, such as the civil rights lawyer Florynce "Flo" Kennedy and the artist-scholar Kate Millett, but mostly they were unknown members of a still largely unknown cause.

They were white, black, Hispanic, old, young, wealthy, poor, fat, thin, aproned and oven-mitted, blue-jeaned and braless, freckled and wrinkled, long-haired, gray-haired, and Afro-haired. They were housewives, grandmothers, college students, artists, actors, lawyers, scholars, and career activists, and they had heard about the protest in a number of ways, through women's consciousness-raising circles, antiwar organizations, and groups advocating birth control and abortion rights. Many were from New Jersey or New

York City, and some came from as far away as Gainesville, Florida, and Bancroft, Iowa, but they had all come to Atlantic City for the same reason: to expose the Miss America Pageant for the sham it really was.

"Atlantic City is a town with class!" they shouted as they marched down the boardwalk. "They raise your morals and they judge your ass!" As passersby gawked, they waved homemade banners, protesting everything from the pageant to the war. MISS AMERICA IS A BIG FALSIE. GIRLS CROWNED—BOYS KILLED. WELCOME TO THE MISS AMERICA CATTLE AUCTION.

Somewhere, a live sheep bleated—and was crowned and festooned with blue and yellow ribbons in a mock ceremony. Elsewhere, a woman wearing a top hat and her husband's suit conducted a mock auction, selling another woman wearing a miniskirt who had chained herself to an eight-foot wooden Miss America puppet in a red-white-and-blue bathing suit. "Step right up, gentlemen, get your late-model woman right here! . . . She sings in the kitchen, hums at the typewriter, purrs in bed!" she yelled at the crowd. "The perfect model, she doesn't talk back . . . you can use her to push your product, push your politics, or push your war."

It was theater of the absurd, but nothing compared with the absurdity of the pageant that they were protesting—a beauty contest that, since its inception in 1921, had never selected a black finalist. (Later that night, the first Miss Black America would be crowned just a few blocks away in a separate pageant.) Inside Convention Hall, fifty life-size Barbie dolls in various shades of white paraded around in swimsuits and zombie smiles, waiting to be judged on their special talents and ding-dong answers to questions like "How can people live together more peaceably?"

Meanwhile, outside on the boardwalk, demonstrators were throwing items of their oppression into the Freedom Trash Can.

"No more girdles, no more pain! No more trying to hold the fat in vain!" someone shouted, dropping a girdle into the can.

"Down with these shoes!" another woman cried, tossing in a high-heeled shoe.

One by one, they stepped up to the can. A woman sick of doing the dishes slammed in a bottle of gooey pink detergent. Another tossed in a pair of falsies. Gradually, the can filled up with bras, false eyelashes, hair curlers, corsets, tweezers, wigs, dishcloths, and pots and pans.

"Why don't you throw yourselves in there!" shouted a man standing on the sidelines, one of several hundred bystanders. "Go home and wash your bras!" shouted another, in a growing chorus of insults.

They were called communists, lesbians, witches, and whores. But they didn't stop. One mother chucked her seventeen-year-old son's copy of *Playboy*. "Women use your minds, not your bodies!" she yelled.

Someone else threw in a copy of *Cosmo*. The October issue wasn't out yet—if it had been, it might have ended up on the top of the heap. "Why I Wear My False Eyelashes to Bed" and "How Not to Get Dumped on *His* Way Up" were just a couple of the stories advertised on the cover that month.

THE DEMONSTRATORS ATTRACTED tons of press, but the cameras never caught their crowning glory inside the Convention Hall. Just as the former Miss America, Debra Barnes, was giving her goodbye speech, Hanisch and another protestor hung a banner over the balcony, announcing their arrival in all caps: WOMEN'S LIBERATION. As security broke up the scene on the balcony, two other women on the convention floor set off two stink bombs by the stage.

The millions of viewers at home didn't see the chaos; they saw just the tearful face of Judith Anne Ford, aka Miss Illinois, when she was crowned as Miss America for 1969. (An eighteen-year-old gymnast, she won over the judges with her skills on the trampoline and her perfectly sculpted platinum-blond hair.) But the message of women's liberation got through in countless articles about the protest that ran in newspapers around the country in the following days.

Some articles reported scenes of bra-burning on the boardwalk, but while a few women tossed their bras into the Freedom Trash Can that afternoon, nobody ever set fire to one. Still, women's lib soon became associated with "bra-burning," and Helen Gurley Brown, always a friend to advertisers, saw an opportunity to come to the rescue of bra manufacturers everywhere.

After the protest, she assigned an article about the bra industry that included a history of bras and a guide to buying the hottest styles. Want to talk about liberation? Then talk about Rudi Gernreich's No-Bra Bra! Want to talk about change? Check out Pucci's new line of mad, eye-popping prints for Formfit Rogers!

"The WLM can put down bras all they like," *Cosmo* told readers; "most American women are still putting them on."

39

BEFORE AND AFTER
1968

' "We had all these young assistants who were basically secretaries, except they couldn't type or take shorthand . . . they were fertile ground for makeovers."

—former *Cosmopolitan* beauty editor Mallen De Santis

Many mornings, Helen and David took a cab together to work. He dropped her off at her office, and then continued on to his own, a few blocks away. When they didn't head in together, Helen took the bus. She loathed the idea of wasting money on a private chauffeur or a taxi for herself, but that wasn't the only reason why she rode the bus. She wanted to be with her girls: to see what they wore, where they went, what they read. She boarded hoping to see women with their noses buried deep inside *Cosmopolitan*, but her market research met with mixed results.

Millions of women read *Cosmo*, but many preferred not to admit it—including Nora Ephron, who took care to remove her glove if she was reading *Cosmo* on the bus so that her fellow passengers would see her wedding ring. "I have not been single for years, but I read *Cosmopolitan* every month," she confessed in her 1970 *Esquire* profile of Helen Gurley Brown. "I see it lying on the newsstands and I'm suckered in. 'How to Make a Small Bosom Amount to Something,' the cover line says, or 'Thirteen New Ways to

Feminine Satisfaction.' I buy it, greedily, hide it deep within my afternoon newspaper, and hop on the bus, looking forward to—at the very least—a bigger bra size and a completely new kind of orgasm. Yes, I should know better. After all, I used to write for *Cosmopolitan* and make this stuff up myself."

In fact, when Nora was still a cub reporter at the *New York Post*, Helen was the first editor to ever offer her a magazine assignment: an article skewering New York's famously catty fashion rag. When "*Women's Wear Daily* Unclothed" appeared in *Cosmopolitan*'s January 1968 issue, it prompted threats of a lawsuit from Fairchild—a sure sign that Ephron had arrived. (Years later, she wrote to thank Helen for giving her the assignment, which she said was "one of the first things I ever did in which I found my voice as a writer.") The same year, Mallen De Santis asked her to undergo a makeover for the magazine.

Nora wrote about her redo in the May 1968 issue in a sequence of short, funny diary entries that accompanied her before-after transformation. In her article, "Makeover: The Short, Unglamorous Saga of a New, Glamorous Me . . . ," she gave a blow-by-blow account of the experience, from deciding on a new "nighttime look" with Mallen to arriving at Lupe's hair salon the following day to be styled by the famous high-society Spanish hairdresser. Flourishing a pair of solid-gold scissors, Lupe told Nora his vision for her hair: "de ringlets in de front and de shaggy in de back."

Nora allowed "de ringlets in de front," but ultimately nixed "de shaggy in de back" because it would take two years to grow back her hair if he chopped it all off. Three hours later, with her hair washed, cut, and set with rollers, she joined Mallen and the photographer in a limo headed to his studio, where the makeup artist would take over. After examining her closely, he decided she was "not pretty-pretty" and pointed out everything that was wrong with her face. ("Told me my face too narrow, eyebrows too arched, chin too long," she later recounted.) He then went about correcting it through the magic of makeup and contour.

At the end of the day, Nora left the photographer's studio with glued-on lashes and bright red lips, as well as a seemingly wider face, softer brows, and shorter chin. She wrote the last entry of her makeover journal the next morning: "Ringlets have lost curls. False eyelashes sitting in medicine cabinet. Old me back in the mirror—the last person I expected to see."

In 1968, Nora Ephron already had a recognizable byline, but many of the makeovers that ran in *Cosmo* were of complete unknowns. For her makeover models, Mallen De Santis didn't go through an agency. She simply walked down the hall.

Day after day, *Cosmo's* young assistants came to the office with oily skin, split ends, and bad dye jobs. "What'll I do? My hair's a mess," a receptionist named Sandy said one day, poking her head into the beauty department. After getting her brown hair professionally streaked with blond highlights, Sandy spent one too many nights home alone with a bleach bottle, and now her hair was three different shades of bad. Sandy's before-and-after makeover story ran with the headline "The Great Hair Disaster . . . And How to Recover!"

Everyone was a potential model, and once in a while, Mallen used someone truly beautiful, like *Cosmo's* art director, Lene Bernbom, who insisted on hiding her thick blond hair under a hat with a chinstrap. (Mallen's stylist gave her a fat ponytail with Dynel sausage curls by Tovar-Tresses.) Mostly, though, she went for plain girls, and the more lackluster the better. "The simple process was to make them look as awful as possible for the 'before' pictures and then make them absolutely glamorous for the 'after' pictures," Mallen says. "The best makeovers were the very bland, mousy girls who you could take and really pile on the makeup and the hair—then they'd look wonderful."

Some girls needed a complete overhaul, like Lynn Foss, "a pretty little mouse of a girl who had all the potential of a sexpot," according to *Cosmo*, "but whose fires were banked by her captain-of-the-girls'-hockey-team exterior." After being further undone for her "before" shot, she was shipped off—along with a blue-sequined dress and a frightening black wig—to the photographer's studio where she was redone by a superstar hair-and-makeup team on loan from Revlon.

Other girls simply needed some fine-tuning and fixing. When Barbara Hustedt walked into a metal stanchion in the subway, chipping her tooth, Mallen saw an opportunity to bring her to a dentist who had just started using epoxy resin as a tooth filler. Someone else's big Dumbo ears were the perfect excuse for a surgical procedure called otoplasty. Another assistant had terrible acne that was cleared up after several visits to Christine Valmy's skincare salon. After her redo story ran, *Cosmo* received more than a thousand letters about it.

Why use real-life models? The idea was that *Cosmo* readers had a lot in common with *Cosmo* staffers and contributors—"same age, same dreams, same potential," Helen explained in one of her columns. But they didn't. Not really. *Cosmo*'s core readers were simple, working-class girls who considered the magazine to be their bible and Helen Gurley Brown to be their savior. *Cosmo*'s editors were sophisticated, college-educated women and men who already knew where to put the dessert fork on a dinner table.

Mallen worked for Helen for almost twenty-five years. During that time, she dramatically expanded *Cosmo*'s beauty coverage to include cosmetics as well as plastic surgery, dentistry, nutrition, and fitness—all important fields for advertisers. She became an expert at channeling Helen's voice through her ear, and she instinctively knew what Helen wanted for articles. Mallen pitched and guided many of them herself.

Are there any stories she's particularly proud of now? "No," she says, after a pause, "I don't think so.

"All the senior editors knew it was kind of a lark, which did not mean that we didn't do our jobs very well," she adds. "My personal life and personal belief had very little to do with the job. It was frivolous, and a lot of my friends thought it was silly that I was working there, but it was a good job. I enjoyed it, I was well paid, and that was it."

A Viper in the Nest
1969

"You can't really talk about bosom techniques without *talking* about them."

—Helen Gurley Brown, "Step Into My Parlour,"
October 1969, *Cosmopolitan*

After Nora Ephron skewered *Women's Wear Daily* in *Cosmopolitan*, *Women's Wear Daily* skewered *Cosmopolitan* right back. How could anyone resist? Helen provided endless material, and along with Jackie O, she soon made regular cameos in the pages of *WWD*'s gossip column, "Eye." In October, the "21" crowd read all about Helen's recent request for her own private john, which Hearst promptly turned down. The exploits of "Mother Brown" were always worth a good laugh.

And so was *Cosmopolitan*. "Nobody took it seriously, let's face it," says Gloria Steinem. "I mean, I would always fight for it on the grounds that it was at least allowing women to be sexual, even though it was to gain approval, and it wasn't exactly self-empowered. But, still, it was a big thing."

Cosmopolitan may have been a joke to the city's media elite, but for countless readers across the country, the magazine was a lifeline, especially when it came to questions about sex and relationships of all kinds. Who else were they going to turn to for answers about how to turn a guy on, or how to cope with an overbearing mother?

At forty-seven, Helen had plenty of advice to give, but she wasn't single, and she wasn't young. When *she* needed answers, she floated down the hall to talk to one of her single-girl assistants or editors: "Robin, would a *Cosmo* girl think like this? . . . or dress like this? . . . or be attracted to this man?" She'd never understand certain attractions—the popularity of the band Cream, for instance—but she counted on her staff to keep her in touch with the times, and they came to expect her informal surveys. "Give me your definition of a bitch," she once prompted. Another time: "Have you ever dated a very wealthy man?"

The press ridiculed *Cosmo* for its endless articles on how to please a man, but Helen was just as interested, if not more, in finding out how men could please women. For the June issue, Gael Greene wrote a feature on how to cope with male impotence—after all, it affected women, too. "Has a woman's magazine ever dealt with the subject of impotency before?" Helen asked her readers in her editor's letter that month. "I'm not sure . . . but we all know it isn't only the *girls* who are 'frigid.' I think you can discuss almost *any* subject if you do it with honesty and in good taste."

Naturally, for a feature on foreplay scheduled for July, she turned to the women on her staff. She wanted to know about their breasts—specifically, how they liked to have them caressed. For too long, men had been mishandling women's breasts, but no one ever talked about it. Well, it was time to fix that. The memo to her female staffers was supposed to be confidential, a private conversation among girls. That's why she addressed it the way she did:

TO   Girl Staff Members

FROM   Helen Brown

SUBJECT

We are doing an article on how men should treat women's

breasts in love-making. It will either help us sell another hundred thousand copies or stop publication of *Cosmopolitan* <u>ALTOGETHER</u>!

They were free to send in their responses anonymously, and if they chose not to respond at all, she would just assume they thought it was none of her business. As for those who did choose to respond, she wanted to know: What pleases them when a man caresses their breasts? What do men do that they think is wrong? Why do they think that some girls don't get as much pleasure as they *should* get out of this kind of foreplay? Perhaps they're too self-conscious about their bosom size, et cetera. Finally, did they have any personal experiences to share? Maybe someone had a friend who didn't like having her bosom caressed, but then learned to enjoy it? "If we do this tastefully and with real insight," she concluded her memo, "the article is going to help a lot of men make a lot of girls more happy."

Helen left it to her senior editors to assign 99 percent of *Cosmo*'s articles to their writers, but the issue of men mistreating women's breasts was too important, and she decided to assign the story herself to a writer in California. The woman took her best shot, musing on love and relationships, but her article lacked what Helen wanted most: specific techniques that men and women could *use*. "This is your personal reminiscence of all your love affairs, and fascinating as it is, it doesn't have *anything* to do with boobs," Helen told her. "I know," the writer conceded, before asking if Helen could supply her with any material.

Shortly after that call, Helen sat down to write her memo.

LINDA COX HAD just started working as an assistant art director when Helen's bosom memo landed in her hands, and she could hardly believe what her new boss was asking of her—it wasn't any of her business! The whole memo really had to be seen to be believed, and on her way out of the office that evening, she quietly tucked it into her bag to share with some of her friends from her last job. They'd get a kick out of seeing how much her life had changed. Before a headhunter sent her to *Cosmopolitan*, Linda had worked as an assistant art director at *Holiday*, a slick magazine for the Jet Set, featuring the best writers and photographers out there. (One photographer, Slim Aarons, became especially well known for shooting the rich and famous in their haute habitats around the world.) Some former coworkers were throwing a dinner party at Trader Vic's in Midtown to say a belated goodbye to her and another former staffer, the writer Marilyn French, who had moved on to *Newsweek*. Linda couldn't wait to see their faces when they heard Helen's request, and as they started to drink, she broke out the memo.

"It was passed around, and we got a lot of laughs out of it, and that's kind of the end of the story," Linda says now. Except it wasn't. As Linda was putting the memo back into her bag, a former coworker from *Holiday*'s art department asked to borrow it. She wanted to show it to her boyfriend. One too many of Trader Vic's famous Scorpions made Linda say, "Sure."

Over the next few days at *Cosmopolitan*, the girls turned in their responses about what they liked ("feathery touches") and what they didn't ("no feeling-the-melons pinching"). Helen was thrilled. All of the girls had written back, except for two, and she had gotten what she had asked for: real feedback from real girls. Bolstered by their insight, she assigned two different writers to the story—the California writer had disowned it by this point—and they produced a fantastic piece, combining their material with hers.

The story was back on track when Helen heard that someone had leaked her memo to *Women's Wear Daily*. Around mid-March, an excerpt of the memo ran in its gossip column. "BROWN STUDY: Eye is in receipt of a 'memo' by Cosmopolitan editor Helen Gurley Brown to her 'girl staff members' announcing preparation of an article on 'how men should treat women's breasts in lovemaking,'" the item began, mocking her serious inquiry into the matter.

All it took was an inch of space to reduce what could have been an act of public service into a public joke—and Helen wasn't laughing. "She was *outraged*," says Barbara Hustedt Crook, who had answered the bosom memo herself. "She stuck a note on the bulletin board—in her own quirky typing—that started, 'THERE'S A VIPER IN THE NEST!!!!!' I can still hear the ice in her voice, discussing it."

"The person responsible would be immediately fired," adds Linda Cox. "We were all shocked that someone would actually leak information to another publication and buzzed about who could possibly have done it. We thought it was a terrible thing to do and anyone who had any connection to *WWD* was suspicious. My friend who had just started at *Newsweek* called when she saw the *WWD* item. I said, 'Isn't that awful? Helen is going to fire whoever leaked it.'"

Helen intended to flush out the culprit, and the staffers had their suspicions.

A few people said it was possibly the decorating editor, Karen Fisher. Other people speculated that Helen herself planted it for the press, but that would have been self-sabotage—*Cosmopolitan* already had printed a teaser for the story in the back of the June 1969 issue, "WHAT MEN SHOULD KNOW ABOUT WOMEN'S BOSOMS."

Along with everybody else on staff, Linda wondered who it

could be. Just to be safe, she called her friend in the art department at *Holiday* and asked her to send the memo back. "She said she would right away. When a few days passed and I still didn't have it, I began to get upset and called her again," Linda says. "She finally admitted what had happened. A photographer, Slim Aarons, had seen it on her desk and picked it up and, as a joke, took it to his pals at *Women's Wear Daily*."

Realizing the part she had played in the whole mess, Linda felt sick. "Helen was still livid, and I was too new and too scared to tell her what had happened. I didn't want to lose my job," she says. "Then *Newsweek* ran the blurb with the additional information that the guilty party would be fired. Oh my God!"

Linda decided not to tell Helen what happened. "I could never, ever face Helen," she says. "Every time she called me into her office, I would almost throw up I was so scared. I never knew when the ax was going to drop."

Not long after the leak, Helen told her version of the story to Nora Ephron in *Esquire*. "This big brouhaha started because this little bitch, whoever she was, sent the memo to *Women's Wear*, and I would still fire her if I knew who she was," she vented.

After Hearst executives got wind of the bosom memo, they demanded to see a copy of the article as soon as it was finished, and now they weren't letting her run it—too graphic. "The actual use of anatomical words bugs them," Helen told Nora. "Well, you cannot talk about love and relationships when you're talking about how to handle a breast. . . . You've got to say a few things about what to do." Helen didn't blame her bosses, at least not publicly. They were just scared of getting too much flak. They were worried about alienating more readers, about stirring up more trouble with conservative supermarkets in the South. She would try running the article again, once the uproar died down.

"We've decided to wait for a bit to publish this one," she explained to her readers after the bosom story failed to appear in the July issue, as advertised. "Now, nobody around here is a puritan (are you kidding?!), but sometimes an article is a bit ahead of its time."

BY NOW HELEN had learned how to work around her bosses instead of working against them. She appeased and pleased, flattered and flirted, and while she frequently got what she wanted for *Cosmo* eventually, her power had its limits in a corporate culture dominated by men.

In June 1969, Hearst threw a party to celebrate company president Richard Berlin's fiftieth anniversary at the corporation. In addition to the Hearst editors and executives who attended the bash, friends like President Nixon, the Duke of Windsor, and J. Edgar Hoover submitted tape recordings to be played for the audience.

Helen wasn't there because she wasn't invited. And she wasn't invited because she was a woman. Even Berlin's own wife, Honey, wasn't welcome. Berlin later wrote a note to Helen, apologizing for the fact that no female executives were allowed to attend the event—the boys, he explained, wanted it to be "a stag affair."

41

WOMEN IN REVOLT
1969–1970

"One of the first things we discover in these groups is that personal problems are political problems. There are no personal solutions at this time. There is only collective action for a collective solution."

—Carol Hanisch, in her 1970 essay, "The Personal Is Political"

On March 21, 1969, nearly three hundred people filled the basement of Washington Square Methodist Episcopal Church to witness an unforgettable event. Located in the heart of Greenwich Village, the church was known for its radical politics, and for sheltering deserters throughout the Vietnam War. On this particular evening, it gave refuge to another maligned group—women who had gotten abortions, many illegally, making them criminals in the eyes of the law. The event was organized by Redstockings, a radical women's group cofounded by Shulamith Firestone and the writer Ellen Willis. The previous month, Redstocking members had infiltrated a New York State legislative hearing on abortion law reform, hoping to be heard as "the real experts on abortion," but the committee rebuked them, depending instead on the testimonies of its own members: fourteen men and one nun. (Ultimately, three women were allowed to address the committee that day, but the protestors were not satisfied with the token coda granted to them.)

Shut out, Redstockings decided to host their own hearing

instead. "Abortion: Tell It Like It Is" was billed as a one-act play that would be followed by personal testimonies. For the first time in public, women would tell the truth about their unplanned pregnancies and illegal abortions—about the borders crossed, the surgeries botched, the fears of being found out and judged.

That March evening in the church basement, the crowd listened to twelve women share their stories over the course of three hours. One woman told how, after a desperate search, she found a hospital that would give her a therapeutic abortion, but only if she agreed to be sterilized at the age of twenty. Another woman had to pretend she was mentally unstable before being granted an abortion—and confessed that going through with it was the sanest thing she'd ever done. At one point a Redstocking commented, "I bet every woman here has had an abortion."

Many women in the audience had endured abortions themselves, but chose not to step up to the microphone, not yet. "I was one of those who kept quiet," Susan Brownmiller later wrote in her memoir, *In Our Time*. "I chose an easier path and played *Village Voice* reporter." Another journalist was there, too. Sitting on a windowsill, wearing aviator glasses and a miniskirt, Gloria Steinem was covering the speakout for her "City Politic" column in *New York*.

Gloria had gotten an abortion in London after graduating from Smith. Like Brownmiller, she wasn't ready to talk about it, but as she listened to the testimonies, she realized that her story fit into a much larger one that hadn't been voiced, until now. After the event, she typed up her article, "After Black Power, Women's Liberation," a witty, well-reported survey of feminist groups and actions around the city, including the abortion speakout hosted by Redstockings. Aiming for objectivity, Gloria left her own emotions, and her own abortion, out of the article—but despite her impersonal tone, this story was very personal. Years later she would look back on that evening in the church basement as a crucial moment in her feminist awakening.

"Suddenly, I was no longer learning intellectually what was wrong. I knew," Steinem later wrote in her book *Outrageous Acts and Everyday Rebellions*. "If one in three or four adult women shared this experience, why were each of us made to feel criminal and alone? How much power could we ever have if we had no power over the fate of our own bodies?"

A FEW DAYS after the speakout, the *Village Voice* published Brownmiller's article, "Everywoman's Abortions: 'The Oppressor Is Man.'" The piece included definitions of new terms for the unenlightened reader. One of those terms was *oppressor*—another word for man. Brownmiller also gave a quick primer on consciousness-raising circles, the leaderless, free-form support groups that encouraged members to tell the truth about their lives—their inner lives, especially—in the company of other women. By the early Seventies, "c.r. groups" and "rap groups" were popping up around the city, in borrowed office spaces downtown, apartments on the Upper West Side, and Brooklyn brownstones. In groups both large and small (but preferably small to create intimacy), women talked about their childhoods, marriages, and sex lives—airing their deepest secrets and insecurities.

It was at her weekly consciousness-raising meeting that Judy Gingold, a Marshall scholar working as a researcher at *Newsweek*, had an epiphany that eventually sparked a revolt. Her group of eight included an assistant at NBC, who voiced her feeling that she could get ahead in her career if only she were better at it. "Everyone was saying the same thing—'if I were better, I would get ahead.' All of us in that room felt inadequate," Gingold later recalled in Lynn Povich's book *The Good Girls Revolt*. "And that's when I thought, wait a minute, that's not right. It's not because we're undeserving or not talented enough that we aren't getting ahead, it's how the world is run. It made me see that the problem wasn't our fault—it was systemic."

At *Newsweek*, Gingold was one of many highly educated women assigned to low-prestige and low-paying jobs. They compiled newspaper clippings, fact-checked articles, sorted mail, fetched coffee, and answered to "sweetheart" and "dolly." Many had ambitions far beyond the research department, but they kept them in check. After all, the writing and editing jobs they coveted weren't available to them—they were given to men. In the fall of 1969, a lawyer friend told Gingold that what *Newsweek* was doing was illegal—the Civil Rights Act of 1964 prohibited segregating jobs by gender. Over the next few months, Gingold discreetly spread the message to her female coworkers around the office, recruiting allies as they passed her desk or reapplied their lipstick in the ladies' room. Soon they had a lawyer—a pregnant civil rights activist named Eleanor Holmes Norton, then assistant legal director at the American Civil Liberties Union—and a solid case. In 1970 there were more than fifty men writing for *Newsweek*, but there was only one woman.

On March 16 of that year, forty-six female employees held a news conference to announce that they were suing *Newsweek* for sexual discrimination, after filing a complaint with the Equal Employment Opportunity Commission. It would take two years and another lawsuit before the case was settled in their favor.

THE SAME DAY that the lawsuit was announced, the new issue of *Newsweek* hit stands. The eye-catching red-yellow-and-blue cover featured an illustration of a naked woman bursting through the female gender symbol ♀ and the headline "Women In Revolt." The former "dollies" who brought the suit against *Newsweek* cleverly timed their press conference to coincide with the release of the magazine's first major article about the burgeoning women's movement—but they were hardly the only women in revolt. Two days after their press conference, Susan Brownmiller (a former *Newsweek* researcher) led another group of women who were ready to confront their oppressors. On March 18, around two hundred women invaded the Hearst offices of *Ladies' Home Journal*, cornering the editor-in-chief, John Mack Carter, at his desk.

The *Journal*'s slogan was "Never Underestimate the Power of a Woman," and yet month after month, the articles and advertisements that typically ran in the magazine underestimated both the power and the intelligence of women readers. Seven years had passed since Betty Friedan had published *The Feminine Mystique*, and magazines like *Ladies' Home Journal* still presumed that women had nothing better to do with their time than clean the house, pretty themselves up, and have dinner and a fresh martini waiting when their husbands got home.

It was time to put an end to celebrity profiles like "Joanne Woodward: The Care and Feeding of Paul Newman" and fashion features like "Dressing for the Men in Your Life." It was time to stop assigning disingenuous self-help articles that were really thinly veiled ads for whatever was the new-and-improved freezer or pantyhose or hair dye of the month. Most important, it was time to hire a staff of women, including nonwhite women, and let *them* determine what kind of stories were important. The protestors were fed up with the image of silly, childish wives depicted in the *Journal*'s recurring column "Can This Marriage Be Saved?" when what women *really* needed to know was how to get a divorce. Or an abortion. Or how to have an orgasm.

"We demand that the *Ladies' Home Journal* hire a woman editor-in-chief who is in touch with women's real problems and needs," Brownmiller began.

One by one, she and another organizer read off the rest of their demands in front of a crowd that included reporters as well as members of Redstockings, New York Radical Feminists (a successor of New York Radical Women), and the National Organization for Women (NOW).

"The Women's Liberation Movement represents the feelings of a large and growing mass of women throughout the country," she continued. "Therefore we demand that as an act of faith toward women in this country, the *Ladies' Home Journal* turn over to the Women's Liberation Movement the editorial content of one issue of the magazine, to be named the *Women's Liberated Journal*."

In the days leading up to the event, Brownmiller and the rest of her sit-in steering committee alerted members of the press about their plans and even cased the *Journal*'s offices. Even if he had caught wind of the plan, Carter, a soft-spoken southern man in his early forties, couldn't have anticipated that he would be spending the next eleven hours in a room with dozens of angry women who had been planning his exit with military precision.

But as they talked, he listened, and his office began to feel more like a giant living room. Clusters of women snacked sitting on the floor and picked through Carter's box of cigars. They also grabbed their fifteen minutes of fame, hanging a "Women's Liberated Journal" banner outside a window and airing their grievances to reporters they had invited from outlets like CBS, NBC, and the *Washington Post*.

Gradually, individual demonstrators spoke up. They talked about their own lives and their mothers' unfulfilled ambitions. At one point, Carter, dressed in a suit, got up to sit on his desk, where he could see the women's faces more clearly.

Everything was going according to plan until Shulamith Firestone and another radical, Ti-Grace Atkinson, barreled toward Carter, shouting that they were going to push him out of the window. "We can do it—he's small," Firestone said, seconds before leaping at his desk. Reacting swiftly, a Redstocking trained in judo intercepted her before she could hurt him. "He was a quiet little man—and he just sat there," says Jacqui Ceballos, a NOW member and mother of four who watched the scene in awe. "They were moving towards him, and Susan and the others pushed them back. They didn't go there to throw him out of the window—they went there to change the magazine and get their articles printed."

Despite their best attempts, they didn't get Carter to resign. But by 6 p.m., the editors of the *Journal* agreed to look into hiring more women. (Three years later, the *Journal*'s managing editor, Lenore Hershey, became its editor-in-chief.) They also agreed to give members of the women's liberation movement eight pages of the August issue and $10,000 to fill it as they pleased. As promised, the summer issue included a special insert—unedited—written by thirty of the protestors, who covered subjects including divorce, childbirth, and consciousness-raising.

Plans were already in the works for a new column, "The Working Woman," by Letty Cottin Pogrebin, who left Bernard Geis Associates after nearly a decade to write her own book, *How to Make It in a Man's World*. (Doubleday published it in 1970, the same year as Kate Millett's *Sexual Politics*. As it happened, Pogrebin and Millett shared an editor, Betty Prashker.)

A mother of three, Letty eventually used her national platform to challenge the idea that a working woman should *have* to adapt herself to a man's world—on the contrary, the world should adapt itself to working women who needed affordable child care, among other considerations—but when she first signed on to write for the *Journal*, she says, she was still just "a baby feminist" with a lot of growing to do.

"My editor at Doubleday warned me that I was going to be attacked by women's libbers and I asked, 'Who are they?' I was oblivious," Letty says. "She gave me Kate Millett's manuscript. . . . I was just learning. I was just opening my eyes." By the time her byline started appearing in the *Journal*, "I was an absolute rabid feminist," she says. "I insisted on being free to say anything I wanted in my column. I wrote it for ten years."

The demonstrators had wanted to target a women's magazine with a man at the helm, and Carter had been an obvious choice, but they threw out other names early on. At one point, someone suggested Helen Gurley Brown.

"I think we passed over it very quickly because we could not say she was the enemy," Brownmiller says. "*Cosmopolitan* was so much one woman's brainchild. She had a successful formula. The circulation statistics were her biggest buttress. Why should she change it?"

42

THE STRIKE
1970

"The feminist movement was so joyous. Even with the shit we
went through, nothing compares to the joy that we felt."

—Jacqui Ceballos, strike organizer

Hardly a day passed when someone didn't ask Helen about
the women's liberation movement. Was it a real movement or just a passing fad? What did she make of all those
man-hating militant feminists? And where did the *Cosmo* Girl fit
into all of it? Was she pro–women's lib or against it?

"Like many other women, I've come to respect it late in the
day, thinking at first it was just an attack by a few hostile nut-
burgers who were giving *all* women a bad name," Helen confided
in her readers in her June 1970 editor's letter. True, women's libbers could be absurd in their attitudes toward men, but thanks
to them, thousands of people were thinking differently about all
kinds of issues. Why, for instance, was it assumed that a woman
should do all the housework, even if she worked, too? When women
made up nearly a third of the workforce, why were so many stuck
with menial jobs like cleaning and clerking? And speaking of double standards, she continued, "Why does a man usually instigate
sex when, where, and the way *he* likes it?"

In her own way, Helen challenged the same system that
she had learned how to manipulate long before the women's

liberation movement existed. She asked many of the same questions asked by the leaders of the women's movement, including Betty Friedan. Not that Friedan would have known. She had been boycotting *Cosmo* for years, and soon she would ask the rest of the country to follow suit.

In the spring of 1970, Friedan announced that she was retiring as the president of NOW, the organization she founded in 1966, and she intended to go out with a bang. The previous year, she divorced her husband, Carl Friedan, after years of his cheating and violence destroyed their marriage and, as she saw it, undermined her authority as a leader of the women's movement. "I was finally too embarrassed," Friedan later wrote in *My Life So Far*. "How could I reconcile putting up with being knocked around by my husband while calling on women to rise up against their oppressors?"

In her farewell address, Betty called for a national demonstration and twenty-four-hour strike for equality on August 26—marking the fiftieth anniversary of women's suffrage. From New York City to San Francisco, she envisioned women taking to the streets to demand equal opportunities for themselves in jobs and education; free twenty-four-hour child care; free abortion on demand; and the end to forced sterilization. (In states around the country, poor women of color were being sterilized without giving consent, often while in hospitals or clinics for otherwise routine procedures; many were minors and deemed to be mentally incompetent or otherwise "unfit" as parents.)

"I propose that women who are doing menial chores in the offices cover their typewriters and close their notebooks, that the telephone operators unplug their switchboards, the waitresses stop waiting, cleaning women stop cleaning, and everyone who is doing a job for which a man would be paid more—stop—and every women pegged forever as assistant, doing jobs for which men get the credit—stop," she told a cheering crowd at the NOW convention. "And by the time those twenty-four hours are ended, our revolution will be a fact."

There were just a few crimps in the plan. They didn't have the tens of thousands of demonstrators that NOW promised to reporters, but New York members soon found ways to raise awareness around the march and larger movement. In early August, when Mayor John Lindsay signed a bill barring sexual discrimination in public places, NOW's vice president for public relations, Lucy Komisar, pushed her way to the bar at McSorley's Old Ale House, an East Village pub that had been serving only men for 116 years. Later that evening, a group of about one hundred libbers including Kate Millett and an eighty-two-year-old former suffragette took over the Statue of Liberty, unfurling a forty-foot banner on the pedestal below her feet: WOMEN OF THE WORLD UNITE!

Seizing the Statue of Liberty was as good a publicity stunt as any, but there was still no guarantee that people would show up for the march and strike in just over two weeks. The day before the march, Betty Friedan held a news conference in New York. Backed by the National Women's Strike Coalition, she once again urged women to strike. The coalition also called for women across the country to ban four products that degraded women: Silva Thins cigarettes, Ivory Liquid detergent, Pristeen feminine deodorant, and *Cosmopolitan*, which they said exploited women and made young girls feel like failures if they didn't look like the models in the magazine.

"I can't believe they've been reading *Cosmopolitan*," Helen told a reporter when she was asked for a comment. The magazine was "very pro lib." Perhaps the coalition was objecting to the idea of women as sexual objects and nothing more, Helen added: "I think it's wonderful that a woman is sexually desirable, and I agree that it would be wrong to suggest that that's her *only* attraction."

ALL OVER NEW York, women organized actions to bring attention to the cause. Many of the activists remained nameless in the press, lumped into the labels "women's libbers" or "militant feminists," but a few names stood out: Gloria Steinem. Ti-Grace Atkinson. Kate Millett.

In August, *Time* anointed Millett as "the Mao Tse-tung of Women's Liberation." Before, much of the movement's literature consisted of mimeographed manifestos, but her book *Sexual Politics*—which grew out of a doctoral thesis she had written at Columbia University—reached the masses. Until this year, "the movement had no coherent theory to buttress its intuitive passions, no ideologue to provide chapter and verse for its assault on patriarchy," *Time* proclaimed. "Kate Millett, 35, a sometime sculptor and longtime brilliant misfit in a man's world, has filled the role through *Sexual Politics*." Drawing examples from literature and psychology, she theorized that women were often helpless and compliant because men controlled society. There was only one way to change the power structure: Women had to destroy the patriarchal system that kept them down. It wasn't enough for women to make it in a man's world; they had to claim the world for themselves. "Whatever the 'real' differences between the sexes may be," Millett wrote, "we are not likely to know them until the sexes are treated differently, that is alike."

Scaling to the top of bestseller lists, *Sexual Politics* was the surprise hit of the summer. In Alice Neel's oil portrait on the cover of *Time*, Millett was the face of resistance with her set jaw, heavy brows, and long, wild dark hair.

Although Millett was a reluctant star of the feminist

movement, she received attention wherever she went, and around the same time her sisters invaded the *Ladies' Home Journal*, Millett and another group of feminists took their fight to *Cosmopolitan*'s editorial offices.

"[They] backed me up against a radiator in COSMO's reception room and demanded that I turn over part of the book to them," Helen later recalled. "I said nobody occupied any editorial space in COSMO unless she could write well, and I would have to be the judge of that—we were already a feminist book."

A women's lib group did send in a couple of articles, but nothing really came of them. Unlike John Mack Carter, Helen had no intention of letting an unedited manifesto slip into her magazine, but in the November 1970 issue—three years before the Supreme Court decided that abortion was a legal right in the landmark case *Roe v. Wade*—Helen published an article on one of the movement's key issues, which happened to be one of hers: abortion. Written by Dr. Selig Neubardt, a New York–based obstetrician and gynecologist with a history of arguing for abortion reform, "All You Need to Know About Pregnancy and Abortion" surely shocked many readers, and helped many more, dispensing the facts about a procedure long considered to be a crime.

In the same issue, Helen ran an excerpt from *Sexual Politics*, along with a personal endorsement of the women's liberation movement. "It's hard for me to understand how *any* self-loving, man-loving woman could really be *against* what the movement is *for*: the realization of woman's full potential as an achiever and the end of the patriarchal system whereby men have most of the power," Helen wrote in her editor's letter. Kate Millett was one of the movement's most eloquent members, she continued, and readers could find an excerpt from her brilliant book in this issue. "Miss Millett's book isn't easy reading, but it's well worth it."

It was a peace offering but not an apology—and Helen's refusal to dismantle the cleavage-baring, makeup-wearing, man-crazy *Cosmo* Girl would inspire other protests over the years. There was, for example, the time a group of about twenty women marched into the General Motors Building with plans to invade *Cosmopolitan*. Security blocked them from entering the editorial offices, so they set up shop in the lobby, where they demanded an end to sexist articles and advertising, as well as $15,000 "in reparation" for damages already done.

Another time, Helen came into the office to find a long, beautifully wrapped box, the kind flowers come in, but when she untied the ribbon and opened the box, she recoiled. "I don't know who sent it because it wasn't signed," Walter Meade says, "but it was filled with dead, long-stemmed roses that were spray-painted black. That really hurt her because she understood that people were wishing her harm. They were wishing her hurt in the worst possible way."

IN WASHINGTON, D.C., Boston, Detroit, and San Francisco, local feminist groups planned their own marches and strikes and made their own Freedom Trash Cans. But the world would be watching New York, and despite what NOW told the press, they still didn't have tens of thousands of demonstrators. They didn't even have permission to use Fifth Avenue. Friedan hadn't been able to convince Mayor Lindsay to clear the whole street for a women's march, especially one starting in the midst of rush hour. They could have the sidewalk—hardly enough room for a revolution.

Despite some initial resistance from many feminist leaders, Friedan and her strike committee found powerful support. Among their ranks: Congresswoman Shirley Chisholm; congressional candidate Bella Abzug; Kate Millett; Gloria Steinem; Flo Kennedy;

Eleanor Holmes Norton, head of New York City's Human Rights Commission; and celebrities like Joan Rivers and Gloria Vanderbilt Cooper. At least for one day, various feminist groups were willing to put aside their differences.

In the days leading up to the event, countless volunteers passed out flyers:

WOMEN'S STRIKE DEMONSTRATION
AUGUST 26
FREE Abortion on Demand
FREE 24 Hour Child Care Centers—Community Controlled
EQUAL Opportunities in Jobs and Education

The plan was to assemble at 5:30 p.m. at Fifty-Ninth Street and Fifth Avenue, where they would march seventeen blocks down to Bryant Park for the rally.

On the morning of the strike, New York's NOW strike coordinator, Jacqui Ceballos, handed out copies of the *Now York Times*—a fake feminist edition with the headline "Women's Strike Emasculates a Stunned Nation"—to reporters and editors at the actual *New York Times*, then raced around the city as various events unfolded. Demonstrating the need for free child care, mothers turned City Hall Park into an impromptu day care center, letting their kids take over the grounds. Other women liberated the men's bar in the Biltmore Hotel, confronted the director of Katharine Gibbs Secretarial School about training secretaries to be office wives, and passed out pamphlets titled "You and Your Marriage" to brides and grooms about to tie the knot at the marriage-license bureau. What exactly *were* the legal rights and responsibilities of each partner—did anyone really know? To get the point across, the page titled "Wife's Responsibilities" was blank except for a giant question mark.

"By five o'clock I was exhausted. I remember walking to join the march, so scared—I was so afraid that I would only see a handful of women," Ceballos says. "I'll never forget it, getting to Fifty-Ninth Street: You couldn't see the end of the line."

Everywhere she looked, there were women—thousands and thousands. Some walked holding hands, others raised bullhorns and banners, such as OPPRESSED WOMEN: DON'T COOK DINNER! STARVE A RAT TODAY!! END HUMAN SACRIFICE! Another read, DON'T GET MARRIED!! WASHING DIAPERS IS NOT FULFILLING!

They walked with their mothers and the ghosts of their grand-mothers. Some marchers had planned to be there. Some stopped whatever they were doing to join in from the sidewalk. Many were young, white, and college educated, but they were joined by their black, Asian, and Latina sisters. Some were nurses in white uni-forms and nuns in black habits. Others wore peasant blouses and bell-bottoms, or midis and heels. Many women carried their ba-bies on their backs or in their arms.

The Socialist Workers Party led the march, followed by the demonstrators who had taken over the Statue of Liberty, holding their banner high: "Women of the World Unite!" The police tried corralling the marchers, but they refused to be contained on the sidewalk. From the first row, the socialists issued instructions: "When the cops blow the whistle, take over the whole avenue."

The whistles blew, and Friedan yelled, "Take the streets!" As the march began, the women overflowed the barricades, spreading across the entire avenue. They pushed past policemen blocking their path, past the honking cars and cursing drivers—"Bitches!" "Baby killers!" "Cunts!"

Fanning across the avenue, they marched down to Fifty-Seventh Street, past Tiffany's and Harry Winston jewelers, past Rockefeller Center and St. Patrick's Cathedral, past the diamond dealers and hot dog vendors, past open windows filled with waving flags and smiling faces.

As they walked, some women took off their heels and marched in their stockings. Men joined, too, carrying signs of their own: "Men for Women's Rights." Some gay men marched for their own rights, but didn't carry signs. And then there were other women's groups like Men Our Masters, or MOM, its members wearing heavy makeup, carrying pink signs, and spouting their love of the opposite sex. What was so wrong with a man lighting a cigarette for a girl? one of the MOMs asked the marchers. "Why can't you light your own fucking cigarettes?" someone replied.

They marched until they made it to the New York Public Library, where a few women scaled the famous marble lions.

Despite the strike committee's call for women to boycott *Cosmopolitan*, Helen Gurley Brown showed up to march along with a ragtag group of women's magazine editors, including Shana Alexander, the first female editor of *McCall's*, and Pat Carbine, who soon would replace Alexander at the helm of *McCall's* after seventeen years at *Look*, where she had risen to the post of executive editor.

"It was exhilarating," Carbine says. "I can't speak for Helen, but I left the office in high heels to walk down Fifth Avenue, which I would not have chosen to do if *Ms.* had already started. I would have had the sense to take those damn shoes off and put on something more comfortable."

In its coverage of the march the next day, the *New York Times* noted that among the demonstrations was a linguistic one. " 'Ms.' is used by women who object to the distinction between 'Miss' and 'Mrs.' to denote marital status," the article read.

43

PITIFUL PEOPLE
1970

"Failure is always at your heels. There is no way to avoid it."

—David Brown, *Let Me Entertain You*

Helen was the first to admit that she wasn't exactly the poster child for women's lib, but a few days after the march, *New York* featured her and David in its cover story, "Living with Liberation." Along with famous couples like Bella and Martin Abzug, Barbara Walters and Lee Guber, and Joan Rivers and Edgar Rosenberg, the Browns talked about the changes that the movement had, and hadn't, brought into their day-to-day lives. As usual, David came off as the doting husband, while Helen painted herself as a dutiful wife who cleaned, cooked, and handed over her paycheck every week. "We definitely have a double standard at home," she admitted. Still, they had managed to create a marriage in which they were both free. "We are totally possessed by each other but we are not each other's possession," as David put it.

Each was also the other's priority, in part because of their decision not to have kids. "I think Helen is taking on a decision that is probably one of mine," David said, explaining that, at his age, it was hard to imagine raising another child, as much as he loved his son Bruce. "I think Helen would have cheerfully had children. She is extremely maternal, but I insist on being the only child."

David gave Helen the attention and stability she needed, and in her he found a lifelong mate and mentee who seemed cosmically connected to his every physical and emotional need. They were a match made in Hollywood, perfect foils for each other, "the Working Girl and the Producer," as Faith Stewart-Gordon, the owner of the Russian Tea Room, would put it in her own memoir. But toward the end of 1970, a seismic shift in their plans threw them off center, leaving them both reeling from the aftershock.

A few days after Christmas, 20th Century Fox fired David for the second time. Trouble had been brewing for a while. As president and executive vice president of the studio, Richard Zanuck (the son of Fox chairman Darryl F. Zanuck) and David had put a lot of time and money into three controversial movies that eventually took them down at Fox: *Beyond the Valley of the Dolls*, *Myra Breckinridge*, and *Portnoy's Complaint*. The screenplay based on Philip Roth's novel made *Cosmo* seem schoolgirlish in comparison, and Zanuck Sr. had had enough. One day in the Fox boardroom, he read off a list of all the offending words in the script: *motherfucker, cocksucker, blow job*. What the hell were they thinking?

After hiring an independent committee to look into ways of restructuring the company, the board of directors at 20th Century Fox asked Richard and David for their resignations, citing the loss of profits as the reason, though David surmised that Darryl Zanuck really wanted them out because he believed they were a potential threat to his power. ("We were—because of our concern over his diminishing ability to run the company," he wrote in *Let Me Entertain You*. Zanuck's habit of creating cinematic showcases for his mistresses cost the company millions and eventually attracted the scrutiny of Fox stockholders, before he resigned in May 1971.) David later likened the firing to an execution. Fox's New York office was located at 444 West Fifty-Sixth Street between Ninth and Tenth Avenues in Hell's Kitchen, a short walk away from the Hearst headquarters at Fifty-Seventh Street and Broadway, but just far enough to edge into a seedier side of Midtown. "It was a dangerous area with a high crime rate," he wrote. "I never experienced any danger on the street compared with the treachery, betrayal, and character assassination that took place within that walnut-paneled boardroom. The rapidity with which one can be reduced to corporate nothingness is amazing and frightening."

It was an ugly story—father pitted against son—and a personal one, soon to become very public, as the Zanucks would be in and out of court over the next two years, battling each other. Before Richard and David even exited the boardroom on the day of their firing, photographers arrived and lay in wait to capture their defeat.

After getting the bad news, Helen and Richard's second wife, Linda Harrison, met their defeated and disoriented husbands in Los Angeles and spent the holiday weekend in Palm Springs. At the last minute, they decided to ring in the New Year at Don the Beachcomber, a popular Polynesian-style bar and restaurant where Frank Sinatra was known to hang out and drink a rum cocktail called the Navy Grog. It was the place to be, but when they got to the restaurant, they didn't get their usual star treatment.

"Look at the table they're giving us," Richard said. "It's the worst table."

"It's chaos here," David said, eyeing the crowd. "The owner of the restaurant is carrying dishes. *He* can't even get the busboy's attention."

But Richard persisted. The reason they were being ignored wasn't that the restaurant was busy or that they had made last-minute reservations. It was that they were no longer studio heads.

"This is Hollywood," he said bitterly, "and phone calls were made."

David didn't think much of the slight that evening—it *was* New Year's Eve, and the place was packed—but many years later, he realized that Zanuck was right.

DAVID HAD BEEN fired before, and knew he would survive, but the swiftness and completeness of this particular severance left Helen reeling. One day, she had been married to a company man, one of the most powerful producers in Hollywood. The next day, the name "David Brown" was erased off his personal parking space in the Fox lot. Helen generally kept it together at work, but after David was fired, she cried her eyes out in George Walsh's office, a place where she went countless times a day to discuss budget issues and production schedules, but rarely went for comfort.

The inescapable truth was that she lived in a near-constant state of anxiety. She worried about falling behind at work, and about David being out of work. She worried about David cheating on her, although, considering her track record, David had more of a reason to worry about her cheating on him. ("She and Jackie Susann had a husband-watch agreement," says Walter Meade. "Jackie kept tabs on David when he was in California, and Helen did the same for her husband when he was in New York. She was wise in the ways of men, so I think she was always suspicious. She once told me if she caught him cheating, she would shoot him.") As usual, Helen worried about Cleo, alone in Osage, and about Mary, who was in Shawnee, Oklahoma, where she had joined a local AA chapter. Helen was thankful to her cousin Lou, who gave her regular updates about the family, but she hated visiting.

She dreaded the flight to Oklahoma City and the drive to Shawnee, where Mary lived in a small, two-bedroom house with her soon-to-be husband, George Alford, whom she had met at a physical rehabilitation center. (A car accident left him with a severe arm injury.) Helen sent small allowances, but she could have done more to help her sister fix the place up. She could have made it wheelchair-accessible inside, at least in the kitchen and bathroom. She could have bought her a new house altogether—she had the money, but she hated spending it. Besides, she never stayed at Mary's. She slept at the Holiday Inn.

Helen with her mother and sister at her sister's house in Shawnee, Oklahoma. (*Family photograph courtesy of Norma Lou Honderich.*)

Back in New York, Helen wrote about her visits home. She told her readers about accompanying Mary to her AA meetings, and about her mother's life in Osage. She came off as the dutiful daughter and a good sport to boot, but occasionally her colleagues saw a different side. "To go home, for her, took a ton and a half of Valium. She loathed her childhood, she loathed her upbringing, she loathed being poor," Meade says. "I rarely talked to her about her family. I never initiated the conversation. I only know anything about it because of what she said. . . . She would complain bitterly about what it cost her emotionally to do it. Home was everything that she was trying to get away from. She wanted a life of accomplishment, recognition, glamour, and fulfillment."

And she had gotten it. So why did she feel the need to constantly prove herself? Why was she so maniacal about working, filling up every free moment with a task? Why wasn't she happy? It was an unanswerable question, like asking, "Why aren't you a natural blonde?"

"Didn't you work in order not to have to work someday?" David asked her once.

"I thought so," Helen said, "but it isn't true. We're on the bread line of success. If somebody gets rid of you or me, we are pitiful people."

Sometimes she felt like a character out of a Kafka story, she told Lyn Tornabene on one of their tapes—this one, Helen recorded alone. If Lyn was surprised that Helen read Kafka, she never said so, but it's likely that David would have been the one to make the literary connection, says Meade: "I can hear him telling her she was just like one of Kafka's characters, and she would have said, 'Who the hell is that?'"

Whether David introduced her to it or not, Kafka's story "The Burrow" resonated with Helen. She felt for the mole-like creature, an ugly, vulnerable little thing that lived under a pile of mud and leaves and spent its life digging and hoarding and burrowing and just-surviving, without ever managing to get anywhere safe. The creature raced around inside its maze, hiding food and strengthening the walls, all the while sensing the approach of some larger, unknown creature—a looming threat. "That's *me!*" Helen recalled thinking. "I'm forever shoring up and trying to protect the trenches. I'm never safe. I'll never be safe."

She had spent her whole life trying to protect her little place in the world—staying later at the office, working harder for her bosses, giving all that she could give—but it never seemed to be enough. All these years later, she was still at it, killing herself to please her Hearst bosses, their wives, and their children.

One simply had to shore up and be ready. The walls could crumble at any moment.

And so she raced. She staved off whatever it was that was coming for her, that faceless, looming thing, with countless treatments and surgeries—nipping, tucking, injecting, peeling, and forever fixing the vulnerable structure that was herself.

She built her shelter not out of mud and leaves—but out of ink and paper. She wrote thousands of letters to celebrities, fashion designers, politicians, and public figures whose support would help strengthen those walls.

She made endless lists documenting what she ate and with whom and how much it cost, always what it cost, what she wore and what her measurements were as of that very moment. She drafted countless memos to her staff, outlining how *Cosmo* could be better, and penned more missives to herself.

She wrote to remind herself which secretary she needed to fire and which editor she wanted to hire, but she also wrote to document her very existence—and to work out her *Cosmo*/cosmic problems on the page.

44

SOME NOTES ON
A NEW MAGAZINE . . .
1971–1972

"We were talking about women who wanted to make their own
decisions and didn't necessarily believe that their fulfillment
lay in the finding, wooing, and marrying of a man."

—Pat Carbine, looking back on *Ms.*

It started with a simple idea that was revolutionary at the
time: What if there could be a magazine created, edited, and
run by women? What if that magazine ran articles that covered women's real problems as opposed to the ones manufactured
by advertisers to sell everything from hair dye to dishwashing
detergent? And rejected ads that insulted women or turned
them into caricatures of themselves? And represented women of
all races and backgrounds? What if that magazine told the truth
about women's lives?

Early in 1971, Gloria Steinem and a feminist lawyer named
Brenda Feigen Fasteau brought together a group of female journalists to brainstorm ideas for such a magazine. Gloria and Brenda
had a history of collaborating on feminist issues, ever since they
met while working to pass the Equal Rights Amendment. In July
1971, along with Bella Abzug, Shirley Chisholm, Betty Friedan,
and Letty Cottin Pogrebin, they cofounded the National Wom-
en's Political Caucus, a group of feminists working to advance the

number of women in office at national and state levels—and to put women's issues on both major parties' platforms.

Around the same time, Gloria asked Letty to join some group discussions about starting a new publication back in New York. Gloria had hosted two of three meetings in her living room. Along with dozens of writers, editors, and other activists, John Lennon and Yoko Ono showed up to discuss the new magazine that didn't yet have a name. Almost everyone agreed that the movement needed a magazine, but what kind?

Gloria had been satisfied with a newsletter format, but Brenda envisioned a slick publication with newsstand appeal, an idea that Letty supported, though not everyone agreed. Radical feminists like Vivian Gornick and Ellen Willis wanted their magazine to look radically different from traditional women's magazines with their perfectly turned-out articles about marriage and motherhood.

Then there was the question of the name. What about "A Woman's Place"? "Lilith"? "Sisters"? "Sojourner"? "The First Sex"? "The Majority"? "Bimbo"?

After those initial meetings, the details began to take shape. In April, Gloria circulated a confidential memo: "Some notes on a new magazine . . ." *Every Woman* was the working title, and it aimed to speak to women who didn't find themselves accurately represented in the pages of magazines like *McCall's*, *Good Housekeeping*, *Ladies' Home Journal*, and *Cosmopolitan*. "All are designed to tell the woman how to better run her household, her husband and her children—save for that unliberated woman's survival kit, *COSMOPOLITAN*, which tells her how to be sexy," the proposal read. "In short, the existing women's magazines simply exalt woman as dependent sex object/wife/mother. . . . There is no magazine that addresses itself specifically to a new identification of American woman."

The modern American woman was someone who realized that her own interests and actions were bound up with those of all women, regardless of race, class, creed, or color. She was part of a "We" that included college students, working women, women on welfare, and frustrated housewives marooned in the suburbs.

Though the magazine would include a range of viewpoints, it would target educated women with above-average incomes and sophisticated reading tastes running the gamut from *Harper's* to *Psychology Today*. Assuming its readers were "intelligent and literate," its editors would inform them on social and political issues directly affecting their lives, and feature content not typically seen in a women's magazine or any magazine. Stories with headlines like:

- ABORTION: MORE DEATHS THAN VIETNAM
- DON'T BELIEVE HIM WHEN HE SAYS POLITICS BEGIN IN WASHINGTON. POLITICS BEGIN AT HOME
- SOMEBODY SHOULD HAVE LIBERATED PAT NIXON
- WHAT WHITE WOMEN CAN LEARN FROM BLACK WOMEN
- WHAT BLACK WOMEN CAN LEARN FROM WHITE WOMEN

With her background in public relations and political organizing, Elizabeth "Betty" Forsling Harris was listed as the publisher, but her commitment wouldn't last a year due to a variety of problems, not the least of which was a major personality conflict. Notoriously difficult and prone to yelling, Betty threw tantrums—and objects—when she didn't get what she wanted. After the fallout with Harris, Pat Carbine came on as publisher, abandoning her brand-new post as editor of *McCall's*. "My plan was to get *Ms.* going with Gloria running it as editor, then to go back to *McCall's*," Carbine says, "but then came the moment when it was clear we would have to do it together if it was going to happen." Joining Carbine and Steinem were cofounders Letty Cottin Pogrebin, Mary Thom, Joanne Edgar, Nina Finkelstein, and Mary Peacock.

Shortly after the proposal made its first rounds, "Battling" Bella Abzug, recently elected to the U.S. House of Representatives in November 1971, agitated for a new piece of legislation. The Ms. Bill would prohibit federal agencies from using prefixes that identified a woman in relation to a man. Women shouldn't have to check a box for "Miss" or "Mrs." on a government form when men weren't required to reveal their marital status. The federal government should start recognizing women as individuals, "not as the wives of individuals," Abzug told the House. The Austrians had adopted *Frau* and the French *madame*. Americans should adopt *Ms.*

"HELLO, I'M CALLING from *Ms.* magazine—"

"Where?"

"*Miizzz*. Em. Es—"

"What?"

It went on like that for a while. Every day, when the founders of *Ms.* magazine made an outgoing call, they got incoming confusion. But part of the beauty of *Ms.* was that it *had* to be explained— more than just a title, it symbolized a mind-set that, if adapted by enough people, could change the very infrastructure of American life. Outlining the magazine and its market potential to possible investors and advertisers proved trickier. Carbine and Steinem borrowed friends from *Look* and *New York* to help train their rookie staff, who grappled with a very basic problem: How do you explain a product that doesn't exist yet?

They started with the basics: *Ms.* would be approximately eighty-eight pages, roughly the size of *Time*, and sold by subscriptions and on newsstands. Still, people wanted to hold something in their hands. They needed an image, so Carbine gave them one: *Cosmopolitan.* "Picture a spectrum of magazines—the Seven Sisters, fashion magazines, food magazines, etc.," she said. "Along the spectrum of magazines not devoted to a single subject, like food or fashion, you could put *Cosmo* on one end of the continuum and *Ms.* would be directly on the other. We would be bookends." Every advertiser knew That *Cosmopolitan* Girl. Well, the *Ms.* woman was her opposite in almost every way.

Cosmo's articles were supposed to help girls get over their hang-ups, but its ads only reinforced them. "Do you have The Globbies?" asked one ad for the Slimmers Glove System: Simply apply some gel onto their two-sided glove to massage and buff those upper-thigh bulges away! Vaginal odor? "Relax," read an ad for Cupid's Quiver—a liquid douche available in champagne and raspberry flavors, among other scents—"And enjoy the revolution."

By 1970, *Cosmo* was full of ads for personal hygiene and beauty products, but Carbine and her team had bigger aspirations for *Ms.* "We did not go for cosmetics *at all*," she says. Instead, they went for cars, financial services, and alcoholic beverages. "I'm talking anything you could have found in *Newsweek* or *Time*," she adds. "I believed that it was time for the advertising and marketing community to realize that women were worth as much as men. We were out there every day as agents of change. I viewed our advertising salespeople as educators."

As Carbine saw it, she and her sales team had to do much more than convince companies like Chevrolet—which targeted only men—to advertise to women. They had to change the way those companies thought about women in the first place, not merely as passengers, but as drivers, literally and figuratively. "Do you have a daughter?" Carbine's team asked more than a few executives. What was she planning to do after college? Might she need a car of her own someday?

"I talked about the spirit that was animating women to want to explore and begin to realize their full potential—and to be able to make choices about their lives that included a job working at home as a mother, but also included the possibility of getting into med school or becoming a lawyer," Carbine says. "I think *Cosmo*'s basic message was, 'Here's how you get a more-than-suitable husband.'"

Just in case the difference between *Ms.* and *Cosmo* still wasn't clear enough, the sales team sought to make it clearer through contrast, Carbine adds: "When push came to shove about comparing us to *Cosmo*, I do remember someone saying, 'This is extreme—but if you want to think about *Cosmo* as the poison, think of us as the antidote.'"

45

ENTER HELEN
1971–1972

*"I'm a materialist, and it's a materialistic world. Nobody is keeping
a woman from doing everything she wants to do but herself."*

—Helen Gurley Brown in *Time*, 1968

Working as a kindergarten teacher in Stillwater, Oklahoma, Helen's cousin Lou wasn't aware that there was a magazine called *Ms.* in the works, but she knew that there were women out there who resented *Cosmo*'s message and derided Helen for it. Lou never considered herself a *Cosmo* Girl, and she took the magazine's articles with a big grain of salt when she read them at all—but she also felt that the feminists were missing something important. "Even back then, as such a young woman, I felt Helen did not get the credit she deserved for freeing women to pursue their dreams," Lou says now. "She was a self-made person, then encouraged and reinvented by David. I think most women will agree she was a feminist regardless of what her critics thought."

Yes, Helen dispensed copious advice on how to catch a man, but for every article in *Cosmo* like "Why (Sob) Didn't He Call and How (Aha!) to Make Him," there was one like "Buying a Used Car Wisely." Ever since Lou could remember, Helen had been ahead of her time when it came to giving women financial advice—she was obsessed with money, and she was also good with it.

Lou never stopped relying on Helen's advice, and in 1971, at the age of twenty-six, she found that she needed it more than ever. Her first husband had left her when she was six weeks pregnant, and Lou soon found herself a single mother, taking care of an infant in a freezing-cold trailer. She knew she needed to move for the sake of both of them, and she found a house that she wanted to buy. She had saved some money toward a down payment, but she would have to borrow the rest. Everyone told her that no bank would lend her the money—that banks didn't give those kinds of loans to single women—and she didn't want a cosigner. She wanted the house to be her own.

"Enter Helen," Lou says. "She told me, 'Nonsense. You go and speak to the bankers, and I know you can convince them you will be a good client. You are great with money, so take a budget you have worked out and *convince* them.'"

Bolstered by Helen's advice, in the summer of 1972, Lou made an appointment at the largest bank in the small town of Stillwater. The loan officer was pleasant enough, though very skeptical. The bank had never loaned money to a single woman before, he explained, but Lou was determined to be the first. On his desk, she noticed a photograph of a little boy and asked if he would be entering kindergarten soon. Yes, the officer said, he would be starting in the fall—at Lou's school. "There was only one class, so I would be his teacher," Lou says. "I asked the man if he would have wanted his little boy in a trailer that was cold in the winter and hot in the summer. Then I asked him if he was ready to take a chance on his son's teacher. Sure enough, I got the loan and was never late on the payment.

"The point is, Helen believed in me," Lou continues. "I felt empowered, and I know countless others did, too, although not from personal experience, but from Helen's writings. She didn't need to tell me to look my best and be as charming as possible; I knew. For whatever reason, that line of thinking went out of favor with many women during the feminist movement. But I'll always remember that Helen was a believer in women."

AROUND THE SAME time that Lou got her bank loan, there were sightings of Helen Gurley Brown at consciousness-raising groups around New York. Someone saw her at an organizer's house, an informal gathering of sisters. Enter Helen: She came in, made a point of taking off all of her jewelry, and sat down with the group. "Somebody who was there, a poet, thought it was remarkable that she came in and took off her earrings, sat down, and got comfortable," says Susan Brownmiller, who heard about it secondhand. "Then, at the end of the meeting, she put her earrings and all her jewelry back on. They thought that was funny.

"She was indicating that women *have* to put up this front, but that wasn't really who she was. But she was also telling the women's liberation women, 'Get real.' The front of decking yourself out glamorously—'You have to do this, grow up.'"

At least that's how the poet conveyed it to Brownmiller. "That's what affected her the most; that this woman came in in costume and wanted everybody to know, 'This is reality, kiddos.'"

46

THE BLUE GODDESS
1971–1972

> "You not only enjoy being a girl—you *thrive* on it! And this quality endears you, naturally, to men. Good thing, too, because you are baby-helpless without them."
>
> —from "How Feminine Are You?"
> a *Cosmo* quiz in the April 1971 issue

Helen didn't always make it easy for feminists to claim her as one of their own, but in 1971, the mother of the movement went to her for help. When Betty Friedan called that spring, Helen braced herself for another diatribe against *Cosmo*, but it never came. Instead Betty asked if Helen would consider attending a press conference with her and some other women to protest the impending repeal of New York's new abortion law—the same one that *Cosmo* had covered in its November 1970 issue, soon after the law passed. "I said a mighty yes," Helen told her readers in the September 1971 issue of *Cosmo*. "Well, whether the press conference had anything to do with it I'm not sure (Betty is a powerful speaker), but the daddy of the abortion repeal bill, New York Senate Majority Leader Earl W. Brydges, decided to kill it. Hooray!"

By 1971, the women's movement was a visible presence on TV, in newspapers, and in magazines, but having a magazine of its own was a different story, and early into their search, the founders of *Ms.* were having a difficult time finding financial backers.

Convincing investors to pour money into an alternative women's magazine was tough enough, but they were asking for a lot more than that. When they told those investors that they also wanted to retain at least 51 percent of the stock, screen ads for content demeaning to women (say, a beer company's depiction of a sexy girl straddling a rocket), and donate 10 percent of the magazine's profits to the women's liberation movement, many potential investors backed off. Others never saw the appeal in the first place. At most there would be 10,000 to 20,000 women interested in the issues they proposed covering, these skeptics said, not nearly enough to support a national magazine; certainly not anywhere near the 100,000 women the founders hoped to reach in the beginning.

Then came a couple of breakthroughs. First, *Washington Post* publisher Katharine Graham contributed $20,000 in seed money to help jump-start *Ms.* Next, Clay Felker came along with an offer too good to refuse. In August he still hadn't committed to a subject for *New York*'s year-end double issue. For a while he had been exploring the possibility of publishing various "one-shots," special issues on a theme that could become ongoing titles, depending on their newsstand success. Felker volunteered to finance a sample issue of *Ms.* in the pages of *New York*, suggesting that the two magazines could split the proceeds fifty-fifty. It was the best of both worlds: *New York* would pay the production costs of the first issue, but *Ms.* would have editorial control. After the debut of the first issue, Felker's financial participation would end, leaving *Ms.* to be as independent as its name suggested.

They took the deal. With Felker's early backing, Gloria Steinem could continue focusing on the editorial side of the operation—assigning articles for the debut issue of *Ms.*, which would preview as a condensed, forty-page insert in *New York* that winter. In a small, cramped workspace, a handful of people worked around the clock putting together the full-length Preview Issue, which would herald their national debut. (Both issues were called previews, which is confusing—the shortened *New York* version came out in December 1971, while the full-length issue of *Ms.* actually came out in January 1972. It was labeled "Spring" just in case it dwelled on shelves until then.)

In addition to an article on "How to Write Your Own Marriage Contract," written by *Eye*'s former editor Susan Edmiston, the full-length *Ms.* included an essay by Anselma Dell'Olio arguing that the sexual revolution was a war waged by men—and not to the benefit of women. ("A sexually liberated woman without a feminist consciousness is nothing more than a new variety of prostitute," she wrote.) Also featured was "We Have Had Abortions," a statement signed by fifty-three women who either had abortions themselves or knew someone who had. Gloria Steinem, Nora Ephron, Anaïs Nin, Susan Sontag, and Billie Jean King were among the names on the statement—soon to be addressed to the White House—which provided a card for readers to fill out and return to *Ms.* to help raise awareness.

Jane O'Reilly, a former colleague of Steinem's from *New York*, turned in her piece about the American housewife who was at once tired of feeling invisible and powerless in her own home and fortified by the knowledge that she was not alone. Women all over the country were having "clicks" of consciousness as they watched the men in their lives wait for dinner to appear and the dishes to be washed and the toys to be picked up off the stairs without lifting a finger to help. Click! Click! Click! "Those clicks are coming faster and faster," she wrote. "They were nearly audible last summer, which was a very angry summer for American women. Not redneck-angry from screaming because we are so frustrated and unfulfilled-angry, but clicking-things-into-place-angry, because we have suddenly and shockingly perceived the basic disorder in what has been believed to be the natural order of things. One little click turns on a thousand others."

Gloria chose to feature "The Housewife's Moment of Truth" on the cover, along with a one-of-a-kind cover girl who happened to be blue. The artist Miriam Wosk painted a cerulean, modern-day version of the famously fierce Hindu goddess, Kali; her multiple arms juggling a typewriter, frying pan, steering wheel, and other objects symbolizing the many demands in a woman's life.

On December 20, 1971, *New York*'s double issue hit newsstands. "Until now, the Women's Movement has lacked an effective national publication to give voice to its ideas. We have placed our knowledge and experience at Gloria's disposal to help shape such a magazine," Felker wrote in his editor's letter that accompanied the insert. "*Ms.*, like *New York*, will concern itself with one of the most significant movements of our time."

Skeptics had laughed off the idea of a women's lib magazine, but that issue set a newsstand record, selling more copies than *New York* had ever sold before. Soon, delivery trucks drove 300,000 full-length issues of *Ms.* around the country.

At $1.50 apiece, the copies were supposed to last for at least eight weeks, but they sold out in eight days, attracting the attention of the industry and investors. If the spring preview had stayed on shelves for a little longer, the blue goddess might have shared a shelf with February's *Cosmo* cover girl, a sultry redhead in a dusty-rose halter dress, posing seductively next to the blurb, "How Good a Lover Are You?"

BY THE EARLY Seventies, the *Cosmo* look was so iconic that humor magazines had no choice but to spoof it (best of all was *Harvard Lampoon*'s parody issue featuring a cross-eyed model in a plunging yellow dress next to cover lines like "10 Ways to Decorate Your Uterine Wall"), but *Cosmopolitan*'s art department was in crisis. Linda Cox, once an assistant art director, quit because she couldn't stand working for the difficult art director, Lene Bernbom. In 1971, Lene left, and Helen began the process of finding a new art director to replace her—she eventually hired several who didn't work out for various reasons.

"Boom-boom-boom, one after the other," Linda says. "One guy would shut the door and screw models on the desk. Another woman had a bottle of bourbon in her lower left-hand drawer. Another person was there . . . they broke her back before she could do anything. Some people just weren't good enough."

Toward the end of 1972, one of Linda's former coworkers at *Cosmopolitan*, a slim, dark-haired woman named Marni, became the next to claim the title of art director when Helen promoted her from an associate position. "Marni called me and said, 'Please come back—you have to help me. I don't know what I'm doing,'" Linda says.

A new mother to an infant son, Linda was ready for a steady job and paycheck. Shortly after Marni called, she came back to *Cosmopolitan* as an associate art director. Marni and Linda worked well together, and Helen was happy, but she was about to lose her art director yet again—this time to a chubby, fifteen-year-old Indian boy who was alternately known to his peace-seeking followers as Guru Maharaj Ji, Lord of the Universe, and the one Perfect Master. By the following year, his American disciples would number in the tens of thousands. Many were young, college educated, and from well-off families, and they were encouraged to give their worldly possessions to the movement.

"She was so completely swept away," Linda says of Marni. "She went to a lecture in New York, and she came in to work the next day and said, 'I've got to leave to go to Switzerland and hear him speak again.' The next week, she went to Switzerland. I kind of covered for her, but she didn't come back, and weeks went by. I called her mother, and her mother was crying: 'Marni's given everything up, everything! She's had to give all her money to the guru, and she's decided to stay.'"

Not long after that, Helen promoted Linda to art director, a position she kept for twenty-four years.

COSMOPOLITAN NUDE MAN

1972

"I thought it was a hoot. A clever takeoff."

—Hugh Hefner on Burt Reynolds's nude centerfold in *Cosmo*

I t was a story made for gossip columns: As early as 1970, *Women's Wear Daily* caught a whiff of the latest *Cosmo* happening, and it had all the makings of a scandal. "Helen Gurley Brown of Cosmopolitan magazine reportedly has a collection of photos of celebrities posing in the nude," *WWD* announced in "Eye" that January. Shortly after the item appeared, Helen sent off a letter to the editors, cutely correcting their report. "You really are so naughty," she began the note, which ran about a week later, typos and all. Besides, where on earth would she go to find pictures of naked famous people? It wasn't as though actors went around with nude photos of themselves in their portfolios, showing them off to magazine editors.

Three days later, "Eye" ran another item about "The Further Adventures of Mother Brown and the Great Male Nude Fold-Out Caper," after getting a phone call from George Walsh, who set the record straight: Yes, it was true that Helen was on the hunt for a suitable movie actor to be photographed in a "relatively coy pose" for a full-color foldout in *Cosmopolitan*, but she still hadn't found the right man for the job. No, it was *not* true that she was "collecting pornography," as "Eye" had implied. It was no longer a secret that *something* was in the works, but even Helen wasn't yet sure what it was.

The idea first came to her a couple of years before. Men liked to look at women's bodies, and women liked to look at men's bodies—it just wasn't as commonly known. And no wonder: Men had been plastering nude pinup girls on their walls ever since the dawn of *Playboy*, but women had no equivalent.

In December 1968, Helen wrote a memo to Dick Deems and John R. Miller titled "COSMOPOLITAN NUDE MAN." Hearst had been trying to deflect the constant comparisons between *Cosmo* and *Playboy*, not encourage them, but Helen had proved again and again that sex sells. Shortly after she raised the idea of a male nude centerfold, she got the money she needed to catch her man—this time, on camera. The only question was: Which man?

She wanted a famous actor, a big Hollywood name, someone like James Coburn, the magnetic tough guy who recently had starred as a suave secret agent in the 1966 James Bond parody, *Our Man Flint. Cosmo* issued the request, and Coburn agreed to pose on the condition that he could select the pictures. Inspired by the Italian painter Caravaggio, the photographer Guy Webster was going for a lush Renaissance feel when he showed up at Coburn's Beverly Hills estate with assorted Moroccan-style rugs, curtains, and velvet pillows in a palette of burgundy and gold.

As a beautiful woman taught a naked yoga class outside in the backyard, Coburn stripped and stretched out on a rug, nude except for his beard and a piece of embroidered maroon fabric draped over his crotch. He was clearly a man who was comfortable with his sexuality, and his confidence translated to the photos, but when Helen saw the slides, she was sorely disappointed. She wanted a beefcake with a big smile, and they gave her Bacchus with a beard. "Apparently he is in his mystical phase right now,"

Helen wrote to Deems and Miller. They had to get the concept just right or else not do it at all.

Despite Helen's best attempts, nobody wanted to be *Cosmo*'s pinup boy. The rejections piled up: Paul Newman. Joe Namath. Robert Redford. Clint Eastwood. Warren Beatty. Tony Curtis. Elliott Gould. Frank Langella. Dustin Hoffman.

Helen was discouraged, but she refused to settle. She wasn't interested in "Mr. Average household face," she told her girls in her January 1971 editor's letter. She wanted someone famous and fun to look at—they deserved no less. "You may or may *not* ever see a male nude centerfold in *COSMO*," she wrote, "but I *hope* you do."

And then, one day when she was not looking, she found him. Burt Reynolds hadn't been on her list of Possibles. He wasn't a star—not yet—but he was sexy. All man and mustache and swagger. The fact that he liked older women—he was dating Dinah Shore, nineteen years his senior—also intrigued her. And he was clearly sharp. Sharp enough to guest-host *The Tonight Show*, where Helen was a regular guest. She and Johnny had a rapport, but her chemistry with Burt Reynolds was explosive. "Like fire and gasoline," Reynolds later recalled in his 1994 memoir, *My Life*.

Under the hot studio lights, they sparred and put on a great show into the commercial breaks. When Reynolds glibly suggested that men bought *Playboy* for its articles, Helen scoffed, and he came back with a joke about *Cosmo*'s inane love advice.

"Are you a sexist?" Helen asked accusingly.

"I bet in ten years that word will be very tired and so dated that you'll sound like a dipshit to ask," he countered.

They swapped barbs to the delight of the audience, and when they were off the air, Helen went for the kill and asked Reynolds to be *Cosmo*'s first male nude centerfold. Reynolds was, for once, speechless.

"Why?" he finally asked.

"Because," she cooed, "you're the only one who could do it with a twinkle in your eye."

Reynolds deflected the offer with more jokes. But Helen wasn't joking. The next day, she called him at his hotel—she wouldn't take no for an answer.

His agent and manager told him not to do it. After years of playing cops on TV in shows like *Hawk* and *Dan August*, he was about to make a name for himself as a serious film actor with his role as a macho Atlanta businessman on a bad canoe trip in *Deliverance*, based on James Dickey's novel. He was thirty-six, and this performance could change his career. Why risk ruining it for a dumb gag?

Reynolds ignored their advice. He thought it sounded like a good send-up. "On the back of the foldout, I told them I wanted to underscore the *Playboy* takeoff with a photograph of me pushing a grocery cart," Reynolds later wrote. "I'd list my favorite colors, hobbies, books, and be quoted saying, 'I'm looking forward to becoming an actress.' But I got screwed."

HELEN LEARNED HER lesson after the Coburn shoot. This time she didn't mess around. Forget Caravaggio. She wanted Scavullo. He was her best man—or rather, her breast man. For seven years now he had been shooting *Cosmo*'s cover girls in slips and body stockings, push-up and padded bras, using masking tape, Vaseline, bobby socks, baseballs, and whatever else he needed to create the illusion of deeper, duskier cleavage. Women had always been sex objects. It was time for a man to have a turn, but the photo shouldn't be too serious, she told Scavullo, nothing soulful. It should be fun.

The day of the shoot, Reynolds's PR rep drove him to Scavullo's studio. On the way over, they stopped at a liquor store so that

Reynolds could buy a few bottles of vodka. He finished one bottle before they even got to the studio, which was colder than an ice bucket. Reynolds tried not to shiver. Or shrivel. After meeting Scavullo and a couple of his assistants, he asked for a glass, went to his dressing room, and cracked open his second fifth of vodka.

He would need the liquid courage soon enough. In the main studio, Scavullo and his assistants made some last-minute adjustments to the set they had created. Somewhat inoculated against the cold, Reynolds took off his clothes and stretched out on a bearskin rug. After letting it all hang out for a moment, he slung a hairy arm over his main attraction, and smiled with just enough teeth to hang on to his cigarillo.

"Fabulous! Fabulous like that!" Scavullo said from behind his Hasselblad camera.

Reynolds knew the exact moment when Scavullo got his shot. "I always know," he later wrote. "I don't have to do forty takes to know when I've got the take I want. I've caught the butterfly. It can feel it flapping around on my finger. I don't have to open my hand to see if it's there."

Still, the session lasted for another hour. Boredom and vodka made him bold. At one point he pretended to hump the bearskin rug. Why not mess around a little and make people laugh? No one would ever see the outtakes of him totally nude and rude. He had been told he'd be getting all the negatives.

THE APRIL 1972 issue sold out instantly. Among the stories advertised on the cover was a profile of Bella Abzug, but that's not the one that stopped thousands of women in their tracks as they shopped for groceries at the supermarket or walked past the newsstand on the way to the subway. They were too busy reading a bright-orange banner slashed across the bottom right corner:

Cosmo's Famous Extra Bonus Takeoff!
AT LAST A <u>MALE</u> NUDE CENTERFOLD
The Naked Truth About Guess Who!!

Helen said who in her editor's letter, but the centerfold needed an introduction all its own, and she assigned features editor Barbara Creaturo to prepare readers for the pages to come. Why was it, Creaturo wondered in her preface, that men had been ogling naked women in magazines forever, but if a girl wanted to catch a glimpse of a nude man, her best bet was to find a copy of *National Geographic*? Naturally, the double standard existed because the men controlling those publications catered to their fellow men, but social mores were changing. Women were becoming bolder in their sexuality, which was not to say they were becoming more promiscuous; they were "just *lusty* and honest in their appetite for an appreciation of attractive men," Creaturo wrote. Fortunately, the modern man was willing, even eager, to show off his body and be a sex object. "As for you (that COSMOPOLITAN girl), we know you don't need any instruction on how to appreciate the look of a beautiful man . . . and now (if you have not already done so), you probably want to flip the page. . . ."

It was a direct invitation. How could a girl resist?

More to the point: Now that *Cosmo* said it was okay to look and even important (in the name of equality!), *why* would she resist?

That thatch of dark hair. Those halfback shoulders. Those straight white teeth, balancing the tip of a tiny cigar . . . Open the rest of the gatefold, and there he was: a man in three sections, from his hairpiece and perfect teeth down to his splenectomy scar and nest of curly pubes. All in full color. Man on bear. Pelt on pelt.

As it turned out, Reynolds was more surprised than anybody

when he saw the photo that ran in *Cosmo*. Helen had invited Reynolds and Dinah Shore to the *Cosmo* offices to look over the pictures with her and about a dozen female editors, who had been running magnifying glasses up and down his furry body ever since the images arrived.

He had liked a shot where he was laughing with a who-gives-a-shit smile on his face, like he was in on the joke. That's the shot that was supposed to have run, but mysteriously, it disappeared. "The original slide was lost," says Mallen De Santis. "It had been on the light box, and it was the first choice. Everyone turned the whole art department inside out, trying to find it. It never turned up."

Reynolds wasn't a fan of their second choice. He thought he looked smug. "Apparently the people at *Cosmo* took this thing more seriously than I did," he told a reporter after the issue came out. "I preferred the shot where I was laughing at myself."

He expected to be in on the joke; he didn't expect to *be* the joke. Reynolds was starring onstage in *The Rainmaker* in Chicago when the new issue came out. The next day, the audience started catcalling. He couldn't go anywhere without being heckled by some smart-ass shouting, "Hey, I didn't recognize you with your clothes on." After shows, screaming women mobbed him with their April issues in hand, opened to "That *Cosmopolitan* Man."

After years of playing bit parts on TV, he was getting offered movie roles—at up to $150,000 per picture. "And a major factor in his ascendancy into the big time is the *Cosmopolitan* photograph as Playmate of the Year," Mary Alice Kellogg wrote for Newsweek Feature Service. But Reynolds worried that he was getting attention for all the wrong reasons. "Face it, these women wouldn't be going crazy over me at the theater if it wasn't for *Cosmo*," he said. "Now when I walk on stage I feel like I'm nude."

Across the country, housewives taped the centerfold to their refrigerators and above their bathtubs. College girls displayed it on the walls of their dorms, and in Huntsville, Alabama, members of the English department at Grissom High School pinned the centerfold to a wall, with a fig leaf covering Reynolds's discreetly placed arm, to see how many teachers would lift it.

After the issue came out, Reynolds received hundreds of Polaroids of naked women, and some of naked men. One fan in Nova Scotia regularly sent her pubic hair encased in wax paper to the actor for the next three years. Once, when Reynolds checked into a hotel, he pulled back the bedcover only to see his own hirsute body printed on the sheets.

The image was reproduced on key chains, coasters, wallpaper, and women's underwear. Every time he stepped onto a plane, women whistled at him. Months later in Denmark, where he was promoting *Deliverance* on its world tour, a woman showed him a porn magazine. Reynolds was surprised to see a photograph of himself on the cover—somehow, someone had gotten an outtake of him humping the bearskin rug.

Back in the States, the Catholic Church issued a critical statement in response to the centerfold. In the South and the Midwest, store clerks hid the issue behind the counter or refused to sell it altogether. Finally, Helen Gurley Brown had gone too far, people said. What was next, a private jet and a *Cosmo* key club for girls?

Meanwhile, high above the hullabaloo, in her office on West Fifty-Seventh Street, Helen watched it all play out, as letters poured in. Writing from a laid-back engineering firm in San Francisco, a group of office girls thanked *Cosmopolitan* for giving them a centerfold to put on *their* section of the wall—why should the guys have all the fun? One male reader accused the magazine of exploiting men, while a married woman from Cupertino, California, lamented ever seeing such an example of poor taste and prayed it would soon be erased from her memory. Donna Visione from Peru, Illinois, was so inspired she wrote a poem:

> *While leafing through COSMO, what did I behold*
> *But a beautiful male in the centerfold.*
> *By a twist of moustache, and with eyes that did flirt*
> *I knew in a moment, it must be—BURT!*
> *He was naked and hairy from head to his feet*
> *Took off his clothes to give us girls a treat*
> *He looked jolly and trim and as dear as an elf*
> *And when I saw him, I ogled—in spite of myself!*

48

PROBLEMS

1973

"Helen saw a shrink all the time I knew her, every week. . . . I
think there were two big things she didn't want anyone to know
about: her insecurities, and her rage. She was profoundly angry."

—Walter Meade

Helen didn't make any New Year's resolutions to usher
in 1973. She simply tried to fulfill the same old ones
she had been making for years: "Relax chin, stay at 105
pounds . . . torture!" she told her readers in her January editor's
letter. She made no mention of taking over the world, but those
plans were also in the works. In 1972 Helen launched the first international edition of *Cosmopolitan* in Britain. Featuring a busty blonde
in a red-hot flamenco-style dress against a matching red-hot cover,
British *Cosmo* was an instant, red-hot success, selling out its 350,000
copies within hours of hitting stands. By early 1973, *Cosmopolitan*
had a new director of international editions—Jeanette Sarkisian
Wagner, who had been the second editor of *Eye*—and plans for a
French version of *Cosmo*, to be followed by editions in Italy, Latin
America, and Australia. "Like Coca-Cola, Helen Gurley Brown
and her message of permissiveness will soon be a ubiquitous international presence," *New York* reported that February. Over the
next two decades, she would expand *Cosmo* into its own universe.

David's profile was about to blast off into space, too. He and
Richard Zanuck finally had started their own production outfit,

the Zanuck/Brown Company, joining MCA/Universal. In 1973, they were getting ready to release a new movie, and it was going to be big. Directed by George Roy Hill and starring Paul Newman and Robert Redford, *The Sting* was scheduled to hit theaters that December, but being the producer's wife, Helen arranged for her senior editors to see an early screening of the film. Soon after she issued the invitation, George Walsh declined. Helen was furious that he didn't have the nerve to tell her to her face. Instead, he asked his secretary to relay the message: He couldn't go because the movie started too late, at 9 p.m., and it just wasn't possible to have a babysitter stay with his kids for so long.

He gave his ticket to his secretary, and shortly afterward, Helen sat down at her typewriter and hammered out some thoughts about George Walsh. He should have come to the screening that night—did he really have a curfew? At the very least, he should have asked if there was *another*, earlier screening he could have attended. But he seemed to think that public relations wasn't a part of his job description; "*screw* that . . . public relations are where it's *at* with your boss," she groused.

Helen titled the document "PROBLEMS," but there was really one problem that was eating away at her—and he happened to be her second in command. Her issues with George Walsh took up fifteen pages. "George Walsh has some kind of personality defect which causes him to be UNABLE to be pleasant," she wrote. "He is patronizing . . . and somehow seems faintly sneering at all times."

A few people on staff knew that Helen had been struggling with George since she first started working at *Cosmo* in 1965. But her readers would have had no idea. Time and time again, she featured him in her editor's column, where *Cosmo* Girls could read all about the man who "runs the office"—still somehow finding the time to study French, renovate his family's Brooklyn brownstone, and help raise the children.

On paper, she cast herself as a shy, self-effacing office wife and George as the man of the house. She created the picture of a lovably odd couple, but in reality, he was more like the odd man out. She wasn't sure where he belonged—maybe *Time* or *Newsweek*—but not at *Cosmo*. He just didn't get the *Cosmo* Girl; "one doesn't want to get personal but probably he is UNABLE to approve or like our kind of lady," Helen wrote, before getting extremely personal and speculative about his private life— "he really *is* a closet chauvinist. . . ."

In all the time they had worked together, Helen couldn't remember him once complimenting her, or even saying "well done." The more she wagged her tail and tiptoed around him, the worse it was between them. Why did she bother courting his approval? If anything, he should be courting hers.

Instead, he played the resigned man. He rarely stayed at the office later than 5:30 p.m., and he cleared the work off his desk every evening. At editorial meetings, he often stared out the window, and he rarely brought in his own original ideas to pitch. He was totally competent when it came to overseeing the magazine's schedule and production, Helen had to admit, but was it too much to ask for a managing editor who cared? Someone who understood her and gave her moral support? Someone more like—David?

"Keep George," David told her. "He is intellectual, high-dome. You are more plebian—you know, girlish material. He is a good foil for you."

Helen took David's advice, but she wasn't happy about it. She knew George sometimes went out on job interviews—maybe one day, he would leave of his own accord. Very soon, his contract would be coming up, and she wasn't sure that she could live with him for another two years.

49

Two Faces of the Same Eve
1974

"*Cosmopolitan* is talking to women one by one.
We're talking about making all women's lives work."

—*Ms.* editor Suzanne Levine, in the *New York Times*,
August 11, 1974

On April 18, 1974, New Yorkers awoke to read the latest installment of news about Watergate on the front page of the *New York Times*—but it was a full-page ad for *Cosmopolitan* in the back pages that really begged for attention. "I think a certain girl who just married a very famous diplomat is a Cosmopolitan girl in every *way*!" read the text next to a photo of a well-coiffed, cleavage-baring model. The ad didn't name the diplomat or the lucky girl who landed him, though anyone with a subscription would have gotten the reference to America's secretary of state, Henry Kissinger, who had tied the knot with his leggy, longtime friend, Nancy Maginnes, just ten days earlier. What made her a *Cosmopolitan* Girl? She was as smart as he was, the girl in the ad proclaimed.

Seeing the ad in the paper, the writer Stephanie Harrington couldn't help but wonder what the staffers over at *Ms.* would make of it. They wouldn't care about *how* Mrs. Kissinger landed her man, she surmised, but they might ask the obvious question: "Why, if she's so smart, isn't *she* Secretary of State?"

As it happened, Harrington was working on an article for the *New York Times* comparing the two magazines, *Ms.* and *Cosmo*, when the ad came out. Around the same time, she arrived at the General Motors Building to meet Helen Gurley Brown.

Harrington had written about her before. As a young writer for the *Village Voice*, she spoofed *Sex and the Single Girl* by writing her own guide to manhunting in Greenwich Village. (She'd also written for Helen—during a period in 1969, Harrington was *Cosmo*'s monthly book columnist, a job that later went to Gloria Vanderbilt.) Helen still made an easy target, but she was also the powerful leader of the most insecure army in the world—the legions of mouseburgers who clung to her every word. To see firsthand how she ruled, Harrington went to an editorial meeting. After making her way up to the fourth floor, she took her place in Helen's small office, along with about a dozen women and two men, who dragged their chairs into a circle, with Helen at the center.

As usual, there were a few announcements, followed by a flourish of blue sheets, as editors read aloud their pitches.

"Have we done anxiety lately?" someone asked.

"That is like asking if you've eaten in the last week," Helen quipped.

"We have depression in the works," someone else mentioned; "this should be separate."

"This one is totally ridiculous—'Are Lesbians Ecological?'"

As the meeting unfolded, Harrington grew increasingly aware of the great disparity between the senior editors, who seemed to be normal, sensible people, and the article ideas they suggested—ideas like "Face-Lift for the Still Young—During Crucial Man-Holding Years" and "Orgasm Is Yours If You Follow These Simple Instructions." Other than conjuring up these ideas, the editors seemed to have little to do with them. For the most part, they were just repackaging the same old formulas that *Cosmo* had been selling for nearly ten years.

Meanwhile, sixteen blocks away, the editors of *Ms.* were packaging a very different set of messages. Early on, Harrington went to an editorial meeting at *Ms.*, located at Forty-First Street and Lexington in a cramped duplex of offices that was about as organized as its staff—which is to say, not very. Sitting in the larger of the two communal offices along with twenty women and one mailman (everyone was invited to meetings), she listened as conversation veered from family-minded urban planning to the Italian left's struggle against sexism to the question of whether equality had killed off romance.

"What is romance?" someone joked. "Is it a magazine?"

"Women's obsession with romance is a displacement of their longings for success," Gloria Steinem cut in, sitting at a desk near the door.

When she sat down to write her article, "Ms. Versus Cosmo: Two Faces of the Same Eve," Harrington didn't overtly identify with one magazine or the other—she criticized and commended both—but she was writing about women who did.

Both magazines had broken the mold of the traditional women's glossy and both were revolutionary, advocating for equal rights in the bedroom and the boardroom. Both attracted fiercely loyal readers who turned to them for a monthly injection of career advice and courage to strike out on their own. But why did it have to be *Ms.* versus *Cosmo*? Why couldn't a woman feel solidarity with both? To illustrate her point, Harrington imagined a young Madame Bovary penning a letter to her favorite magazine:

To the Editor:

I am a survivor. (What woman isn't?) Of a suffocating marriage,
two destructive affairs, even thoughts of suicide. (I suppose that sounds
melodramatic—arsenic after black lace.) I was brought up to believe
that a woman could live only through a man. And social and economic
realities make it hard to do anything else. But your magazine let me
know that I wasn't alone, that I am not crazy, that there are women
all across the country who are determined to start considering their
own needs and to accomplish something for themselves by themselves.
The support I find in your magazine has given me the courage to
finally reorder my priorities.

Right on!

The letter was signed "Emma Bovary, Yonville Parish," but
which editor was she writing to—and at which magazine? Was
Emma Bovary a *Cosmo* Girl or a *Ms.* woman? It was a clever con-
struction, mirroring a very real divide. On the one hand, there
was *Cosmopolitan*, the working girl's self-help guide with its aging
not-so-single-girl editor, Helen Gurley Brown (now fifty-two and
still wearing miniskirts); its endless advice on how to be sexy and
how to catch a man, explained in baby-simple prose; its cover girls
with bursting cleavage; its staff of men and women, all versed in
Cosmo-speak (which is to say Helen-speak, a language all its own);
its readership of nearly two million; and its ever-expanding reach
around the globe, with twelve foreign editions and counting.
(Helen regularly critiqued foreign editions, which often repurposed material from American *Cosmo*, to make sure that international editors stayed true to the original's optimistic, sex-positive
message and now famous *Cosmo* style.)

On the other hand, there was *Ms.*, the feminist free-for-all with its glamorous, unofficial spokeswoman, Gloria Steinem (now forty and wearing flared jeans); its sometimes heavy-handed advice on how to start a consciousness-raising group or a revolution; its edited-by-committee prose "as riveting as the telephone directory—the gray, not the yellow pages," as Harrington quipped; its "coverpersons" like George McGovern and Bella Abzug; its majority female staff and resistance to editorial hierarchy; and its readership of 400,000, including many highly educated women. "More than twice as many *Ms.* readers as *Cosmopolitan* readers attended college, and more than a third of *Ms.* readers hold advanced degrees," Harrington reported. "And only 5.5 per cent of *Ms.* readers also read *Cosmopolitan.*"

Two very different magazines, and readerships—and two very different revolutions. But what if some of those differences could be bridged? What if the so-called two faces of Eve could come together as a united front?

Occasionally, they did—on issues like reproductive freedom. After the Supreme Court's 1973 *Roe v. Wade* decision to legalize abortion came under attack, Helen attended yet another press conference, organized by the National Abortion Rights Action League, along with Gloria. Helen later described the day in her July editor's letter: "Before the press conference we went to the ladies' room where I glued on my false lashes and anchored my fall while Gloria ran a comb through her hair and put on some Chap Stick!"

Helen found a lot to admire about Gloria, but the feeling wasn't always mutual. "She was the most unconfident, ingratiating person, constantly referring to herself as a mouseburger," Steinem says. "If anything, we felt sorry for her because she was working so hard, and she so clearly lacked faith in herself, so nobody blamed her. At least I certainly didn't blame her for *Cosmopolitan*. We just referred to it as the Unliberated Woman's Survival Kit."

"Helen really created a little money-printing press for Hearst. A *big* one. Strike the word 'little,'" adds Pat Carbine. "And here comes something down the highway that is calling into question one of the basic premises of the magazine, which is that if you just follow this formula that we'll give you every month, you can catch a man, and that's what it's all about. Issue by issue, dissecting that premise—which one could say *Ms.* is all about—Helen *had* to pay attention."

HELEN TRIED TO educate herself about feminism. She frequently asked Gloria for updates on the women's movement, and over time they developed a friendly rapport. In April 1974, Helen wrote to Gloria to thank her for calling the office to "reassure us that you and the other leaders of the Women's Liberation movement were *not* against us." She was glad to have an ally in the movement, and yet, as many questions as Gloria answered, as many times as she signed her letters to Helen "in sisterhood," somehow the message never got through. Helen understood the movement and didn't. "She would say 'Now, your movement says this, your movement says that . . . ,'" Pat Carbine recalls. "Gloria would stop her in her tracks and say, 'Helen it's *our* movement.'"

As much as Gloria wanted to support Helen in theory, some chasms were too wide to be bridged. In the mid-Seventies, Helen once again attracted the ire of feminists when a former *Esquire* secretary, Julie Roy, revealed that she had been abused by Dr. Renatus Hartogs, a prominent New York psychiatrist and psychoanalyst who wrote *Cosmo*'s monthly column "Analyst's Couch." Over the years, Dr. Hartogs had answered readers' questions about everything from losing their virginity to dealing with frigidity. It later came out that he had been using his actual analyst's couch to have sex with patients, under the guise of sexual therapy.

Once again, protestors showed up in the lobby of the General Motors Building, but Helen was not there. She was in her office four floors above—on the phone with Gloria.

"Gloria, you have to do something, you have to do something! There are demonstrations in the lobby!" Helen said frantically.

As usual, Gloria was calm. "Well, who's demonstrating?"

"Your people are demonstrating!" Helen sputtered.

"What do you mean, 'my people'?" Gloria asked, confused.

"Women!" Helen cried.

Retelling the story forty years later, Steinem lets the irony settle in, before going on. "She was most alarmed. I said, 'But Helen, what are they demonstrating about?' Well, it turned out that the sex advice column in *Cosmopolitan* was being written by a psychiatrist who was on trial for sexually abusing his patients. And Helen didn't fire him. He continued to write the sex column. I said, 'Well, Helen, no wonder they're demonstrating. Why don't you fire him?' And Helen said, 'Oh, he's such a nice man.'

"I do not remember feeling angry at her," Steinem says. "I just felt sad."

Barbara Hustedt Crook saw it a little differently. There were times when she felt embarrassed to work at *Cosmo*. Walking through the protestors who occasionally gathered in the lobby, "it felt like breaking the picket line," she says. "I was sort of with them in spirit." She had worked for the editor who oversaw "Analyst's Couch," and her personal opinion of Hartogs was that he was kind of a jerk. "I wasn't surprised by the accusations," she says. "What did surprise me was Helen's initial refusal to fire him on the grounds, as she explained in a staff meeting, with real passion and eloquence, that he was innocent until proven guilty. On the one hand, it seemed ludicrous and icky to keep him on, while on the other, I quite admired her for it, because her position seemed principled rather than personal, and fairly courageous."

Hartogs later was found guilty by a state supreme court jury. In March 1975 he was convicted of malpractice and ordered to pay $350,000 to his victim, one of several women who eventually came forward. His final column for *Cosmo* appeared four months later.

50

ERA AND YOU

1975

"The advent of the women's movement changed us all,
including Helen."

—Gloria Steinem

In March 1975, a great white shark terrorized residents of Dallas. Richard Zanuck and David Brown wanted to preview their new movie, *Jaws*, in a landlocked city far away from the film's real location in Martha's Vineyard, Massachusetts, and they chose a suburban theater that was packed by the time the opening credits rolled. David sweated in his seat. From the start, the production had been plagued with problems—the most difficult being the star of the film, or rather stars: three different versions of a plastic, twenty-four-foot mechanical shark that the cast and crew named Bruce.

Everything hinged on that shark, including the career of their young director, Steven Spielberg. By now it was no secret that the shark was a fake, but if it seemed like a fake—if it made people laugh instead of scream—it was game over. On the other hand, if it seemed real . . . they got their answer when the shark burst through an otherwise still, sunlit sea, causing one woman to jump out of her seat, accidentally spilling her Coke on another audience member in front of her. "The audience screamed and screamed," David later wrote in *Let Me Entertain You*. "The cards they filled out to rate the picture made *us* scream—with pleasure: 95 percent rated the film 'excellent.'"

A couple of nights later, they screened the movie in Long Beach, California, and got a similar reaction. It dawned on David that they had a blockbuster on their hands—and, in part, he had *Cosmo* to thank. A couple of years earlier, Peter Benchley's manuscript had landed on the desk of the books editor, who passed it along to Helen with a short note, suggesting that it might make a good movie. Soon after that, David and Richard bought the rights.

Helen visited David in the Vineyard while they were filming, and she tagged along for some of the promotion of *Jaws*, but she had to hold down the fort back at the office. She got considerable help from Walter Meade, whom she rehired, this time to replace George Walsh as her managing editor. George's exit, though delayed, was inevitable. "She knew that he had to go. He knew that he had to go," says Meade, who regarded Walsh as very professional, but also saw that he was conflicted about working for Helen. "It was circumstance that ended their relationship. It was oil and water." (Walsh went on to become editor-in-chief of the general books division of Macmillan Publishing Company.)

Walter came back just in time to celebrate a landmark event: *Cosmo*'s tenth anniversary under Helen. Since he first walked into her office a decade earlier, a lot had changed, including Helen herself. When she showed up at *Cosmo* for her first-ever job as a boss, "it seemed to me there were *no* guidelines for being or trying to *get* to be a woman executive," she wrote in her February 1975 editor's letter. "If you *were* one, you'd simply 'fallen in' (like I did) or were one of those rare creatures who somehow instinctively knew how to go after the same glittery work-prizes men did."

Around the same time, Helen met Letty Cottin Pogrebin for lunch. It had been years since they had seen each other, and Letty had changed, too. When they first met, she was all of twenty-two, a baby book-publicist and swinging single girl who wanted a life as adventurous as Holly Golightly's. A decade later, Letty was an editor at *Ms.*, a columnist at *Ladies' Home Journal*, a prominent author, speaker, and activist, and the mother of three children with her labor-lawyer husband—to some, she was a model of the modern woman. Helen relished the chance to ask Letty all about *her* experience as a feminist, and over the next two and a half hours, they talked about what was happening in the women's movement, what still needed to happen, what women wanted, what men wanted, and what women and men wanted from each other. They didn't talk much about husbands, kids, houses, or jobs that day, but they met for other lunches, and Letty had the opportunity to ask Helen a question on one subject she never quite addressed in *Sex and the Single Girl* and rarely included in *Cosmo*.

"We used to go to lunch for old times' sake. I guess we were both drinking, though we tried not to, and I was glad because it sort of oiled her gears," Letty says. "She was asking me about my children, and I said, 'Helen, did you ever miss having children?' She said, 'Well, between you and me, I stopped using birth control. I wanted a child, and I didn't want David to know, so I left it in the hands of fate, and I never got pregnant.' I just think she was so completely invested in this framed photograph of the elegant, hip, pioneering sexologists and single-single-single."

Her public image failed to capture the complexity that was always just out of frame. "If she hadn't created her own trademark, I think she would have been happy to be a feminist," Letty says. "It was too late for her to be a feminist, or at least an out-feminist. She had created this tribe of so-called liberated women through sex— which was precisely the opposite of what we at *Ms.* would say— but I think she related on a deep level. She just couldn't go back."

◆   ◆   ◆

SO SHE WENT forward—Helen eventually did identify as a "devout feminist"—and she aligned herself with other women who were moving in the same direction. At the end of 1975, a group of editors including Pat Carbine from *Ms.* and Ruth Whitney from *Glamour* met to discuss the role that women's magazines could play in getting the Equal Rights Amendment to the Constitution ratified. Helen promised to try to reel in the help of John Mack Carter, the former editor of *Ladies' Home Journal* who recently had become the editor of another Hearst title, *Good Housekeeping.*

She kept her word and wrote to Carter. They needed four more states to make the ERA the Twenty-Seventh Amendment to the Constitution, and rounding up enough votes to make that happen wouldn't be easy, considering local defeats of the bill in New York and New Jersey. They needed to rally all the support they could get. "This may not be a subject you feel passionately about, John," Helen wrote, perhaps anticipating a lukewarm reaction, but she urged, "the group feels passionately that you should *join*!" She quickly outlined the plan. Each magazine would publish something about the ERA in an upcoming issue. Whether the magazines chose to run a major feature about it or just a sidebar was up to them. They didn't have to endorse the bill. They only had to disseminate the information about it to their readers. Might John consider running such an article in *Good Housekeeping*, a magazine that reached millions of readers?

In her own whispery way, Helen made a bold request, and it worked. Carter joined the cause, along with the editors of more than thirty other women's magazines, whose combined circulation reached nearly 60 million. Each magazine devoted a part of its July 1976 issue to the ERA.

For *Cosmo*, that meant running a two-page feature called "ERA

& YOU," explaining why ratifying the amendment was both so important and so controversial. "Puzzled and confused about the Equal Rights Amendment?" *Cosmo* asked. Staunch opponents saw the bill as threatening to families and the very moral fiber of American life, but many women didn't support ERA because they weren't sure what having equal rights really meant. They were afraid of being saddled with responsibilities they didn't want in the name of equality: being drafted if there were another war, for instance, losing Social Security benefits if they were widowed, or no longer being entitled to child support if they were divorced. After all, if men and women were equal . . .

Cosmo's writer, Linda Wolfe, addressed those fears head-on. Maybe women *would* be expected to join the army someday. Maybe they would lose some child support. Maybe they would have more obligations. But equality was worth it. "We cannot hope to grab all the goodies and give nothing in return," Wolfe wrote. "Men and women will have equal rights or they will have unequal ones, as they have today."

RATIFICATION OF THE ERA proved to be a long and continuing battle. (Congress passed the amendment in 1972, but to become a part of the Constitution, it needed to be approved by a three-fourths majority of thirty-eight states. A decade after it was proposed, the ERA missed the mark by three states.) Still, Helen persisted in using *Cosmo*'s pages to educate her readers on issues that directly affected their lives. She was a fierce and lifelong supporter of birth control and a woman's right to choose. Most of all, she was a fierce and lifelong supporter of women.

"She seemed to understand long before anybody else that women supporting each other—older women supporting younger women—was a form of feminism," says Erica Jong, who developed

a friendship with Helen after the publication of her groundbreaking 1973 novel, *Fear of Flying*. "I believe that it is the very essence
of feminism: helping each other, which, when I was young, was
very rare. Helen seemed to know that nurturing younger women
was part of what could make her important." At the same time,
Jong adds, "We did not think of her as a great feminist leader. We
thought of her as a very successful advertising woman who ap-
pealed to a more down-market group, a pop culture person who
found a way to make money out of women and their needs. Now I
do think she was a feminist, in that she promoted women."

As she got older, Helen went out of her way to nurture young
female executives, publishers, editors, and writers—and she took
great interest in *Ms*. It wasn't "*Ms*. versus *Cosmo*," except for when
the two staffs played each other in a game of softball. The two
magazines shared freelance writers, contributing editors, even
article ideas. When *Cosmo* rejected an article making the case for
embracing au naturel body hair, *Ms*. took it and ran it in a summer issue. When David Brown came across a *Ms*. cover line that
he particularly liked—"Is it different with a younger man?"—he
called up Pat Carbine and asked her if he could buy it for *Cosmo*.
She didn't sell it, but Carbine says now, "I regarded the call as the
consummate compliment."

Over the years, Helen and Gloria became allies, if not exactly
lunch buddies. Helen wrote Gloria long fan letters on *Cosmopolitan*
stationery, confessing her eternal admiration and devotion. Did
Gloria know how wonderful she was? How inspiring? Was it okay
to tell her she looked smashing the other night? She courted Gloria
relentlessly: to let *Cosmo* profile her, to write for *Cosmo*, to speak at
Cosmo's International Conference. Gloria never stopped being critical of Helen. She challenged Helen openly and publicly, but she
also came to see the value in joining forces with her.

"I can imagine the same woman reading both our magazines," Gloria wrote to Helen in September 1978, "and in any case, I would like very much to be able to say some of the things to your readers that I wish had been said to me much earlier."

Thanks to Helen, Gloria could get her message across to more people through the pages of *Cosmo*. And when she needed more funding for *Ms.*, Helen introduced her to a Hearst executive, who discussed with her the possibility of applying to the Hearst Foundation. "That you made the first call was especially important in underlining the fact that we each serve a different purpose with our publications; that *Ms.* has a complementary function as a kind of early warning system on emerging issues that is helpful to other women's magazines, and vice versa," Gloria wrote.

It was a mutually beneficial arrangement. One of the most famous feminists of her generation, Gloria gave Helen the sense of belonging to a cause that didn't always want her. In return, Helen supported Gloria wholeheartedly—with money, time, constant encouragement, and the occasional care package, like a shipment of bran muffins. She sent checks to the Ms. Foundation for Women, and she gave advice, often unsolicited.

The overall look of *Ms.* could be much better, Helen told Gloria again and again. The layouts tended to be messy and hard to read, the headlines uninviting. "She came to an editorial meeting once and tried to jazz up our cover lines," Steinem says. "It was very generous of her to do that."

In August 1978, Gloria Steinem visited the *Cosmo* offices at Helen's request. "She called me up and said, 'My staff needs to understand the women's movement. Will you come over and explain it?'" Steinem says. "I thought it was brave because, one, she was admitting she knew nothing about the women's movement; and, two, she was understanding that her *staff* should understand."

Helen regularly invited celebrities to sit in on editorial meetings. In addition to Barbara Walters, a personal friend, Elizabeth Taylor, Jane Fonda, Henry Kissinger, and Woody Allen were just a few of the guests who graced *Cosmo* staffers with their presence, though no one knew why. Some staffers guessed the visits were an ego trip for Helen, who wanted to show off her connections to her employees and vice versa. "We were supposed to ask questions, and it was excruciatingly awful," Mallen De Santis says. "I mean, these were major people who couldn't have had less interest in talking to a bunch of civilians. You had to really exert yourself, so they didn't feel like they were casting their pearls before swine. You had to be nice swine."

Most of the visitors went on about some element of their own personal success, but Gloria came to *Cosmo* to talk about a movement that affected them all, men and women alike.

"I was trying to explain, as we were all trying to explain, that this was not a reform; this was a revolution; this was long and deep and connected to the suffragists' and abolitionists' era; that that had been one big leap forward, and now we were trying to accomplish another one," Steinem says, adding that feminists wanted to call attention to the fact that there weren't enough women in politics— or in medical schools, for that matter. "We were saying, 'But it could be different. It could be different . . . that's the vision.'"

Helen was so grateful for Gloria's visit that she wrote to thank her for it the very same day: "We *are* all sisters . . . that's the overpowering message we got . . . and there is much for all of us to do."

51

HAVING IT ALL
1982

"Having It All sounds so fucking cliche to me."

—Helen Gurley Brown, in a 1982 memo to her book editors

In 1982, Gloria Steinem walked into *Cosmopolitan*'s editorial offices to interview Helen Gurley Brown for a cable television special. It was a bracingly cold day in late winter, and the wind howled along Broadway.

Helen began with a tour, showing Gloria a black-and-white picture of herself as a baby ("I think I was a darling baby—I have not seen a better baby picture, ever!") and another one of herself as a young woman of twenty-two. "I am wearing falsies. You know people *wore* falsies in those days." She moved on to a more recent color photograph of herself in a flattering red dress and pearls, standing in front of a tree in a residential neighborhood, along with two gray-haired women: one in a wheelchair, the other in a housedress, attempting, and failing, to smile.

"This is my family, my mother Cleo Bryan, my sister Mary Alford. Mary got polio when she was nineteen and I was fourteen. My mother passed away last year, this was taken just a few months before that time," Helen told Gloria, moving along to a picture of herself and David in black tie at a Hearst dinner dance. "This is the first cover of *Cosmopolitan* when I came aboard," she said, pointing out the July 1965 issue, featuring Renata Boeck. "I got the sexiest picture I could find."

Cut to Helen and Gloria sitting down across from each other. Gloria wears a short-sleeved purple blouse and large-framed glasses; she looks confident and relaxed with one arm resting on a pinkish-beige floral couch that matches the wallpaper behind it. Helen wears a tweed jacket with pink piping and a plaid scarf tied into a giant bow around her throat and sits on a cane chair, her back straight as a pin. As the camera closes in on her bronzed face and sprayed hair, she purses her lips, nods, smiles, and almost seems to flinch as she waits for the first question.

"Ever since I've known that we were scheduled to have this conversation, I've been asking people questions and asking what they would like me to ask you," Gloria begins. "But I think the biggest mistake about you is that you are a glamorous person who—"

"Come on!" Helen protests, shimmying her shoulders and laughing for the camera. "I'm glamorous! I'm glamorous!"

"You are glamorous," Gloria says smoothly. "But I think they feel that you arrived here without effort. They don't understand the work that went into it. And I think most especially they would be surprised to hear about your childhood."

Not everyone knew, for instance, that she grew up "without much money."

"Not much money!" Helen interrupts. "Not much money doesn't even describe it!"

Over the next few minutes, Helen recited the same story she had been telling for the past twenty years with slight variations. This time, her family wasn't "dirt-poor," a description David sometimes used to describe her Arkansas roots; the Gurleys were "genteel poor." Her father died when she was ten, leaving her mother, "a pitiful little creature," to take care of one daughter with polio and another with unsightly acne.

Gloria listened patiently, occasionally sharing pieces of her own story. In Toledo, Ohio, her family also had been genteel poor, living off the unpredictable income of her father, a traveling antiques dealer. She, too, had taken care of her mother, who suffered from debilitating depression but still made sure that both of her daughters went to college.

"I'm more pitiful!" Helen said, and laughed. "You were able to go to college. You got the money somehow to get there so I feel that I'm more pitiful than you. How did you get there?"

"Well, my mother wanted very much to have both her daughters go to college and she saved money and sold the family house. And I got scholarships and worked as a salesgirl," Gloria answered. "I think that most women in the country probably have had the kinds of experiences you and I have had, and they don't identify with women who surmount them because they think they must be special." A pause. "Actually, we're the same people."

Whatever Helen had been expecting, it probably wasn't that statement. But sitting in her office on that blustery day, Helen and Gloria discovered they had a lot in common. They both had rough childhoods and grew up with unhappy mothers who felt trapped in their lives. They both knew women whose lives had been ruined by getting pregnant out of wedlock—a crime that used to be punishable by society, as Gloria reminded the audience. They both knew women whose spirits had been crushed by an unfair system, Gloria continued, but Helen refused to talk about women as victims.

"I understand your point, which is that women could go a lot further if we were not victimized by a system that pays us less, penalizes us for having children that keep us away from our jobs," Helen said. "Yes, we would do better. But then we also are acknowledging—or at least I am—that, regardless of the breaks, you can do pretty well anyway. You can rise above it."

"Regardless of the bad breaks, a *few* people can do pretty well," Gloria corrected her. "We're just trying to make a world in which *more* people can do pretty well."

As the film rolled, Gloria Steinem's interview with Helen Gurley Brown sometimes seemed more like Helen Gurley Brown's interview with Gloria Steinem, with Helen interjecting, "Can we talk about you?" She wanted to know Gloria's thoughts on marriage—always a subject of interest to her *Cosmo* Girls—but she also opened the floor to talk about a subject close to Gloria's heart.

"Would you like to tell me where we are right now with the women's movement?" Helen asked.

"I think partly where we are is the ability for you and I to come here and talk to each other and talk to a lot of people in their living rooms, most of whom are probably women, who hear us saying things that were in their heads, too—in all of our heads—and we didn't think we were supposed to say," Gloria answered. "Like, in your case, 'I didn't want to have children.' Or in my case, 'I didn't want to get married.' Or whatever. Or that we would like equal pay."

Speaking of equality, why didn't Helen have a spot on the Hearst board when she made millions for the company? People talked about that, you know.

"It's such a tricky thing. It's a privately owned, family-owned company," Helen began, but Gloria wasn't satisfied with her response.

"It's good for the country to see talent rewarded," she said.

"I *am* rewarded!" Helen protested.

"It's bad for the country to see it not sufficiently rewarded."

"Oh, Gloria!"

And so it went. After defending her position at the company—they let her do whatever she wanted!—Helen defended her magazine when Gloria asked if she would ever consider putting "more reality about the sadness of life" into *Cosmopolitan.*

"That's a very tough question. Because unlike you, I want my magazine to sell tremendously well, and I do tend to accent the positive," she said. She could publish almost anything she wanted in *Cosmo*, she added—she could turn it into *U.S. News & World Report*—but she liked the shallow stuff. She cared about beauty and fashion.

"No, we both care about it," Gloria conceded. "But I think you have secrets and a seriousness and a worth that *Cosmo* as a magazine doesn't adequately reflect. That your public image doesn't adequately reflect. That's why we're here."

"To try to *change* all that," Helen purred, deflecting the issue, but Gloria kept her on course. It was interesting how Helen acted on TV talk shows—giggling and flirting with the host—when, in reality, she was a much more serious person than she presented herself to be.

Helen delivering one of her trademark TV performances in an appearance with reporter and commentator Cleveland Amory. (*Copyright © Ann Zane Shanks.*)

"Gloria, you're trying so hard to make it seem as though I'm victimized or put upon. . . ."

"No . . ." Gloria said. "I'm just suggesting that we as women go on playing certain roles when we have the power to change, and I would like other people to know you as I know you."

"Yes, I would like to be known as a serious person. I'm a very serious little person," Helen said. "I'm no good at all at a party."

Why did she have to call herself "little"? Gloria pressed. Why did she have to put herself down?

Helen simpered and sidestepped and sighed, but Gloria wouldn't let her off the hook. For once she wanted to see the real Helen Gurley Brown—and she wanted the rest of the world to see her, too. Why was it so hard for her to be truly honest about herself? Why couldn't she show the complexity of who she really was?

The thought dangled in the air for a moment, but Helen didn't bite—or rather, she bit for just long enough to slide right off the hook. And then, they moved on again. Helen's new book, *Having It All*, would be coming out soon. What would she like to do after that?

Well, Helen said, she expected to continue editing *Cosmopolitan*; she had a contract, though she didn't want to be a "doorjamb case."

"That's when you get your foot in the door and you refuse to be removed no matter what's happening," she said. "I don't want to be one of those."

She planned to stay at *Cosmo* for as long as she could. After that, who knew?

"Everybody says, 'I want to go to Cyprus' or 'I want to write my book' or 'I want to look at the sunset' or 'I want to spend more time with my children,'" she told Gloria. "None of those things exist for me. . . . It's hard for me to think ahead and say, 'What is going to fill up my life?'"

What about a new book or a new magazine? Gloria asked.

"No," Helen said, she had squeezed every last drop of wisdom she could think of into *Having It All*. And she didn't want to deal with the next subject, the obvious one: age. It was so cliché. So . . . predictable. She had been cheering up young single girls and plain girls and poor girls with their noses pressed against the glass forever. She wasn't interested in cheering up old girls about the same issues. She wanted to do something different. Something more meaningful for society, maybe. Something global.

"Women over sixty are the single poorest group in the whole country," Gloria said. Wouldn't it be worth her while to help them?

"Maybe that's the next phase," Helen said unconvincingly, as they wrapped up.

It was time to go. She had places to be and people to see. Somewhere in Manhattan on that cold, glittery night, twenty people from Estée Lauder were waiting at a restaurant to meet Helen Gurley Brown—and hear all about That *Cosmopolitan* Girl.

EPILOGUE

"Home. I'll go home, and I'll think of some way to get him back.
After all, tomorrow is another day."

—Scarlett O'Hara (Vivien Leigh), *Gone with the Wind*

In 1993, That *Cosmopolitan* Girl went into forced retirement at the suggestion of a new ad agency hired to work on the magazine's image. Going forward, *Cosmo* would eschew the word *girl* and be known as "the largest selling young women's magazine in the world." For two decades, feminists had been protesting *Cosmo*'s insistence on calling women "girls," and Martin H. Landey, chairman and chief executive of New York's Cox Landey & Partners, thought they had a point. "I don't think the advertising should talk like that anymore,'" Landey told the *New York Times*. "The world changes."

The world changes, and Helen Gurley Brown helped change it, selling sex without guilt in the Sixties, sex as liberation in the Seventies, and sex with power in the Eighties, along with power hair. British hairstylist Harry King created the iconic *Cosmo* style—big hair fanned out and sprayed on the sides—on the model Kelly Emberg for the December 1980 cover, starting an instant trend. "It became known as the Cobra Look," he says. "I could not believe I was getting away with this hair. . . . I was making a goof, and it became mainstream."

In 2015, the Browns' brainchild turned fifty under a new

editor, the British-born Joanna Coles, who, since her appointment in 2012, has been honoring Helen's sex-loving brand of feminism while using the magazine and its website to educate readers (see: "Your *Cosmo* Guide to Contraception: How Not to Get Pregnant") and to endorse political candidates. In the United States, *Cosmopolitan* is the bestselling magazine for young women, reaching approximately 18 million readers a month, and it is one of the biggest magazines in the world, with more than sixty international editions distributed in more than one hundred countries, from Finland to Mongolia.

Helen oversaw many of *Cosmo*'s international incarnations herself, especially during her final years at the magazine. She didn't want to be a doorjamb case, but sure enough she became one. Though her initial engagement with Hearst was for a couple of years, she remained *Cosmo*'s editor-in-chief for more than three decades, and her later years were some of her most controversial ones, though not for the reasons she intended.

In 1988, Helen made national headlines thanks to a hugely controversial article she ran in *Cosmo*'s January issue, "Reassuring News About AIDS: A Doctor Tells Why You May Not Be at Risk." According to Dr. Robert E. Gould—a psychiatrist with no proven medical or research expertise regarding HIV—straight women could rest easy about the virus, which was most commonly associated with young gay men. "There is almost no danger of contracting AIDS through ordinary sexual intercourse," Gould wrote. Playing down the importance of using a condom during vaginal intercourse, he argued that in many cases "a healthy vagina" (without lesions, for instance) was sufficient protection against the virus.

As soon as the issue hit stands, medical authorities denounced Gould's article for spreading false information, a charge that was later supported by then–surgeon general C. Everett Koop. But Gould wasn't the only one to blame. In mid-January, three hundred activists organized by the New York chapter of the AIDS group ACT UP picketed outside of the Hearst Magazine Building, bearing signs that read "The *Cosmo* girl CAN get AIDS," "CONDOMS *NOT* COSMO," and "HELEN GURLEY BROWN—DOES *HAVING IT ALL* INCLUDE AIDS?" Distributing flyers that tore apart Gould's claims, they called for a boycott of the magazine, asking the public to "Say No to *Cosmo*."

What was Helen thinking when she approved the article? It's impossible to say, but the same year, it was reported that only 4 percent of AIDS patients contracted the virus through heterosexual intercourse. Still, telling straight women that they didn't have to worry about contracting AIDS wasn't just shortsighted; it was delusional and potentially catastrophic. Helen's vision for single women to enjoy sex without consequence blinded her to very real, very deadly consequences that didn't exist when she was young— and believing she was right, she refused to apologize.

About a week after the protest, Helen went on the air, defending the article to Ted Koppel of ABC's *Nightline*. "We have come so far in relieving women of fear and fright and guilt," she said, "and now along comes this thing to scare the daylights out of everybody forever. And since there isn't too much proof that AIDS is spread through heterosexual intercourse, I think our side should be presented, too."

"When your readership, ten million mostly young women, read an article like that, and draw the conclusion that, therefore, maybe they don't need to urge their partners to use condoms," Koppel pressed, "do you feel entirely comfortable with that?"

"I feel quite comfortable with this," Helen replied, sending chills down the spines of her closest allies.

"People would always say to me 'How can you work for her?' and 'She's a terrible person.' And I would say, 'No, she isn't,'" Liz Smith says. "She was wrong about a lot of things. She never believed that straight women could get AIDS, and we all went to the ground wrestling with her that AIDS was a international disease, and it wasn't just a disease of gay men. She never saw that, and it caused the women's movement to move away from her, but she didn't mean any harm."

Feminists further distanced themselves from Helen in the Nineties, when she downplayed sexual harassment in a decade full of high-profile charges against powerful men, such as Supreme Court nominee Clarence Thomas and Senator Bob Packwood. When asked if any of her female *Cosmo* staffers had been sexually harassed at work, Helen quipped, "I certainly hope so."

And in October 1991, she wrote an op-ed in the *Wall Street Journal* that was as disturbing as it was infuriating. "I *know* about sexual harassment," Helen began, before suggesting that people lighten up about a little horseplay at work. To make her point, she described a game her office mates used to play at Los Angeles's KHJ radio station when she worked there in 1940. Here's how Scuttle worked: A guy (usually an announcer or engineer) would chase a girl (a secretary or an assistant) around the office until he caught her and tore off her panties. "While all this was going on, the girl herself usually shrieked, screamed, flailed, blushed . . . but to my knowledge no scuttler was ever reported to the front office. *Au contraire*, the girls wore their prettiest panties to work," Helen wrote, confessing that she used to hope to be scuttled herself, but she was too plain to attract the attention.

ONCE, HELEN GURLEY Brown led the way for the single girl, but by the mid-Nineties she was old enough to be That *Cosmopolitan*

Girl's grandmother—and her ideas seemed to get battier every year. In 1996, at the age of seventy-four, she finally agreed to step down so that she could be replaced by a much younger editor, Bonnie Fuller, coming from another Hearst title, *Marie Claire*. "I think it was difficult for her," says Laurence Mitchell, who worked as Helen's photo director for fifteen years, starting in 1981. "Her biggest fear in life was that, if she were to retire, no one would ever ask her to lunch—but the point is, she never went to lunch anyway!"

Shortly after the announcement was made, some critics rushed to knock Helen down even further. The *Wall Street Journal* ran an unflattering front-page story by media reporter Patrick Reilly, suggesting that Brown had overstayed her welcome and that the company couldn't wait to replace her. It was the most hurtful article she had read about herself in the thirty-four years she had been in the public eye, and for once, Helen put aside her diplomacy and furiously typed up one of the few angry letters that she actually *sent*—on her signature cotton-candy pink letterhead:

"If it gives you any satisfaction.

1. i cried my eyes out for an hour today
2. i think you are a TOTAL SHIT!"

Exit Helen.

ONLY SHE DIDN'T leave that easily. In addition to giving her a car and a new office, Hearst gave Helen Gurley Brown a new title: editor-in-chief of *Cosmopolitan*'s international editions. If she was hurt by the forced retirement, she didn't really complain, at least not publicly. Privately, she confided in a few friends, admitting that the ugly publicity that surrounded her exit—and the exit it-self—was hard on her.

"The company has been insanely good to me until these last 15 minutes," she wrote to Walter Meade in February 1996, "and they didn't mean me to get hurt, though I was." Since she couldn't imagine not working, she would commit herself to im-proving *Cosmo*'s international editions, and see whatever else came her way.

She did what she promised. She still traveled, appearing at *Cosmo* launch parties around the world. She still came to work and made endless notes on *Cosmo*'s foreign-language editions, but after a while, "they didn't really want to hear her comments," says one longtime colleague. "They accepted it, but it wasn't something that they necessarily took into consideration." What did she really know about single women in Russia or in the Middle East?

When she wasn't writing notes for the international editions of *Cosmo*, Helen worked on preserving her legacy. In 1972 she be-gan sending her papers to the Sophia Smith Collection at Smith College, the alma mater of Gloria Steinem and Betty Friedan. Helen had been saving letters, photos, and other memorabilia ever since she could remember. For a long time, she stored ev-erything in her building's basement, but gradually she began moving the contents of her life to the college's women's history archives. Being at Smith meant a great deal to her. It pained her to think of her lifework ending up in a paper shredder some-where after she died. "I don't have children, and it sort of hurts me to think that I just have to throw it away," Helen wrote. At Smith, she added, "I feel I have a home."

When Helen left *Cosmo* in 1997, one of her first thoughts was to visit Smith, in Northampton, Massachusetts. As early as 1975, she proposed talking to Smithies in their natural habitat—perhaps in their own dormitories. Surely she would benefit as much as the students would. It was so important to keep *Cosmo* young and vital, and she wanted to hear what they had to say.

One of Helen's biggest insecurities was that she never had a formal college experience. "She was ashamed of being sort of from the sticks and not having an education. She was always covering that," says Erica Jong. "She admired people who had graduated from college and graduate school and were more intellectual than she was." Shortly before she died, Helen visited Smith. The college made her an honorary member of the Class of 1962, the year that *Sex and the Single Girl* was first published, and she finally earned membership in an exclusive club she never could have dreamed of entering when she was college-age.

Once, Helen had dismissed the idea of writing a book about getting older, but in 1993 she published *The Late Show*, an advice book for women over fifty, followed by yet another rehashing of her life story in 2000's *I'm Wild Again*, a reflective book that includes a letter to the daughter she never had, as well as more tender portraits of her mother and sister.

Still, people seemed to prefer the sensational Helen Gurley Brown, who was still doling out blow-job tips into her late seventies, not the serious person whom Gloria Steinem had tried, and failed, to unearth. "I don't know that she counted her own reality as serious and important enough to share it," Steinem says. "I don't know. I hope so, with somebody, I hope so."

As always, Helen had David, and David had Helen, whom he needed more than ever after his son Bruce Brown died after years of struggling with drugs. Bruce had been troubled ever since Helen could remember, and those troubles never went away.

Articles described the Browns as "childless," but that's not accurate. People forgot that David was a father, Helen a step-mother. They just remembered that the Browns never wanted children, though they didn't necessarily know why. "Because she had to raise herself," says Lyn Tornabene, recalling one of the last conversations with Helen she ever had. "There was no room for any other baby. She needed the attention and wanted it. That was it."

ON FEBRUARY 1, 2010, David died at home in Manhattan at the age of ninety-three. By then the Browns had amassed a fortune—in 2015, the Browns' estate was worth around $105 million, minus $73 million worth of donations—and Helen asked Hearst CEO Frank A. Bennack Jr. to oversee her affairs. Along with Hearst general counsel and senior vice president Eve Burton, he soon became a co-trustee and co-executor of her will.

In David's absence, the walls of Helen's burrow finally began to cave in. Her mind dulled, her memory dimmed, and she relied on someone else to remind her of her story. Toward the end of her life, she started talking to her cousin Lou on the phone every Sunday night, and frequently those conversations turned toward her childhood in Arkansas. "Helen talked to me about Cleo in her old age. During those times, she was not so dismissive; rather, she showed an understanding. Perhaps it was always there, but it was more 'catchy' to do the whole hillbilly bit," Lou says. "It warmed my heart when she would confide in me over the years, the last ones in particular. I think she needed a person to talk to who had nothing to gain by being nice to her and could talk to her about her family. She told me in her last year, one night, 'I feel happy when we are talking. I don't feel happy very often.' I know that was true because she missed David so much.

Fortunately, toward the end she thought he was on a long trip. At least, I think that was fortunate."

Before David died, he and Helen had a macabre little chat about where they should be buried. Southampton, Long Island, or in the Ozarks? "Take me to the Ozarks," David told her. "I want to be wherever you are, and besides, I've always liked to go to new places." To many people who knew the Browns in New York, the idea of Helen and David being buried in Arkansas seemed absurd, but Cleo's side of the family, the Siscos, had a family cemetery in Osage, and Helen wanted to be buried there along with her mother and Mary, who died in 1997. "I think she just remembered it as being so pretty. She said over and over, 'This is where I'm from, these are my roots, my grandparents are here,'" Lou says. "She always wanted to be buried here, and David was so in love, he wanted to be buried beside her." After David died, Lou helped Helen design his gravestone. At a certain point, Helen told Lou, "Someday you'll be doing this for me."

Helen entrusted her estate to Hearst executives, but she asked Lou to bring David's ashes to Arkansas. After he died, Lou offered to take care of Helen as a daughter would, back in Arkansas, but Helen didn't want to leave their home in the Beresford building on Central Park West—a palatial four-story penthouse apartment worth millions. She still showed up for work, long after she lost her ability to do it. Day after day, a driver picked her up and took her to the office, where she either slept or flipped through magazines for a few hours, before being driven home.

When Lou came to visit her in New York, she tried to look at Helen the way Helen had looked at her as a young girl—without judgment. "She always wanted her makeup on, and although she let her aides do most of it, she put on her own lipstick! Not a single

tremor in her hands," Lou says. "We talked about the fact that neither of us drank coffee, and that's why her hands were so steady."

Other people focused on Helen's thinning hair. She had a bald
spot in the back that she no longer bothered to cover with a wig,
as she slipped further into dementia. The biggest shock of all
was her weight. She had spent most of her adult life starving
herself; she bragged to friends that she allowed herself to eat one
cookie a year, on Christmas. Now she ate cookies all the time.
She loved cookies: chocolate-chip cookies, sugar cookies. You
name it, she ate it all.

"A few years before she died, she was very heavy," says former
Cosmo photo director Laurence Mitchell. "When I called to say, 'I
want to come and see you,' she would say, 'Now I *insist* you bring
me cookies.' And she would really eat them! She wasn't herself
those last few years."

TOWARD THE END of her life, Helen looked for meaningful ways
to allocate all that money she had been saving up for years, and
she put much of it toward education. In addition to establishing
an endowed fund at Smith College for students who return to
school later in life, in 2012 Helen left $30 million to Stanford and
Columbia—David's alma maters—to create the Brown Institute
for Media Innovation.

Shortly after visiting with the dean of the Columbia Journalism School, Helen died on August 13, 2012, following a brief stay
at New York–Presbyterian Hospital/Columbia. She was ninety
years old, "though parts of her were considerably younger," read
her obituary in the *New York Times*.

In October, a who's who of the city's media elite—Hearst executives, magazine editors and writers, gossip columnists and

the gossiped-about—attended her memorial at Lincoln Center's Alice Tully Hall, where waiters served pink champagne and warm chocolate-chip cookies to guests including Mayor Michael Bloomberg and Brooke Shields. Helen never liked the idea of memorial services—she thought they were boring—but Hearst put on a great show, screening clips from *Gentlemen Prefer Blondes* and bringing in Matthew Broderick and Kelli O'Hara to sing a couple of Helen's favorite show tunes on a stage bathed in pink light and decorated with hundreds of pink roses arranged into a perfect mound, like a scoop of ice cream.

Amid the crowd were many people who knew Helen personally, and people who just felt like they did. People like Patricia Myles, a retired police officer from Virginia who first read *Sex and the Single Girl* when she was in college and credited Helen Gurley Brown for inspiring her to move to a big city, get her own apartment, and pursue her career. "In the back of my mind, Helen would say 'Do it, do it!' So I did," Myles says. "She gave me the courage for so many things. She impacted my life something fierce."

One by one, friends and former colleagues took to the stage to say goodbye to the quintessential *Cosmo* Girl.

Mayor Bloomberg credited Helen for changing the world, and changing it for women in particular.

Barbara Walters told the crowd that Helen and David "never had children and never regretted it," which may have been only partly true. "She believed she didn't have to follow a traditional path, and *Cosmopolitan* was her child."

Hearst CEO Frank A. Bennack Jr. remembered Helen's odd habit of taking off one earring and resting it on the table at four-star restaurants—invariably the earring would disappear. "Can you see me on all fours under the table at La Caravelle?" he joked. Like several other speakers, he also noted Helen's penny-pinching ways, telling the crowd that she "threw her nickels around like manhole covers."

It was a predictable theme, but others close to Helen felt that her fears about money weren't funny at all. "It's not a joke. It was kind of an obsession," says Lou, who was also in the crowd that day.

Lou couldn't hear the speeches herself. She is mostly deaf now, a condition she has dealt with for years, but her family later told her that of all nine speakers, Liz Smith was the best. She was also kind, Lou adds: "She made me feel so great when she told me Helen talked about her 'little cousin Norma Lou.' She even said 'Norma Lou,' although I introduced myself as Lou, so I know it was true."

When it was her turn on the podium, Liz started with a question she had been trying to answer for nearly fifty years. "People have asked me since 1965, 'What is, what was, Helen really like?'" Liz began. "Well, friends, I've been in entertainment for sixty-two years. I have known Elizabeth Taylor, Katharine Hepburn, Madonna, Eleanor Roosevelt, Hillary Clinton, and Barbara Walters. But what can one say about Helen being the person most people ask about?"

Liz went on to share some funny, crowd-pleasing anecdotes about Brown's lettuce-leaf diet and much larger appetite for sex, well into her older age. And yet she never answered the question, *What was Helen* really *like?* At least not publicly. "She may have thought she had it all, but I always thought she kind of led a spiritually empty life," Smith says now. "I always considered her my intellectual inferior, if you can believe it, and she was one of the smartest, shrewdest people I'd ever known."

For all her confessions, Helen remained unknowable, even to those who knew her best. For all the work she did on her physical self in the name of self-improvement, toward the end of her life Helen wondered if maybe she hadn't transformed herself so much at all. "I'm afraid we continue in life to be who we *were*," she wrote in *I'm Wild Again*. "I started as insecure as a jelly doughnut—isn't that how we *all* start?"

AFTER FASHION WEEK in New York, Helen was cremated wearing her favorite perfume, a Pucci dress, and a purse containing a twenty-dollar bill. Many months later, in May 2013, she ended up right back where she began. In Arkansas with Mother and Mary. Only this time she was with David, too.

After a lifetime of tunneling up, she chose a resting spot of quiet anonymity in her family's cemetery, its iron gate decorated with an *S* for Sisco. It is as pretty a corner of the world as one could imagine, with wide-angle views of grazing cattle, distant mountains, and hay-strewn fields hemmed in by oaks, cedars, and black walnut trees. Near the cemetery is a small pond. It rarely freezes over, but in winter the grass turns gold, glinting in the sun. The relative who oversees the cemetery, and who dug Helen's grave by hand, lives across the street.

The day of Helen's burial, it snowed in Arkansas—an unusual occurrence in May. The weather was so bad, they had to set up a tent, and due to the icy roads, some of the guests couldn't make it, but those who did joined the small graveside service to say goodbye to a woman they had known, and hadn't known at all, for many years. As promised, Lou designed Helen's gravestone (in pinkish desert rose), choosing a fancy *Cosmo*-esque pussycat for the front and inscribing the full names of David, Ira, Cleo, and Mary on the back. It stands beside David's granite gravestone, featuring an Oscar, a nod to his storied and wildly successful producing career. (After *Jaws*, David went on to produce films such as *Cocoon*, *Driving Miss Daisy*, and *A Few Good Men*.) When Lou asked Helen for the names of David's closest relatives to put on the back of his stone, Helen said she had trouble remembering them.

Some relatives traveled to the cemetery from other towns around Arkansas. Also among the small group were a few Hearst executives from New York: Frank Bennack and his wife; Eve Burton; and the senior vice president and editorial director of Hearst Magazines International, Kim St. Clair Bodden. In death, Helen's two lives finally merged together as everyone waited for the priest to start.

Before Helen died, she and Lou talked about the possibility of her having a "somewhat religious service," and that is what they had. Lou asked an Episcopal priest from her church to lead it, and after pouring her ashes from an urn, the Rev. Roger Joslin invited individuals to come forward and shovel the earth.

"As far as I know, Helen Gurley Brown didn't read a lot of what we call Holy Scripture. But if she had, I suspect that the 'Song of Solomon,' the Song of Songs, would have been her favorite book," he began, reading aloud a few lines.

Granted, as a little girl in Little Rock, Helen wouldn't have heard a sermon on the Song of Solomon, with its racy imagery, he said. "God is not even mentioned, and the language is every bit as erotic as anything you would find on the pages of *Cosmopolitan* . . . But it can also be understood in a more literal way—as poetry, graphically depicting erotic love between a man and a woman."

> *Your lips are like a crimson thread,*
> *And your mouth is lovely. . . .*

Your two breasts are like two fawns,
Twins of a gazelle that feed among the lilies.

As the sun peeked out, the priest described a woman they all recognized—she was a different kind of preacher who once declared that "skinny is sacred," but also had more meaningful truths to deliver about love, sexuality, and self-realization.

"Helen's fierce honesty, her willingness to explore and depict the sensual nature of modern love, has moved us all toward a deeper and more expansive conception of what is truly sacred," he continued.

Everyone knew that Helen hated it when people went on for too long, so he decided to end early.

"I'll let the Song of Solomon give voice to former lovers, to her departed husband, David, to friends and family and to all that loved her," the priest said.

You have ravished my heart, my sister, my bride,
You have ravished my heart
With a glance of your eyes.

It was a beautiful sermon that captured something important and essential about Helen Gurley Brown, but again, perhaps not the whole picture.

Just out of frame was David Brown's gravestone, which bears no mention of his mother, father, or son. There is only the inscription that Helen wrote for it—one cover line he didn't approve, his final credit:

MARRIED TO HELEN GURLEY BROWN

When Helen died in 2012, about two and a half years after David, she was laid to rest beside him in rural Arkansas, where her mother and sister are also buried. (*Photos courtesy of Norma Lou Honderich and the author.*)

ACKNOWLEDGMENTS

Not long after Helen Gurley Brown died in August 2012, I read her book *Sex and the Single Girl* for the first time. Like millions of women before me, I loved her funny, frank voice from the very first page, but I couldn't help but note the irony of my own introduction to her groundbreaking book, fifty years after its publication.

There I was, a new mom, pushing my baby jogging stroller along a wooded bike path, reading Helen's snappy writing with great pleasure—my hot-pink paperback copy was splayed against the stroller's hood. I wasn't young, single, or dreaming of the big city—so I was hardly her target reader—but her advice has stuck with me nevertheless. If you haven't read *Sex and the Single Girl* in a while (or if you've never read it, period), pick up a copy sometime. Sex is a surprisingly small part of it. At its heart, *Sex and the Single Girl* is really a guide to becoming an individual.

In the five decades since it was written, a lot has changed. I never experienced a world in which a woman couldn't lease an apartment on her own. I've never been discriminated against while applying for a job. I first want to thank my parents, Terry and Michelle Hauser, for raising me to believe that I could do anything I wanted, as long as I worked hard for it. We didn't really talk about "feminism" in my house while I was growing up, but looking back, I now realize that we lived by its principles.

I also want to thank my husband and best friend, Addison MacDonald, for the endless love, support, and patience—and the occasional wine run. As a working mom (to our son Marlow, whose sweetness and sense of humor are a daily tonic), I am grateful to have such a wonderful partner in life, and such awesome in-laws, Greg MacDonald and Wendy Soliday, whom I now look to as examples for how to raise a caring, kind son.

Flannery O'Connor said a good man is hard to find (Helen would agree), but I've been fortunate. This book wouldn't have happened without my longtime literary agent, Larry Weissman, who one day several years ago took me out for drinks and asked if I'd ever thought about writing a book. Over time, Larry has become a mentor and a friend, a someone so valuable to me that I don't even know what to call him anymore—but "agent" doesn't begin to cover it all. His wife, Sascha Alper, defies classification as well. A skilled chef and baker, she is also a talented writer and editor who read my manuscript early on, and gave me priceless advice and edits.

My smart and seasoned editor, Claire Wachtel, helped me see the big picture. Shortly after I turned in my first draft, we met in a lunch booth at HarperCollins, and talked for hours about how Helen Gurley Brown tapped into the cultural zeitgeist of the 1960s. Hours turned into days when I returned to her office the next morning to share a carton of blueberries and talk some more. After our conversation, I expanded the focus of the book to include more about the era that Helen lived in—and helped define—and those passages were some of the most fun to research and report. I'm also thankful to the indefatigable associate editor Hannah Wood, my savvy and heroic guide through the production process, and researcher Rebekah Call, as well as HarperCollins deputy general counsel, Beth Silfin, for her cool, calm judgments.

Since I first read *Sex and the Single Girl* on the back of a baby stroller, dozens of people have come forward to help me bring this book to life. I am grateful to Katherine Heintzelman, a close friend and an early reader; Julia Holmes, a copy editor and novelist who helped me fact-check the book; my film agent, Josie Freedman, who thought it would make a good movie; Barbara Hustedt Crook, Eileen Stukane, and Sheila Weller, all of whom made important introductions to sources; Sharon Harkey and Amber Rounds, who transcribed interviews; and of course the dozens and dozens of people who participated in those interviews, many of them writers and editors themselves whom I greatly admire.

I must give special thanks to Lou Honderich, one of Helen's last remaining relatives and a talented author in her own right. (Look up her young-adult novel, *Ricki.*) Thanks largely to Lou, *Enter Helen* doesn't tell the same old "rags to riches" story that Helen told time and time again; she helped me see all the complexities of her beloved cousin as well as all the nuances of her family's history.

Lou also gave me wonderful photos of Helen and David Brown to use in the book. Thanks, as well, to legendary TV producer Robert Shanks, who shared his photos of Helen Gurley Brown in the 1960s taken by his wife, Ann Zane Shanks, and to the photographer I. C. Rapoport, who also captured Helen on film during her early years at *Cosmopolitan*. Finally, thanks to Eve Rockett, the widow of Canadian photographer Paul Rockett, who took the cover photo of Helen, as well as to GNP Crescendo Records, at gnpcrescendo.com, who provided the high-resolution image.

Last but not least, I would like to acknowledge Smith College, and the special collections staff in particular. What an education I have gotten here—and for free! My heartfelt thanks to Elizabeth Myers, Maida Goodwin, Karen Kukil, Joyce Follet, Amy Hague, Kelly Anderson, Kathleen Banks Nutter, Nanci Young, Kate Sumner, Margaret Jessup, and Nichole Calero. The women's archives that are housed here are world-renowned, and the women who work here are world-class.

NOTES

Dating from 1938 to 2001, the Helen Gurley Brown Papers are housed at the Sophia Smith Collection at Smith College in Northampton, Massachusetts, and will hereafter be referred to as HGB Papers, SSC. The SSC also houses the Gloria Steinem Papers and the *Ms.* Magazine Records, as well as back issues of *Cosmopolitan*, *Ms.*, *Good Housekeeping*, and *Ladies' Home Journal*.

A note on the notes that follow: The author re-created scenes based on the recollections of interview sources as well as material found in articles and other documents, including the writings of Helen Gurley Brown. Whenever Helen's inner thoughts are expressed, they are based on dialogue or descriptions from her own notes, letters, journals, columns, memoirs, etc., as cited.

EPIGRAPH

VII "Funny business, a woman's career": *All About Eve*, 20th Century Fox, 1950.
VII "She is such a feeling person": Runner Associates, 1957 job evaluation of Miss Helen Marie Gurley, then a copywriter at Foote, Cone & Belding, HGB Papers, SSC.

PROLOGUE

1 "Oh well he's got that je ne sais quoi": Helen Gurley Brown, poem written circa early 1960s, HGB Papers, SSC.
1 "a lady who knew . . . the power of sex": Helen Gurley Brown and Lyn Tornabene, *Helen*, 1970–71, HGB Papers, SSC.
1 "Enter, Helen": Ibid.
2 "Anybody can be me": Ibid.

2 They called this song, "Look at Me," aka "The Mouseberger Blues": Ibid. Note: In later years, the spelling changed from *mouseberger* with an *e* to *mouseburger* with a *u*.

2 "she made supper": Quotes and impressions from Lyn Tornabene, interview with the author, November 2014.

3 During those sessions: Summary of subjects discussed gleaned from collected taped interviews recorded by Helen Gurley Brown and Lyn Tornabene, 1970–72, HGB Papers, SSC.

3 "It was too soon"; "I'm still trying": Lyn Tornabene, interview with the author, November 2014.

1: REAL ESTATE

5 "All my life, ever since I was a little girl": *How to Marry a Millionaire*, 20th Century Fox, 1953.

5 Helen loved the idea of David Brown; "gentle as a baby lamb": Descriptions of Helen Gurley Brown's impressions of David; and his house; career, background, and their courtship are from her unpublished autobiography, 1962–63, HGB Papers, SSC.

5 "collector's-item age": Ibid.

6 "It's too soon": Ibid.

6 Helen was a lousy legal secretary: Descriptions of Helen's early jobs, such as working for Paul Ziffren, are from her unpublished autobiography, 1962–63, as well as from *I'm Wild Again: Snippets from My Life and a Few Brazen Thoughts* (New York: St. Martin's Press, 2000), p. 282.

7 "Helen, the kind of man you are thinking of": Helen Gurley Brown, *I'm Wild Again*, p. 283.

7 He interviewed her on a Monday: Ibid., p. 14.

7 It was a simple arrangement: Helen described her affair with the wealthy builder and the liquor, cash, and gifts he gave her in Helen Gurley Brown and Lyn Tornabene, audio recording file no. 2551b, tape 7, "Haring (?) Saga" (side B), Lyn Tornabene, HGB Papers, SSC.

8 "I was like a prostitute": Ibid.

9 According to Ruth's thumbnail sketch: Helen Gurley Brown, unpublished autobiography, 1962–63.

10 He was seriously impressed: Accounts of Helen and David's early courtship are from Helen Gurley Brown's unpublished 1962–63 autobiography and *I'm Wild Again*, pp. 25–26.

10 he, too, had been abandoned by his father: Details about David Brown's family and childhood are from his memoir, *Let Me Entertain You* (New York: William Morrow & Co., 1990), pp. 60–71.

10 "We were a secret"; "He was the worst kind of snob": Ibid.

11 "He's only 42"; "I feel more like a something with other people": Helen Gurley Brown, early unpublished notes about David Brown, HGB Papers, SSC.

11 His house was more run-down: Descriptions of David's Pacific Palisades house and Helen's living situation are from Helen Gurley Brown's unpublished autobiography, 1962–63.

2: GROUND RULES

13 "Don't you know that a man being rich is like a girl being pretty?": *Gentlemen Prefer Blondes*, 20th Century Fox, 1953.

13 Sol Spiegel, Sam Siegel: Helen described struggling to learn names in Hollywood in her unpublished autobiography, 1962–63, HGB Papers, SSC.

13 a little mnemonic device: Ibid.

14 Helen spent at least half her salary buying black-tie dresses: Ibid.

14 "Tell me, Ernest": Ibid.

14 "You simply don't ask a screenwriter . . . What would you think": Ibid.

15 "She's supposed to have a clean house . . . but I just have a *feeling*": Helen Gurley Brown and Lyn Tornabene, dialogue from audio recording file no. 2549b, "General Personality" tape 5, (side B), 1970–71, HGB Papers, SSC.

15 "Nobody ever asks me": Helen Gurley Brown, unpublished autobiography, 1962–63.

15 "Look, you are not a Radcliffe undergraduate . . . You must simply act": Ibid.

3: SEX AND THE NOT-SO-SINGLE GIRL

16 "It's useful being top banana": *Breakfast at Tiffany's*, Jurow-Shepherd, 1961.

16 She was not beautiful, or even pretty: Helen Gurley Brown, *Sex and the Single Girl* (Fort Lee, NJ: Barricade Books, 2003), p. 3.

16 painfully plain: Letty Cottin Pogrebin, interview with the author, January 2014.

17 "the type who'd ravage females": Cindy Adams, "He Made Her a Married Woman," *Pageant*, December 1963.

17 it was David who had come up with the idea: Ibid.

17 It was up to Mrs. Neale: Descriptions of David's house and housekeeper are from Helen Gurley Brown's unpublished autobiography, 1962–63, HGB Papers, SSC.

17 it dawned on Letty: Letty Cottin Pogrebin, interview with the author, January 2014.

18 A natural showman: Impressions of Bernard Geis's appearance and showmanship, Ibid.

18 his particular genius was in advertising, promotion, and publicity: Background on Bernard Geis Associates from Dick Schaap, "How to Succeed in Publishing Without Really Publishing," *New York Times*, August 13, 1967; and from Amy Fine Collins, "Once Was Never Enough," *Vanity Fair*, January 2000.

18 "Berney Geis was an original. An innovator": Letty Cottin Pogrebin's eulogy for Bernard Geis, shared during interview with the author, January 2014.

18 he was a lovable scamp; "How many times a week do you have sex?": Descriptions of Geis's flirtatiousness and the famous fireman's pole in the office, Ibid.

19 she nearly passed out: Information on Letty's responsibilities and promotion at Bernard Geis Associates, Ibid.

19 "I'd like to publish this": Ibid.

19 "What *is* a sexy woman?": Quotes from Helen Gurley Brown, *Sex and the Single Girl*, p. 65.

19 She had just gotten her own prescription: Letty Cottin Pogrebin, "What 'The Pill' Did," CNN.com, May 7, 2010. Background on Enovid from "The Pill," American Experience, www.pbs.org.

20 "Folksingers Are Promiscuous": Stephanie Gervis (later Harrington) cited this sign in her fantastic spoof of *Sex and the Single Girl*, "Guidelines for Village Girls: In Greenwich Village, Sex Is Where You Find It," *Village Voice*, July 26, 1962.

20 "The average man with an urge": Helen Gurley Brown, *Sex and the Single Girl*, p. 21.

20 "Don Juan would curl his lip": Ibid.

20 "Carry a controversial book": Ibid., p. 63.

20 "A lady's love *should* pay": Ibid., p. 239.

20 "Should a man think you are a virgin?": Ibid., p. 231.

21 Helen's funny, forthright voice spoke to Letty: Descriptions of Letty's reaction to *Sex and the Single Girl* and her own single-girl lifestyle are from Letty Cottin Pogrebin, interview with the author, January 2014.

21 "the newest glamour girl of our time": Helen Gurley Brown, *Sex and the Single Girl*, p. 5.

21 "Berney, you won't believe it": Letty Cottin Pogrebin, interview with the author, January 2014.

22 "Listen to voices in movies": Helen Gurley Brown, *Sex and the Single Girl*, p. 81.

22 "Not everyone is going to be charmed": Dialogue and descriptions of media-training Helen Gurley Brown are from Letty Cottin Pogrebin, interview with the author, January 2014.

4: THE STORY EDITOR

25 "If you would please your woman": David Brown, "Sex and the Single Girl as Seen by David Brown," *Cavalier*, April 1964.

25 David also discovered some love letters: Helen gave a brief account in a note she wrote prefacing her letters to Bill Peters, written in the late 1940's, HGB Papers, SSC.

25 "what an intolerable waste of gin": Helen Gurley Brown to Bill Peters, June 15, 1949, HGB Papers, SSC.

25 "With a ukulele and a striped blazer": Helen Gurley Brown to Bill Peters, August 8, 1949, HGB Papers, SSC.

25 "I swam and ate fried chicken": Ibid.

26 She really could write: Helen recalled this story to Art Berman in "Helen's Book Was a Shock to Her Mother," *Los Angeles Times*, June 24, 1962, HGB Papers, SSC.

26 David was essentially a talent scout: Information about David Brown Associates and David's early projects is from David Brown, *Let Me Entertain You* (New York: William Morrow & Co., 1990), pp. 19–22.

27 David reported to Herbert R. Mayes: Background on David Brown's years at *Cosmopolitan*, Ibid., pp. 27–34.

27 Originally called *The Cosmopolitan*: Background on *Cosmopolitan*'s founding and colorful history is from James Landers, *The Improbable First Century of*

"Cosmopolitan" Magazine (Columbia: University of Missouri Press, 2010), passim.

27 For a while, *Cosmopolitan* enjoyed great success: Ibid. Additional background from David Brown, *Let Me Entertain You*, p. 28.

28 he became a mentor to David: Account of David Brown's relationship with Herbert R. Mayes from *Let Me Entertain You*, pp. 28–30.

28 "the best editor in New York": Ibid.

28 "I said, 'No, Herb, the truth is": Ibid.

29 David soon built a reputation in Hollywood: Background on David Brown's early career in film from Herb Stein, "Hollywood: Brown No Newcomer to Picture-Making; Producer Versatile in Story 'Know-How,' " *Morning Telegraph*, February 9, 1961; and from Hollywood columnist Joan Dew, "Joan Dew's Male Call: A Producer Who Isn't Stereotyped," publication and date unknown, HGB Papers, SSC.

29 Wayne, a leggy brunette: David Brown discussed his ex-wife Wayne's unhappiness in Los Angeles, and the decline of their marriage, in *Let Me Entertain You*, p. 250; he later wrote about the importance of a wife having her own career in "Sex and the Single Girl as Seen by David Brown," *Cavalier*, April 1964.

29 she and David finally married: Helen gave an account of their wedding in David Brown's memoir, *Let Me Entertain You*, p. 40, as well as in her unpublished autobiography, 1962–63, in which she described the later outing to see stripper Candy Barr, HGB Papers, SSC.

30 something of a little mascot: Helen Gurley Brown and Lyn Tornabene, audio recording file no. 2552a, tape 8, "3/25/72" (side A), HGB Papers, SSC. Helen described her comfortable position at Foote, Cone & Belding.

30 Working on the Max Factor account: Helen described this naming process in Helen Gurley Brown, *Sex and the Office* (Fort Lee, NJ: Barricade Books, 2004), p. 308.

30 WHIPPED CHERRY *and following names*: Helen Gurley Brown, "SHADE NAMES," circa 1959, early advertising copy, HGB Papers, SSC.

30 She doubted herself: Accounts of Helen's frustrations at Kenyon & Eckhardt from Helen Gurley Brown and Lyn Tornabene, audio recording no. 2552a, tape 8, "3/25/72" (side A), HGB Papers, SSC; and from Helen Gurley Brown, *Sex and the Office*, p. 308.

31 "What am I going to do?": Dialogue from Helen Gurley Brown's version of the story told in David Brown's memoir, *Let Me Entertain You*, pp. 104–5.

31 "There's a chapter on the apartment": Ibid.

31 "that sounds like my book": Ibid.

31 "It won't work": Helen Gurley Brown and Lyn Tornabene, dialogue from audio recording no. 2552a, tape 8, "3/25/72" (side A), HGB Papers, SSC.

32 the stigma of the single woman: Eleanor Harris, "Women Without Men," *Look*, July 5, 1960.

32 "There are two sound ways": Betsy Marvin McKinney, "Is the Double Standard Out of Date?" *Ladies' Home Journal*, May 1961.

33 "I think you've got it": Helen Gurley Brown and Lyn Tornabene, dialogue and account from audio recording no. 2552a, tape 8, "3/25/72" (side A), HGB

Papers, SSC. Helen talked about how David made her rewrite three times. She also cited the article "Women Without Men" as a motivating force.

33 It was David who told Helen: David explained how he wanted Helen to write the book under her married name, sharing her own experiences, in "Sex and the Single Girl as seen by David Brown."

5: A Fun Scam

34 "An extra woman is a problem": Marjorie Hillis, *Live Alone and Like It: A Guide for the Extra Woman* (London: Virago Press, 2005), chapter 1.

34 "Your very kind, very superlative comments": Letty Cottin to Helen and David Brown, February 6, 1962, HGB Papers, SSC.

35 "When the clock says Charlie's due home": Michael Drury, "Live the Life You Love," *Good Housekeeping*, April 1962.

36 In 1960, there were an estimated 21 million: Eleanor Harris, "Women Without Men," *Look*, July 5, 1960.

36 "I think marriage is insurance for the *worst* years of your life": Helen Gurley Brown, *Sex and the Single Girl* (Fort Lee, NJ: Barricade Books, 2003), p. 4.

36 Letty would pull off a lot of stunts: Descriptions based on Letty Cottin Pogrebin's interview with the author, January 2014; Letty's eulogy for Bernard Geis; and description of billboard from Barbara Seaman's excellent biography *Lovely Me: The Life of Jacqueline Susann* (New York: William Morrow, 1987), p. 325.

38 "She worked very hard to create this package": Letty Cottin Pogrebin, interview with the author, January 2014.

6: Single Women of the World, Unite!

39 "Should Men Be Allowed?": Letty Cottin, press release for *Sex and the Single Girl*, April 16, 1962, HGB Papers, SSC.

39 "It's the old '*Everybody* is talking about *Sex and the Single Girl*' approach": Letty Cottin to Helen Gurley Brown, March 14, 1962, HGB Papers, SSC.

40 "We're not getting too far": Ibid.

40 "Maybe a Catholic ban!": Helen Gurley Brown to Letty Cottin, March 19, 1962, HGB Papers, SSC.

40 Mary Magdalene, pre-salvation: Letty Cottin to Helen Gurley Brown, March 30, 1962, HGB Papers, SSC.

40 No, Helen wrote back, her semi-famous exes were out: Helen Gurley Brown to Letty Cottin, March 19, 1962, HGB Papers, SSC.

40 "I know you worked like a dog": Letty Cottin to Helen Gurley Brown, March 14, 1962.

41 "I just don't think there would be anything *in* it for them": Helen Gurley Brown to Letty Cottin, March 19, 1962, HGB Papers, SSC.

41 "Douse the perfume on cotton": Helen Gurley Brown, *Sex and the Single Girl*, p. 80.

41 On her pink paper, Helen drafted a note to Max Factor: Helen Gurley Brown to Letty Cottin, May 2, 1962, HGB Papers, SSC.

42 "You are that *rara avis*": Letty Cottin to Helen Gurley Brown, March 14, 1962, HGB Papers, SSC.

42 "There are just too few single girls browsing through book stores": Helen Gurley Brown to Letty Cottin, March 19, 1962, HGB Papers, SSC.

43 "Don't Knock It, Girls, Says Author": Letty Cottin, press release for *Sex and the Single Girl*, April 16, 1962, HGB Papers, SSC.

44 "What *The Best of Everything* did": Letty Cottin to Jerry Wald, April 24, 1962, HGB Papers, SSC.

44 "Naturally, not all of your girls will become the wife of a Hollywood producer": Letty Cottin to Director, Katherine Gibbs Schools, April 27, 1962, HGB Papers, SSC.

45 "The book may shatter conventional shibboleths" *and following*: Letty Cottin to editor, *Record Chronicle*, Denton, Texas, April 26, 1962, HGB Papers, SSC.

7: THE DECLINE OF WESTERN CIVILIZATION

46 "As tasteless a book": Robert Kirsch, "Sex and the Single Girl Falls Short of Its Promising Title," *Los Angeles Times*, July 6, 1962, HGB Papers, SSC.

46 "HEARTIEST CONGRATULATIONS": Bernard Geis Associates to Helen Gurley Brown at the Hotel Madison, 15 East 58th St., New York, NY, HGB Papers, SSC. Reproduced with the permission of Bernard Geis Associates. *Note:* The telegram is dated "23 1050 EDT," which author interpreted to mean May 23 at 10:50 eastern daylight time. Letty Cottin Pogrebin confirmed that Bernard Geis sent his book authors a congratulatory telegram on their publication dates.

46 Godless Gotham: Letty Cottin Pogrebin, eulogy for Bernard Geis.

46 Helen's book tour had begun: Details taken from various correspondence between Helen Gurley Brown and Bernard Geis Associates, as well as from collected book tour itineraries and miscellany, 1962–69, HGB Papers, SSC.

48 *Sex and the Single Girl* instead of *Sex for the Single Girl*: "Playboy Interview: Helen Gurley Brown," *Playboy*, April 1963.

48 "How does it feel to be on top of Richard Nixon?" Letty Cottin Pogrebin to Helen Gurley Brown, June 21, 1962, HGB Papers, SSC.

49 "Now, I don't have to go out and promote": Ron Fimrite, "The Single Girl's Expert on Sex," *San Francisco Chronicle*, July 6, 1962, HGB Papers, SSC.

49 "Of course you feel alone sometimes": Joy Miller, AP, reprinted as "Former Little Rockian Analyzes Spinsterhood," *Arkansas Democrat*, June 7, 1962.

49 "So do murder and rape!": Cleo Bryan to Helen Gurley Brown, May 3, 1962, HGB Papers, SSC.

49 "When Mrs. Cleo Bryan": Art Berman, "Helen's Book Was a Shock to Her Mother," *Los Angeles Times*, June 24, 1962, HGB Papers, SSC.

50 Helen didn't mention that she thought her mother was being totally selfish: Helen aired her true feelings about her mother's reaction to Lyn Tornabene years later in audio recording no. 2552b, "Emotions," tape 8 (side B), HGB Papers, SSC.

50 "My mother is quite a dame": Art Berman, "Helen's Book Was a Shock to Her Mother."

50 "David put me up to writing the book": Ibid.

51 "HUSBAND SAID 'WRITE'": Ibid.

52 Pickwick's in Hollywood devoted a window display: "How to Promote a Book and Sell 1,000 Copies," *Publishers Weekly*, October 1962, HGB Papers, SSC.

52 "There are no girls that age down here": Stephanie Gervis, "In Greenwich Village, Sex Is Where You Find It," *Village Voice*, July 26, 1962, HGB Papers, SSC.

53 "a libel against womanhood": reader letter, *San Francisco Chronicle*, July 12, HGB Papers, SSC.

53 "Miss Brown provides the blueprint of a female so phony": Robert Kirsch, "Sex and the Single Girl Falls Short of Its Promising Title."

53 "At long last someone has written a book": Anne Steinert, "Being a Single Girl Can Be Fun," *New York Journal-American*, May 23, 1962, HGB Papers, SSC.

53 "sometimes shocking but always stimulating philosophy": Mildred Schroeder, " 'Sex and the Single Girl'—Startling, Stimulating," *San Francisco Examiner*, May 30, 1962, HGB Papers, SSC.

53 "racy and sassy": Initials T. M., "1962 Baedeker for 'Les Girls,' *Houston Chronicle*, date unknown, HGB Papers, SSC.

53 " 'Do I dare go on?' " *and following*: Miss Zora Ann Krneta, "Handbook for 'The Chase,' " *Charleston Gazette*, West Virginia, June 10, 1962, HGB Papers, SSC. Quote is slightly condensed.

54 "David Brown in for new scrutiny": Information about *Sex and the Single Girl*'s success is from Helen Gurley Brown's memo, "Brief Resume of What's Happened With the Book So Far," July 1962, HGB Papers, SSC.

54 "Now it's time to get down to work": Diane Patrick, "Royal Correspondence: PW Talks with Helen Gurley Brown," *Publishers Weekly*, February 23, 2004. Helen spoke about her Royal manual typewriter in this interview as well.

8: SOMETHING'S GOT TO GIVE

55 "Honey, nothing can live": *The Misfits*, Seven Arts Productions, 1961.

55 The film was troubled from the start: Background on *Something's Got to Give* and David's impressions of Marilyn Monroe taken from David Brown's memoir, *Let Me Entertain You* (New York: William Morrow & Co., 1990), p. 53.

56 they didn't know her: Background on Marilyn Monroe's life from Donald Spoto, *Marilyn Monroe: The Biography* (New York: Cooper Square Press, 2001), passim.

56 "She used to come into my office and sit on my lap": David Brown, *Let Me Entertain You*, p. 53.

56 Unfortunately, it didn't last: Background on Monroe's psychiatrist's meddling and the Fox lawsuit from Donald Spoto, *Marilyn Monroe*, passim.

56 David had committed to producing a historic drama: Murray Schumach, "Fox Will Step Up Filming for 1963," *New York Times*, March 26, 1962.

56 There were many other films on Fox's list: Ibid.

57 "the greatest grossing film of all times": Kenneth S, Smith, "Skouras Defends 'Cleopatra' to Stockholders," *New York Times*, May 16, 1962.

57 Costs for *Cleopatra* . . . skyrocketed: Ibid. Additional background on *Cleopatra* remake from David Kamp, "When Liz Met Dick," *Vanity Fair*, April 2011.

57 "intemperate vamp who destroys families": Referenced by Kitty Kelley, *Elizabeth Taylor: The Last Star* (New York: Simon & Schuster, 2011), chapter 17. Also, reference to pope: David Bret, *Elizabeth Taylor: the Lady, the Lover, the Legend, 1932–2011* (Vancouver, Canada: Greystone Books, 2011), p. 156.

57 "a big picture" on "a big subject": Background on *Cleopatra* movies from David Brown, *Let Me Entertain You*, p. 73.

58 "Only the Romans left more ruins in Europe": Ibid., p. 76.

58 Warner Bros. was offering $200,000: Information on the film option and adaptation challenges of *Sex and the Single Girl* from Shana Alexander, "Singular Girl's Success," *Life*, March 1, 1963.

59 also busy trying to sell the stage rights: Lucy Kroll to David Brown, June 25, 1962, HGB Papers, SSC.

59 "You're old enough, do you want a little sip?": Impressions, descriptions, scenes, and dialogue in this chapter taken from extensive interviews and email exchanges between author and Helen's cousin Lou Honderich, 2013–15.

61 "Do you think you might possibly be homesick?": Ibid.

62 "We're going to go shopping!": Ibid.

63 "Where are all the bags?": Ibid.

63 "What do boys at your age do?": Ibid.

64 Lou could tell that David liked her company: Impressions, descriptions, scenes, and dialogue, ibid.

64 Her cousin had been her "glamorous go-to": Ibid.

65 "You don't have to be perfect": Ibid.

66 the friends and relatives who had read it were shocked: Ibid.

66 "She sold her family down the river": Cleo's comment, per Lou Honderich, from an email exchange with the author.

66 "Would your mother mind if you read it?" Lou Honderich, interview with the author, November 2013.

66 "Absolutely . . . I believe the things I said": Ibid.

9: THE WOIKING GIRL'S FRIEND

67 "She's a phony": *Breakfast at Tiffany's*, Jurow-Shepherd, 1961.

67 "I've never been able to flirt before": David Brown described some of the fan mail that Helen received in "Sex and the Single Girl as Seen by David Brown," *Cavalier*, April 1964.

68 "The best way to get this across": Bernard Geis to Helen Gurley Brown, June 8, 1962, HGB Papers, SSC. Reproduced with the permission of Bernard Geis Associates.

68 She said yes to all kinds of meet-and-greets: Details are from various correspondence between Helen Gurley Brown and Bernard Geis Associates, as well as from collected book tour itineraries and miscellany, 1962–69, HGB Papers, SSC.

68 "female-type supervisors": "FEMALE DAY," Jack Mauck, circa 1962, HGB Papers, SSC.

68 "Once a year the dimly illuminated S.H.I.T. Society": Ibid.

69 Among the ideas Helen and Berney discussed, over time: From collected

memos between Helen Gurley Brown and Bernard Geis, March 1962 and later, HGB Papers, SSC.

70 "not too old nor too unattractive": Helen Gurley Brown, "The Girls of Beverly Hills" (in addition to the treatment for this novel, Helen saved her other early book proposals, including ones for "Topic A" and "Executive Wives"), early 1960s, HGB Papers, SSC.

70 "She is not the performer with her husband": Helen Gurley Brown, "The Girls of Beverly Hills," HGB Papers, SSC.

70 "The doctors I've talked to tell me": Helen Gurley Brown to Bernard Geis, March 5, 1962, HGB Papers, SSC.

71 "The book I could write best": Helen Gurley Brown to Bernard Geis, March 14, 1962, HGB Papers, SSC.

71 "We are beginning to get fervent letters": Bernard Geis to Helen Gurley Brown, June 7, 1962, HGB Papers, SSC. Reproduced with the permission of Bernard Geis Associates.

71 the post office in Pacific Palisades refused to deliver the mail: Jennifer Scanlon, *Bad Girls Go Everywhere* (New York: Penguin Books, 2009), p. 149.

71 "Hold onto your lovely wig": Bernard Geis to Helen Gurley Brown, October 9, 1962, HGB Papers, SSC. Reproduced with the permission of Bernard Geis Associates.

72 "I am something of a little *star* now!": Helen Gurley Brown to Bernard Geis, October 10, 1962, HGB Papers, SSC. Helen detailed the hassle of her recent appearances.

72 Eventually, "Woman Alone" would reach: Background on the offer and Helen Gurley Brown's syndicated newspaper column gathered from collected "Woman Alone" correspondence, clippings, and financial material, 1962–65, HGB Papers, SSC.

73 To pay for *Cleopatra*: Background on the cost of *Cleopatra*, the crumbling of Fox, the iron hand of Darryl F. Zanuck, and David Brown's eventual firing taken from David Brown, *Let Me Entertain You* (New York: William Morrow & Co. 1990), pp. 73–77. Additional background on *Cleopatra* remake from David Kamp, "When Liz Met Dick," *Vanity Fair*, April 2011.

73 "The 'We' explains why he oozes security": Cindy Adams, "He Made Her a Married Woman," *Pageant*, December 1963.

73 David was offered a position: Helen Gurley Brown in David Brown's memoir, *Let Me Entertain You*, p. 106.

10: NEW YORK, NEW YORK

75 "I was a country girl from Los Angeles": Helen Gurley Brown, quoted in an unidentified publication in collected clippings about her apartments and offices, November 22, 1993, HGB Papers, SSC.

75 extensive newspaper strike: Background information from Scott Sherman, "The Long Good-Bye," *Vanity Fair*, November 30, 2012; Sheldon Binn, "114-Day Newspaper Strike Ends as Engravers Ratify Contract; Loss Is in Excess of $190,000,000," *New York Times*, April 1, 1963; and "Newspaper Panel to Hear Disputes," *New York Times*, February 14, 1964.

76 "These were costumes for women with energy to burn": Jeanne Molli, "Balenciaga and Givenchy Styles Offer Last Word on Spring," *New York Times*, Western Edition, March 1, 1963.

76 She barely left the apartment: David Brown described Helen's fearful reluctance to leave the apartment in *Let Me Entertain You* (New York: William Morrow & Co., 1990), p. 255. Helen wrote about her earlier visit to New York with David, recalling how Bruce's mother brought her a scarf and mittens, in her unpublished autobiography, 1962–63, HGB Papers, SSC.

77 Outside, it was gray, always gray: Helen documented her early impressions of New York that spring in "NEW YORK NEW YORK NEW YORK," March 11, 1963, HGB Papers, SSC.

77 She wondered how New Yorkers felt when they went out west: Ibid.

78 The day they were supposed to leave 515 Radcliffe Avenue: David Brown, *Let Me Entertain You*, p. 254–55.

78 Once in the city: Ibid.

78 she stood in the doorway of No. 17C and cried: Background on Helen's first days in 17C from unidentified publication in collected clippings about her apartments and offices, November 22, 1993, HGB Papers, SSC.

79 she missed the feeling of having somewhere to *be*: Helen Gurley Brown, *Sex and the Office* (Fort Lee, NJ: Barricade Books, 2004), p. 281. Helen confided in the reader that, while at home writing *Sex and the Office*, she missed office life.

79 "CALLING ALL WIDOWS, DIVORCEES, BACHELOR GIRLS": Helen Gurley Brown, "Woman Alone," Los Angeles Times Syndicate, reprinted in *Helen Gurley Brown's Outrageous Opinions* (New York: Bernard Geis Associates in Cooperation with Avon Books, 1966), p. 17.

79 Her efforts to win over doormen: Helen Gurley Brown, "NEW YORK NEW YORK NEW YORK."

81 "In many ways it's like Pittsburgh": Ibid.

81 "The west is for the babies": Helen Gurley Brown, untitled, undated notes on New York (different from above), HGB Papers, SSC.

11: THE MEANING OF LUNCH

82 "Lunchtime is fraught with possibilities!": Helen Gurley Brown, *Sex and the Office* (Fort Lee, NJ: Barricade Books, 2004), p. 96.

82 "You see them every morning at a quarter to nine": Rona Jaffe, *The Best of Everything* (New York: Penguin Books, 2005), p. 1.

83 She would suggest two Brown Paper Bag Plans: Helen observed the lunchtime habits of working girls and then offered these solutions in *Sex and the Office*, pp. 100–4.

83 "American Beauty Lunches": Ibid., p. 100.

83 "My idea is that a kind of secretarial handbook": Helen Gurley Brown to Bernard Geis, November 8, 1962, HGB Papers, SSC.

84 "I'm best when I'm angry": Ibid.

84 "The girl is sent as a bribe": Helen Gurley Brown, *Sex and the Office*, p. 257.

84 "office wolves"; "If your instinct goes 'sniff, sniff—peculiar, peculiar'": Ibid., pp. 220–21.

84 "It makes me feel small and helpless": Details about the material that Bernard Geis cut out of *Sex and the Office* are taken from "Three Little Bedtime Stories," a chapter not used, from an early draft of *Sex and the Office*, HGB Papers, SSC.

85 "full of sincerity and friendship": The story of Claudia and the young model is also from "Three Little Bedtime Stories."

85 "and then her mouth was THERE": Ibid.

86 "Boys Will Be Girls . . . and Vice Versa": Helen Gurley Brown, outline for a draft of *Sex and the Office*, undated, HGB Papers, SSC.

86 "I thought it was going to be about how to handle temperamental homosexuals": Bernard Geis to Helen Gurley Brown, February 19, 1964, HGB Papers, SSC. Reproduced with the permission of Bernard Geis Associates.

86 It was the idea of a matinee that was truly "icky": Helen Gurley Brown to Bernard Geis, February 8, 1964.

86 "No objection was made by me": Bernard Geis to Helen Gurley Brown, February 19, 1964, HGB Papers, SSC. Reproduced with the permission of Bernard Geis Associates.

87 On an average day, 2,700 people entered the Playboy Club: Background information on the Playboy Club from Thomas Buckley, "Playboy Club Busiest in City Despite Its Failure to Win Cabaret License," *New York Times*, April 5, 1963.

87 "I get a lot of mail about how to keep from having a baby": "*Playboy* Interview: Helen Gurley Brown," *Playboy*, April 1963.

87 "There is some chance of becoming barren": Ibid.

88 "It's outrageous that girls can't be aborted here": Ibid.

88 "I just hit the roof": Ibid.

88 "*Au contraire*. She's asking for it": Ibid.

88 "I don't know of anything more ruthless": Ibid.

12: A STRANGE STIRRING

89 "The truth is that I've always been a bad-tempered bitch": Betty Friedan, *Life So Far* (New York: Simon & Schuster, 2000), p. 379.

89 "top money": From the *Playboy* ad that ran in Gloria Steinem's article, "A Bunny's Tale," *Show*, May 1963.

89 Pretending to be a former waitress: Ibid.

90 "all women are Bunnies": Steinem detailed the aftermath of her *Show* exposé in her book *Outrageous Acts and Everyday Rebellions*, 2nd ed. (New York: Holt, 1995), p. 75.

91 "It was a strange stirring": Betty Friedan, *The Feminine Mystique*, 50th anniversary edition (New York: Norton, 2013), p. 1.

91 Originally from Peoria, Illinois: Background on Betty Friedan's upbringing, career, and family life from Friedan, *Life So Far*, passim.

91 "I later learned he was having an affair": Ibid., p. 78.

92 "one night, he hit me": Ibid., p. 87.

92 Betty was asked to conduct a survey of her Smith classmates: Background on the survey that led to *The Feminine Mystique* is taken from Betty Friedan's account in *Life So Far*, pp. 97–105.

92 The final survey asked about: Ibid.

93 After that meeting, Betty got a $3,000 book advance: Ibid., p. 109.

93 "Sometimes a woman would tell me": Betty Friedan, *The Feminine Mystique*, p. 8.

94 "The only way for a woman . . . to know herself as a person": Ibid., p. 416.

94 "I'll tell you *this*": Helen Gurley Brown, original first chapter for *Sex and the Office*, "Come with Me to the Office," which was later cut. HGB Papers, SSC.

94 "They call her brilliant, this highly paid Circe": Philip Wylie, "The Career Woman," *Playboy*, January 1963.

95 "We haven't been introduced": Helen Gurley Brown's original first chapter for *Sex and the Office*, "Come with Me to the Office."

96 "Most girls—probably 90 per cent": Bernard Geis to Helen Gurley Brown, February 4, 1964, HGB Papers, SSC. Reproduced with the permission of Bernard Geis Associates.

96 She was willing to tone down that chapter, not to lose it entirely: Background is from Helen Gurley Brown's letter to Bernard Geis, February 8, 1964, HGB Papers, SSC.

96 "Tell her she not only *isn't* unfortunate": Ibid.

97 "Explain to your husband": Helen Gurley Brown, *Sex and the Office* (Fort Lee, NJ: Barricade Books, 2004), p. 276.

97 "The Inquiring Camera Girl": Background from "The Inquiring Camera Girl camera," www.jfklibrary.org, John F. Kennedy Presidential Library and Museum, Columbia Point, Boston, MA; and Dorothy McCardle, "Jackie Kennedy—Ex-Girl Reporter, Part 3: She Found Out What It Takes to Be Nation's No. 1 Hostess," *St. Petersburg Times*, September 30, 1960.

13: WOMEN ALONE

98 "No matter how accustomed to your own community": Max Wylie, *Career Girl, Watch Your Step!* (New York: Dodd, Mead, 1964), p. 92.

98 a massive crowd of 250,000 people: Accounts of the march and the Rev. Dr. Martin Luther King Jr.'s speech from James Reston, " 'I Have a Dream . . .' Peroration by Dr. King Sums Up a Day the Capital Will Remember," *New York Times*, August 29, 1963; and "The March on Washington; March Returns to Site of Dr. King's Great Dream," *New York Times*, October 16, 1995.

98 "I have a dream": Rev. Martin Luther King Jr. at the March on Washington, 1963, www.archives.gov/press/exhibits/dream-speech.pdf.

99 That same day, two young women were brutally stabbed: Selwyn Raab, "30-Year-Echoes from Slaying of 2," *New York Times*, August 29, 1993.

99 On the floor, the bodies of the two roommates: Background on the murders largely taken from T. J. English, *The Savage City: Race, Murder, and a Generation on the Edge* (New York: HarperCollins, 2011), passim.

99 "The Career Girls Murders lit up the city like a hit Broadway show": Ibid, p. 25.

100 tabloids found new ways to package the stories: Ibid.

100 "girls were asking superintendents about double locks": Gay Talese, "Air of Fear Grips Sedate East Side," *New York Times*, August 31, 1963.

100 "a wave of fear ran through single women in New York": Jane Maas, interview
      with the author, February 2015.

101 "The police [are] under intense pressure": Homer Bigart, "Killing of 2 Girls
      Yields No Clue," *New York Times*, September 27, 1963.

101 The headline was . . . not subtle: Helen Gurley Brown, "Woman Alone," Los
      Angeles Times Syndicate. "HOW DO YOU KEEP FROM GETTING MUR-
      DERED?" was reprinted in *Helen Gurley Brown's Outrageous Opinions* (New York:
      Bernard Geis Associates in Cooperation with Avon Books, 1966), pp. 280–82.

101 "Scream," he advised: Ibid.

102 "Is there so much more crime": Ibid.

102 "Well, maybe girls alone should stay away"; "it will have nothing to do with
      where she lives": Ibid.

102 "the fringe element" *and following*: Max Wylie, *Career Girl, Watch Your Step!*
      p. 68.

102 "Don't think of yourself as being safe": Ibid., p. 58.

103 "You're Helen Gurley Brown": Barbara Seaman told the story of the meeting
      between Helen and Jacqueline Susann in *Lovely Me* (New York: William Mor-
      row, 1987), p. 282.

103 "truck driver in drag": Referenced by Abby Hirsch, "Novels and Stories,
      Kitsch and Quality," *New York Times*, July 11, 1976.

104 "I loved the way she looked": Helen Gurley Brown quoted in Barbara Seaman's
      biography of Susann, *Lovely Me*, p. 283.

104 He had taken her here shortly after they married: Helen Gurley Brown, un-
      published autobiography, 1962-63, HGB Papers, SSC.

104 New York intimidated her: Helen mused about her gradual New Yorkification
      in *I'm Wild Again: Snippets from My Life and a Few Brazen Thoughts* (New York:
      St. Martin's Press, 2000), pp. 37–42.

104 Some nights in her apartment, she wondered: Ibid., p. 41. Helen wrote about
      imagining the goings-on in the apartments and lives around her, a theme she
      sometimes explored in her notes.

104 More than a few of her neighbors were famous: Details about Helena Rubin-
      stein's apartment taken from Thomas W. Ennis, "Helena Rubinstein's Apart-
      ment Is for Rent at $50,000 a Year," *New York Times*, February 6, 1966.

105 New York wasn't interested in little girls: Helen Gurley Brown, early notes
      about New York, HGB Papers, SSC.

105 "Jacqueline Kennedy orders mostly from sketches": John Fairchild, front-page
      editorial, *Women's Wear Daily*, July 13, 1960.

106 "Why the fuck does this have to happen to me?": Barbara Seaman, *Lovely Me*,
      p. 284.

106 "As we have seen through our tears": Helen Gurley Brown, "Woman Alone,"
      Los Angeles Times Syndicate, "Envy Not, Columnist Advises," reprinted in
      Pittsburgh Post-Gazette, December 9, 1963.

14: Peace Through Understanding

107 "It was the perfect time to think silver": Andy Warhol and Pat Hackett, *POP-
      ism: The Warhol Sixties* (Harcourt Brace Jovanovich, 1990), p. 64.

107 the NYPD finally arrested a suspect: Background on George Whitmore Jr. and Richard Robles from T. J. English, *The Savage City: Race, Murder, and a Generation on the Edge* (New York: HarperCollins, 2011); and Paul Vitello, "George Whitmore Jr., Who Falsely Confessed to 3 Murders in 1964, Dies at 68," *New York Times*, October 15, 2012.

108 Gernreich's topless bathing suit: Bernadine Morris, "Topless Suits Go on Sale This Week," *New York Times*, June 16, 1964.

108 the nation's first topless bar: David Allyn, *Make Love, Not War: The Sexual Revolution—An Unfettered History* (New York: Routledge, 2011), p. 25.

109 As a girl, she had been to the World's Fair in Chicago, twice: Helen Gurley Brown, unpublished autobiography 1962–63, HGB Papers, SSC.

109 The tension between them had been building up: Helen talked about Cleo's visit to New York City during the World's Fair in Helen Gurley Brown and Lyn Tornabene, audio recording no. 2552b, "Emotions," tape 8 (side B), HGB Papers, SSC.

109 "Don't pay any attention to her": Helen recalled this story in the "Emotions" tape with Tornabene and in a later *Cosmopolitan* article idea memo, "NOTES ON GIRLS WHO GET HIT OR VICE VERSA," alternately titled, "FAMILY FISTICUFFS," *Cosmopolitan* article ideas, 1970s–1980s, HGB Papers, SSC. Dialogue is from the *Cosmopolitan* memo.

109 She hit Cleo right there in the taxi: Ibid.

110 "Practically everybody in the world is coming to the fair!": "Stock Footage—TO THE FAIR! 1964 World's Fair in New York City," YouTube.

110 For a ticket price of two dollars, fairgoers could visit pavilions: Background on the World's Fair from Liz Robbins, "Around the Unisphere at the World's Fair, Lives Changed," *New York Times*, April 18, 2014; "Look Closer: 1964 New York World's Fair," waltdisney.org, June 16, 2012; Annie Colbert, "Travel Back 50 Years to 1964 New York World's Fair," mashable.com, April 23, 2014; Alan Taylor, "1964: The New York World's Fair," *Atlantic*, June 2, 2014.

111 In states throughout the South, blacks tested their new rights: Peter Millones, "Negroes in South Test Rights Act: Resistance Light," *New York Times*, July 4, 1964.

111 what should have been a simple haircut: Ibid; and "Utilize Places Opened by Law," *CORE-lator* (newsletter published bimonthly by the Congress of Racial Equality), no. 107, July–August 1964.

111 Frequently, the testing met strong, sometimes violent resistance: Peter Millones, "Negroes in South Test Rights Act: Resistance Light."

112 "When these slick woman's magazines": Service of *Chicago Daily News*, "Equality for Women May Be Biggest Problem Raised for Employer by Rights Act," *Kansas City Times*, October 2, 1964, HGB Papers, SSC.

112 "Despite the thoroughness of your course program": Letty Cottin Pogrebin to Mrs. Marjorie Brick, Berkeley School of Secretarial Training, August 7, 1964, press release for *Sex and the Office*, HGB Papers, SSC.

113 "A publisher asked me to write a 'me-too' book": Gloria Steinem, interview with the author, December 2013.

113 "Both have suffered allegations"; "knowledge by nature"; "an ingenious combination"; "*Sex and the Office* doesn't quite fit into George Orwell's category of

'good-bad-books'": Gloria Steinem, "Very Basic Training," a double review of *Sex and the Office* by Helen Gurley Brown, and *Nine to Five and After: The Feminine Art of Living and Working in the Big City* by Irene Silverman, *New York Herald Tribune*, October 18, 1964, HGB Papers, SSC.

15: IN THE MAIL

115 "What is it like to be the little princess": Joan Didion, "Bosses Make Lousy Lovers," *Saturday Evening Post*, January 30, 1965, HGB Papers, SSC.

115 On TV, she wore a wig: Helen Gurley Brown, *Sex and the Office* (Fort Lee, NJ: Barricade Books, 2004), p. 37.

115 "I'm kind of outspoken": Helen Gurley Brown and Joe Pyne in conversation on *The Joe Pyne Show*, YouTube, www.youtube.com/watch?v=nGl-yrGYs98.

115 "terrible woman": Ibid.

115 "Well, Joe, it's just that I think": Ibid.

116 One day, she climbed into a white, two-door Volkswagen Beetle: Accounts of this tour are from Joan Didion, "Bosses Make Lousy Lovers"; and Skip Ferderber, "Sex and the Single Back Seat Observer," Crosscut.com, August 14, 2012, in which Ferderber recalled driving Helen and Joan around in the White Angel.

117 "a very tired woman indeed": Joan Didion, "Bosses Make Lousy Lovers."

117 "a twilight world": Ibid.

118 "over exposure signals on HGB": Letty Cottin and Carol Hill to Helen and David Brown, November 17, 1964, HGB Papers, SSC.

118 Among their ideas that never made it to screen: The food-themed quiz show was called *Cook's on the Fire*, and the invention show was called *Invention, Please*, early 1960s, collected television scripts, HGB Papers, SSC.

118 "EXPLAIN PLEASE!"; "how to change a tire"; "How it started with the Jews and the Arabs": Helen and David Brown, *Frankly Female*, early 1960s, collected television scripts, HGB Papers, SSC.

119 Nor did they have success with a comedy-drama series: *Sandra (The Single Girl)*, early 1960s, collected television scripts, HGB Papers, SSC.

119 "It is a series built around a female lead": American Broadcasting Company (letter writer's name not provided on copy), Mrs. Lucy Kroll, November 23, 1962, HGB Papers, SSC.

119 "The only possible harm": Helen and David Brown, *The Unwind Up*, early 1960s, collected television scripts, HGB Papers, SSC.

120 "in the mail": David wrote about this theory in his memoir, *Let Me Entertain You* (New York: William Morrow & Co., 1990), p. 132.

16: FEMME

121 "Here's a proposal for you": Bernard Geis to Richard Deems, December 23, 1964, HGB Papers, SSC. Reproduced with the permission of Bernard Geis Associates.

121 Helen's epic tour finally slowed to a halt: Details taken from various correspondence between Helen Gurley Brown and Bernard Geis Associates, as well as from collected book tour itineraries and miscellany, 1962–69, HGB Papers, SSC.

122 "It's not the worst picture ever made": A. H. Weiler, "Movie Review: Sex and the Single Girl (1964)," *New York Times*, December 26, 1964.

122 "It was ridiculous, a horrible movie": Rex Reed, interview with the author, 2014.

123 "You know, Helen, you really ought to have a magazine for these girls": Helen Gurley Brown and Lyn Tornabene, tape no. 10, "HGB Interview," 1970–71, HGB Papers, SSC. Helen also described the process in David Brown's memoir, *Let Me Entertain You* (New York: William Morrow & Co., 1990), p. 106.

123 At a certain point, Charlotte Kelly: David Brown, *Let Me Entertain You*, p. 111.

123 Among their ideas for monthly departmental features: Headlines and short quotes are from the Browns' *Femme* prospectus, 1964, HGB Papers, SSC.

123 Among their suggested headlines for major articles: Ibid.

124 "The bathing-suit girl": Helen Gurley Brown, undated introductory note, presumably for archive visitors, to the *Femme* prospectus.

125 "For the woman on her own"; "U.S. Presidents Who Liked Girls"; "Where the Men Are": *Femme* prospectus.

125 "as a first class citizen"; "independent attitude": Ibid.

126 "This woman's magazine will *never* deal with the problems of school lunches": This quote, and following excerpt, ibid.

127 What if the Browns told you: Ibid.

128 "Spec said that he and Hefner would be glad to look at the prospectus": Bernard Geis to David Brown, November 11, 1964, HGB Papers, SSC. Reproduced with the permission of Bernard Geis Associates. Geis wrote other notes to the Browns that fall about his attempts to shop the prospectus around to magazines including *Esquire*.

129 "It looks as though they may fold it": David Brown gave a detailed account of shopping around the *Femme* prospectus in *Let Me Entertain You*, p. 111–13.

129 "You're to telephone Deems": Ibid.

129 Hearst didn't want to replace *Cosmopolitan*: Ibid.

129 "How many copies does 'Our Unadoptable Children' sell": Helen Gurley Brown, *Cosmopolitan* proposal, 1965, HGB Papers, SSC.

130 "One of the first things Helen said to me": Ruth Manton, interview with the author, March 2013.

131 "I think Helen was cowering in a corner somewhere": David Brown, *Let Me Entertain You*, p. 112.

17: FOR THE GIRL WITH A JOB

132 "Helen Gurley got browner, browner, and browner": From "Helen Gurley Wins a Holiday in Hawaii," *Glamour*, May 1953, HGB Papers, SSC.

132 Growing up, Helen inhaled magazines: Despite David's comment that he'd never seen her read a magazine, Helen often wrote about loving movies and movie stars whose pictures she saw in magazines.

132 ten women with modest incomes who still managed to show impeccable taste: Jennifer Scanlon referenced the *Glamour* contest qualifications in *Bad Girls Go Everywhere* (New York: Penguin Books, 2009), p. 29.

132 Helen entered for the first time in 1951: Helen Gurley Brown, early notes on entering *Glamour*'s contest, and the application process, HGB Papers, SSC.

133 Helen gave it her all: Ibid.

133 "starts with that most basic commodity—one's own self": "Helen Gurley Wins a Holiday in Hawaii."

134 It also made her true ambitions known: Jennifer Scanlon, *Bad Girls Go Everywhere*, p. 29.

134 it was her first time in a magazine office: Helen Gurley Brown's account in David Brown's memoir, *Let Me Entertain You* (New York: William Morrow & Co., 1990), p. 107.

18: THE MOST EXCITING WOMAN IN THE WORLD

135 "She has no intention": "Sex & the Editor," *Time*, March 26, 1965.

135 "FIRST DAY AT HEARST": Helen Gurley Brown, entry in red diary, HGB Papers, SSC.

135 David's old mentor Herb Mayes was the first to call: David Brown, *Let Me Entertain You* (New York: William Morrow & Co., 1990), p. 30.

135 David negotiated for a total annual compensation package of $35,000: In a letter to Richard Deems dated February 11, 1965, David Brown negotiated for Helen to be allotted $35,000 annually. James Landers confirmed this number in *The Improbable First Century of "Cosmopolitan" Magazine* (Columbia: University of Missouri Press, 2010), p. 224.

135 "a spokeswoman for single women and girls with jobs": Hearst press release, 1965, HGB Papers, SSC.

135 "A lot of people will think we hired her": "Sex & the Editor," *Newsweek*, March 29, 1965, HGB Papers, SSC.

136 "I don't want to be a magazine editor!": Helen Gurley Brown, *I'm Wild Again: Snippets from My Life and a Few Brazen Thoughts* (New York: St. Martin's Press, 2000), p. 171.

136 Just in case, her contract included a stipulation: David Brown referenced this agreement in a letter to Richard Deems, February 11, 1965.

136 become an astronaut or a brain surgeon: Helen Gurley Brown's account in David Brown's memoir, *Let Me Entertain You*, p. 107.

136 "Ask the managing editor to have lunch with you": Helen Gurley Brown and Lyn Tornabene, tape no. 10, "HGB Interview," 1970–72, HGB Papers, SSC.

136 she still went to bed feeling like she would be starting a prison term: From Helen's account in David Brown, *Let Me Entertain You*, p. 107.

136 In 1965, what is known today as the Hearst Tower: Background on Hearst Magazine Building from Landmarks Preservation Commission, February 16, 1988, Designation List 200, LP-1625; background on collaboration between William Randolph Hearst and Joseph Urban from Anthony Ramirez, "An Urban Landmark in Manhattan Grows by 46 Stories," *New York Times*, September 18, 2005.

138 a simple light-blue jersey dress: Helen recalled her outfit in David Brown, *Let Me Entertain You*, p. 108.

138 a rumor pinballed around the offices: Account and dialogue from former *Cosmopolitan* secretary Vene Spencer, interview with the author, September 2014.

139 "It came as a complete shock": Ibid.

139 she started by inviting her new employees into her office: Account of meeting Helen Gurley Brown for the first time, and what he office looked like, ibid.

139 She did her homework: Ibid.

140 Betty promptly turned her down: Helen spoke about her early challenges with the staff at *Cosmopolitan* in Helen Gurley Brown and Lyn Tornabene, audio recording file no. 2553b, tape no. 9 (side B), 1970–71, HGB Papers, SSC.

140 "The magazine is bubbling with enthusiasm": "Sex & the Editor," *Time*.

140 Almost instantly, there was mutiny: Helen Gurley Brown and Lyn Tornabene, audio recording file no. 2553b, tape no. 9 (side B).

141 When she asked to see what was scheduled for future issues: Helen Gurley Brown's account in David Brown, *Let Me Entertain You*, p. 108.

142 "You don't need literary people": Helen Gurley Brown and Lyn Tornabene, audio recording file no. 2553b, tape no. 9 (side B).

142 "I went to sleep but it didn't take": Helen Gurley Brown's account in David Brown, *Let Me Entertain You*, p. 108.

143 "That wasn't her"; "When it seems to you as though she's being a storyteller": Walter Meade, interview with the author.

19: The July Issue

144 "I hope to have a magazine that reflects life": "Sex & the Editor," *Newsweek*, March 29, 1965, HGB Papers, SSC.

144 Apparently mailroom runs were beneath her: Helen spoke about her early challenges with the staff at *Cosmopolitan* in Helen Gurley Brown and Lyn Tornabene, audio recording file no. 2553b, tape no. 9 (side B), 1970–71, HGB Papers, SSC.

144 "Mrs. Brown," Robin said: Ibid.

145 At some point every day, Helen picked up the phone and called David: Helen detailed her struggles and reliance on David early on at *Cosmopolitan* in David Brown, *Let Me Entertain You* (New York: William Morrow & Co., 1990), p. 109.

146 "a bosom she doesn't make much of a fuss about": "Are You a JAX Girl": *Cosmopolitan*, July 1965.

146 "What's this one?": Helen Gurley Brown and Lyn Tornabene. Helen recalled finding her first cover girl in audio recording file no. 2553b, tape no. 9 (side B).

147 she was the first *Cosmo* cover girl under Helen Gurley Brown: Biographical details about Renata Boeck per Renata Boeck, interview with the author, August 2014.

147 "They were looking for someone famous": Ibid.

147 "Ten minutes later, I got a call": Ibid.

148 "She wanted cleavage": Ibid.

148 "It is the case of the untreated woman": Robert A. Wilson, *Feminine Forever* (New York: M. Evans and Company, 1966); and Joe Neel, "The Marketing of Menopause," NPR, August 8, 2002.

149 "from puberty to the grave": Robert A. Wilson, *Feminine Forever*.

149 "honey of a hormone": Lin Root, "Oh What a Lovely Pill!" *Cosmopolitan*, July 1965. (Even though Lin Root is the credited writer, Helen told Lyn Tornabene

that she rewrote the article in audio recording 553b, tape no. 9 [side B], 1970–71, HGB Papers, SSC.)

149   "My skin is fresher": Lin Root, "Oh What a Lovely Pill!"

149   years later, studies showed: Joe Neel, "The Marketing of Menopause."

150   "I mainlined Premarin for years": Meryl Gordon, "Hormonal Imbalance," *New York*, July 22, 2002.

150   Above all, she wanted *Cosmopolitan* to feel personal: Helen described *Cosmo*'s tone as being like the voice of an older sister in an article by John J. Goldman, *Los Angeles Times*, reprinted as "Ask Helen Gurley Brown: "Can a Small Town Girl Achieve Fame in the City," *Tuscaloosa News*, May 5, 1971.

150   In a rush to fill the position of managing editor: Helen told Lyn Tornabene about offering the job to various staffers, audio recording file no. 2553b, tape no. 9 (side B).

150   several other editors had worked at the magazine for years: A. R. Roalman gave a great overview of *Cosmopolitan*'s staff and modus operandi in "The New Cosmopolitan," *Writer's Digest*, August 1966.

151   "For information on children": Ibid.

151   Helen used to call her "a white-knuckle girl": Walter Meade, interview with the author.

151   "Don't come at me with the inexpensive, off-season vacation story": A. R. Roalman, "The New Cosmopolitan."

151   she wanted the fiction to reflect this new demographic: Ibid.

152   Liz had been writing about movies and movie stars: Biographical details about Liz Smith per her memoir *Natural Blonde* (New York: Hyperion, 2000), passim.

152   "She was just a little girl from Arkansas like I was just a little girl from Texas": Liz Smith, interview with the author, May 2013.

152   "like icebergs—only partly visible to mortals" *and following*: Liz Smith, "Mr. and Mrs. Burton One Year Later," *Cosmopolitan*, February 1965.

153   Liz Smith had come in to work expecting to be fired: Smith described job-hunting along with her colleagues in *Natural Blonde*, p. 199.

153   "Well, Lizzie, what shall we do with you?": Ibid., p. 200.

153   "a glorious unfettered, sexy and seductive paean": Ibid.

154   "I'll never forget—she was so shy and deferential": Liz Smith, interview with the author, May 2013.

20: TECHNIQUES

155   "In an ideal world": Helen Gurley Brown, *Sex and the Office* (Fort Lee, NJ: Barricade Books, 2004), "Come Fly with Me."

155   Another was hiring Walter Meade: Biographical details about Meade, impressions of Helen Gurley Brown, descriptions of her office, and dialogue from Walter Meade, interviews and email exchanges with the author.

155   "We need an articles editor" *and following dialogue*: Ibid.

156   That was the mind-set Walter was in when Bill called: Ibid.

156   "I don't know what I'm doing either": Ibid.

158   Meade never forgot the memo that Helen sent back with the manuscript: Ibid.

158   Lyn Tornabene had been the magazine's entertainment editor: Biographical

details about Lyn Tornabene, anecdotes about office life at *Cosmopolitan* pre–Helen Gurley Brown, impressions of Helen, descriptions of her office, and dialogue from Lyn Tornabene, interview with the author, November 2014.

159 "Why should I do that?: Liz Smith fondly recalled Tornabene in her memoir, *Natural Blonde* (New York: Hyperion, 2000), 198.

159 "It was a very strange meeting": Lyn Tornabene, interview with the author, November 2014

159 "She called on Thanksgiving": Ibid.

160 "I don't think Helen needed to see how far she could get": Ibid.

21: PIPPY-POO COPY

161 "What was so marvelous about Helen": Lyn Tornabene, interview with the author, November 2014.

161 "You don't just fall into a job like this": Dialogue and descriptions in this scene from Dick Schaap, "Now It's the Cosmo Club," *Providence Journal-Bulletin* and *New York Herald Tribune*, 1965.

162 "She did not look like most editors": Ibid.

162 "I always thought I was smarter than she was": Liz Smith, interview with the author, May 2013.

163 "the magazine for people who can read": David Brown, *Let Me Entertain You* (New York: William Morrow & Co., 1990), p. 28.

163 "We don't want very many cosmic pieces": Helen Gurley Brown in a Q&A, "New Direction for *Cosmopolitan*," *Writer*, July 1965.

163 "You are censoring me!": Liz Smith, *Natural Blonde* (New York: Hyperion, 2000), p. 200.

163 The writer of the review: Biographical details about Rex Reed per Reed, interview with the author, 2014.

164 A few days later, Liz called Rex: Liz Smith and Rex Reed told slightly different versions of how he came to be *Cosmopolitan*'s movie critic; this telling is based on Reed's account.

164 "Car lovers will drool": Rex Reed, "Drama Takes a Back Seat," *Cosmopolitan*, June 1965, HGB Papers, SSC.

164 When Helen called Rex in for a meeting: Impressions of Helen Gurley Brown, descriptions of her office and her outfit, and dialogue from Rex Reed, interview with the author, 2014.

164 "you write pippy-poo copy": Ibid.

165 "Because, my dear," Helen cooed, "I *was* that girl": Ibid.

22: DADDY'S LITTLE GIRL

166 "Have *you* a rotten family": Helen Gurley Brown, *Having It All: Love, Success, Sex, Money, Even If You're Starting with Nothing* (New York: Simon & Schuster, 1982), p. 34.

166 "the girl with her nose pressed against the glass": Nikki Finke, "The Times Are Changing, but Not Cosmo, Still Hot After 25 Years," *Los Angeles Times*, April 20, 1990.

166 You have to start in Carroll County: Descriptions of Helen Gurley Brown's birthplace, Green Forest, Arkansas, and surrounding areas are per author, who visited in January 2014.

167 "That's sort of a misconception": Lou Honderich, interview with the author.

168 "I think it helped sell books": Ibid.

169 Born in 1893 in the tiny nearby village of Alpena: Biographical details about Cleo Bryan per Helen Gurley Brown, "Memories of Mother and Early Life in Little Rock," unpublished, late 1990s, HGB Papers, SSC; and per Lou Honderich, interview with author.

169 Newt has assumed the role of unofficial town historian: Information about the history of Osage Clayworks and Cleo's house per Newton Lale, interview with the author, January 2014.

170 "Our mothers and our grandmothers grew up": Ibid.

170 Cleo had wanted to get out once herself: Biographical details about Cleo, including her education, early career, courtship with Ira Gurley, marriage, and childbirth experiences, from Helen Gurley Brown, "Memories of Mother and Early Life in Little Rock."

170 "I think Ira was smart": Lou Honderich, interview with the author, 2015.

171 "devout male chauvinist": Helen Gurley Brown, "Memories of Mother and Early Life in Little Rock."

171 "Having babies isn't everything": Ibid.

172 "It was before the depression when money didn't *consume* people so": Ibid.

173 Cleo was the homemaker, the caretaker. Ira was the fun-maker, the thrill-seeker: Ibid.

173 By 1932, he was preparing to run for secretary of state: Ibid.

173 Helen was ten years old: Ibid. Helen gave a heartrending account of her father's death and the aftermath in "Memories of Mother and Early Life in Little Rock."

175 "One last time" happened a few times: Ibid.

176 the one-story white farmhouse was simple: Descriptions of Cleo's parents' house per Lou Honderich, email exchange with the author, July 2014.

176 For Helen and Mary, it was a time of escape: Helen Gurley Brown, "Memories of Mother and Early Life in Little Rock."

176 Cleo tried to keep her own hands busy, too: Ibid.

177 Looking for some answers: Ibid.

177 Later, Cleo found out: Ibid.

23: GOING WEST

178 "Helen may have come to the false conclusion about her looks after moving to California": Lou Honderich, email exchange with the author.

179 "The days were somewhat pleasant, despite our being daddyless": Ibid.

179 Helen found a happier home nearby: Ibid.

181 "the most beautiful breasts anybody ever aspired to," "loving Elizabeth," "loving *boys*": Ibid.

182 "If Elizabeth and I were going through a homosexual phase": Ibid.

182 Going to Chicago was the most thrilling adventure: Ibid.

182 When Cleo returned, she confessed: Ibid.

182 "It's been three years since we lost your daddy" *and following*: Helen recalled this dialogue in Helen Gurley Brown and Lyn Tornabene, audio recording file no. 2545a, tape no. 1, Scene II (side A), 1970–71, HGB Papers. SSC.

183 In 1936, Cleo took the girls on a road trip: Helen Gurley Brown, "Memories of Mother and Early Life in Little Rock."

24: GOOD TIME GURLEY

185 "'Guppie' likes having her back scratched": Untitled short profile of Helen Gurley, publication unknown (possibly *The Optimist*), circa spring 1939.

185 On a Sunday afternoon in April 1937: Helen Gurley Brown wrote about Mary's polio diagnosis in multiple sources; this account is from *I'm Wild Again: Snippets from My Life and a Few Brazen Thoughts* (New York: St. Martin's Press, 2000), p. 5.

185 "[We] were formed from the same gene pool" *and following*: Helen Gurley Brown, *I'm Wild Again*, p. 5.

186 Mary lived at the clinic: Ibid.

186 "Dear Mr. President": Helen Gurley Brown, *Dear Pussycat: Mash Notes and Missives from the Desk of Cosmopolitan's Legendary Editor* (New York: St. Martin's Press, 204), p. 2.

186 Starting classes at John H. Francis Polytechnic High School: Helen Gurley Brown, "Memories of Mother and Early Life in Little Rock," unpublished, late 1990s, HGB Papers, SSC.

186 Anxious that something would happen to her: Ibid. Helen described Cleo's mounting neurosis, and her own unhappiness, which was also tied up with her acne and plain-girl looks.

188 At home, Helen became a part-time caretaker to Mary: Ibid.

188 At school, Helen was determined to become more social: Helen Gurley Brown, *I'm Wild Again*, p. 6.

188 They were as "close as stitches" . . . and they both wielded the power to wound: Helen Gurley Brown, "Memories of Mother and Early Life in Little Rock."

188 She was elected president: Helen Gurley Brown's class stats are from various article clippings that she saved from her high-school newspaper, *The Optimist*, John H. Francis Polytechnic High School, late-1930s, HGB Papers, SSC.

188 Hal didn't have a date: Helen Gurley Brown, *I'm Wild Again*, p. 7.

189 luck had little to do with Helen's high school success: Background from various article clippings that she saved from *The Optimist*.

189 "It lowers the respect of other fellows": "Slacks on Campus Out of Place, Say Students," publication unknown (possibly *The Optimist*), circa spring 1939.

189 "I've dreamed of being an Ephebian": Untitled short profile of Helen Gurley, publication unknown (possibly *The Optimist*), circa spring 1939.

189 she soon lined up big plans: Account of Helen's attempt at attending college; Cleo and Mary's move to Warm Springs, Georgia; and Helen's consequent move back home from Jennifer Scanlon, *Bad Girls Go Everywhere* (Penguin Books, 2009), pp. 18–19.

191 Helen became attuned to the clawing sounds of the gophers: Helen Gurley Brown, *I'm Wild Again*, p. 8.

192 She found him to be embarrassing: Ibid., p. 9.

192 Sometimes it felt like believing in Santa Claus: Helen Gurley Brown, *Dear Pussycat*, p. 308.

193 "If I'd been beautiful I might be a gold digger": Ibid.

194 "She really did it because she saw me being a semi-nurse-companion": Helen Gurley Brown, *I'm Wild Again*, p. 10.

25: TURNING POINTS

195 "The world that shaped Helen": Walter Meade, email exchange with the author, February 2014.

195 They should just use Helen as the girl: Helen Gurley Brown and Lyn Tornabene, audio recording no. 2268, tape 10, "HGB interview," 1970–71, HGB Papers, SSC.

196 "That nearly killed me": Ibid.

196 "I learned very early to be good in bed": Helen Gurley Brown and Lyn Tornabene, audio recording no. 2547a, "Sex Is Power" tape no. 3, (side A) 1970–71, HGB Papers, SSC.

196 She didn't lose her virginity until she was twenty: Helen Gurley Brown interview with David Allyn for his book, *Make Love, Not War: The Sexual Revolution: An Unfettered History* (New York: Routledge, 2011).

196 "It was the most *marvelous* feeling": Helen Gurley Brown and Lyn Tornabene, audio recording no. 2268, tape 10, "HGB interview."

197 In no particular order; "the boys in the band" "devastating": Helen described her conquests in Helen Gurley Brown and Lyn Tornabene, audio recording file no. 2547a, tape 3, "Sex Is Power" (side A).

198 Psychoanalysis, hypnosis, touch therapy—Helen tried it all: Helen described her various therapists and therapy sessions in Helen Gurley Brown and Lyn Tornabene, audio recording no. 2268, tape 10, "HGB Interview."

198 he told her she didn't have the right looks; "What about your mother?": Ibid. Helen recalled this disturbing session and dialogue to Lyn Tornabene.

198 It wasn't until she went to group therapy: Helen talked about Charles Cooke and group therapy with Lyn Tornabene. Milton H. Erickson's assessment of Cooke is from Milton H. Erickson, Jeffrey K. Zeig, and Brent B. Geary, eds., *The Letters of Milton H. Erickson* (Phoenix, AZ: Zeig, Tucker & Theisen, 2000), p. 249.

199 Standing there, naked and vulnerable: Helen Gurley Brown and Lyn Tornabene, audio recording no. 2268, tape 10, "HGB Interview."

199 Another time, when Charles brought a "potty" to a session: Ibid.

26: SELF-PORTRAIT

200 "God damn it, Helen, you aren't a mouseburger anymore": Lyn Tornabene to Helen Gurley Brown, January 20, year unknown (possibly circa 1982-83), HGB Papers, SSC; "hillbilly stock": Helen Gurley Brown quoted in Janet Cawley. "Yes, a Feminist Can Love Men," *Chicago Tribune*, June 12, 1994.

200 she believed that she was: Helen wrote extensively about her insecurity. In *I'm Wild Again: Snippets from My Life and a Few Brazen Thoughts* (New York: St. Martin's Press, 2000), she revisited her humble roots, plain-girl looks, and "average" IQ, in the section "Insecurity—a Girl's Good Friend."

201 "I thought they'd *interest* you": Helen Gurley Brown, "Step Into My Parlour," *Cosmopolitan*, July 1965.

201 "A guy reading *Playboy*": Helen Gurley Brown in *Providence Journal*, 1965, HGB Papers, SSC.

201 "to the point of ridiculousness"; "a bona-fide genius": Helen Gurley Brown, "Step Into My Parlour," *Cosmopolitan*, August 1971, SSC.

202 "We like our apartment" *and following*: Hugh Hefner, *Playboy*, December 1953.

202 he liked the idea of there being "a female version of *Playboy*": Hugh Hefner, interview with the author, November 2013.

202 "It was the beginning of the sexual revolution" *and following*: Ibid.

203 "Playmates," Hefner says, "were often *Cosmo* Girls": Ibid.

203 "I think magazines are the most personal form of mass communication": Ibid.

204 "She seems constantly aware of her lack of fulfillment": Runner Associates, 1957 job evaluation of Miss Helen Marie Gurley, HGB Papers, SSC.

204 "a woman's 3 worst odor problems": Ad in July 1965 *Cosmopolitan*, SSC.

205 "You also want to be inspired": Helen Gurley Brown, "Step Into My Parlour," *Cosmopolitan*, July 1965, SSC.

27: PARLOUR GAMES

206 "Desk accessories should be female": Helen Gurley Brown, *Sex and the Office* (Fort Lee, NJ: Barricade Books, 2004), p. 48.

206 "I always thought that when Helen decided to call her column": Walter Meade, email exchange with the author, February 2014.

207 "About every four weeks": Linda Cox, interview with the author, June 2015.

207 From the start, David edited "Step Into My Parlour": In David Brown, *Let Me Entertain You* (New York: William Morrow & Co., 1990), pp. 109–10, Helen says that David still edited her column every month.

207 He wanted her to cut a risqué cover line: Helen recalled this episode ibid., p. 110.

207 Like the company itself, Berlin was conservative: Description of Berlin and his position at Hearst draws from James Landers's comprehensive history of *Cosmopolitan*, *The Improbable First Century of "Cosmopolitan" Magazine* (Columbia: University of Missouri Press, 2010), pp. 211–13.

208 "The new pill that makes women more responsive to men": Helen in David Brown, *Let Me Entertain You*, p. 110.

208 "Why don't you try this on Mr. Berlin?" he asked: Helen Gurley Brown and Lyn Tornabene, audio recording file no. 2553b, tape no. 9 (side B), 1970–71, HGB Papers, SSC.

208 Helen learned something about power: Ibid.

209 "The new pill that promises to make women more responsive": *Cosmopolitan* cover, July 1965.

209 The July issue sold approximately 954,000 newsstand copies: Jeannine Locke, "The Pippy-Poo World of Helen Gurley Brown," *Star Weekly*, Toronto, January 1, 1966.

209 "Guess how much?": Walter Meade, interview with the author.

209 "I think she said, 'We're on the Yellow Brick Road'": Ibid.

210 "I will not have it in my home": Reader letter, "Dear Cosmopolitan," *Cosmopolitan*, October 1965, SSC.

210 "whorish" model on the cover; "nothing but a stupid, idiotic *cow* of a sexpot": Reader letters, "Dear Cosmopolitan," *Cosmopolitan*, September 1965; October 1965, SSC.

210 advertising giants like AT&T and Coca-Cola backed away or bailed: Helen Gurley Brown and Lyn Tornabene, audio recording file no. 2553b, tape no. 9 (side B).

210 "The July issue of *COSMO* is alive": Reader letter, "Dear Cosmopolitan," *Cosmopolitan*, October 1965.

210 "I feel that you have given career girls a 'laughing look'": Reader letter, *Cosmopolitan*, October 1965, SSC.

211 One of those magazines was *Look*: Background on Gardner "Mike" Cowles Jr., Fleur Fenton Cowles, *Look* magazine, and Samuel "Shap" Shapiro from the following sources: Online biography of Gardner Cowles Jr. (Mike) by Herb Strentz, www.lib.drake.edu, Cowles Family Publishing Legacy, Drake University, Cowles Library; Amy Fine Collins, "A *Flair* for Living," *Vanity Fair*, October 1996; "Cowles Closing Look Magazine After 34 Years," *New York Times*, September 17, 1971; and "Samuel O. Shapiro, 87, a Circulation Director," obituary, *New York Times*, September 6, 1990.

211 even he had never seen anything quite like the newsstand sales figures: Patricia Carbine recalled this episode in the conference room at *Look*, interview with the author, January 2014.

211 "I thought she was talking about somebody I didn't know": Ibid.

212 "What she had managed to do was turn her book into a magazine": Ibid.

28: JAMES BOND ON A BUDGET

213 "She had flattery down to a high art": Liz Smith, interview with the author, May 2013.

213 A few weeks into her appointment as editor: Descriptions of Helen's walk per Walter Meade, interview with the author.

214 "How's your summer going?": Barbara Hustedt Crook, interview with the author.

214 "She always made me nervous": Ibid.

214 Richard Berlin had been reluctant to hire Helen: James Landers, *The Improbable First Century of "Cosmopolitan" Magazine* (Columbia: University of Missouri Press, 2010), p. 224.

214 Deems monitored *Cosmopolitan*'s editorial content: Background on the supervising roles of Richard Deems and Frank Dupuy Jr., ibid, pp. 224, 230.

215 She also needed to cut costs, drastically: Chris Welles, "Soaring Success of the Iron Butterfly," *Life*, November 19, 1965.

215 "Well, I don't understand it": Helen Gurley Brown and Lyn Tornabene, audio recording file no. 2553b, tape no. 9 (side B), 1970–71, HGB Papers, SSC.

215 "Well," they huffed, "if Herb Mayes": Ibid.

215 "Those two-faced bitches": Ibid.

216 It was amazing how sloppy writers could be: Helen outlined some of her writing pet peeves in memos to the staff, beginning with "Memo 1," January 18, 1967, *Cosmopolitan* editing and writing, HGB Papers, SSC.

216 "One thing I decided": Liz Smith, "Cosmo Goes to the Movies," *Cosmopolitan*, August 1965.

217 Helen penciled in: Red diary, 1965, HGB Papers, SSC.

217 People wanted to see only the "after," he said: Helen Gurley Brown, "Step Into My Parlour," *Cosmopolitan*, October 1965.

217 Typically, there might be around thirty articles: Helen occasionally explained how the magazine was put together in "Step Into My Parlour." Additional background from Walter Meade and Linda Cox, interviews with the author.

217 George made up a schedule for an upcoming issue: Ibid.

218 "How can you have a hole": Helen Gurley Brown, "Step Into My Parlour," *Cosmopolitan*, August 1965, SSC.

218 "Have you written anything recently?": Ibid.

29: MR. RIGHT IS DEAD

219 "The girl of the fifties would stay home": Associated Press, reprinted as "The Bookshelf: 'Romance Wanes in Cynical Sixties,'" *Milwaukee Sentinel*, September 13, 1965.

219 "How would you go about telling your date": Referenced by Lily Rothman, "The Surprisingly Feminist Roots of *The Bachelorette*," *Time*, May 18, 2015.

220 "The Girl Ghetto": Paul Stewart, "The Girl Ghetto: Manhattan's Swingiest Square Mile," *Cosmopolitan*, September 1966.

220 At night they gathered at singles bars: Background from Malachy McCourt, *A Monk Swimming* (New York: Hachette Books, 1998), passim; and Nicola Twilley, "A Cocktail Party in the Street: An Interview with Alan Stillman," *New City Reader*, November 12, 2010, available at www.ediblegeography.com/a-cocktail-party-in-the-street-an-interview-with-alan-stillman/.

220 "passion pads": Background on singles housing from "Housing: Pads for Singles," *Time*, August 26, 1966.

221 "Many single women take cruises or head alone": Thomas Meehan, "New Industry Built Around Boy Meets Girl," *Cosmopolitan*, September 1965, SSC.

221 "Don't listen to the pessimists. You can do it!": Lyn Tornabene, "Do Be an Actress!" *Cosmopolitan*, September 1965.

221 "What's new this month, pussycat?": Helen Gurley Brown, "Step Into My Parlour," *Cosmopolitan*, September 1965.

222 "If you hate being away from *your* darlings": Ibid.

222 "rumple-proof" sari; "Of course I'm purring, pet" *and following caption excerpt*: "Husband-Coming-Home Clothes," *Cosmopolitan*, September 1965.

223 The merchandising editor: Helen Gurley Brown, "Step Into My Parlour," *Cosmopolitan*, September 1965.

223 "I never paid much attention to them": Melvin Sokolsky, interview with the author, September 2014.

30: That *Cosmopolitan* Girl

224 "A color photograph of a pretty brunette": Eugenia Sheppard, "'Any Woman Can Get a Man . . . ,'" *New York Herald Tribune*, September 9, 1965.

224 The stretchy, red-jersey wraparound dress: Melvin Sokolsky, interview with the author, September 2014.

224 "Basically, that red dress is selling the most beautiful set of breasts": Ibid.

225 Working in a spotless, white-walled studio: Background on Scavullo, his studio, and his style of working from *Scavullo: Francesco Scavullo Photographs 1948–1984* (New York: Harper & Row, 1984). Also per Harry King, interview with the author, September 2014.

225 "I don't know what other models ate": Kecia Nyman described her first *Cosmopolitan* session with Scavullo in an interview with the author, August 2014.

226 "We all loved Scavullo": Ibid.

226 It was a place of legend and extraordinary leverage: History and legend of "21" drawn from H. Peter Kriendler with H. Paul Jeffers, *"21": Every Day Was New Year's Eve* (Dallas: Taylor, 1999).

227 "just another 102-pound nobody in a Pucci dress": Gael Greene detailed Helen Gurley Brown's relationship with "21" and her famous *Cosmopolitan* luncheons in "That Cosmo Girl at '21,'" *New York*, January 18, 1971.

227 Playing the hostess, Helen used her charms: Description of Helen's hosting skills per former *Cosmo* beauty editor Mallen De Santis, interview with the author, October 2012.

227 "She would go through the dummy": Ibid.

228 Change didn't necessarily mean improvement: Helen Gurley Brown, statement for advertisers, 1965, HGB Papers, SSC.

228 a woman between the ages of eighteen and thirty-four: Helen Gurley Brown described her target reader in many articles, including an early Q&A she did with *The Writer*, "New Direction for *Cosmopolitan*," *Writer*, July 1965.

229 The *Cosmopolitan* cover girl was a different species altogether: Jennifer Scanlon wrote about this disconnect between the *Cosmo* reader and the *Cosmo* cover girl in *Bad Girls Go Everywhere* (New York: Penguin Books, 2009), p. 170.

31: The Iron Butterfly

230 "The U.S. Weather Bureau did *not* track": Chris Welles, "Soaring Success of the Iron Butterfly," *Life*, November 19, 1965.

230 By November, the magazine would average about a million copies per issue: Ibid.

230 "Congratulations, Chieftess": Helen saved the actual gold record, HGB Papers, SSC. There are also great photos of the champagne party accompanying Welles's story.

230 Shortly after penciling "Life Mag": Helen Gurley Brown, red diary, 1965, HGB Papers, SSC.

231 "It's just a half-baked crusading idea, I guess": Chris Welles, "Soaring Success of the Iron Butterfly."

231 "Helen's terribly polite, terribly innocent": Ibid.

231 "She had a nickname: the Iron Butterfly": Vene Spencer, interview with the author, September 2014.

232 "quite obscene"; "utter contempt for women," and *following quotes*: Chris Welles, "Soaring Success of the Iron Butterfly."

32: RESOLUTIONS

233 "This is it. The turning point": David Lachenbruch, "Everything's Coming Up Color," "TV Set Buyers Guide," *TV Guide*, 1966.

233 In the beginning of 1966: Charles Mohr, "Raids on North Vietnam Resumed by U.S. Planes as 37-Day Pause Is Ended," *New York Times*, January 31, 1966.

234 screen-tested potential book covers: Martin Kasindorf, "Jackie Susann Picks Up the Marbles," *New York Times Magazine*, August 12, 1973.

234 "A new book is just like any new product": Requoted by David Streitfeld in "Book Report: Writing to Sell," *Washington Post*, March 25, 1990.

234 "Take 3 yellow 'dolls' before bedtime": Letty Cottin Pogrebin, press release for *Valley of the Dolls*, 1966, requoted by Barbara Seaman in *Lovely Me: The Life of Jacqueline Susann* (New York: William Morrow & Co., 1987), p. 303

234 Using *Sex and the Single Girl* as a model: Barbara Seaman, *Lovely Me*, p. 282.

234 In early May, *Dolls* took the number-one slot: Amy Fine Collins, "Once Was Never Enough," *Vanity Fair*, January 2000.

234 "What matters to *me* is telling a *story* that *involves* people": Jane Howard, "Happiness Is Being Number 1," *Life*, August 19, 1966.

235 "He must have gotten very far down the list": Gloria Steinem, interview with the author, December 2013.

235 "MADDENINGLY SEXY": Helen Gurley Brown's blurb on the back of the *Valley of the Dolls* paperback (New York: Grove Press, 1997).

235 Helen titled the last talk "What Business Men Should Know About Girls": John W. Fisher, "Packed House Hears Helen Gurley Brown's Tips on Making Ads Appeal to Distaff Side," *Adcrafter*, March 25, 1966.

235 "Women are interested in everything men are interested in" *and following*: Ibid.

236 Toward the end of 1966, they went to Europe: Helen wrote about her trip in detail in "Step Into My Parlour," *Cosmopolitan*, December 1966.

236 London was such a *male* city: Ibid.

236 From London, they continued on to: Ibid.

237 In 1966 alone, Helen spent $3,343.30: Helen recorded her expenditures and her measurements in a file, "Clothes: drawings, measurements, and expenditures," 1966–71, HGB Papers, SSC.

237 "We lunched at the Tea Room": Lyn Tornabene, interview with the author, November 2014.

237 "fewer but better clothes"; "There's no use resolving anything major, of course": Helen Gurley Brown, "Step Into My Parlour," *Cosmopolitan*, January 1967.

237 "None of us had ever been there": Vene Spencer recalled Helen taking her and Les Girls out for lunch at "21" in interview with the author, September 2014.

238 "But you ladies stay": Ibid.

238 "Where do you live?"; "Do you have a boyfriend?"; "Do you want to get married?": Helen Gurley Brown and Lyn Tornabene, audio recording file no. 2549b, "General Personality" tape 5, (side B), 1970–71, HGB Papers, SSC. Note: Dialogue is slightly altered, but meaning is similar.

239 Helen had her nose done at age forty: Helen Gurley Brown, *I'm Wild Again Snippets from My Life and a Few Brazen Thoughts* (New York: St. Martin's Press, 2000), p. 266.

239 "Both Robin and I got our noses fixed": Vene Spencer, interview with the author, September 2014.

239 In December 1966, along with show mainstays: *What's My Line?* Season 18, Episode 16, 1966.

240 "She wasn't taking any chances": Vene Spencer recalled this "dress rehearsal" of *What's My Line?* in interview with author, September 2014.

240 "I hope you will accept this as a little token": Ibid.

240 "I was laughing to myself": Ibid.

240 "Loosen my tie!": Story of Bill Guy's heart attack per Vene Spencer, his former assistant, told to the author in interview, September 2014.

240 "I was buying the fiction, negotiating with the agents": Ibid.

241 In a matter of months, Helen had lost her fiction editor, her articles editor, and a resourceful assistant: Timeline and details of their departures per Vene Spencer and Walter Meade, interviews with the author.

241 the office couldn't stop talking about her: Helen Gurley Brown to Vene Spencer, undated, courtesy of Vene Spencer.

33: THE 92 PERCENT

242 "Everyone has an identity": Jacqueline Susann, *Valley of the Dolls* (New York: Grove Press, 1966), p. 111.

242 "You're the first lady analyst": Judy Klemesrud, "Mrs. Brown, Your Subject Is Showing," *New York Times*, December 31, 1967.

242 a failure, one of the few Helen ever had: Jennifer Scanlon, *Bad Girls Go Everywhere* (New York: Penguin Books, 2009), p. 147.

242 A tall and striking woman: Information about Mallen De Santis's career per De Santis, interview with the author, October 2012.

243 "I did what Helen referred to as 'material evaluation' ": Ibid.

243 "She really relied on Mallen being her guidepost": Eileen Stukane, interview with the author, January 2013.

244 Every four weeks, they reviewed the *last* issue: Helen described this evaluation process, and her doubts about the current issue, in "Step Into My Parlour," *Cosmopolitan*, May 1967, SSC.

244 "Every time an editor sees": Ibid.

245 "Everybody—and especially me—needs editing!": Helen Gurley Brown, "Memo 1," January 18, 1967, *Cosmopolitan* editing and writing, HGB Papers, SSC.

245 "RULE 1. WRITING SHOULD BE CLEAR": Ibid.

245 "She was always interested in clarity": Nat Hentoff, interview with the author, 2014.

246 "All instructions for making *anything*": Helen Gurley Brown, "Memo 1."

246 "She edited the magazine for three Helens": Walter Meade, email exchange with the author, January 2015.

246 "I just didn't get David in his boutonnière": Lyn Tornabene, interview with the author, November 2014.

247 "RULE 22. *DON'T ATTACK THE ADVERTISER!*": Helen Gurley Brown, "Memo 1."

247 "25 men will follow you down the street": Ibid.

247 "Show no mercy toward sloppiness": Ibid.

248 "It wasn't that we didn't get letters": Barbara Hustedt Crook, email exchange with author, February 2014.

248 "We made up things all the time!" Mallen De Santis, interview with the author, October 2012.

248 "It's pretty tough, as you know": Helen Gurley Brown, "Memo 1."

249 "Very good!": Ibid.

249 "Only 8 per cent of our readers": Ibid.

249 "Hey, beautiful dark girl": Ruth Ross, "The Negro Girl Goes Job Hunting," *Cosmopolitan*, March 1967. Information about Mary, who worked in the mailroom, per various *Cosmo* staffers, interviews with the author.

249 "a true story, told by a young woman": "I Didn't Have the Baby, I Had the Abortion," *Cosmopolitan*, July 1967.

250 "I'm still shaking!": Anonymous reader letter, *Cosmopolitan*, October 1967.

250 "The boys think we're pretty special"; "It's not that we're all beautiful": Iris George, "Could *You* Work in Vietnam?" *Cosmopolitan*, July 1967.

34: NOBODY OVER THIRTY

252 "The trouble with most teen magazines": Eugenia Sheppard, "Nobody over Thirty," *Women's Wear Daily*, December 11, 1967, access to article courtesy of ProQuest.

252 They came by thumb and by Greyhound bus: A great history of the Summer of Love was provided by Sheila Weller in "Suddenly That Summer," *Vanity Fair*, July 2012.

252 "The word 'hip' translates": Hunter S. Thompson, "The 'Hashbury' Is the Capital of the Hippies," *New York Times Magazine*, May 14, 1967.

253 "turn on, tune in, drop out": Timothy Leary. Accounts of the Human Be-In and the Diggers from Sheila Weller, "Suddenly That Summer"; and the Digger Archives, www.diggers.org.

253 "We wanted to signal that this was the end": From transcript for "Summer of Love," *American Experience*, PBS, pbs.org/wgbh/amex/love/filmmore/pt.html.

253 "We hope that we have something here for the artists and the industry": Jann Wenner, "Letter from the Editor," *Rolling Stone*, November 9, 1967.

254 "If you want to swing college": Smith-Corona Electric Portable.

254 "Pick a flower": Hanes nylons.

254 "Join the cola dropouts": Wink by Canada Dry.

254 "Join the Youth Quake": Diet Rite Cola.

254 A kind of *Life* for college kids, *Eye*: Eugenia Sheppard, "Nobody over Thirty."

254 One of their first hires: Information about Judith Parker and Susan Szekely (now Susan Edmiston) per Susan Edmiston, interview with the author, May 2015.

255 "a dozen girls and men all under 30": Eugenia Sheppard, "Nobody over Thirty."

256 like *Rolling Stone* meets young *Cosmo*: Susan Edmiston detailed Helen's involvement with *Eye* and her clashing vision for the magazine, interview with the author, May 2015.

256 "in the quiet setting of Woodstock, an artists' colony in New York State": "Night Creatures," *Eye*, March 1968.

256 "Helen and Richard Deems would come down in the limousine": Susan Edmiston, interview with the author, May 2015.

256 "I was not directly involved": Susan Edmiston, email exchange with the author, May 2015.

257 "You could call it cosmetics of the soul": Lillian Roxon, "Cosmetics of the Soul," *Eye*, September 1968.

257 "I had a meeting with her once": Donna Lawson Wolff, interview with the author, June 2015.

258 "Raquel Welch was to have been shot in full figure": Helen Gurley Brown, untitled, undated, *Cosmopolitan* art and photography, HGB Papers, SSC. Note: Even though this memo is undated, Helen provided enough information to confirm that she wrote it shortly after the Welch cover was shot.

258 "From lack of communication"; "costumes": Ibid.

259 "*SOFTLY SEXY*"; "'chippily' sexy" : Helen Gurley Brown, "Memo to the ART DEPARTMENT—also Fashion, Decorating, Food, Beauty and Travel," November 14, 1967, *Cosmopolitan* art and photography, HGB Papers, SSC.

259 "more boy-and-girl-*together*-pictures"; "We are the one magazine for women which can show so much love": Ibid.

260 "they were always off somewhere in an office being treated like gods": David McCabe, interview with the author, January 2015.

260 "No, silly boy": Ibid.

35: The World's Most Beautiful Byline

261 "We just wanted *one* cover with somebody with small breasts": Barbara Hustedt Crook, interview with the author.

261 "Girls must ALWAYS look man-loving": Helen Gurley Brown, "Fashion Photography Rules," August 17, 1970, *Cosmopolitan* art and photography, HGB Papers, SSC.

262 "For a jazzy company": Rex Reed, "Girls in the Publishing Business," *Cosmopolitan*, November 1966.

262 "That's it, that's her, that's who": Harvey Aronson, "The World's Most Beautiful Byline," *Newsday*, September 25, 1965.

262 Gloria took the assignment for one simple reason: Gloria Steinem, interview with the author, December 2013.

262 "'Oh, God, we spent ten dollars'": Ibid.

263 "I *always* wear a center part": Gloria Steinem essay in "Brunettes: A Touch of Evil Is Required . . . ," *Cosmopolitan*, July 1968.

263 "Gloria and Barbara didn't try": "At a Holiday Disco Party," *Glamour*, December 1964.

263 "How do I get to be Gloria Steinem?": Reader letter, *Glamour*, October 1965.

264 "Audrey Hepburn in the CIA . . . with bosoms": "A Girl—Signed Herself," *Glamour*, February 1964.

265 her life and her lifework truly began to merge: Steinem described the disconnect between the fluffy articles she was writing and the activist's life she was living in her essay "Life Between the Lines" in *Outrageous Acts and Everyday Rebellions*, 2nd ed. (New York: Holt, 1995).

265 "I *knew* him," Gloria says now: Steinem's account of expecting to pose with Jim Brown, in her own clothes, per interview with the author, December 2013.

265 "some truly ridiculous costume": Ibid. Photographer Gordon Munro provided additional background information about this shoot in an interview with the author, November 2013.

265 "I remember her saying, 'You mean I've really got to do this?' ": Gordon Munro, interview with the author, November 2013.

266 "I'm trying to think of an analogy": Steinem, interview with the author, December 2013.

266 "I didn't really know who Gloria Steinem was at the time": Descriptions, dialogue, and quotes that follow are from Gordon Munro and Gloria Steinem, interviews with the author.

267 "onetime Playboy bunny": Steinem, "Brunettes: A Touch of Evil Is Required . . . ," *Cosmopolitan*, July 1968.

267 "It was a nightmare": Gloria Steinem, interview with the author, December 2013.

268 "I wanted to make amends": Gordon Munro, interview with the author, November 2013.

36: FAKE PICTURES

269 "That's the whole enchilada, darling": Liz Smith, "The Park Avenue Call Girl," *Cosmopolitan*, July 1968.

269 "We'll tape it," Liz said: Liz Smith, *Natural Blonde* (New York: Hyperion, 2000), p. 205. Additional background information on trying to find a call girl as a source per interview with the author, May 2013; and in Helen Gurley Brown, "Step Into My Parlour," *Cosmopolitan*, July 1968.

270 sweet "civilian girls"; "Too much free stuff around": Liz Smith, "The Park Avenue Call Girl."

270 "The day before at lunch": Ibid.

270 Liz got a call from the director Alan Pakula: Liz Smith, *Natural Blonde*, p. 205.

271 "It was a great feat of imagination on my part": Liz Smith, interview with the author, May 2013.

271 blood on the streets: Account of the Democratic National Convention in Chicago from Anthony Lukas, "Police Battle Demonstrators in Streets," *New York Times*, August 29, 1968.

271 it was meant for simple, small-town girls: Helen Gurley Brown, "chat with david" memo, December 9, 1973, HGB Papers, SSC.

272 "On *this* cruise, you can even board ship": Harriet La Barre, "The Travel Bug," *Cosmopolitan*, September 1968.

272 "Oh, hundreds! Hundreds!": Mallen De Santis, interview with the author, October 2012.

272 George Walsh brought the fewest: Helen Gurley Brown complained about Walsh's lack of original story ideas in a miscellaneous note to herself, "PROBLEMS," November 1973, HGB Papers, SSC.

272 "One day I found myself taking a swipe at my <u>mother</u>": Helen Gurley Brown, "NOTES ON GIRLS WHO GET HIT OR VISA VERSA," alternatively titled, "FAMILY FISTICUFFS," *Cosmopolitan* article ideas, 1970s–1980s, HGB Papers, SSC.

273 "major emo" or "major non-emo": Account of *Cosmo*'s story-assigning process came from various interviews done by the author, as well as from a folder labeled "article ideas," in which Helen collected examples of pitches for *Cosmopolitan*, HGB Papers, SSC. In addition to explaining her filing process in a separate note, Helen labeled many of the sheets according to these designations of "major" emotional stories, etc.

273 "THOSE <u>OTHER</u> PEOPLE . . . the ones who <u>belong</u>"; "more intellectual"; "even when you <u>belong</u> at them": *Cosmopolitan* article ideas, 1970s–1980s, HGB Papers, SSC.

273 "now, the reason all this is occurring to me is that *i* am one of the kinky ones": Helen Gurley Brown, "THE YOU NOBODY KNOWS," *Cosmopolitan* article ideas, 1972, HGB Papers, SSC.

274 "She grew up in an age when movie stars": Walter Meade, email exchange with author, February 2014.

274 "I think Scarlett is closer to Helen": Ibid.

37: THE ACTRESS

275 "To be a woman is to be an actress": Susan Sontag, "The Double Standard of Aging," *Saturday Review*, September 23, 1972.

275 "too serious a step": Background on Linda LeClair story per Judy Klemesrud, "An Arrangement: Living Together for Convenience, Security, Sex," *New York Times*, March 4, 1968.

276 they handed out leaflets calling their case "a Victorian drama": Background on the LeClair Affair from Paul Starr, "LeClair Trial Set for Today; Seen as Housing Rule Test," *Columbia Daily Spectator*, April 11, 1968; Deirdre Carmody, "Barnard Considering Decision on Student Living with a Man," *New York Times*, April 17, 1968; Deirdre Carmody, "President Delays Action on Defiant Girl," *New York Times*, May 9, 1968; William A. McWhirter, "'The Arrangement' at College," *Life*, May 31, 1968; and David Allyn, *Make Love, Not War: The Sexual Revolution: An Unfettered History* (New York: Routledge, 2011), pp. 96–98.

277 "A sexual anthropologist of some future century"; "unalluring": William A. McWhirter, "'The Arrangement' at College."

277 What connection did Helen . . . "*None*": Susan Edmiston, interview with the author, May 2015.

278 Shulamith Firestone, a twenty-three-year-old rabble-rouser: Background on Firestone from Martha Ackelsberg, "Shulamith Firestone: 1945–2012," *Jewish Women's Archive Encyclopedia*, jwa.org; Margalit Fox, "Shulamith Firestone, Feminist Writer, Dies at 67," *New York Times*, August 30, 2012; and Susan Faludi, "Death of a Revolutionary," *New Yorker*, April 15, 2013.

278 She also called pregnancy "barbaric"; "shitting a pumpkin": Shulamith Firestone, *The Dialectic of Sex: The Case for Feminist Revolution* (New York: William Morrow, 1970); referenced by Susan Faludi in "Death of a Revolutionary."

278 "WE SUPPORT"; "AUNT TOM OF THE MONTH": New York Radical Women, "NOTES FROM THE FIRST YEAR," June 1968, Duke University Digital Collections.

278 Susan didn't especially like Helen: Susan Edmiston and Donna Lawson Wolff provided background on Helen's relationship with young staffers, including art director Judith Parker.

278 "on the blink": "Eye's Alright," "Eye," *Women's Wear Daily*, May 17, 1968, access to article courtesy of ProQuest.

279 "I remember hearing that they were on acid": Donna Lawson Wolff, interview with the author, June 2015. Additional background information from Sheila Weller's book *Girls Like Us: Carole King, Joni Mitchell, Carly Simon—and the Journey of a Generation* (New York: Washington Square Press: 2008), p. 265; Jeanette Wagner spoke of the locks being changed in "Master Class: Jeanette Wagner," *Women's Wear Daily*, February 1, 2001, access to article courtesy of ProQuest.

279 "Perhaps they were handicapped in handling the boat": Susan Edmiston, email exchange with author, May 2015.

280 Along with Richard Deems, Helen personally interviewed: Helen Gurley Brown to John R. Miller, August 9, 1968, 7:30 p.m., HGB Papers, SSC.

280 Sitting at her desk one night at seven thirty: Ibid.

280 Helen estimated that *Eye* was taking up nearly a third of her time: Ibid.

280 "Dear John, I'm in trouble" *and following*: Ibid.

281 "Where is George Walsh": Ibid.

281 "John, I have told you before": Ibid.

282 Hearst suspended publication after the May 1969 issue: "A Dropout," "Eye," *Women's Wear Daily*, March 26, 1969, access to article courtesy of ProQuest.

38: A GROOVY DAY ON THE BOARDWALK

283 "As they glide back and forth": Penelope Orth, "There She Is . . . ," *Eye*, April 1968.

283 Helen eventually used *Cosmo*'s newsstand success as a bartering chip: Helen Gurley Brown to John Miller, September 27, 1968; and to Richard Deems and Miller, November 26, 1968, HGB Papers, SSC.

283 In 1968, a civil rights activist: Susan Brownmiller gave an excellent account of the hatching and actualizing of the idea for the Miss America protest in her book *In Our Time: Memior of a Revolution* (New York: Dial Press, 1999), pp. 35–41.

283 "the Annual Miss America Pageant will again crown 'your ideal'" *and follow-ing*: Robin Morgan, "No More Miss America!" August 22, 1968; the press release available at www.redstockings.org/index.php/42-uncategorised/65-no-more-miss-america.

284 "woman-garbage"; "Lots of other surprises": Ibid.

284 "Ain't she sweet, makin' profits": Lyrics by Bev Grant. Reproduced with permission.

285 "Atlantic City is a town with class"; "WELCOME TO THE MISS AMER-ICA CATTLE AUCTION": Background is from Marcia Cohen, *The Sisterhood: The Inside Story of the Women's Movement and the Leaders Who Made It Happen* (New York: Fawcett Columbine, 1988), p. 150; and "Miss America: People & Events: The 1968 Protest," *American Experience*, PBS, pbs.org/wgbh/amex/missamerica/peopleevents/e_feminists.html.

285 Elsewhere, a woman wearing a top hat and her husband's suit: Susan Brown-miller, *In Our Time*, pp. 35–41.

285 "Step right up, gentlemen": Ibid. Brownmiller wrote about the mock auction, performed by an artist named Florika and another protestor, Peggy Dobbins. For online footage, see: "Miss America, Up Against the Wall" (also known as "Ms. America, Up Against the Wall"), a women's liberation documentary available at www.youtube.com/watch?v=awCRaGkowjY.

285 Later that night, the first Miss Black America: Judy Klemesrud, "There's Now Miss Black America," *New York Times*, September 9, 1968.

285 "How can people live together more peaceably?": Miss America 1969—Judith Ford, Pageant Center, pageantcenter.com; Alumna Judi Ford Nash, Miss America 1969, ultoday.com (covering the University of Louisiana and the UL District), October 12, 2011.

286 "No more girdles, no more pain!"; "Down with these shoes!": Susan Brown-miller, *In Our Time*, p. 39; Charlotte Curtis, "Miss America Pageant Picketed by 100 Women," *New York Times*, September 8, 1968.

286 A woman sick of doing the dishes: Charlotte Curtis, "Miss America Pageant Picketed by 100 Women."

286 "Why don't you throw yourselves in there!"; "Go home and wash your bras!": Ibid.

286 "Women use your minds": Jacqui Ceballos, interview with the author, October 2014.

286 Someone else threw in a copy of *Cosmo*: Robin Morgan, "No More Miss America!"; the press release invited protestors to throw out their copies of *Cosmopolitan*.

286 Hanisch and another protestor hung a banner: Susan Brownmiller vividly re-called this scene in *In Our Time*, p. 40.

287 nobody ever set fire to one: Ibid., p. 37.

287 "The WLM can put down bras all they like": Deedee Moore, "Take It Off, Push It Up, Fill It Out: The Mad, Mad Bra Industry," *Cosmopolitan*, March 1969.

39: BEFORE AND AFTER

288 "We had all these young assistants": Mallen De Santis, interview with the author, October 2012.

288 She wanted to be with her girls: Liz Smith, eulogy for Helen Gurley Brown, October 18, 2012, available at "Liz Smith Remembers Helen Gurley Brown," wowowow.com/culture/liz-smith-remembers-helen-gurley-brown/, October 24, 2012.

288 "I have not been single for years" *and following excerpt*: Nora Ephron, "Helen Gurley Brown Only Wants to Help," *Esquire*, February 1970.

289 "one of the first things I ever did in which I found my voice as a writer": Nora Ephron to Helen Gurley Brown, undated (possibly circa 1996), HGB Papers, SSC. Background on threatened lawsuit by Fairchild per Ephron in her introduction to her reprinted essay, "*Women's Wear Daily* Unclothed," in *Wallflower at the Orgy* (New York: Bantam Books, 2007), p. 60.

289 "nighttime look"; "de ringlets in de front and de shaggy in de back": Nora Ephron, "Makeover: The Short, Unglamorous Saga of a New, Glamorous Me," *Cosmopolitan*, May 1968, SSC.

289 "not pretty-pretty"; "Told me my face too narrow": Ibid.

290 "Ringlets have lost curls": Ibid.

290 "What'll I do? My hair's a mess": Edited by Mallen De Santis, "The Great Hair Disaster . . . And How to Recover!" *Cosmopolitan*, February 1968.

290 "The simple process was to make them look as awful as possible": Mallen De Santis, interview with the author, October 2012.

291 "a pretty little mouse of a girl": "Mouse into Sexpot," *Cosmopolitan*, September 1968.

291 Other girls simply needed some fine-tuning: Background provided by Mallen De Santis, interview with the author, October 2012; and Barbara Hustedt Crook.

291 "same age, same dreams, same potential": Helen Gurley Brown, "Step Into My Parlour," *Cosmopolitan*, February 1968.

292 "All the senior editors knew it was kind of a lark": Mallen De Santis, interview with the author, October 2012.

40: A VIPER IN THE NEST

293 "You can't really talk about bosom techniques": Helen Gurley Brown, "Step Into My Parlour," *Cosmopolitan*, October 1969, SSC.

293 Helen's recent request for her own private john: "The Press," "Eye," *Women's Wear Daily*, October 7, 1969, access to article courtesy of ProQuest.

293 "Nobody took it seriously": Gloria Steinem, interview with the author, December 2013.

294 "Robin, would a *Cosmo* girl think like this?": Helen Gurley Brown, "Step Into My Parlour," *Cosmopolitan*, April 1968.

294 "Give me your definition of a bitch"; "Have you ever dated a very wealthy man?": From Nora Ephron, "Helen Gurley Brown Only Wants to Help," *Esquire*, February 1970.

294 "Has a woman's magazine" *and following*: Helen Gurley Brown, "Step Into My Parlour," *Cosmopolitan*, June 1969.

294 "TO—Girl Staff Members" *and following excerpt*: Helen Gurley Brown, to Girl Staff Members, undated ["(1969)"? notation], HGB Papers, SSC.

295 "If we do this tastefully": Ibid.

295 "This is your personal reminiscence": Nora Ephron, "Helen Gurley Brown Only Wants to Help."

295 Linda Cox had just started working as an assistant art director: Backstory and career details provided by Linda Cox, interview with the author, June 2015.

296 "It was passed around": Per Linda Cox, who wrote up an account of the bosom-memo debacle and shared it with the author, June 2015.

296 "feathery touches"; "no feeling-the-melons pinching": Barbara Hustedt Crook, email exchange with the author, October 2014.

296 she assigned two different writers: Nora Ephron, "Helen Gurley Brown Only Wants to Help."

297 "BROWN STUDY: Eye is in receipt": "BROWN STUDY," "Eye," *Women's Wear Daily*, March 13, 1969, access to article courtesy of ProQuest.

297 "She was *outraged*": Barbara Hustedt Crook, email exchange with the author, October 2014.

297 "The person responsible would be immediately fired": Linda Cox account, June 2015.

297 "WHAT MEN SHOULD KNOW ABOUT WOMEN'S BOSOMS": *Cosmopolitan*, June 1969.

298 "She said she would right away": Linda Cox account, June 2015.

298 "Helen was still livid"; "I could never, ever face Helen": Ibid.

298 "This big brouhaha started": Nora Ephron, "Helen Gurley Brown Only Wants to Help."

298 "The actual use of anatomical words bugs them": Ibid.

299 "We've decided to wait": Helen Gurley Brown, "Step Into My Parlour," *Cosmopolitan*, October 1969, SSC.

299 the boys, he explained, wanted it to be "a stag affair": Richard Berlin to Helen Gurley Brown, June 25, 1969, HGB Papers, SSC.

41: WOMEN IN REVOLT

300 "One of the first things we discover": Carol Hanisch, "The Personal Is Political," in *Notes from the Second Year: Women's Liberation—Major Writings of the Radical Feminists*, ed. Shulamith Firestone and Anne Koedt (New York: Radical Feminism, 1970), available on Hanisch's website, www.carolhanisch.org/CHwritings/PIP.html.

300 On March 21, 1969, nearly three hundred people filled the basement: Background is from Susan Brownmiller, *In Our Time* (New York: Dial Press, 1999), pp. 107–9; Susan Brownmiller, "Everywoman's Abortions: 'The Oppressor Is Man,'" *Village Voice*, March 27, 1969; and Jennifer Nelson, *Women of Color and the Reproductive Rights Movement* (New York: New York University Press, 2003), chapter 1.

300 "the real experts on abortion": Redstockings. Jennifer Nelson gave a thorough account of the disruption in *Women of Color and the Reproductive Rights Movement*, chapter 1.

301 "I bet every woman here has had an abortion": Susan Brownmiller, *In Our Time*, p. 109.

301 "I was one of those who kept quiet": Ibid.

301 Gloria had gotten an abortion in London: Ibid.

301 After the event, she typed up her article: Gloria Steinem, "After Black Power, Women's Liberation," *New York*, April 4, 1969.

302 "Suddenly, I was no longer learning intellectually what was wrong": Gloria Steinem, *Outrageous Acts and Everyday Rebellions*, 2nd ed. (New York: Holt, 1995), p. 21.

302 A few days after the speakout: Susan Brownmiller, "Everywoman's Abortions."

302 "Everyone was saying the same thing": Judy Gingold in Lynn Povich, *The Good Girls Revolt: How the Women of Newsweek Sued Their Bosses and Changed the Workplace* (New York: PublicAffairs, 2013), p. 52.

303 They compiled newspaper clippings: Background on sexism at *Newsweek* from Lynn Povich, *The Good Girls Revolt;* and Jessica Bennett and Jesse Ellison, "Young Women, Newsweek, and Sexism," *Newsweek*, March 18, 2010.

303 In the fall of 1969, a lawyer friend told Gingold: Lynn Povich, *The Good Girls Revolt*, p. 55.

303 On March 16 of that year: Background ibid., chapter 1.

304 Susan Brownmiller . . . led another group of women: Brownmiller gave another vivid account, this time of the *Ladies' Home Journal* sit-in that she helped organize, in *In Our Time.*

305 "We demand that the *Ladies' Home Journal* hire a woman editor-in-chief": Ibid., p. 86.

305 "The Women's Liberation Movement represents": Ibid.

306 "We can do it—he's small": Ibid., p. 91.

306 "He was a quiet little man": Jacqui Ceballos, interview with the author, October 2014.

306 They also agreed to give members: Susan Brownmiller, *In Our Time*, p. 92.

306 Plans were already in the works for a new column, "The Working Woman": Per Letty Cottin Pogrebin, follow-up interview, May 2015.

307 "a baby feminist"; "My editor at Doubleday warned me": Letty Cottin Pogrebin, interview with the author, January 2014.

307 "I think we passed over it very quickly": Susan Brownmiller, interview with the author, January 2014.

42: THE STRIKE

308 "The feminist movement was so joyous": Jacqui Ceballos, interview with the author, October 2014.

308 Hardly a day passed: Helen Gurley Brown, "Step Into My Parlour," *Cosmopolitan*, June 1970.

308 "Like many other women": Ibid.

308 "Why does a man usually instigate sex": Ibid.

309 "I was finally too embarrassed": Betty Friedan, *Life So Far* (New York: Simon & Schuster, 2000), p. 224.

309 "I propose that women who are doing menial chores": Ibid, pp. 232–33.

310 They didn't have the tens of thousands of demonstrators: Ceballos, interview with the author, October 2014. Ceballos recalled a conversation she had with a fellow activist about recruiting demonstrators, after hyping the upcoming

march and strike to the press: "I said, 'How are we going to get fifty thousand to march?' "

310   In early August: Account of Lucy Komisar at McSorley's from Grace Lichten-stein, "McSorley's Admits Women Under a New City Law," *New York Times*, August 11, 1970; and background about Statue of Liberty takeover from Ceballos's recollections of events leading up to August 26, 1970, posted on Veteran Feminists of America's website, vfa.us, as well as from Ceballos's interview with the author, October 2014.

310   The coalition also called for women across the country to ban four products: Background from Linda Charlton, "Women Seeking Equality March on 5th Ave. Today," *New York Times*, August 26, 1970; and photo, "Betty Friedan Speaking at Press Conference," Corbis Images, www.corbisimages.com, August 25, 1970.

310   "I can't believe they've been reading *Cosmopolitan*": "Boycott of Products Amazes Beholders," UPI, republished in *Lebanon Daily News*, August 26, 1970.

311   "the Mao Tse-tung of Women's Liberation": "Who's Come a Long Way, Baby?" reported by *Time* women staffers, led by Ruth Mehrtens Galvin, *Time*, August 31, 1970.

311   "the movement had no coherent theory" *and following*: Ibid.

311   "Whatever the 'real' differences between the sexes may be": Kate Millett, *Sexual Politics* (Urbana and Chicago: University of Illinois Press, 2000), p. 29.

312   "[They] backed me up against a radiator": Helen Gurley Brown, "Step Into My Parlour," *Cosmopolitan*, November 1985.

312   "It's hard for me to understand how *any* self-loving, man-loving woman": Helen Gurley Brown, "Step Into My Parlour," *Cosmopolitan*, November 1970.

313   they demanded an end to sexist articles . . . as well as $15,000 "in reparation": "Women's Lib Pickets Meet with Editor," UPI, republished in *Milwaukee Journal*, December 3, 1970.

313   "I don't know who sent it because it wasn't signed": Walter Meade, interview with the author.

313   They didn't even have permission: Background is from Marcia Cohen, *The Sisterhood: The Inside Story of the Women's Movement and the Leaders Who Made It Happen* (New York: Fawcett Columbine, 1988), p. 280.

313   Among their ranks: Ibid.

314   "WOMEN'S STRIKE DEMONSTRATION": August 26 Strike Committee, undated, 1970 flyer, Phyllis Birkby Papers, SSC.

314   On the morning of the strike: Jacqui Ceballos, interview with the author, October 2014.

314   Other women liberated: Mary Breasted gave a great play-by-play of these events in her article, "Women on the March: 'We're a Movement Now!'" *Village Voice*, September 3, 1970.

315   "By five o'clock I was exhausted": Jacqui Ceballos, interview with the author, October 2014.

315   "OPPRESSED WOMEN: DON'T COOK DINNER!": "Women Strike for Equality March," photo by Michael Abramson, August 26, 1970, Getty Images, www.gettyimages.com.

315   "When the cops blow the whistle": Betty Friedan, "Women Take the Streets,"

"Voice of New York," *New York*, April 11, 1988.

315 "Take the streets!": Ibid.

315 They pushed past policemen . . . "Bitches!": Background is from Marcia Cohen, *The Sisterhood*, p. 285.

316 "Why can't you light your own fucking cigarettes?": Mary Breasted, "Women on the March: 'We're a Movement Now!'"

316 a ragtag group of women's magazine editors: Mary Thom, *Inside Ms.* (New York: Henry Holt, 1997), p. 11.

316 "It was exhilarating": Pat Carbine, interview with the author, January 2014.

316 "'Ms.' is used by women who object": Linda Charlton, "Women March Down Fifth Avenue in Equality Drive," *New York Times*, August 27, 1970.

43 : PITIFUL PEOPLE

317 "Failure is always at your heels": David Brown, *Let Me Entertain You* (New York: William Morrow & Co., 1990), p. 131.

317 "We definitely have a double standard"; "We are totally possessed by each other": Helen and David Brown, respectively, in Diana Lurie, "Living with Liberation," *New York*, August 31, 1970.

317 "I think Helen is taking on a decision" *and following*: Ibid.

318 cosmically connected to his every physical and emotional need: David Brown, *Let Me Entertain You*, p. 70.

318 "the Working Girl and the Producer": Faith Stewart-Gordon, *The Russian Tea Room: A Love Story* (New York: Simon & Schuster, 1999), p. 146.

318 20th Century Fox fired David for the second time: David Brown, *Let Me Entertain You*, pp. 123–25.

318 three controversial movies: Ibid., p. 128.

318 "We were—because of our concern": Ibid., p. 124.

318 Zanuck's habit of creating cinematic showcases: Background on Darryl Zanuck from Martha Smilgis, "In Darryl Zanuck's Last Drama, a Forgotten French Lover Sues for $15 Million," *People*, July 14, 1980; and Steven Daly, "Myra Breckinridge: Swinging into Disaster" in *Vanity Fair's Tales of Hollywood: Rebels, Reds, and Graduates and the Wild Stories Behind the Making of 13 Iconic Films*, ed. Graydon Carter (New York: Penguin Books, 2008).

319 "It was a dangerous area with a high crime rate": David Brown, *Let Me Entertain You*, p. 124.

319 the Zanucks would be in and out of court: Ralph Blumenthal, "End of Fox Suits Is Indicated," *New York Times*, May 15, 1973.

319 After getting the bad news: David Brown, *Let Me Entertain You*, p. 125.

319 "Look at the table they're giving us" *and following dialogue*: Ibid.

320 she cried her eyes out in George Walsh's office: Helen briefly recounted this scene in a memo that she wrote to herself and titled "PROBLEMS," November 1973, HGB Papers, SSC.

320 "She and Jackie Susann had a husband-watch agreement": Walter Meade, email exchange with author, January 2015.

322 "To go home, for her, took a ton and a half of Valium": Walter Meade, interview with the author.

322 "Didn't you work in order not to have to work someday?" *and following dialogue*: David Brown, *Let Me Entertain You*, p. 252.

322 she felt like a character out of a Kafka story: Helen Gurley Brown and Lyn Tornabene, audio recording no. 2268, tape 10, "HGB Interview," 1970–71, HGB Papers, SSC.

322 "I can hear him telling her she was just like one of Kafka's characters": Meade, email exchange with author, January 2015.

323 "That's *me!*" *and following*: Helen Gurley Brown and Lyn Tornabene, audio recording no. 2268, tape 10, "HGB Interview."

323 countless treatments and surgeries: These are well documented by Helen Gurley Brown herself in her books, *I'm Wild Again: Snippets from My Life and a Few Brazen Thoughts* (New York: St. Martin's Press, 2000) and *The Late Show: A Semiwild but Practical Survival Plan for Women Over 50* (New York: William Morrow, 1993).

44: Some Notes on a New Magazine . . .

324 "We were talking about women who wanted to make their own decisions": Pat Carbine, interview with the author, January 2014.

324 It started with a simple idea that was revolutionary at the time: The bulk of the historical background in this chapter comes from two major sources: Mary Thom's personal and well-observed *Inside Ms.: 25 Years of the Magazine and the Feminist Movement* (New York: Henry Holt, 1997); and Abigail Pogrebin's fascinating and deeply researched oral history, "How Do You Spell Ms.," *New York*, October 2011.

325 Around the same time, Gloria asked Letty: Letty Cottin Pogrebin, follow-up interview with the author, May 2015.

325 Gloria had hosted two of three meetings: Patricia Cronin Marcello, *Gloria Steinem: A Biography* (Westport, CT: Greenwood Press, 2004), p. 120.

325 Gloria had been satisfied, but: Abagail Pogrebin, "How Do You Spell Ms."

325 Then there was the question of the name: Ibid.

325 "All are designed to tell the woman": "Some Notes on a New Magazine . . .," April 1971, *Ms.* Magazine Records, SSC.

326 Assuming its readers were "intelligent and literate": Ibid.

326 Stories with headlines like *and following headlines as examples*: Ibid.

326 Notoriously difficult and prone to yelling: Abigail Pogrebin, "How Do You Spell Ms."

326 "My plan was to get *Ms.* going": Pat Carbine, interview with the author, January 2014.

327 The Ms. Bill would forbid federal agencies: Carl C. Craft, Associated Press, "Sex Prefix Is New Target of Bella Abzug," *Gettysburg Times*, July 27, 1971.

327 "not as the wives of individuals": Ibid.

327 "Hello, I'm calling from *Ms.* magazine": Abigail Pogrebin, "How Do You Spell Ms."; and Mary Thom, *Inside Ms.*, p. 14. Thom explained how anyone working for *Ms.* in the beginning had to pronounce it and spell it repeatedly. Author based dialogue on these accounts.

327 Carbine and Steinem borrowed friends: Pat Carbine, interview with the author, January 2014.

328 *Ms.* would be approximately eighty-eight pages: Stats from "Some Notes on a New Magazine . . .".

328 "Do you have The Globbies?": Slimmers Glove System.

328 "Relax": *and following*: Cupid's Quiver. *Time* wrote about the ad for Cupid's Quiver in "Advertising: The Unlikeliest Product," December 26, 1969.

328 "We did not go for cosmetics *at all*": Pat Carbine, interview with the author, January 2014.

329 "I talked about the spirit that was animating women": Ibid.

329 "When push came to shove about comparing us to *Cosmo*": Ibid.

45: ENTER HELEN

330 "I'm a materialist": Helen Gurley Brown, "Big Sister," *Time*, February 9, 1968.

330 Working as a kindergarten teacher: Biographical details about Lou Honderich per Honderich, email exchange with the author, January 2014.

330 "Even back then, as a such a young woman": Ibid.

331 Lou never stopped relying on Helen's advice, and in 1971: Ibid.

331 "Enter Helen," Lou says: Ibid.

331 "The point is, Helen believed in me": Ibid.

332 Someone saw her at an organizer's house: Susan Brownmiller shared this secondhand story in interview with the author, January 2014.

332 "She was indicating that women *have* to put up this front": Ibid.

332 " 'This is reality, kiddos' ": Ibid.

46: THE BLUE GODDESS

333 "You not only enjoy being a girl—you *thrive* on it!": "How Feminine Are You?" *Cosmopolitan*, April 1971.

333 "I said a mighty yes": Helen Gurley Brown, "Step Into My Parlour," *Cosmopolitan*, September 1971.

334 the founders of *Ms.* were having a difficult time: Background on the beginnings of *Ms.* and securing financial backers is from "Personal Report from *Ms.*" *Ms.*, July 1972, SSC.

334 Then they had a couple of breakthroughs: Background from "Personal Report from *Ms.*"; Mary Thom, *Inside Ms.* (New York: Henry Holt, 1997), p. 15; and Clay Felker, "Editor's Letter: What Is Ms. and What Is It Doing in New York?" *New York*, December 20, 1971.

334 In a small, cramped workspace: Stephanie Harrington provided a great description of the *Ms.* headquarters in "Ms. Versus Cosmo: Two Faces of the Same Eve," *New York Times*, August 11, 1974.

335 labeled "Spring" just in case: Abigail Pogrebin, "How Do You Spell Ms.," *New York*, October 2011.

335 "A sexually liberated woman without a feminist consciousness": Anselma Dell'Olio, "The Sexual Revolution Wasn't Our War," *Ms.*, Spring 1972 preview issue.

335 "Those clicks are coming faster and faster": Jane O'Reilly, "The Housewife's Moment of Truth," *Ms.*, Spring 1972 preview issue.

336 The artist Miriam Wosk painted: "Remembering Miriam Wosk, First Ms. Cover Artist," *Ms.* magazine blog, December 22, 2010; and Abigail Pogrebin, "How Do You Spell Ms."

336 "Until now, the Women's Movement has lacked": Clay Felker, "Editor's Letter: What Is Ms. and What Is It Doing in New York?"

336 they sold out in eight days: Abigail Pogrebin, "How Do You Spell Ms."

337 *Cosmopolitan*'s art department was in crisis: Linda Cox, interview with the author, June 2015.

337 "Boom-boom-boom, one after the other": Ibid.

337 "Marni called me and said, 'Please come back' ": Ibid.

337 By the following year, his American disciples: Background on Guru Maharaj Ji from Ted Morgan, "Middle-Class *Premies* Find Oz in the Astrodome," *New York Times*, December 9, 1973.

337 "She was so completely swept away": Linda Cox, interview with the author, June 2015.

338 Not long after that, Helen promoted Linda: Ibid.

47: COSMOPOLITAN NUDE MAN

339 "I thought it was a hoot": Hugh Hefner, interview with the author, November 2013.

339 "Helen Gurley Brown of Cosmopolitan": "Knees Up, Mother Brown," "Eye," *Women's Wear Daily*, January 29, 1970, access to article courtesy of ProQuest.

339 "You really are so naughty": "Letter to Eye," "Eye," *Women's Wear Daily*, February 9, 1970, access to article courtesy of ProQuest.

339 "The Further Adventures of Mother Brown and the Great Male Nude Foldout Caper"; "relatively coy pose"; "collecting pornography": "Phone Call to Eye," "Eye," *Women's Wear Daily*, February 12, 1970, access to article courtesy of ProQuest.

340 Men liked to look at women's bodies, and women: Irin Carmon, "Helen Gurley Brown, Objectifier of Men," *Salon*, August 13, 2012.

340 Inspired by the Italian painter Caravaggio: Photographer Guy Webster told the story of shooting James Coburn for *Cosmo* in a video online: "Jim Whitney Documentary on Guy Webster," YouTube.com, September 12, 2014.

340 "Apparently he is in his mystical phase": Helen Gurley Brown to Richard Deems, "COSMOPOLITAN NUDE MAN," December 4, 1968.

341 The rejections piled up: Helen Gurley Brown, "Step Into My Parlour," *Cosmopolitan*, January 1971.

341 "Mr. Average household face"; "You may or may *not* ever see a male nude": Ibid.

341 "Like fire and gasoline": Burt Reynolds, *My Life* (New York: Hyperion, 1994), p. 173. The bulk of what follows—dialogue, descriptions, scenes—is per Reynolds's version of the story in chapter 33 of his book.

341 "Are you a sexist?"; "I bet in ten years": Ibid.

342 "Why?" he finally asked; "Because," she cooed, "You're the only one": Ibid.

342 "On the back of the foldout": Ibid., p. 174.

342 using masking tape, Vaseline, bobby socks, baseballs: Booth Moore, "Cosmo's Eyes," *Los Angeles Times*, January 9, 2004.

342 The day of the shoot: Burt Reynolds, *My Life*, p. 174.

343 "Fabulous! Fabulous like that!": Per photographer Harry King, this is what Scavullo regularly exclaimed during shoots; interview with the author, September 2014.

343 "I always know . . . I've caught the butterfly": Burt Reynolds, *My Life*, p. 174.

343 he pretended to hump the bearskin rug: Ibid., p. 175.

344 "*Cosmo*'s Famous Extra Bonus Takeoff!" *and following*: *Cosmopolitan* cover, April 1972, SSC.

344 "just *lusty* and honest in their appetite for an appreciation of attractive men"; "As for you (that COSMOPOLITAN girl)": Barbara Creaturo, "Cosmo's Playmate of the Year!—Why?" *Cosmopolitan*, April 1972.

345 He had liked a shot where he was laughing: Burt Reynolds wrote about visiting *Cosmo* and seeing the images in *My Life*, 174.

345 "The original slide was lost": Mallen De Santis, interview with the author, October 2012.

345 "Apparently the people at *Cosmo* took this thing more seriously than I did": Mary Alice Kellogg, Newsweek Feature Service, "Redskin to Bearskin: Burt Reynolds Soars," *Boca Raton News*, April 13, 1972.

345 "Hey, I didn't recognize you with your clothes on": Burt Reynolds, *My Life*, 175.

345 "And a major factor in his ascendancy"; "Face it, these women wouldn't be going crazy": Mary Alice Kellogg, "Redskin to Bearskin: Burt Reynolds Soars."

346 and in Huntsville, Alabama, members of the English Department: This detail and others collected from readers' letters, "Dear Cosmopolitan," *Cosmopolitan*, July 1972.

346 After the issue came out: Burt Reynolds described the frenzy that followed his *Cosmo* appearance in *My Life*, pp. 174–76.

346 Back in the States, the Catholic Church issued a critical statement: Ibid., p. 175.

346 letters poured in: "Dear Cosmopolitan," *Cosmopolitan*, July 1972.

347 "While leafing through *COSMO*, what did I behold": Ibid., poem by Donna Visione, reprinted with permission.

48: Problems

348 "Helen saw a shrink all the time I knew her": Walter Meade, interview with the author.

348 "Relax chin, stay at 105 pounds . . . torture!": Helen Gurley Brown, "Step Into My Parlour," *Cosmopolitan*, January 1973.

348 British *Cosmo* was an instant, red-hot success: Linda Grant, *Sexing the Millennium: Women and the Sexual Revolution* (New York: Grove Press, 1994), p. 124.

348 "Like Coca-Cola, Helen Gurley Brown and her message": James Brady, "La Fille Cosmopolitaine," "New York Intelligencer," *New York*, February 12, 1973.

348 He and Richard Zanuck finally had started their own production outfit: David Brown, *Let Me Entertain You* (New York: William Morrow & Co., 1990), pp. 143–44.

349 George Walsh declined: Still furious, Helen detailed her version of the story in

a miscellaneous note to herself, "PROBLEMS," November 1973, HGB Papers, SSC.

349   "*screw* that . . . public relations are where it's *at*": Ibid.

349   "George Walsh has some kind of personality defect": Ibid.

349   *Cosmo* Girls could read all about the man who "runs the office": Helen Gurley Brown, "Step Into My Parlour," *Cosmopolitan*, August 1970.

350   "one doesn't want to get personal": Helen Gurley Brown, "PROBLEMS," November 1973.

350   Helen couldn't remember him once complimenting her, or even saying "well done": Ibid.

350   Instead, he played the resigned man: Ibid.

350   "Keep George": Ibid.

49: Two Faces of the Same Eve

351   "*Cosmopolitan* is talking to women one by one": Suzanne Levine in Stephanie Harrington, "Ms. Versus Cosmo: Two Faces of the Same Eve," *New York Times*, August 11, 1974.

351   "I think a certain girl who just married": *Cosmopolitan* ad in *New York Times*, April 18, 1974.

351   "Why, if she's so smart": Stephanie Harrington, "Ms. Versus Cosmo: Two Faces of the Same Eve."

352   After making her way up to the fourth floor: Ibid.

352   "Have we done anxiety lately?"; "That is like asking if you've eaten in the last week"; "We have depression in the works"; "This one is totally ridiculous— 'Are Lesbians Ecological?' ": Ibid.

353   Harrington went to an editorial meeting at *Ms.*: Ibid.

353   "What is romance?"; "Women's obsession with romance": Ibid.

354   "I am a survivor": Ibid.

354   The letter was signed "Emma Bovary, Yonville Parish": Ibid.

354   Helen regularly critiqued foreign editions: Per Linda Cox, interview with the author, June 2015.

355   "as riveting as the telephone directory"; its "coverpersons": Stephanie Harrington, "Ms. Versus Cosmo: Two Faces of the Same Eve."

355   "More than twice as many *Ms.* readers as *Cosmopolitan* readers": Ibid.

355   "Before the press conference we went to the ladies' room": Helen Gurley Brown, "Step Into My Parlour," *Cosmopolitan*, July 1974.

355   "She was the most unconfident, ingratiating person": Gloria Steinem, interview with the author, December 2013.

356   "Helen really created a little money-printing press for Hearst": Pat Carbine, interview with the author, January 2014.

356   "reassure us that you and the other leaders": Helen Gurley Brown to Gloria Steinem, April 11, 1974, HGB Papers, SSC.

356   "She would say, 'Now, your movement says this' ": Pat Carbine, interview with the author, January 2014.

356   a former *Esquire* secretary, Julie Roy: Julie Roy and Lucy Freeman later wrote a book about Roy's relationship with Renatus Hartogs, *Betrayal* (New York:

Stein and Day, 1976); reviewed by Susan Braudy, "Betrayal," *New York Times Book Review*, August 8, 1976.

357 "Gloria, you have to do something": Steinem recalled this story and conversation in interview with the author, December 2013.

357 "I do not remember feeling angry at her": Ibid.

357 "it felt like breaking the picket line": Barbara Hustedt Crook, interview with the author.

357 "I wasn't surprised by the accusations": Barbara Hustedt Crook, email exchange with the author, October 2014.

358 Hartogs later was found guilty: "N.Y. Psychiatrist Ordered to Pay $350Gs for Sex," *Jet*, April 3, 1975; and AP, "Patient Awarded $350,000," republished in *Milwaukee Journal*, March 20, 1975.

50: ERA AND YOU

359 "The advent of the women's movement": Gloria Steinem, interview with the author, December 2013.

359 David sweated in his seat: Account of screening *Jaws* in Dallas is from David Brown, *Let Me Entertain You* (New York: William Morrow & Co., 1990), p. 15. Additional background on the plagued production is from Jeff Labrecque, "The 20 Best Summer Blockbusters of All Time: 'Jaws' is No. 1," *Entertainment Weekly*, www.ew.com, April 9, 2014.

359 "The audience screamed and screamed": David Brown, *Let Me Entertain You*, p. 15.

360 in part, he had *Cosmo* to thank: Jennifer Scanlon, *Bad Girls Go Everywhere* (New York: Penguin Books, 2009), p. 206.

360 "She knew that he had to go. He knew that he had to go": Walter Meade, interview with the author, July 2015.

360 "it seemed to me there were *no* guidelines": Helen Gurley Brown, "Step Into My Parlour," *Cosmopolitan*, February 1975.

361 Helen relished the chance to ask Letty: Helen fondly recalled her lunch with Letty in her April 1975 "Step Into My Parlour" column in *Cosmopolitan*.

361 "We used to go to lunch for old times' sake": Letty Cottin Pogrebin recalled this conversation with Helen in interview with author, January 2014.

361 "If she hadn't created her own trademark": Ibid.

362 Helen eventually did identify as a "devout feminist": Emanuella Grinberg, "Helen Gurley Brown's Complicated Feminist Legacy," CNN.com/2012/08/17/living/helen-gurley-brown-legacy/index.html (August 19, 2012; (post includes a link to the 1996 video).

362 Helen promised to try to reel in the help of John Mack Carter: Helen Gurley Brown to John Mack Carter, December 30, 1975, HGB Papers, SSC.

362 "This may not be a subject you feel passionately about, John": Ibid.

362 Each magazine devoted a part of its July 1976 issue to the ERA: Jennifer Scanlon, *Bad Girls Go Everywhere* (New York: Penguin Books, 2009), p. 195.

363 "Puzzled and confused": Linda Wolfe, "ERA & YOU," *Cosmopolitan*, July 1976.

363 "We cannot hope to grab all the goodies": Ibid.

363 Ratification of the ERA proved to be a long and continuing battle: Background

from Adam Clymer, "Time Runs Out for Proposed Rights Amendment," *New York Times*, July 1, 1982; and Roberta W. Francis, Chair, ERA Task Force, National Council of Women's Organizations, "The History Behind the Equal Rights Amendment," www.equalrightsamendment.org.

363 "She seemed to understand long before anybody else": Erica Jong, interview with the author, January 2014.

364 The two magazines shared freelance writers, contributing editors, even article ideas: Mary Thom, *Inside Ms.* (New York: Henry Holt, 1997), p. 41.

364 "I regarded the call as the consummate compliment": Pat Carbine, interview with the author, January 2014.

364 Helen wrote Gloria long fan letters: Collected letters from Helen Gurley Brown to Gloria Steinem, HGB Papers, SSC.

365 "I can imagine the same woman reading both our magazines": Gloria Steinem to Helen Gurley Brown, September 21 (possibly 1978; no year provided), HGB Papers, SSC.

365 "That you made the first call was especially important": Gloria Steinem to Helen Gurley Brown, September 11 (no year provided), HGB Papers, SSC.

365 "She came to an editorial meeting once": Gloria Steinem, interview with the author, December 2013.

365 "She called me up and said, 'My staff needs to understand the women's movement' ": Ibid.

366 "excruciatingly awful": Mallen De Santis, interview with author, October 2012. Barbara Hustedt Crook and Linda Cox also talked about these celebrity visits to *Cosmo*.

366 "I was trying to explain . . . that this was not a reform": Steinem, interview with the author, December 2013.

366 "We *are* all sisters": Helen Gurley Brown to Gloria Steinem, August 10, 1978, HGB Papers, SSC.

51: HAVING IT ALL

367 "*Having It All* sounds so fucking cliche to me": Helen Gurley Brown, letter to Joni Evans and Michael Korda, July 29, 1982, HGB Papers, SSC.

367 Helen began with a tour; "I think I was a darling baby"; "I am wearing falsies": "Gloria Steinem in Conversation with Helen Gurley Brown," *A Moment in Time: Conversations with Legendary Women*, Enduring Freedom Productions, Starlight Home Entertainment, 2006.

367 "This is my family"; "This is the first cover of *Cosmopolitan*"; "I got the sexiest picture I could find": Ibid.

368 Cut to Helen and Gloria sitting down across from each other: Information and dialogue that follows are from video, "Gloria Steinem in Conversation with Helen Gurley Brown." Author used the unedited transcript of the interview, part of the HGB Papers at SSC; some quotes that appear may not be in the edited version. Author edited and condensed parts of the interview to include here, but all meaning is kept intact.

373 twenty people from Estée Lauder were waiting at a restaurant: Ibid.

Epilogue

375 "Home. I'll go home": Scarlett O'Hara in *Gone with the Wind*, 20th Century Fox, 1940.

375 would eschew the word *girl* and be known as "the largest selling young women's magazine in the world"; "I don't think the advertising should talk like that anymore": Stuart Elliott, " 'That Cosmopolitan Girl' Won't Be a Girl Anymore," *New York Times*, January 4, 1993.

375 "It became known as the Cobra Look": Harry King, interview with the author, September 2014.

376 In the United States, *Cosmopolitan* is the bestselling magazine for young women: Statistics per Hearst, www.hearst.com/magazines/cosmopolitan.

376 "There is almost no danger of contracting AIDS"; "a healthy vagina": Robert E. Gould, "Reassuring News About AIDS: A Doctor Tells Why You May Not Be at Risk," *Cosmopolitan*, January 1988.

377 "The *Cosmo* girl CAN get AIDS"; "Say No to *Cosmo*": Background from ACT UP: Oral History Project, a program of MIX: The New York Lesbian & Gay Experimental Film Festival, 2003; and video of actual protest, www.jeancarlo musto.com/doctorsliars&women.html.

377 was reported that only 4 percent of AIDS patients: Associated Press, "AIDS Risk Articles Criticized," *New York Times*, February 20, 1988.

377 "We have come so far in relieving women of fear and fright" *and following*: Helen Gurley Brown interview with host Ted Koppel on ABC's *Nightline*, January 21, 1988; referenced by Jeff Cohen and Norman Solomon, "Cosmo's Deadly Advice to Women About AIDS," *Seattle Times*, July 31, 1993.

378 "People would always say to me 'How can you work for her?' ": Liz Smith, interview with the author, May 2013.

378 downplayed sexual harassment in a decade full of high-profile charges: Jennifer Scanlon, *Bad Girls Go Everywhere* (New York: Penguin Books, 2009), pp. 223–24.

378 "I certainly hope so": Helen Gurley Brown quoted herself in her op-ed, "At Work, Sexual Electricity Sparks Creativity," *Wall Street Journal*, October 29, 1991.

378 "I *know* about sexual harassment"; "While all this was going on": Ibid. Shortly thereafter, Roger Simon wrote a column about Helen Gurley Brown's *Wall Street Journal* column, quoting her in horror, "Odd Ideas from the Original Cosmo Girl," *Los Angeles Times*, November 3, 1991.

379 replaced by a much younger editor, Bonnie Fuller: Jennifer Scanlon, *Bad Girls Go Everywhere*, pp. 226–28.

379 "I think it was difficult for her": Laurence Mitchell, interview with the author, October 2013.

379 "If it gives you any satisfaction" *and following excerpt*: Helen Gurley Brown to Patrick Reilly, February 2, 1996, HGB Papers, SSC, in response to his article "Spiked: Helen Gurley Brown Finds That 'Nice Girls' Sometimes Finish Last," *Wall Street Journal*, February 1, 1996.

379 In addition to giving her a car and a new office: Jennifer Scanlon, *Bad Girls Go Everywhere*, p. 227.

380 "The company has been insanely good to me until these last 15 minutes":

Helen Gurley Brown to Walter Meade, February 1996, HGB Papers, SSC.

380 "I don't have children, and it sort of hurts me to think that I just have to throw it away"; "I feel I have a home": Helen Gurley Brown to Sophia Smith Collection, donor file.

381 "ashamed of being sort of from the sticks and not having an education": Erica Jong, interview with the author, January 2014.

381 Helen visited Smith, and the college made her an honorary member of the Class of 1962: Per Smith College website, www.smith.edu.

381 "I don't know that she counted her own reality": Gloria Steinem, interview with the author, December 2013.

382 "Because she had to raise herself": Lyn Tornabene, interview with the author, November 2014.

382 On February 1, 2010, David died at home: Bruce Weber, "David Brown, Film and Stage Producer, Dies at 93," *New York Times*, February 2, 2010.

382 By then, the Browns had amassed a fortune: Katherine Rosman, "Who Owns Helen Gurley Brown's Legacy," *New York Times*, August 22, 2015.

382 "Helen talked to me about Cleo in her old age": Lou Honderich, email exchange with the author.

383 "Take me to the Ozarks": David Brown, *Let Me Entertain You* (New York: William Morrow & Co., 1990), p. 259.

383 "I think she just remembered it as being so pretty": Background on Helen and David's burial arrangements per Lou Honderich, interview with the author.

383 "She always wanted her makeup on": Ibid.

384 "A few years before she died, she was very heavy": Laurence Mitchell, interview with the author, October 2013.

384 Helen looked for meaningful ways to allocate: Rosman, "Who Owns Helen Gurley Brown's Legacy."

384 after visiting with the dean of the Columbia Journalism School: Ibid.

384 She was ninety years old, "though parts of her were considerably younger": Margalit Fox, "Helen Gurley Brown, Who Gave 'Single Girl' a Life in Full, Dies at 90," *New York Times*, August 13, 2012.

384 In October, a who's who of the city's media elite: Mike Vilensky, "Cosmo Girl's Homage."

385 "In the back of my mind, Helen would say 'Do it, do it!'": Patricia Myles, interview with the author, September 2013.

385 Mayor Bloomberg credited Helen for changing the world: Mike Vilensky, "Cosmo Girl's Homage."

385 "never had children and never regretted it"; "She believed she didn't have to follow a traditional path": Ibid.

385 "Can you see me on all fours under the table at La Caravelle?"; she "threw her nickels around like manhole covers": "A fond earful for Helen," PageSix.com, NYPost.com, October 21, 2012; and Abigail Alderman, "David & Helen Gurley Brown Institute Comes to Life," Hearst.com, November 15, 2012.

386 "It's not a joke": Lou Honderich, interview with the author.

386 "She made me feel so great": Ibid.

386 "'What is, what was, Helen really like?'": Liz Smith, eulogy for Helen

Gurley Brown, posted under "Liz Smith Remembers Helen Gurley Brown," wowowow.com/culture/liz-smith-remembers-helen-gurley-brown/, October 24, 2012.

386 "She may have thought she had it all": Liz Smith, interview with the author, May 2013.

387 "I'm afraid we continue in life to be who we *were*": Helen Gurley Brown, *I'm Wild Again: Snippets from My Life and a Few Brazen Thoughts* (New York: St. Martin's Press, 2000), p. 63.

387 wearing her favorite perfume, a Pucci dress, and a purse containing a twenty-dollar bill: Per Lou Honderich.

387 The relative who oversees the cemetery: Ibid.

387 The day of Helen's burial, it snowed in Arkansas: Ibid.

388 When Lou asked Helen for the names of David's closest relatives: Ibid.

388 "As far as I know, Helen Gurley Brown didn't read a lot of what we call Holy Scripture": Rev. Roger Joslin, burial sermon, May 3, 2013.

388 "and the language is every bit as erotic": Ibid.

388 "Your lips are like a crimson thread": Song of Solomon 4:3.

389 "skinny is sacred": Helen Gurley Brown, *I'm Wild Again*, p. 157.

389 "Helen's fierce honesty"; "I'll let the 'Song of Solomon' give voice to former lovers": Rev. Roger Joslin, burial sermon, May 3, 2013.

389 "You have ravished my heart": Song of Solomon 4:9.

389 "MARRIED TO HELEN GURLEY BROWN": Gravestone of David Brown, Sisco Cemetery, Osage, Arkansas.

INDEX

Page numbers in italics refer to illustrations.

ABOUT THE AUTHOR

BROOKE HAUSER often covers women in media and entertainment. Her work has appeared in the *New York Times*, the *Los Angeles Times*, *Allure*, *Parade*, and *Premiere*, among other publications. As a journalist, she has written about a wide range of subjects, including female corrections officers, Baptist preachers, Chinese beauty queens, and a former secretary of state. Hauser's first book, about young newcomers to America, *The New Kids: Big Dreams and Brave Journeys at a High School for Immigrant Teens*, was a winner of the American Library Association's 2012 Alex Award. Originally from Miami, Florida, Hauser recently moved to western Massachusetts, where she lives with her family and occasionally teaches nonfiction writing at Smith College.

About the author

About the book

Insights,
Interviews
& More . . .

Meet Brooke Hauser

Photograph by Isabella Casini

BROOKE HAUSER is the author of *Enter Helen: The Invention of Helen Gurley Brown and the Rise of the Modern Single Woman*, which has been optioned for film and won Best Nonfiction Book at the National Arts & Entertainment Journalism Awards. A longtime journalist, she has written for *Allure* (where she was also a contributing editor), *Glamour*, *Marie Claire*, the *New*

York Times, *The New Yorker*, and the *Los Angeles Times*, among other publications.

Her first book, *The New Kids: Big Dreams and Brave Journeys at a High School for Immigrant Teens*, won the American Library Association's 2012 Alex Award. *People* selected *The New Kids* as one of its "Great Reads," *Parade* chose it as a "Parade Pick," and the *New York Post* called it "required reading." Says the *New York Times*: "Ms. Hauser's book is a refreshing reminder of the hurdles newcomers to this country still face and how many defy the odds to overcome them."

For several years, Hauser covered the film industry as an editor and writer-at-large at *Premiere*. In 2005, her interest in profiling characters not usually featured in the mainstream media led her to the City section of the *New York Times*. Her article, "This Strange Thing Called Prom," was optioned by Miramax.

As a reporter, Hauser has written about a wide range of subjects, including female corrections officers, Baptist preachers, Chinese beauty queens, and a Vermont dairy farmer with a screenwriting career on the side. Other profile subjects include a former Secretary of State (Colin Powell), and dozens of film, TV, and pop stars.

Originally from Miami, Florida, Hauser recently moved to western Massachusetts, where she lives with her family. She frequently teaches nonfiction writing at Smith College. Learn more about her at her website, www.brookehauser.com. ◡

A Q & A with Brooke Hauser

Enter Helen *is not a typical biography because it diverges from a linear timeline to hone in on a specific period of Helen Gurley Brown's life. Why did you structure it this way?*

I could have started at the very beginning, with Helen Gurley Brown's birth in Green Forest, Arkansas, in 1922, but I decided to enter her story right before the publication of *Sex and the Single Girl* to give readers an immediate picture of who she was, what she believed, and why her ideas were considered so scandalous at the time. The 1960s and 1970s were some of the most exciting and transformative years of her life and career, and also an incredibly transformative time for America. I wanted to show how she tapped into the zeitgeist of the era, particularly the sexual revolution and the women's movement. I enjoyed weaving in passages about the invention of the Pill and the publication of *The Feminine Mystique*, which notably hit shelves a year after *Sex and the Single Girl*. Particularly thinking of readers who are unfamiliar with HGB, I felt it was important to establish her place in the culture early on. It shaped her, but she also influenced the culture. These detours further serve as an important reminder for Baby Boomers who may have forgotten—or never realized—just how revolutionary Helen really was. Once I felt that I had firmly fixed the image of Helen Gurley Brown in the reader's mind, I wanted to slowly chip away at it to expose the real person underneath. I saw my perfect opportunity midway through the book, in the scene where Helen fires the movie critic Rex Reed because he doesn't understand the simple, small-town Cosmo Girl. "How do you know such a girl exists?" he asks. "Because," Helen says, "I *was* that girl." She was, and yet she wasn't. It's hard to say who the "real" Helen was, because she was different Helens to different people in different areas (and eras) of her life, from Arkansas to Los Angeles to New York, and then back to Arkansas, where she was laid to rest. Her friend and former *Cosmo* colleague Walter Meade once described her as being like a Picasso portrait—she had so many faces and fragments—and I didn't think a traditional chronological narrative could do her justice.

During your research for the book, you discovered inconsistencies in Helen's story that she told about herself. How did these revelations change the way you viewed her?

As a reader, it was impossible for me not to get sucked into the rags-to-riches drama of Helen's autobiographical narrative, but as a reporter, it was my duty to fact-check it. Yes, Helen came from a small town originally, and she played up her "nowhere looks," but otherwise, there was nothing simple about her. Unraveling the legend she spun about herself, and discovering just how complicated, and constructed, she really was, made me distrust her—and that's probably a good thing. As a biographer, part of my job is to examine "the truth." Like everyone else, I love Nora Ephron's 1970 *Esquire* profile of her, "Helen Gurley Brown Only Wants to Help." But Ephron never really questions Helen's sincerity in the piece. Rereading it now, I have to wonder: Were those real tears that Helen shed, relating the story of her depressed mother and wheelchair-bound sister for the umpteenth time? Or was she putting on a bit of a show for *Esquire*? Did she really care about her Cosmo Girls as much as Ephron and everyone else seemed to believe? I can't say for sure, but I have learned enough ▸

about Helen's motivations and manipulations to know that it's worth casting some doubt. Her own family felt that she threw them under the bus on the road to reinventing herself. And one has to wonder if she would have cared about the Cosmo Girl had the magazine not been so profitable. Helen was smarter than people knew. And more selfish. I look at her legend with a mix of admiration and suspicion. I found the most unvarnished versions of Helen in the audio-tape interviews she did with Lyn Tornabene, as well as in her own unpublished writings. In her *Cosmo* article memo, "The You Nobody Knows," Helen herself admitted that she sometimes presented "a fake picture." I tried to keep that in mind. I still find it fascinating that someone so confessional could remain so unknowable. I asked people who had been close to her whether they felt Helen was a genuine person. Several friends and colleagues shared a story of some interaction with her that left them wondering. Meade recalled being invited over to Helen's Central Park West apartment. Inside, there was a foyer with photographs mounted on the walls—mostly celebrities that she knew personally. But on this occasion, Walter's picture was mounted on the wall, too. "There I was," he told me, "and then I noticed that where my photograph was, the spacing around it was just slightly different than all the others, and I realized, 'That's the space she has for whoever is coming to dinner.'"

What other discoveries did you make while working on the book?

Early on, my editor asked me to broaden the scope of the book to incorporate more about the era in which Helen lived. Her rise to fame and notoriety is a great lens through which to view the '60s, but I wanted to capture a different side of the decade than what we usually see. The civil rights movement, Vietnam, Woodstock, and the violence of 1968 are well-remembered in America's collective consciousness, but I also wanted to show lesser-known events that would have been on Helen Gurley Brown's radar. For instance, the Career Girl Murders. It was chilling to learn that on August 28, 1963, the same day that Martin Luther King gave his "I Have a Dream" speech in

Washington, two young women were killed in their apartment in Manhattan, setting off a citywide panic. Around the same time, I found one of Helen's newspaper columns, "How Do You Keep From Getting Murdered?" A passionate champion of the career woman, Helen was not about to let a freakish double homicide frighten her "girls," and she sought to assuage some of the hysteria. Her article, coupled with Max Wylie's safety 1964 manual, *Career Girl, Watch Your Step*, gives a fascinating glimpse into what it felt like to be a "woman alone" in New York City at that time. The story of Linda LeClair also was new to me. She was the Barnard student who was kicked out of school for living with her boyfriend off-campus—making national news. This happened in 1968, a year after the Summer of Love in San Francisco. To me, the so-called LeClair Affair speaks volumes about the puritanical attitude that Helen was up against. It also conveys the spirit of the youth movement, which rejected so much of what she symbolized as a rich, older woman who was part of the Establishment. By the late '60s, Helen, once a pioneer, was falling behind the times.

Is there anything you left out of the book that you wish you could have included?

Oh, there are so many wonderful anecdotes that didn't make the cut because they would have interrupted the flow of the narrative, which is really anchored in the '60s and '70s. There is one piece of juicy intel that I stumbled across soon after *Enter Helen* was published: In 1989, Helen wrote a letter to Donald Trump, asking if he would consider posing nude for a *Cosmo* centerfold, à la Burt Reynolds, for the magazine's upcoming twenty-fifth anniversary under her editorship. Trump declined, even though Helen floated the idea of covering his manhood with a stack of books or a flowerpot. I laughed out loud when I read her letter. Curiosity led me to look up whether Helen ever corresponded with Hillary Clinton—they shared an Arkansas connection—and, well, of course she did. Helen was pen pals with everyone. ▶

A Q & A with Brooke Hauser (*continued*)

How are women responding to the book?

It's funny, when I first started considering this project, I heard a common refrain about Helen Gurley Brown: "Nobody cares." Well, several years later, people care. They might not always like her; they might find her ideas to be passé, ridiculous, at times even grotesque; but they recognize her cultural significance. Lena Dunham piqued millennials' interest in Helen Gurley Brown with her memoir, *Not That Kind of Girl*, which was partly inspired by *Having It All*. And as I was putting the finishing touches on *Enter Helen*, it was announced that Dunham would be developing a new HBO series, *Max*, set in the world of a 1960s women's magazine. Since then, there have been numerous think pieces about HGB's "complicated" and "imprecisely feminist" legacy. There's also a movie based on *Enter Helen* in the works. On a personal level, I have enjoyed engaging with readers who engage with the book. After *Enter Helen* came out, I gave a private reading at a women's clothing store in my town of Northampton, Massachusetts. I actually got the idea from Helen's book promotion: In the spring of 1962, an L.A. boutique featured *Sex and the Single Girl* paired with a fetching black bikini in its window display. We skipped the bikini for this event, but served cosmopolitans to the customers in attendance. I also did an event with Kate Bolick, the author of *Spinster: Making a Life of One's Own*, at a brewery in western Massachusetts. We talked about love, singledom, and bad dating advice—and took a vintage *Cosmo* quiz with the audience, which included quite a few men. I appreciate these creative approaches, and I especially love hearing about book-club nights featuring *Enter Helen*. While women in particular are embracing the book, I also have heard from guys who have picked up copies belonging to their girlfriends or wives and found themselves unexpectedly pulled into the life and times of HGB. She always did know how to catch a man.

Do you think Helen was a feminist? What's your take?

People have a hard time labeling Helen Gurley Brown as a feminist because she didn't always label herself that way. She carved out her own path in a man's world long before the Women's Liberation Movement caught fire in the 1970s, and she knew how to manipulate men to her personal and professional advantage. I think everyone can agree that she was an opportunist, working to make conditions better for herself, if not for her entire gender. But I also would argue that she was a feminist (or a proto-feminist, if you want to get technical about it), in that she believed women and men should have equal rights and opportunities, and that women should have autonomy over their own bodies. Perhaps the writer Caitlin Moran put it best in her book *How to Be a Woman*: "Here is the quick way of working out if you're a feminist. Put your hand in your pants.

    a. Do you have a vagina? and
    b. Do you want to be in charge of it?

If you said 'yes' to both, then congratulations! You're a feminist." ∽

Reading Group Guide
Discussion Questions for
Enter Helen

1. Helen Gurley Brown broke barriers as a career woman and a leader of the sexual revolution before the Women's Liberation Movement caught fire. And while she knew how to manipulate her way through "a man's world," she later came to identify as a feminist. Do you think she was a feminist—why or why not?

2. "*Cosmopolitan* is talking to women one by one," *Ms.* editor Suzanne Levine told the *New York Times* in 1974. "We're talking about making all women's lives work." Which magazine do you think has had more of a direct impact on women's lives, *Cosmopolitan* or *Ms.*, and how so?

3. In her own writings, Helen portrayed her background as poor and hillbilly. But according to her cousin Lou, Helen's childhood in Little Rock was "solidly middle class," and her parents were educated: Cleo had been a school teacher, Ira had a law degree. Why do you think Helen exaggerated her story?

4. Helen's father was killed when she was very young, and she had a complicated relationship with her mother as well as with her older sister Mary. How do you think his premature death, Cleo's depression and Mary's early illness shaped Helen's mindset and message?

5. According to her friend Lyn Tornabene, Helen once said she slept with 178 men. She believed that "sex is power." Do you think that sex empowered Helen as much as she claimed?

6. David Brown was a producer, and Helen Gurley Brown may have been his biggest and best production of all time. He came up with the idea for *Sex and the Single Girl*, and helped her become editor of *Cosmopolitan*, where he had been a